TAKING SIDES

Clashing Views on Controversial

Issues in World History, Volume II

TAKING SIDES

Clashing Views on Controversial

Issues in World History, Volume II

Selected, Edited, and with Introductions by

Joseph R. Mitchell
Howard Community College

and

Helen Buss Mitchell
Howard Community College

McGraw-Hill/Dushkin
A Division of The McGraw-Hill Companies

For Jason, our first successful collaboration

Photo Acknowledgment
Cover image: © 2002 by PhotoDisc, Inc.

Cover Art Acknowledgment
Charles Vitelli

Portions of this material were published in *Taking Sides: Clashing Views on Controversial Issues in World Civilizations,* 2d ed. and *Taking Sides: Clashing Views on Controversial Issues in Western Civilization,* 1st ed.

Manufactured in the United States of America

First Edition

123456789BAHBAH5432

Library of Congress Cataloging-in-Publication Data
Main entry under title:
Taking sides: clashing views on controversial issues in world history, volume ii/selected, edited, and with introductions by Joseph R. Mitchell and Helen Buss Mitchell.—1st ed.
Includes bibliographical references and index.
1. World history. 2. History, modern. I. Mitchell, Joseph R., ed. II. Mitchell, Helen Buss, ed. III. Series.
909
0-07-254857-6
ISSN 1538-716X

Printed on Recycled Paper

Preface

In *Taking Sides: Clashing Views on Controversial Issues in World History Volume II,* we identify the issues that are typically covered in the teaching of world history, using scholarly and readable sources that argue these issues. We have taken care to choose issues that will make this volume multicultural, gender based, and reflective of current historical scholarship. We frame these issues with preview and follow-up sections that are user-friendly for both teachers and students. Students who use this volume should come away with a greater understanding and appreciation of the value of studying history as well as enhanced skills in critical thinking.

Plan of the book   This book is made up of 18 issues that argue pertinent topics in the study of world history. Each issue has an issue *introduction,* which sets the stage for the debate as it is argued in the yes and no selections that follow. Each issue concludes with a *postscript* that makes some final observations and points the way to other questions related to the issue. In reading the issue and forming your own opinions, you should not feel confined to adopt one or the other of the positions presented. There are positions in between the given views or totally outside them, and the *suggestions for further reading* that appear in each issue postscript should help you to find resources to continue your study of the subject. We have also provided Internet site addresses (URLs) in the *On the Internet* page that accompanies each part opener. At the back of the book is a listing of all the *contributors to this volume,* which will give you information on the historians and commentators whose views are debated here.

Using the book   Care has been taken to provide issues that are in various ways related. They could be used to (a) compare/contrast those with like content, (b) show relationships between and among some topics across time, geographic, and cultural boundaries, and (c) make connections between past historical events and their contemporary relevance. For example, Issues 1 and 9 analyze the effects of two revolutions—one economic (Industrial), one political (Russian)—on the lives of women. Issues 2 and 4 deal with the effects of revolution on nineteenth-century France and Japan respectively. Issues 3, 5, and 6 cover nineteenth-century British imperialism and its effects on colonial populations in Ireland, Africa, and Asia. Issues 4 and 11 trace the rise to power of Japan during the 19th-century Meiji Restoration and its fall from grace during World War II. Issues 4 and 7 analyze the different responses of Japan and China to Western imperialism. Issues 5 and 15 deal with Africa's current problems and colonialism's responsibility for them. Issues 8, 10, and 11 cover the causes of war and its horrendous consequences. Issues 11 and 12 evaluate the responsibility of two men—Russian premier Josef Stalin and Japanese emperor Hirohito—in the conduct of two major wars. Issues 13, 14, 15, and 18 deal with important questions facing much of the non-Western world in this postcolonial era. Finally, Issues 16 and 17 cover the prospects for an economically united Western Europe and review how it used its military power to bring peace to one of the continent's troubled regions.

A word to the instructor An *Instructor's Manual With Test Questions* (multiple-choice and essay) is available through the publisher for the instructor using *Taking Sides* in the classroom. A general guidebook, *Using Taking Sides in the Classsroom,* which discusses methods and techniques for integrating the pro-con approach into any classsroom setting, is also available. An online version of *Using Taking Sides in the Classroom* and a correspondence service for *Taking Sides* adopters can be found at http://dushkin.com/usingts/.

Taking Sides: Clashing Views on Controversial Issues in World History is only one title in the Taking Sides series. If you are interested in seeing the table of contents for any of the other titles, please visit the Taking Sides Web site at http://www.dushkin.com/takingsides/.

Acknowledgments We would like to thank Larry Madaras of Howard Community College—fellow teacher, good friend, coeditor of *Taking Sides: Clashing Views on Controversial Issues in American History,* and editor of *Taking Sides: Clashing Views on Controversial Issues in American History Since 1945*—for his past and present assistance in making our work possible. Special acknowledgment also goes to David Stebenne of Ohio State University—friend, scholar, teacher, and author of *Arthur J. Goldberg: New Deal Liberal* (Oxford University Press, 1996)—for his suggestions and advice. Thanks also go out to the library staffs of Howard County, Maryland; University of Maryland, College Park; University of Maryland, Baltimore County (UMBC); and Howard Community College—especially Ela Ciborowski, who secured interlibrary loans.

At McGraw-Hill/Dushkin, a debt of gratitude is owed to list manager Ted Knight and developmental editor Juliana Gribbins, who guided us through the publishing side of the book and gave encouraging words and positive feedback.

A final word We would appreciate any questions, comments, or suggestions regarding our work, especially which issues work best in your classroom and which issues you never use. Please contact us at joemitch@bigjar.com. We promise a quick response.

Joseph R. Mitchell
Howard Community College

Helen Buss Mitchell
Howard Community College

Contents In Brief

Contents

Historian Edward Shorter argues that employment opportunities outside the home that opened up with industrialization led to a rise in the illegitimacy rate, which he attributes to the sexual emancipation of unmarried, working-class women. Historians Louise A. Tilly, Joan W. Scott, and Miriam Cohen counter that unmarried women worked to meet an economic need, not to gain personal freedom, and they attribute the rise in illegitimacy rates to broken marriage promises and the absence of traditional support from family, community, and the church.

Peter Kropotkin (1842–1921), a Russian prince, revolutionary, and anarchist, argues that the French Revolution eradicated both serfdom and absolutism and paved the way for France's future democratic development. Columbia University professor Simon Schama counters that not only did the French Revolution betray its own goals, it also produced few of the results that it promised.

Christine Kinealy, fellow of the University of Liverpool, argues that the British government's response to the Irish potato famine was deliberately inadequate. The British government's "hidden agenda" of long-term economic, social, and agrarian reform was accelerated by the famine, and mass emigration was a consequence of these changes. Historian Hasia R. Diner documents large-scale emigration both before and after the Irish potato famine. Diner credits the Irish people with learning from their famine experiences that the reliance of the poor on the potato and the excessive subdivision of land within families were no longer in their own best interests.

Issue 4.   Did the Meiji Restoration Constitute a Revolution in Nineteenth-Century Japan?   62

Historian Thomas M. Huber states that the Meiji Restoration was responsible for the most dramatic change in Japan's history and deserves to be referred to as a revolution. Historian W. G. Beasley argues that when compared with other revolutions such as the French and Russian, the Meiji Restoration did not constitute a revolution in the classical sense.

Issue 5.   Were Economic Factors Primarily Responsible for British Imperialism?   82

Professor Lance E. Davis and Robert A. Huttenback state that, although statistics prove that British imperialism was not a profitable venture, it was supported by an economic elite that was able to promote and derive profits from it. Professor John M. MacKenzie argues that the motivation for British imperialism was multicausal and that most of the causes can be found in the general anxiety crisis permeating British society in the late nineteenth century.

Issue 6.   Were Indigenous Sex Workers in the British Empire Always Powerless?   104

British historian Denis Judd finds that throughout the British Empire sexual contact with "native" women was one of the perks of the imperial system. He documents the abuse and exploitation of indigenous sex workers, or prostitutes, calling it part of a pattern of conquest wherever the British flag was raised. Historian of African history Luise White interviewed indigenous sex workers in Nairobi, Kenya, and concluded that rather than being passive victims, these women acted as historical agents, doing through prostitution what in better times they would have done through marriage—stock their fathers' herds and keep livestock values competitive.

Professor Paul A. Cohen contends that while antiforeign and anti-Christian attitudes played a role in the start of the Boxer rebellion, a more immediate cause was a severe drought and its impact on Chinese society. Historian Henrietta Harrison concedes that while the Boxers were motivated by more than a single factor, opposition to Christian missionary activity was at the core of their rebellion.

History professor V. R. Berghahn states that, although all of Europe's major powers played a part in the onset of World War I, recent evidence still indicates that Germany's role in the process was the main factor responsible for the conflict. History professor Samuel R. Williamson, Jr., argues that the factors and conditions that led to the First World War were a shared responsibility and that no one nation can be blamed for its genesis.

History professor Richard Stites argues that in the early years of the Bolshevik Revolution, the Zhenotdel, or Women's Department, helped many working women take the first steps toward emancipation. Film historian Françoise Navailh contends that the Zhenotdel had limited political influence and could do little to improve the lives of Soviet women in the unstable period following the revolution.

Issue 10.   Was German "Eliminationist Antisemitism" Responsible for the Holocaust?   184

Professor of political science Daniel Jonah Goldhagen states that due to the nature of German society in the twentieth century—with its endemic, virulent antisemitism—thousands of ordinary German citizens became willing participants in the implementation of Holocaust horrors. Holocaust historian Christopher R. Browning argues that Goldhagen's thesis is too simplistic and that a multicausal approach must be used to determine why ordinary German citizens willingly participated in the Holocaust

Issue 11.   Should Emperor Hirohito Have Been Held Responsible for Japan's World War II Actions?   206

Professor Peter Wetzler states that Emperor Hirohito bears responsibility for World War II because he did not oppose the war effort. This was in order to guarantee the continued rule of his Japanese imperial family. Author Stephen S. Large argues that Emperor Hirohito's lack of real political power to effect change absolves him from any direct responsibility for World War II.

Issue 12.   Was Stalin Responsible for the Cold War?   228

Historian John Lewis Gaddis states that after more than a half a century of cold war scholarship, Joseph Stalin still deserves most of the responsibility for the onset of the cold war. Historian Martin J. Sherwin counters that the origins of the cold war can be found in the World War II diplomacy involving the use of the atomic bomb, and he places much of the blame for the cold war on the shoulders of Franklin D. Roosevelt, Harry S. Truman, and Winston Churchill.

own incompetent, corrupt, power-hungry leaders. African history professor A. Adu Boahen argues that major problems left to Africa by the departing colonial powers are at the root of many of the continent's current problems.

Career diplomat Warren Zimmermann, the United States' last ambassador to Yugoslavia, argues that the republic's ethnic leaders, especially Slobo-dan Milosevic, bear primary responsibility for the nation's demise. Political science professor Steven Majstorovic contends that while manipulation by elite ethnic leaders played a role in the death of Yugoslavia, the fragile ethnic divisions, formed by memory and myth, also played an important role in the country's demise.

Steven Everts, research fellow at the Centre for European Reform in London, argues that the emergence of the *euro* as a world currency and Euroland as a united voice may lead to increasing rivalry between Europe and the United States, as both seek economic and political influence in the rest of the world. Werner Weidenfeld, director of the Munich Center for Applied Policy Research, sees the European Union as a vehicle for restructuring the transatlantic relationship between Europe and the United States. If they develop a partnership between equals, they will be positioned for international crisis management and other global challenges.

World policy analyst Anatol Lieven states that dated United States cold war policies and despair-inducing political, economic, and social conditions have contributed to the rise of radical Islamists, some of whom were responsible for the September 11, 2001, attacks. International relations specialist Mark Juergensmeyer contends that the roots of the September

11, 2001, attacks lie in the radical views of the terrorists, especially the symbolism of cosmic war and the battle between good and evil.

Contents

Introduction

The Study of World History

Joseph R. Mitchell

Helen Buss Mitchell

What Is History?

History is a dialogue between the past and the present. As we respond to events in our own world, we bring the concerns of the present to our study of the past. What seems important to us, where we turn our attention, how we approach a study of the past—all these are rooted in the present. It has been said that where you stand determines what you see. This is especially the case with history. If we stand within the Western tradition exclusively, we may be tempted to see its story as the only story or the only one worth telling. And whose perspective we take is also critical. From the point of view of the rich and powerful, the events of history take one shape; through the lens of the poor and powerless, the same events can appear quite different. If we take women or non-Western cultures or the ordinary person as our starting point, the story of the past may present us with a series of surprises.

Tools of the Historian

Much of the raw material of history consists of written sources. Original sources —from a period contemporary with the events or ideas described—are called *primary sources*. These may consist of documents of all kinds, including official records as well as personal letters and diaries. The writings of historians reflecting on the past are called *secondary sources*. It is important to keep in mind that primary sources may not automatically be assumed to be free from bias. Each contains historical and personal perspectives. Their principal limitation, however, is that they record what people considered noteworthy about their own age and not necessarily what would most interest us today. As the concerns of the present evolve, the questions we bring to our study of the past will also change. Much of what you read in this book will reflect differences in focus between one historian and another. As Edward Hallett Carr points out, the historian constructs a working model that enables him or her to understand the past. It would be a great mistake to confuse this working model with a photocopy.

Traditional History

Only recently has history considered itself a social science and striven for a kind of scientific accuracy in speaking about the past. For much of human history, until perhaps the late nineteenth century, history was considered a branch of literature rather than a kind of science. It was concerned first of all with narrative, with the telling of a compelling story, and its focus was on the fascinating characters whose lives shaped and defined the past.

Biography, the recounting of the life and times of a powerful man, was regarded as one of the most reliable windows on the past. The so-called "great man" was credited with shaping and defining his own time. As a result, studying Emperor Hirohito of Japan or Soviet premier Josef Stalin was assumed to offer one of the most reliable keys to unlocking a specific historical time period.

And, traditional history looked relatively uncritically at the great men from the past. Military heroes, for example, were lauded for their conquests with little or no focus on the carnage that made those conquests possible. Another unspoken assumption was the dominance and superiority of the West as the creator and bearer of human civilization. Divine power was sometimes seen as directing, or at least approving, the actions of powerful nations and men.

The traditional areas of focus for the historian have been political, diplomatic, and constitutional. Political history considers how power has been organized and enforced by the state within human societies. Diplomatic history looks at what influenced the power struggles between states as they continually struggled for dominance. Constitutional history examines the evolution of national states with special attention to who ruled and who or what conferred the right to rule. These questions continue to intrigue historians as Issues 4 (concerning reasons for the Meiji Restoration in Japan) and 8 (concerning German militarism and World War I) illustrate. In the present, the prospect of a united Europe raises interesting questions for the United States, which are explored in Issue 17 on the European Economic and Monetary Union.

A related domain of the traditional historian has been that of intellectual history, or the history of ideas— in the fields of politics, economics, sociology, theology, and science. Taking this approach to its widest scope, one might explore the intellectual climate of an age, such as the Age of Imperialism, the rise of communism, the period of the cold war, or the dominance of capitalism. This question has become complicated by the psychological insights of Sigmund Freud. Are we really motivated chiefly by our primal, internal drives no matter how high-minded we might wish to appear? And, especially since the economic theories of Karl Marx have become widely known, the influence of both ideas and economic forces on individuals and civilizations has been widely explored. See Issue 5 on the motivation of British imperialism: Which was more prominent, economic factors or national anxiety?

Revisionism

However, history is not a once-and-for-all enterprise. Each generation formulates its own questions and brings new tools to the study of the past, resulting in a process called *revisionism*. Much of what you will read in this book is a product of revisionism as historians reinterpret the past in the light of the present. One generation values revolutions, the next focuses on their terrible costs. One generation assumes that great men shape the events of history, the next looks to the lives of ordinary people to illuminate the past. There is no final answer, but where we stand will determine which interpretation seems more compelling to us. Issues 11 and 12 introduce the tension between traditional and revisionist interpretations of Hirohito and Stalin.

As new tools of analysis become available, our ability to understand the past improves. Bringing events into clearer focus can change the meaning that we assign to them. Many of the selections in this book reflect new attitudes and new insights made possible by the tools that historians have borrowed from the other social sciences. For instance, studies of climate and its historical consequences can shed new light on what motivates people to act as they do. To explore this question, see Issue 7 on the Boxer Rebellion in China. Were the disaffected motivated primarily by antireligious feelings or left with nothing meaningful to do by the drought?

Presentism

While we stand in the present, we must be wary of what historians call *presentism,* that is, reading the values of the present back into the past. If we live in a culture that values individualism and prizes competition, we may be tempted to see these values as good even in a culture that preferred communalism and cooperation. And we may miss a key component of an ancient civilization because it does not match what we currently consider worthwhile. We cannot and should not avoid our own questions and struggles. They will inform our study of the past; and yet, they must not warp our vision. Ideally, historians engage in a continual dialogue in which the concerns, but not the values, of the present are explored through a study of the past.

At the same time, though, we might bring the moral standards of the present to bear on the past. Cultural relativism, pioneered in the field of anthropology, made us sensitive to the many and varied ways in which civilizations define what is "normal" and what is "moral." So, we remain appropriately reluctant to judge individuals from other times and places by our standards since they were or are, in fact, behaving perfectly normally and morally by the standards of their own time and place. However, from the perspective of the present, we do not hesitate to condemn slaveholding, genocide, or even the hidden costs of revolutions. Issue 2, for instance, explores whether or not the French Revolution could be said to be worth its human costs.

Changing Historiographical Focuses

All cultures are vulnerable to the narrow-mindedness created by *ethnocentrism* —the belief that one's own culture is superior to all others. From inside a particular culture, certain practices may seem normative—that is, we may assume that all humans or all rational humans must behave the way we do or hold the attitudes we hold. When we meet a culture that sees the world differently from ourselves, we may be tempted to write it off as inferior or primitive. As an alternative to ethnocentrism, we might want to enter the worldview of another and see what we can learn from expanding our perspective. These issues will offer you many opportunities to try this thought experiment.

Stepping outside the Western tradition has allowed historians to take a more globocentric view of world events. Accusing their predecessors of Eurocentrism, some historians have adopted an Afrocentric view of world history that emphasizes Africa's seminal role in cultural evolution. Within the Western tradition, women have challenged the male-dominated perspective that studied war but ignored family. Including additional perspectives complicates our interpretation of past events but permits a fuller picture to emerge. We must be wary of *universalism*—assuming, for example, that patriarchy has always existed or that being a woman was the same for every woman no matter what her historical circumstances. What similarities exist between women swept up in the European Industrial Revolution and Kenyan women who turned to prostitution under a period of extreme environmental stress? Are there ways in which their sexual lives have parallels? And in what ways are their lives and circumstances profoundly different? If cultures other than the West have been dominant or influential during the past, what did the world look like under those circumstances?

Social History

Some historians have moved beyond political, diplomatic, and constitutional history to explore economics and demographics as well as to study social processes. Moving from a focus on nations and rulers to a close examination of forces that can be studied analytically has opened up the realms of business and the family to the historian. Proponents of the so-called new social history rejected what they called history from the "top down." Instead of the great man whose influence shaped his age, they looked to the lives of ordinary people and called what they were doing history from the "bottom up." The previous generation of historians, they asserted, had sometimes acted as if only the influential had a role in shaping history. Social history assumes that all people are capable of acting as historical agents rather than being passive victims to whom history happens. With this shift in attitude, the lives of slaves, workers, women of all kinds, and children, too, become worthy subjects of historical investigation.

Because the poor and powerless seldom leave written records, other methods must be used to understand their lives. Applying the methods of social scientists to their own discipline, historians have broadened and deepened their field of study. Archaeological evidence, DNA analysis, the tools of paleoanthropology, computer analysis of demographic data—all these have allowed the voiceless to speak across centuries. Fossil evidence, for instance, and the analysis of mitochondrial DNA—the structures within cells we inherit only from our mothers—may each be employed, sometimes with strikingly different results, to trace the migrations of preliterate peoples.

What historians call *material culture* reveals the everyday lives of people by analyzing what they discarded as well as the monuments and other material objects they intended to leave as markers of their civilizations. And, the high-speed comparative functions of computers have allowed the historian to analyze vast quantities of data and look at demographic trends. How old are people when they marry for the first time, have a child, or die? Only with the expanded life expectancy made possible by the modern world has it been possible for people to see their children's children—to become grandparents. If we study weather patterns and learn that certain years were periods of drought, we can imagine ourselves into the lives of those living under drought conditions. Would disaffected young men with nothing meaningful to occupy their labor turn to protest? Issue 7 on the Boxer Rebellion explores this question.

Race, Class, and Gender

The experience of being a historical subject is never monolithic. That is, each of us has a gender, a race, a social class, an ethnic identity, a religion (even if it is atheism or agnosticism), an age, and a variety of other markers that color our experiences. At times the most important factor may be one's gender, and what happens may be more or less the same for all members of a particular gender. Under other circumstances, however, race may be predominant. Being a member of a racial minority or of a powerful racial majority may lead to very different experiences of the same event. At other times social class may determine how an event is experienced; the rich may have one story to tell, the poor another. And other factors, such as religion or ethnic identity—even age—can become the most significant piece of a person's identity, especially if prejudice or favoritism is involved. Historians try always to take into account how race, class, and gender (as well as a host of other factors) intersect in the life of a historical subject. Issue 9 examines the lives of Bolshevik women who discovered that the revolution that they hoped would benefit their gender was first and foremost devoted to issues of class.

Issues Involved in Historical Interpretation

Often historians will agree on what happened but disagree about why or how something happened. Sometimes the question is: Were internal or external causes more responsible? Both may have contributed to an event, but one or the other may have played the more significant role. Looking at differing evidence may lead historians to varying interpretations. A related question is: Was it the circumstances that changed or only the attitudes of those who experienced them? Issue 1 debates the cause for a rise in illegitimacy rates. Was the capitalist Industrial Revolution responsible for changing young women's attitudes in a more sexually permissive environment? Or did they retain traditional attitudes but find the external circumstances dramatically altered?

Periodization

Even more basically, the student of the past must wonder whether the turning points that shape the chapters in our history books are the same for all historical subjects. The process of marking turning points is known as *periodization*. It is the more or less artificial creation of periods that chunk history into manageable segments by identifying forks in the road that took people and events in a new direction. Using an expanded perspective, we may learn that the traditional turning points hold for men but not for women or reflect the experiences of one ethnic group but not another. And, if periodization schemes conflict, which one should we use? Were there sharp breaks at the periods we designate the Renaissance, the Scientific Revolution, or the Industrial Revolution? If there were, did women and men experience these breaks identically?

It is also important to keep in mind that people living at a particular moment in history are not aware of labels that later historians will attach to their experience. People who lived during the Middle Ages were surely not aware of living in the middle of something. Only much after the fact were we able to call a later age the Renaissance. To those who lived during what we call the Middle Ages or the Renaissance, marriage, childbirth, work, weather, sickness, and death were the real concerns, just as they are for us. Our own age will certainly be characterized by future historians in ways that might surprise and shock us. As we study the past, it is helpful to keep in mind that some of our assumptions are rooted in a traditional periodization that is now being challenged.

Continuity or Discontinuity?

A related question concerns the connection or lack of connection between one event or set of events and another. When we look at the historical past, we must ask ourselves whether we are seeing continuity or discontinuity. In other words, is the event we are studying part of a normal process of evolution or does it represent a break from a traditional pattern? Questions of continuity versus discontinuity are the fundamental ones on which the larger issue of periodization rests. The first issue in this volume explores whether the Industrial Revolution took the lives of workers in wholly new directions or whether traditional behaviors continued, albeit in a radically different context.

Sometimes events may appear continuous from the point of view of one group and discontinuous from the point of view of another. Suppose that factory owners found their world and worldview shifting dramatically, whereas the lives and perspectives of factory workers went on more or less as they had before. When this is the case, whose experience should we privilege? Is one group's experience more historically significant than another's—and how should we decide?

Issue 6 looks at young women from the countryside in Kenya who engaged in prostitution during the rule of the British Empire. Drought and a loss in cattle value had rendered young men unable to afford the traditional bride price. Short-term prostitution saved the family economy by bringing wealth in cattle—exactly what a bride price would have done. Do the choices made by these young women represent continuity or discontinuity? And, in Issue

13, is modern capitalism continuous with traditional capitalism or does the modern version represent such a strong discontinuity with its historical past that Confucian values appear incompatible with it?

The Power of Ideas

Can ideas change the course of history? People have sometimes been willing to die for what they believe in, and revolutions have certainly been fought, at least in part, over ideas. Some historians believe that studying the clash of ideas or the predominance of one idea or set of ideas offers the best key to understanding the past. Issue 3 looks at how much British policy decisions during the Irish potato famine of the mid-nineteenth century were justified by prevailing ideas—such as those of laissez-faire capitalism and the contrast between the deserving and the undeserving poor.

What do you think? Do ideas shape world events? Would devotion to a political or religious cause lead you to challenge the status quo? Or, would economic conditions be more likely to send you to the streets? Historians differ in ranking the importance of various factors in influencing the past. Do people challenge the power structure because they feel politically powerless, or because they are hungry, or because of the power of ideas?

The Timeliness of Historical Issues

When we read the newspaper or listen to the evening news, we find numerous and confusing political, economic, religious, and military clashes that can be understood only by looking at their historical contexts. The role of the United States in world events, the perennial conflicts in the Middle East, the horror and enigma of the Holocaust (see Issue 10), the nature and future of terrorism (see Issue 18), the threat posed by religious revivalism (see Issue 14), Africa's political future (see Issue 15), the question of whether ancient ethnic hatred can ever be quenched (see Issue 16)—these concerns of the global village have roots in the past. Understanding the origins of conflicts gives us the possibility of envisioning their solutions. The issues in this book will help you think through the problems facing our world and give you the tools to make an informed decision about what you think is the best course of action.

In a democracy, an informed citizenry is the bedrock on which a government stands. If we do not understand the past, the present will be a puzzle to us and the future may seem out of our control. Seeing how and why historians disagree can help us to determine what the critical issues are and where informed interpreters part company. This, at least, is the basis for forming our own judgments and acting upon them. Looking critically at clashing views also hones our analytic skills and makes us thoughtful readers of all our textbooks as well as magazines and newspapers.

Why Study World History?

You may be wondering why this book deals with world history rather than exclusively with Western civilization. At times the West has felt its power and dominance in the world made only its own story worth studying. History, we are sometimes told, is written by the winners. For the Chinese, the Greeks, the Ottoman Turks, and many other victors of the past, the stories of other civilizations seemed irrelevant, unimportant, not nearly as valuable as their own triumphal saga. The Chinese considered their Middle Kingdom the center of the world, the Greeks labeled all others barbarians, and the Ottoman Turks expected never to lose their position of dominance. From our perspective in the present these stories form a tapestry. No one thread or pattern tells the tale, and all seem to be equally necessary for a complete picture of the past to emerge.

Any single story—even that of a military and economic superpower—is insufficient to explain the scope of human history at a given moment in time. Our story is especially interesting to us and you will find issues specific to Western civilization in this book. However, as we are learning, our story achieves its fullest meaning only when it is told in concert with those of other civilizations that share an increasingly interconnected planet with us. As communications systems shrink the Earth into a global village, we may be ignoring the rest of the world at our own peril. At the very least the study of civilizations other than our own can alert us to events that may have worldwide implications. And, as we are beginning to learn, no story happens in isolation. The history of the West can perhaps be accurately told only within a global context that takes into account the actions and reactions of other civilizations as they share the world stage with the West. As you read the issues that concern non-Western civilizations, stay alert for what you can learn about your own.

Your textbook may take a global focus, or it may be restricted to the study of Western civilization. In either case, the readings in this book will enrich your understanding of how the peoples of the world have understood themselves and their relationships with others. As we become a more clearly multicultural society, we have an additional reason for studying about other civilizations that have blended with our own through immigration. Perhaps the biggest challenge for an increasingly diverse United States of America is to understand its own role in world affairs and its relationship with other countries, which may have different histories, value systems, and goals.

On the Internet . . .

Industrial Revolution

This Web site is a clearinghouse for major sites on the Industrial Revolution. It covers a variety of subjects, including several on women, and contains much primary source materials.

http://www.sau29.k12.nh.us/library/KHS/indusrev.htm

Internet Modern History Sourcebook: French Revolution

The Internet Modern History Sourcebook: French Revolution Web site looks at the French Revolution from the perspective of those who experienced it. The site breaks the revolution into phases and presents relevant primary source materials for each.

http://www.fordham.edu/halsall/mod/modbook13.html

The Irish Potato Famine

The Irish Potato Famine Web site presents a collection of useful sites on the "Great Famine"; some contain primary source materials, including visuals.

http://www.seark.net/~sabra/potato.html

Schauwecker's Guide to Japan: Meiji Period, 1868–1912

Part of a larger site on the history of Japan, Schauwecker's Guide to Japan: Meiji Period, 1868–1912, contains a brief article. If considered with the many links contained within it, this section presents a detailed account of history during the Meiji period.

http://www.japan-guide.com/e/e2139.html

History of Imperialism

The History of Imperialism Web site contains six pages of links to all sorts of information, including articles, definitions, timelines, maps, political cartoons, study questions, and book resources—all nicely organized for easy use.

http://members.aol.com/TeacherNet/World.html

Images of the African Woman in Victorian Literature

"Images of the African Woman in Victorian Literature" is a well-written article that shows that the British sexual exploitation of African women was reflected in Victorian literature, which portrayed African women as possessing "savage sexuality."

http://www.ssmu.mcgill.ca/journals/latitudes/
3vsez.htm

PART 1

The Modern World

T his section traces the development of capitalism and democracy and the influence that they had on the modern world. It also covers the rise of nationalism and how countries were affected by it in both positive and negative ways, including the change brought about by various types of revolutions and their effects.

- Did the Industrial Revolution Lead to a Sexual Revolution?

- Was the French Revolution Worth Its Human Costs?

- Did British Policy Decisions Cause the Mass Emigration and Land Reforms That Followed the Irish Potato Famine?

- Did the Meiji Restoration Constitute a Revolution in Nineteenth-Century Japan?

- Were Economic Factors Primarily Responsible for British Imperialism?

- Were Indigenous Sex Workers in the British Empire Always Powerless?

ISSUE 1

Did the Industrial Revolution Lead to a Sexual Revolution?

YES: Edward Shorter, from "Female Emancipation, Birth Control, and Fertility in European History," *The American Historical Review* (June 1973)

NO: Louise A. Tilly, Joan W. Scott, and Miriam Cohen, from "Women's Work and European Fertility Patterns," *Journal of Interdisciplinary History* (Winter 1976)

ISSUE SUMMARY

YES: Historian Edward Shorter argues that employment opportunities outside the home that opened up with industrialization led to a rise in the illegitimacy rate, which he attributes to the sexual emancipation of unmarried, working-class women.

NO: Historians Louise A. Tilly, Joan W. Scott, and Miriam Cohen counter that unmarried women worked to meet an economic need, not to gain personal freedom, and they attribute the rise in illegitimacy rates to broken marriage promises and the absence of traditional support from family, community, and the church.

Historians agree that between 1750 and 1850, the illegitimacy rate rose across Europe. In many of the European countries this time period coincides with industrialization. Did the arrival of capitalism change the living and working habits of unmarried women and introduce new attitudes that made them more interested in sex? When the result is agreed upon, what matters most is the evidence offered to explain the cause.

In the selection that follows, Edward Shorter asserts that a nineteenth-century sexual revolution that had its roots in industrial capitalism occurred. In his view the market economy, with its values of self-interest and competitiveness, changed the value system of the proletarian subculture—the young men and women working for wages in industrializing countries. Earning their own money, says Shorter, gave these workers the means to live independently. Young women in particular, he argues, declared their independence from family control, struck out in pursuit of personal freedom, and began to enjoy sex as a way of finding individual self-fulfillment. The predictable result was a rise in illegitimacy rates.

Louise A. Tilly, Joan W. Scott, and Miriam Cohen, in reply, fault Shorter for offering little or no hard evidence for his hypothesis. Citing the work of other historians, they assert that family interest rather than self-interest led women to work. Women moved very slowly into industrial work, and, even by the end of the period (1850), most women who were employed were doing domestic service, dressmaking, laundering, and tailoring, not factory work. Many women earned far too little to permit them to live independently. Those who did probably kept the traditional assumption that premarital intercourse with an intended bridegroom would be followed by marriage. Tilly, Scott, and Cohen argue that what changed was not the attitudes but the external context. In the absence of traditional pressures, young men moved on to other work or better opportunities, leaving the women they had impregnated behind.

As you read these two conflicting interpretations, look for the explanation offered by each selection and, most important, at what evidence is offered to support the interpretation. It may seem logical to assume that an increase in rates of illegitimacy must be due to a sexual revolution. But is that the only or the best explanation that existing information can support? There is a real temptation to use our "common sense" to fill in the gaps, but the historian insists on evidence.

For centuries history was written exclusively from the point of view of the rich, the powerful, and the literate. For some, understanding the "great man" —Alexander the Great, Julius Caesar, and Napoleon, for example—was the key to understanding the age in which he lived. This is often called history "from the top down." Many scholars, however, have begun to uncover the lives of the poor, the powerless, and the illiterate—what some call history "from the bottom up." Borrowing the methods of the social sciences, such as archaeology, anthropology, sociology, and psychology, and using quantitative analyses of economic and demographic data, historians are trying to fill in the missing pieces of the past. The selections in this issue take on the challenge of assessing the motives of people who left few, if any, written records. Since we cannot read their diaries and letters, we must use the evidence that we do have about the lives these women led and attempt to imagine how they might have seen the world.

In this issue, the chief question concerns continuity versus discontinuity. What changed? What remained the same? Did the attitudes of working women change as they entered the capitalist labor force, as Shorter states? And did these attitudes lead them to pursue personal pleasures such as sex, which, in the absence of birth control, resulted in higher rates of illegitimacy? Or, as Tilly, Scott, and Cohen argue, did the attitudes stay the same (premarital sex, as usual, in the context of courtship and with the expectation of marriage), while the context changed, leaving women pregnant and with no expectation of marriage?

Edward Shorter **YES**

Female Emancipation, Birth Control, and Fertility in European History

The conventional wisdom about female emancipation is that it originated among upper-class women in the mid-nineteenth century, surfacing first in tandem with the movement for emancipation of the slaves, then moving forward independently as the suffrage movement. While this account may be substantially correct as involves women's participation in national political life, it is, in my opinion, inapplicable to family history. I suggest that the position of women within the family underwent a radical shift starting late in the eighteenth century; furthermore, the change progressed from young and lowly women to older women of higher status. The logic of this chronology sees involvement in the economy of the market place as the principal motor of emancipation.

What exactly is meant by "female emancipation"? General statements about the position of women within early modern European families are uncertain in the extreme because, at the same time, so many impressions of individual famous women are to be found in the literature and so little is known in a systematic, quantitative way about the cultural rules and norms of women in the popular classes. Yet one might fairly characterize the situation of most women as one of subordination. In the first place, both young men and women were subordinated to the authority of their parents, so that parental intervention in the mating market customarily replaced romantic love in bringing young couples together. In the second place, both social ideology and the force of events conspired to make the husband supreme over the woman in the household, his obligation being merely to respect her, hers, however, to serve and obey him. In most matters of sex, economics, or family authority the woman was expected to do the husband's bidding. Clearly individual exceptions existed, yet the rule seems to have been powerlessness and dependency for the woman.

Thus female emancipation involves, quite simply, the replacement of this subordination with independence. In the nineteenth and twentieth centuries married women acquired for themselves first, practical leverage on household political power, and second, a family ideology stressing their own rights to sexual gratification and emotional autonomy. And unmarried women became

From Edward Shorter, "Female Emancipation, Birth Control, and Fertility in European History," *The American Historical Review*, vol. 78, no. 3 (June 1973). Copyright © 1973 by The American Historical Association. Reprinted by permission. Notes omitted.

increasingly convinced of the impropriety of family and community restraints upon social and sexual relations, so that they came to ignore the strictures of both parents and community in order to gratify their own personal needs. Therefore women's emancipation at the popular level means disregarding outside controls upon personal freedom of action and sexuality for the sake of individual self-fulfillment.

What evidence exists that the years 1750–1850 saw a movement toward female emancipation among the popular classes? We are, alas, at the beginning of the investigation rather than the end, and so I can merely anticipate the findings of future research. Yet even within the existing literature strong hints may be found that crucial changes in the status and authority of women were under way after 1750 and that these changes were linked in some way to economic modernization. The search for evidence may be aided by considering the nature of the change in the relationship between married woman and husband as well as that between the young, unmarried woman and parental and communal authority. To demonstrate that there is in fact an *explicandum,* let us briefly review some previous findings on these questions.

Least studied to date has been the family life and authority relationships of lower-class women in the years before 1900. Save for tiny pinpricks of information here and there the subject is uncharted, yet those studies that exist converge to demonstrate a radical upheaval in popular family life in the wake of capitalism. Neil Smelser, in a classic study of the British cotton industry, describes "the reversal of traditional age and sex roles as wives and children went to the factory." Industrial growth fragmented the customary "family economy" by making individual producers of its separate members. And, for the children at least, independence accompanied wage labor. Peter Stearns has recently reviewed the German literature, finding toward the end of the nineteenth century (a period inconveniently late for the case I wish to present here) "recognition of greater independence for the woman.... There is suggested here a new sentiment within the family, the possibility of greater affection for the children, who were not underfoot all the time, and greater sensuality and equality in the relationship between man and wife." And Rudolf Braun, in his sensitive reconstruction of life among cottage and factory workers in the Zurich highlands, notes massive shifts in family patterns, starting with the eighteenth century. While Braun is silent on specific changes in the relationships between married men and women, he pulls back the canvas for a brief instant to reveal, for example, women forgetting how to cook. Why, Braun asks, were ready-made foods in such great demand in factory towns?

> It was not merely the pressure to eat at the workplace that accelerated the demand for prepared dishes, nor the lack of time at home, but also the woman factory worker's lack of skill in cooking. Bound to the machine and the factory since earliest childhood, she inadequately learned the arts of cooking and homemaking. We have seen these complaints since the woman cottage workers of the *ancien régime,* but with factory workers they become even more urgent.

One can imagine that the authority patterns among traditional petit-bourgeois families were as different from those of worker couples out on the frontier of economic advance as night is from day.

Evidence is more abundant that young unmarried women were rebelling against parental and social authority in the period from 1750 to 1850. To draw upon my own research, I noted in early nineteenth-century Bavaria an absolute squall of outrage from middle-class observers of popular life, seated for the most part in lower levels of the governmental bureaucracy, about a new spirit of independence among young women in agricultural labor and domestic service. Through this chorus of complaints ran the themes of escape and experimentation, of throwing off old superordinates and codes, and of, in general, what a much later generation of emancipators was to call "liberation."

There was the theme of escape from old jobs. Young women wanted, when possible, to forsake domestic service for employment that would safeguard personal independence. The unpopularity of service may be seen in the cries about a shortage of rural labor *(Dienstbotenmangel)* that became a constant theme in social criticism from the mid-eighteenth century onward. Or, to take another sort of example, Munich's police chief noted in 1815:

> It is sad, and most difficult for the police to prevent, that so many young girls leave service when they grow tired of waiting on people and under one pretext or another take a room somewhere, living from their own industry. But they do little real work and let themselves be supported by boyfriends; they become pregnant and then are abandoned.

And there was the theme of escape from old residences. Young women wanted to live alone, in their own quarters and away from the oppressive supervision of either parents or employers. In the late 1830s the indignant provincial government of Würzburg observed:

> In our province the so-called practice of *Eigenzimmern* is quite customary, according to which the deflorated daughter leaves the parental house and rents a room elsewhere, not necessarily to avoid the reproaches of the parents for her misdeeds, but in order to move more freely, to accommodate the visit of the boyfriend *[Zuhälter]* and with him to live in concubinage *[wilde Ehe]*.

On the matter of escape from old personal styles, let Joseph Maria Johann Nepomuck Freiherr von Frauenberg, archbishop of Bamberg, speak:

> A most detrimental alteration in the character of the female gender [has taken place]. Earlier, women distinguished themselves through their soft, withdrawn, modest, and chaste being, while nowadays they take part in all public entertainments, indeed providing some, set the tone *[den Ton angeben]*, and so have entirely departed from their natural situation. Thus has female morality disappeared.

The archbishop noted this development had occurred principally in the cities. There were other complaints about how female servants and hired hands would squander their entire wages in buying expeditions to the cities, returning to the farm with clothes alien to native folkways. Still other laments were voiced about feminine indifference to pastoral authority and about newly grasping, calculating female attitudes to wage matters. All these threads led back in the opinion of contemporaries—and rightly so I think—to sexuality and thus ultimately to fertility: "In the countryside a young girl who has preserved her virgin purity until age twenty is exceptional, and moreover encounters even among her girlfriends no recognition."

Perhaps Bavaria was not typical of the rest of Europe, though I believe that it was, for within its frontiers the kingdom harbored a remarkable diversity of social and economic arrangements. Perhaps, even more serious for the case I wish to make, male complaints about "moral breakdown" among young women reflected sooner the beholder's own libidinal preoccupations than a change in objective social conditions. Perhaps, too, nostalgia is close to being a historical constant, so that most men who search their own memories invariably see behind the outlines of a gray, disorganized present the golden harmony of an idealized past. Yet in this case I doubt it. And I suspect that future research will verify that this particular set of social critics at this particular point in time—the years 1800–40—were onto something. The objective order of the real world was in fact changing, and a shift in the position of women was moving the ground directly from under the feet of these "patriarchs."

These changes in the mentalities and sexual comportment of women may ultimately be linked to a variety of changes in economic structure that one might summarize under the label "capitalism." Three salients of industrial advance mattered to fertility, and two of the three made more of a difference to women than to men....

First, capitalism meant the formation of a proletarian subculture. Large numbers of people who had in common the fact that they were wage laborers found themselves living together in the same communities. Because the material conditions of their lives differentiated them clearly from the surrounding social order of small proprietors, these newly aggregated workers in both agriculture and industry began to develop their own rules for doing cultural business, which is, after all, the essence of a subculture. A way of life specific to the working classes began to elaborate itself within the large farm areas of modernizing agriculture, upon the upland slopes where the putting out of textiles and nail manufacture was thriving, and within the newly blossoming industrial cities themselves.

The subculture would sooner or later matter to fertility by providing alternative sets of rules for sexual comportment, target family sizes, and new techniques for contraception and abortion. But subcultures are especially important in the area of legitimation of behavior about which the individual might otherwise feel uneasy. It is now common knowledge that the charter culture of traditional Europe had internalized within young people a host of restraints against intercourse. So that if before 1750 there was relatively little premarital intercourse, it was not necessarily because external supervision was totalitarian in its strictness but because most people within the culture shared the belief that premarital sex was wrong. When in later years sex before marriage became commonplace, it was because a new generation of sexually active young men and women felt their behavior was socially accepted, at least by their peers. The point is that if an individual is going to bend the operating rules of the dominant culture, he must feel that members of his own group, whose good opinion he treasures, will support his venturesomeness.

The proletarian subculture was, of course, indulgent of eroticism. Yet this particular indulgence must not be attributed without further argument to the industrial origins of the subculture. The fact that a subculture exists does not automatically mean that its specific operating rules must be libertine. Indeed many subcultures with quite repressive sexual values have flourished in the past, such as the colonies of nineteenth-century pietists in the United States. Some additional aspect of industrialism must therefore be adduced to explain the expressly permissive sexual content of the European proletarian subculture.

The second important dimension of capitalism lay in the mentality of the market place. In the eighteenth and early nineteenth centuries the market economy encroached steadily at the cost of the moral economy, and the values of individual self-interest and competitiveness that people learned in the market were soon transferred to other areas of life. It was this process of the transfer of values that gave the proletarian subculture its libertine moral caste.

The years after 1750 saw the intrusion of the principles of the market place into popular life. In early modern Europe trade in foodstuffs and in most nonagricultural products was tightly regulated by communal and corporate bodies, so that the Continent was fragmented into countless tiny local markets, kept through a complot of regulation and poor transportation as hermetically sealed compartments. Of course long-distance trade existed, yet most of the labor force was involved in local production along noncapitalistic lines. German political economists made a classic distinction between *Export-* and *Lokalgewerbe,* and most of the population lived from the latter. Then late in the eighteenth century these locally administered economies began to be engulfed by free markets of vast territorial scope. The struggle over free trade in grain in France has been often told; the losing battle of German guilds against pack pedlars, retail merchandise shops, unlicensed competitors, and the Customs Union is similarly familiar. Everywhere the moral economy regulated by the village fathers lost out to free competition regulated only by the invisible hand of the price mechanism.

Contact with these new labor markets was the most direct source of personal autonomy. As women became immersed in the market, they learned its values. I have elsewhere suggested that capitalism's mental habits of maximizing one's self-interest and sacrificing community goals to individual profit transfer easily to other thought processes. It seems a plausible proposition that people assimilate in the market place an integrated, coherent set of values about social behavior and personal independence and that these values quickly inform the noneconomic realms of individual mentalities. If this logic holds true, we may identify exposure to the market place as a prime source of female emancipation, for women who learned autonomy and maximization of self-interest in the economy would quickly stumble upon these concepts within the family as well. Men would also have learned these values, but then it was men who had traditionally been the dominant sex; a more sensitive attunement to questions of individuality left men, if anything, less able to defend themselves against the demands for autonomy of their wives and daughters. The moral authority of traditional society was of a piece; the same communitarian principles that held together the moral economy also maintained the authoritarian family. And they crumbled together as well.

Thus a second crucial consequence of capitalism for women came in the area of personal values: an unwillingness to accept the dictates of superordinates and a new readiness to experiment with personal freedom and gratification. The reader should at this point bear in mind that we have to juggle simultaneously three different effects of capitalism: the first dimension of subculture weakened traditional moral taboos and destroyed internalized antisexual values; the second dimension, which we have just considered, quickened interest in intercourse as an aspect of personality development; and the third dimension of capitalism, to which we now turn, removed many of the external controls upon female sexual emancipation.

This last principal salient of industrial advance worked in the interest of women by modifying with wage labor the balance of power in the family. Paid employment meant that women would bring a distinct, quantifiable contribution to the family's resources, and accordingly would probably be entitled to a greater voice in the disposal of these resources. As many sociologists of the family have noted, the wife's (or daughter's) influence within the conjugal unit is a direct function of the status she enjoys in the outside world and of the resources she is able to import from that world into the family circle. Richard F. Tomasson has convincingly explained the historical development and the present-day international singularity of the Swedish family with such an approach, arguing also that, "Where females have greater equality and are subject to less occupational and social differentiation, the premarital sex codes will be more permissive than where the female's status is completely or primarily dependent on the status of her husband." Altogether, capitalism entailed a quite material source of female independence and autonomy, increasing vastly the leverage formerly obtained from customary, dependent, unpaid, "women's work."

Popular involvement in the market economy started with the young and the poor and ended with the older and more prosperous. It was the most marginal whom capitalism could first detach from their traditional economic moorings, and so in the eighteenth century the young members of the proletarian classes that population growth had been creating went first to the cottage looms and spinning wheels. Thereafter ever more prosperous groups of the traditional economy found themselves pulled into the flux of the market, so that by the late nineteenth century even the most isolated sectors of the old middle class had been plunged into price competition and profit rationality. Immersion in the market progressed by stages.

Early in the eighteenth century the putting-out system began its conquest of the countryside, drawing in the landless poor. Then, in the course of the century agricultural capitalism began to encroach upon traditional subsistence and manorial farming, recruiting from among the landless and especially from the youth, for often unmarried laborers would live in the farmer's house, or newly married couples in nearby cottages. Next came migration to the newly rising factories and mills. The timing varied from one region to another, but normally it was the youth whom the fresh modern sector pulled from small farms and craft shops into factories.

In the nineteenth century industrial growth created a prosperous new middle class of administrators and clerks, of technicians and professionals. Because these people had often to endure long delays before marriage, women entered their childbearing periods at relatively advanced ages and largely abstained from intercourse beforehand. Finally, in the nineteenth century capitalism tore at the heart of the traditional old middle class itself, rather than merely at the supernumary poor. Across the Continent the masters of craft shops had to accommodate themselves to industrial capitalism, either by servicing the new factories or by going to work in them. And the depopulation of the countryside on the threshold of the twentieth century is an oft-told tale. It was frequently as mature men and women that these families were forced out of the traditional sector, of which they had constituted the backbone.

Thus the market started with the youngest and lowliest on the age-status spectrum and concluded with the most established and mature. It was also in this order that, I suggest, the spirit of female emancipation spread, from young and poor to well to do and middle-aged.

⋅❀⋅

How, precisely, did these massive shifts in economic structure, culture, and individual mentalities affect either marital or nonmarital fertility? The linkages between emancipation and the increase in illegitimacy seem crisp and strong; those between capitalism and marital fertility are largely artifacts.

For the unmarried woman capitalism meant personal freedom, which meant in turn sexual freedom. The young woman could withstand parental sanctions against her sexual and emotional independence because the modern sector promised employment, economic self- sufficiency, and if need be, migration from home to another town. Such independence meant often, as we have seen, a paramour and therewith, in the absence of birth control, illegitimacy.

Louise A. Tilly, Joan W. Scott,
and Miriam Cohen

Women's Work and European Fertility Patterns

According to [Edward] Shorter, a change in fertility rates can only mean a change in sexual practices, which has to mean a change in attitudes, particularly of women. The sequence must be linear and direct. As Shorter argues:

> It seems a plausible proposition that people assimilate in the market place an integrated, coherent set of values about social behavior and personal independence and that these values quickly inform the noneconomic realm of individual mentalities. If this logic holds true, we may identify exposure to the market place as a prime source of female emancipation.

This statement, as its language clearly reveals, is based on a claim of reasoning, not on evidence. Shorter offers nothing to prove that more women worked in the capitalist marketplace in this period. He merely assumes that they did. Similarly, he assumes that women at the end of the eighteenth century had different family roles and attitudes from their predecessors. And he assumes as well that changes in work opportunities immediately changed values. Ideas, in his opinion, instantly reflect one's current economic experience. Shorter employs a mechanistic notion of "value transfer" to explain the influence of changes in occupational structure on changes in collective mentalities: "In the eighteenth and early nineteenth centuries the market economy encroached steadily at the cost of the moral economy, and the values of individual self-interest and competitiveness that people learned in the market were soon transferred to other areas of life."

For Shorter, sexual behavior echoes market behavior at every point. "Emancipated" women gained a sense of autonomy at work that the subordinate and powerless women of pre-industrial society had lacked. That work, created by capitalist economic development, necessarily fostered values of individualism in those who participated in it, and individualism was expressed in part by a new desire for sexual gratification. Young women working outside the home, Shorter insists, were by definition rebelling against parental authority. Indeed, they sought work in order to gain the independence and individual fulfillment that could not be attained at home. It follows, in Shorter's logic, that sexual behavior, too, must have been defiant of parental restraint. As the

Excerpted from Louise A. Tilly, Joan W. Scott, and Miriam Cohen, "Women's Work and European Fertility Patterns," *Journal of Interdisciplinary History,* vol. 6, no. 3 (Winter 1976), pp. 447–476. Copyright © 1976 by The Massachusetts Institute of Technology and the editors of the *Journal of Interdisciplinary History.* Reprinted by permission of MIT Press Journals. Notes omitted.

market economy spread there arose a new, libertine, proletarian subculture "indulgent of eroticism." Once married, the independent young working women engaged in frequent intercourse because they and their husbands took greater pleasure in sex. Female "emancipation" thus began among the young and poor. In the absence of birth control, the sexual gratification of single working girls increased the illegitimate birthrate; that of married women (who worked or had worked) inflated the legitimate birthrate. In this fashion Shorter answers a central question of European historical demography. The fertility increase in the late eighteenth century was simply the result of the "emancipation," occupational and sexual, of working-class women....

It is now time to examine the historical evidence that Shorter neglected on women's role in pre-industrial society; on the effects of industrialization on women's work and on their attitudes; and on the motives which sent young girls out into the "marketplace" at the end of the eighteenth and beginning of the nineteenth century. None of the evidence that we have found supports Shorter's argument in any way. Women were not powerless in "traditional" families; they played important economic roles which gave them a good deal of power within the family. Industrialization did not significantly modernize women's work in the period when fertility rates rose; in fact, the vast majority of working women did not work in factories, but at customary women's jobs. Women usually became wage earners during the early phases of industrialization not to rebel against their parents or declare independence from their husbands, but to augment family finances. Indeed, women in this period must be studied in their family settings, for the constraints of family membership greatly affected their opportunities for individual autonomy. No change in attitude, then, increased the numbers of children whom working women bore. Rather, old attitudes and customary behavior interacted with greatly changed circumstances—particularly in the composition of populations—and led to increased illegitimate fertility.

Women eventually shed many outdated priorities, and by the end of the nineteenth century some working women had clearly adopted "modern" life styles. But these changes involved a more gradual and complex adaptation than Shorter implies. The important point, however, is that the years around 1790 were not a watershed in the history of women's economic emancipation —despite the fact that the locus of women's work began to move outside the home. These *were* the crucial years for the increases in fertility in Europe. All of the evidence is not in, by any means; what we offer, however, indicates that in this period, women of the popular classes simply were not searching for freedom or experiencing emancipation. The explanation for changed fertility patterns lies elsewhere.

Women's Place in "Traditional" Families

In the pre-industrial family, the household was organized as a family or domestic economy. Men, women, and children worked at tasks which were differentiated by age and sex, but the work of all was necessary for survival. Artisans' wives assisted their husbands in their work as weavers, bakers, shoemakers, or tailors. Certain work, like weaving, whether carried on in the city or the country, needed the cooperation of all family members. Children and women did the spinning and carding; men ran the looms. Wives also managed many aspects of the household, including family finances. In less prosperous urban families, women did paid work which was often an extension of their household chores: They sewed and made lace; they also took odd jobs as carters, laundresses, and street cleaners.

Unmarried women also became servants. Resourcefulness was characteristic of poor women: When they could not find work which would enable them to contribute to the family income, they begged, stole, or became prostitutes. Hufton's work on the Parisian poor in the eighteenth century and Forrest's work on Bordeaux both describe the crucial economic contribution of urban working-class women and the consequent central role which these women played in their families.

In the country, the landowning peasant's family was also the unit of productive activity. The members of the family worked together, again at sex-differentiated tasks. Children—boys and girls—were sent to other farms as servants when their help was not needed at home. Their activity, nonetheless, contributed to the well-being of the family. They sent their earnings home, or, if they were not paid wages, their absence at least relieved the family of the burden of feeding and boarding them. Women's responsibilities included care of the house, barnyard, and dairy. They managed to bring in small net profits from marketing of poultry and dairy products and from work in rural domestic industry. Management of the household and, particularly, of finances led to a central role for women in these families. An observer in rural Brittany during the nineteenth century reported that the wife and mother of the family made "the important decisions, buying a field, selling a cow, a lawsuit against a neighbor, choice of future son-in-law." For rural families who did not own land, women's work was even more vital: From agricultural work, spinning, or petty trading, they contributed their share to the family wage—the only economic resource of the landless family.

In city and country, among propertied and propertyless, women of the popular classes had a vital economic role which gave them a recognized and powerful position within the household. It is impossible to guess what sort of sexual relations were practiced under these circumstances. We *can* say, however, that women in these families were neither dependent nor powerless. Hence, it is impossible to accept Shorter's attempt to derive women's supposed sexual subordination from their place in the pre-industrial household.

Why Women Worked

Shorter attributes the work of women outside the home after 1750, particularly that of young, single women, to a change in outlook: a new desire for independence from parental restraints. He argues that since seeking work was an individualistic rebellion against traditionalism, sexual behavior, too, reflected a defiance of parental authority. The facts are that daughters of the popular classes were most often sent into service or to work in the city by their families. Their work represented a continuation of practices customary in the family economy. When resources were scarce or mouths at home too numerous, children customarily sought work outside, generally with family approval.

Industrialization and urbanization created new problems for rural families but generated new opportunities as well. In most cases, families strategically adapted their established practices to the new context. Thus, daughters sent out to work went farther away from home than had been customary. Most still defined their work in the family interest. Sometimes arrangements for direct payment in money or foodstuffs were made between a girl's parents and her employer. In other cases, the girls themselves regularly sent money home. Commentators observed that the girls considered this a normal arrangement—part of their obligation to the family.

In some cases the conditions of migration for young working girls emphasized their ties to family in many ways limited their independence. In Italy and France, factory dormitories housed female workers, and nuns regulated their behavior and social lives. In the needle trades in British cities, enterprising women with a little capital turned their homes into lodging houses for piece-workers in their employ. Of course, these institutions permitted employers to control their employees by limiting their mobility and regulating their behavior. The point is not that they were beneficent practices, but that young girls lived in households which permitted them limited autonomy. Domestic service, the largest single occupation for women, was also the most traditional and most protective of young girls. They would be sent from one household to another and thus be given security. Châtelain argues that domestic service was a safe form of migration in France for young girls from the country. They had places to live, families, food, and lodgings and had no need to fend for themselves in the unknown big city as soon as they arrived. It is true that servants often longed to leave their places, and that they resented the exploitation of their mistresses (and the advances of their masters). But that does not change the fact that, initially, their migration was sponsored by a set of traditional institutions which limited their individual freedom.

In fact, individual freedom did not seem to be at issue for the daughters of either the landed or the landless, although clearly their experiences differed. It seems likely that peasant families maintained closer ties with their daughters, even when the girls worked in distant cities. The family interest in the farm (the property that was the birthright of the lineage and not of any individual) was a powerful influence on individual behavior. Thus, farm girls working as domestics continued to send money home. Married daughters working as domestics in Norwegian cities sent their children home to be raised on the farm by grandparents. But even when ties of this sort were not maintained, it was seldom from rebellious motives. Braun describes the late eighteenth-century situation of peasants in the hinterland of Zurich. These peasants were willing to divide their holdings for their children because of new work opportunities in cottage industry. These young people married earlier than they would have if the farm had been held undivided, and they quickly established their own families. Braun suggests that the young workers soon lost touch with their parents. The process, as he describes it, however, was not rebellion; rather, the young people went into cottage industry to lessen the burden that they represented for the family. These motives were welcomed and encouraged by the parents. Family bonds were stretched and broken, but that was a consequence, not a cause, of the new opportunities for work.

Similarly, among urban artisans, older values informed the adaptation to a new organization of work and to technological change. Initially, artisans as well as their political spokesmen insisted that the old values of association and cooperation could continue to characterize their work relationships in the new industrial society. Artisan subculture in cities during the early stages of industrialization was not characterized by an individualistic, self-seeking ideology, as Thompson, Hufton, Forrest, Soboul, Gossez, and others have clearly shown. With no evidence that urban artisans adopted the values of the marketplace at work, Shorter's deduction about a "libertine proletarian subculture" has neither factual nor logical validity. It seems more likely that artisan families, like peasant families, sent their wives and daughters to work to help bolster their shaky economic situation. These women undoubtedly joined the ranks of the unskilled who had always constituted the urban female work force. Wives and daughters of the unskilled and propertyless had worked for centuries at service and manufacturing jobs in cities. In the nineteenth century there were more of them because the proportions of unskilled propertyless workers increased.

Eighteenth- and early nineteenth-century cities grew primarily by migration. The urban working class was thus constantly renewed and enlarged by a stream of rural migrants. Agricultural change drove rural laborers and peasants cityward at the end of the eighteenth century, and technological change drove many artisans and their families into the ranks of the unskilled. Women worked outside the home because they had to. Changed attitudes did not propel them into the labor force. Family interest and not self-interest was the underlying motive for their work.

Women's Work

What happened in the mid-eighteenth century with the spread of capitalism, the growth of markets, and industrialization? Did these economic changes bring new work experiences for women, with the consequences which Shorter describes? Did women, earning money in the capitalist marketplace, find a new sense of self that expressed itself in increased sexual activity? In examining the historical evidence for the effects on women's work of industrialization and urbanization, we find that the location of women's work did change—more young women worked outside the home and in large cities than ever before. But they were recruited from the same groups which had always sent women to work.

The female labor force of nineteenth-century Europe, like that of seventeenth- and eighteenth-century Europe, consisted primarily of the daughters of the popular classes and, secondarily of their wives. The present state of our knowledge makes it difficult to specify precisely the groups within the working classes from which nineteenth-century women wage earners came. It is clear, however, that changes in the organization of work must have driven the daughters and wives of craftsmen out of the family shop. Similarly, population

growth (a result of declining mortality and younger age at marriage due to opportunities for work in cottage industry) created a surplus of hands within the
urban household and on the family farm. Women in these families always had
been expected to work. Increasingly, they were sent away from home to earn
their portion of the family wage.

Shorter's notion that the development of modern capitalism brought new
kinds of opportunities to working-class women as early as the middle of the
eighteenth century is wrong. There was a very important change in the location
of work from rural homes to cities, but this did not revolutionize the nature
of the work that most women did. Throughout the nineteenth century, most
women worked at traditional occupations. By the end of the century, factory
employment was still minimal....

Shorter is also incorrect in his assumption that the working woman was
able to live independently of her family because she had the economic means to
do so. Evidence for British working women indicates that this was not the case.
Throughout the nineteenth century, British working women's wages were considered supplementary incomes—supplementary, that is, to the wages of other
family members. It was assumed by employers that women, unlike men, were
not responsible for earning their own living. Female wages were always far lower
than male. In the Lancashire cotton mills in 1833, where female wages were the
highest in the country, females aged 16–21 earned 7/3.5 weekly, while males
earned 10/3. Even larger differentials obtained among older workers. In London in the 1880s, there was a similar differential between the average earnings
of the sexes: 72 percent of the males in the bookbinding industry earned over
30/– weekly; 42.5 percent of women made less than 12/–. In precious metals, clocks, and watch manufacturing, 83.5 percent of the males earned 30/
– or more weekly; females earned 9–12/–. Women in small clothing work-
shops earned 10–12/– weekly, while women engaged in outwork in the clothing
trades made only 4/– a week. In Birmingham, in 1900, the average weekly wage
for working women less than age 21 was 10/–, for men 18/–. Women's work
throughout this period, as in the eighteenth century, was for the most part unskilled. Occupations were often seasonal and irregular, leaving women without
work for many months during the year. Is it possible that there were many single women who could enjoy a life of independence when the majority could
not even afford to live adequately on their personal wages?...

Women's work from 1750 to 1850 (and much later) did not provide an
experience of emancipation. Work was hard and poorly paid and, for the most
part, it did not represent a change from traditional female occupations. Those
women who traveled to cities did find themselves free of some traditional village and family restraints. But, as we shall see, the absence of these restraints
was more often burdensome than liberating. Young women with inadequate
wages and unstable jobs found themselves caught in a cycle of poverty which
increased their vulnerability. Having lost one family, many sought to create
another.

The Origins of Increased Illegitimacy

The compositional change which increased the numbers of unskilled, property-less workers in both rural and urban areas and raised their proportion in urban populations also contributed to an increase in rates of illegitimacy. Women in this group of the population always had contributed the most illegitimate births. An increase in the number of women in this group, therefore, meant a greater incidence of illegitimacy.

A recent article by Laslett and Oosterveen speaks directly to Shorter's speculations: "The assumption that illegitimacy figures directly reflect the prevalence of sexual intercourse outside marriage, which seems to be made whenever such figures are used to show that beliefs, attitudes and interests have changed in some particular way, can be shown to be very shaky in its foundations." Using data from Colyton, collected and analyzed by E. A. Wrigley, they argue that one important component in the incidence of illegitimacy is the existence of illegitimacy-prone families, which bring forth bastards generation after generation. Nevertheless, they warn, "this projected sub-society never produced all the bastards, all the bastard-bearers."

The women who bore illegitimate children were not pursuing sexual pleasure, as Shorter would have us believe. Most expected to get married, but the circumstances of their lives—propertylessness, poverty, large-scale geographic mobility, occupational instability, and the absence of traditional social protection—prevented the fulfillment of this expectation. A number of pressures impelled young working girls to find mates. One was the loneliness and isolation of work in the city. Another was economic need: Wages were low and employment for women, unstable. The logical move for a single girl far from her family would be to find a husband with whom she might re-establish a family economy. Yet another pressure was the desire to escape the confines of domestic service, an occupation which more and more young women were entering.

Could not this desire to establish a family be what the domestic servants, described by the Munich police chief in 1815, sought? No quest for pleasure is inherent in the fact that "so many young girls leave service.... But they do little real work and let themselves be supported by boyfriends; they become pregnant and then are abandoned." It seems a sad and distorted version of an older family form, but an attempt at it, nevertheless. Recent work has shown, in fact, that for many French servants in the nineteenth century, this kind of transfer to urban life and an urban husband was often successful.

Was it a search for sexual fulfillment that prompted young women to become "engaged" to young men and then sleep with them in the expectation that marriage would follow? Not at all. In rural and urban areas premarital sexual relationships were common. What Shorter interprets as sexual libertinism, as evidence of an individualistic desire for sexual pleasure, is more likely an expression of the traditional wish to marry. The attempt to reconstitute the family economy in the context of economic deprivation and geographic mobility produced unstable and stable "free unions."

... The central point here is that no major change in values or mentality was necessary to create these cases of illegitimacy. Rather, older expectations operating in a changed context yielded unanticipated (and often unhappy) results.... Women's work in the late eighteenth and early nineteenth centuries was not "liberating" in any sense. Most women stayed in established occupations. They were so poorly paid that economic independence was precluded. Furthermore, whether married or single, most women often entered the labor force in the service of the family interest. The evidence available points to several causes for illegitimacy, none related to the "emancipation" of women: economic need, causing women to seek work far from the protection of their families; occupational instability of men which led to *mariages manqués* (sexual intercourse following a promise of marriage which was never fulfilled). Finally, analysis of the effects of population growth on propertied peasants and artisans seems to show that the bifurcation of marriage and property arrangements began to change the nature of marriage arrangements for propertyless people.

POSTSCRIPT

Did the Industrial Revolution Lead to a Sexual Revolution?

In the world of the "great man," women, racial and ethnic minorities, and the poor are nearly invisible. They appear as passive participants in the historical drama; it is as if history happens to them. Revisionist historians, however, insist that even the apparently powerless have the potential to act as agents of historical change rather than as passive victims. Both Shorter and Tilly et al. assume that working-class, European women in the years between 1750 and 1850 made decisions and acted upon them. For reasons that may never be completely clear, there was a rise in illegitimacy rates, evidence that more babies than in the past were being born outside of marriage. What changed? A higher illegitimacy rate can mean that more sexual activity is taking place, but it can also mean that fewer unmarried, pregnant women are marrying.

To help you to make your own decision, you may wish to consider the evidence offered in the following books and essays. For a Marxist interpretation, see Friedrich Engels, *The Origin of the Family, Private Property and the State* (International Publishers, 1972). Ivy Pinchbeck, in *Women Workers and the Industrial Revolution, 1750–1850* (F. Cass, 1969), argues that occupational changes played a significant role in women's legal and political emancipation. Rudolf Braun, in "The Impact of Cottage Industry on an Agricultural Population," in David Landes, ed., *The Rise of Capitalism* (Macmillan, 1966), describes an economic system in rural Switzerland in which the daughters in a family learned to spin and weave, contributing their earnings to the family economic unit as a matter of course. Olwen Hufton makes a similar point about the Parisian poor in the eighteenth century in "Women in Revolution, 1789–1796," *Past and Present* (vol. 53, 1971) and about a broader segment of the population in "Women and the Family Economy in Eighteenth-Century France," *French Historical Studies* (vol. 9, 1975). Whether or not young working women kept their own wages and had enough money to support an independent lifestyle is a key historiographic question. For more work by this issue's authors, students may wish to read "Women's Work and the Family in Nineteenth-Century Europe," *Comparative Studies in Society and History* (vol. 17, 1975) and *Women, Work, and Family* (Holt, Rinehart & Winston, 1978) by Scott and Tilly. Essays by Shorter include "Illegitimacy, Sexual Revolution and Social Change in Modern Europe," *Journal of Interdisciplinary History* (vol. 2, 1971) and "Sexual Change and Illegitimacy: The European Experience," in Robert J. Bezucha, ed., *Modern European Social History* (D. C. Heath, 1972).

ISSUE 2

Was the French Revolution Worth Its Human Costs?

YES: Peter Kropotkin, from *The Great French Revolution, 1789–1793*, trans. N. F. Dryhurst (Schocken Books, 1971)

NO: Simon Schama, from *Citizens: A Chronicle of the French Revolution* (Alfred A. Knopf, 1989)

ISSUE SUMMARY

YES: Peter Kropotkin (1842–1921), a Russian prince, revolutionary, and anarchist, argues that the French Revolution eradicated both serfdom and absolutism and paved the way for France's future democratic development.

NO: Columbia University professor Simon Schama counters that not only did the French Revolution betray its own goals, it also produced few of the results that it promised.

Few historical events have created the emotional responses and concomitant debates as has the French Revolution. Taking advantage of one of the largest bodies of historical data gathered, historians of the past two centuries have analyzed, synthesized, and evaluated every facet of this seminal event in the history of the Western world.

From this scholarship has come a myriad of important questions regarding the political, economic, social, religious, cultural, and intellectual aspects of the Revolution—questions involving causation, behavior, outcomes, and assessments. Each generation of historians has taken the work of its predecessors and used it to shape an understanding of the Revolution that emanates from the uncovering of new sources of information, the creation of new tools to assist in the process, and the development of new schools of historical thought that attempt to give a more contemporary, relevant slant to this important event. As a result of this historiographical process, many major questions regarding the French Revolution have been raised and plausible answers given.

One of the most important questions that French Revolution scholarship has raised, a double-edged one that is both elemental and significant is, What were its outcomes, and were they worth the human cost that was paid to achieve them?

The debate began before anyone knew what course the Revolution would take. In a 1790 treatise entitled *Reflections on the Revolution in France*, English statesman Edmund Burke (1729–1797) uncannily predicted the future course of the Revolution and its catastrophic consequences for both France and Europe. He also argued in favor of a slow, evolutionary style of political change that was taking place in his own country, rather than the spasmodic one that was beginning to envelop France. Burke's message was clear: the revolution in France will be costly and counterproductive.

A year later, the French Revolution gained an articulate defender in Thomas Paine (1737–1809), an English-born American citizen. In *Common Sense* (1776), a stirring call-to-arms for American colonists to throw off the yoke of English oppression, Paine acquired a reputation as a foe of tyrannical government and as a strong supporter of human freedom and equality. In Part 1 of his political pamphlet *The Rights of Man*, published in 1791, Paine argued that revolution was necessary to purge civilization of those elements that stood in the way of democratic reform. According to Paine, no price was too high to pay for the realization of these cherished goals.

As generations passed, the basic question debated by Burke and Paine faded into the background as historians began to explore other fertile areas of historical research. There was either a general acceptance of the French Revolution's importance in changing the course of history or a quiet acquiescence in its outcomes, regardless of the consequences.

Peter Kropotkin (1842–1921) was an early historical defender of the French Revolution. Obviously influenced by his radical, anarchistic background and his desire to see all people freed from the yoke of oppression, his view of the Revolution was somewhat simplistic and uncritical. Coming from a ninteenth-century environment, in which revolutions were commonplace and were viewed by many as an inevitable part of political evolution, his opinions on the French Revolution are representative for his time—and for generations to come.

Of all the books written about the French Revolution in recent years, none have been as popular as Simon Schama's *Citizens: A Chronicle of the French Revolution*, which is excerpted in the second selection of this issue. Published in the midst of the Revolution's bicentennial celebration, the book aroused much controversy for many reasons; among them was his view that the French Revolution was not worth its human costs. Seeing violence as an endemic part of the revolutionary process, Schama also states that the French Revolution produced few of the tangible results that it had promised. Coming from the twentieth century when false political promises, revolutions that turned into dictatorships, and resultant massive losses of human lives were commonplace, Schama's work is as much a product of that century as Kropotkin's is of his.

Together the two readings provide not only opposing viewpoints on whether or not the French Revolution was worth its human costs, but also a clear example of how different eras can have different values, which can affect how the past is interpreted.

Peter Kropotkin  **YES**

The Great French Revolution, 1789–1793

When one sees that terrible and powerful Convention wrecking itself in 1794–1795, that proud and strong Republic disappearing, and France, after the demoralising *régime* of the Directory, falling under the military yoke of a Bonaparte, one is impelled to ask: "What was the good of the Revolution if the nation had to fall back again under despotism?" In the course of the nineteenth century, this question has been constantly put, and the timid and conservative have worn it threadbare as an argument against revolutions in general.

... Those who have seen in the Revolution only a change in the Government, those who are ignorant of its economic as well as its educational work, those alone could put such a question.

The France we see during the last days of the eighteenth century, at the moment of the *coup d'état* on the 18th Brumaire, is not the France that existed before 1789. Would it have been possible for the old France, wretchedly poor and with a third of her population suffering yearly from dearth, to have maintained the Napoleonic Wars, coming so soon after the terrible wars of the Republic between 1792 and 1799, when all Europe was attacking her?

The fact is, that a new France had been constituted since 1792–1793. Scarcity still prevailed in many of the departments, and its full horrors were felt especially after the *coup d'état* of Thermidor, when the maximum price for all foodstuffs was abolished. There were still some departments which did not produce enough wheat to feed themselves, and as the war went on, and all means of transport were requisitioned for its supplies, there was scarcity in those departments. But everything tends to prove that France was even then producing much more of the necessaries of life of every kind than in 1789.

Never was there in France such energetic ploughing, Michelet tells us, as in 1792, when the peasant was ploughing the lands he had taken back from the lords, the convents, the churches, and was goading his oxen to the cry of *"Allons Prusse! Allons Autriche!"* Never had there been so much clearing of lands—even royalist writers admit this—as during those years of revolution. The first good harvest, in 1794, brought relief to two-thirds of France—at least in the villages, for all this time the towns were threatened with scarcity of food. Not that it was scarce in France as a whole, or that the *sans-culotte* municipalities neglected to take measures to feed those who could not find employment, but from the

From Peter Kropotkin, *The Great French Revolution, 1789-1793*, trans. N. F. Dryhurst (Schocken Books, 1971).

fact that all beasts of burden not actually used in tillage were requisitioned to carry food and ammunition to the fourteen armies of the Republic. In those days there were no railways, and all but the main roads were in the state they are to this day in Russia—well-nigh impassable.

A new France was born during those four years of revolution. For the first time in centuries the peasant ate his fill, straightened his back and dared to speak out. Read the detailed reports concerning the return of Louis XVI. to Paris, when he was brought back a prisoner from Varennes, in June 1791, by the peasants, and say: "Could such a thing, such an interest in the public welfare, such a devotion to it, and such an independence of judgment and action have been possible before 1789?" A new nation had been born in the meantime, just as we see to-day a new nation coming into life in Russia and in Turkey.

It was owing to this new birth that France was able to maintain her wars under the Republic and Napoleon, and to carry the principles of the Great Revolution into Switzerland, Italy, Spain, Belgium, Holland, Germany, and even to the borders of Russia. And when, after all those wars, after having mentally followed the French armies as far as Egypt and Moscow, we expect to find France in 1815 reduced to an appalling misery and her lands laid waste, we find, instead, that even in its eastern portions and in the Jura, the country is much more prosperous than it was at the time when Pétion, pointing out to Louis XVI. the luxuriant banks of the Marne, asked him if there was anywhere in the world a kingdom more beautiful than the one the King had not wished to keep.

The self-contained energy was such in villages regenerated by the Revolution, that in a few years France became a country of well-to-do peasants, and her enemies soon discovered that in spite of all the blood she had shed and the losses she had sustained, France, in respect of her *productivity,* was the richest country in Europe. Her wealth, indeed, is not drawn from the Indies or from her foreign commerce: it comes from her own soil, from her love of the soil, from her own skill and industry. She is the richest country, because of the subdivision of her wealth, and she is still richer because of the possibilities she offers for the future.

Such was the effect of the Revolution. And if the casual observer sees in Napoleonic France only a love of glory, the historian realises that even the wars France waged at that period were undertaken to secure the fruits of the Revolution—to keep the lands that had been retaken from the lords, the priests and the rich, and the liberties that had been won from despotism and the Court. If France was willing in those years to bleed herself to death, merely to prevent the Germans, the English, and the Russians from forcing a Louis XVIII. upon her, it was because she did not want the return of the emigrant nobles to mean that the *ci-devants* would take back the lands which had been watered already with the peasant's sweat, and the liberties which had been sanctified with the patriots' blood. And France fought so well for twenty-three years, that when she was compelled at last to admit the Bourbons, it was she who imposed conditions on them. The Bourbons might reign, but the lands were to be kept by those who had taken them from the feudal lords, so that even during the White

Terror of the Bourbons they dared not touch those lands. The old *régime* could not be re-established.

This is what is gained by making a Revolution.

◦◦◉◦◦

There are other things to be pointed out. In the history of all nations a time comes when fundamental changes are bound to take place in the whole of the national life. Royal despotism and feudalism were dying in 1789; it was impossible to keep them alive; they had to go.

But then, two ways were opened out before France: reform or revolution.

At such times there is always a moment when reform is still possible; but if advantage has not been taken of that moment, if an obstinate resistance has been opposed to the requirements of the new life, up to the point when blood has flowed in the streets, as it flowed on July 14, 1789, then there must be a Revolution. And once the Revolution has begun, it must necessarily develop to its conclusions—that is to say, to the highest point it is capable of attaining— were it only temporarily, being given a certain condition of the public mind at this particular moment.

If we represent the slow progress of a period of evolution by a line drawn on paper, we shall see this line gradually though slowly rising. Then there comes a Revolution, and the line makes a sudden leap upwards. In England the line would be represented as rising to the Puritan Republic of Cromwell; in France it rises to the *Sans-culotte* Republic of 1793. However, at this height progress cannot be maintained; all the hostile forces league together against it, and the Republic goes down. Our line, after having reached that height, drops. Reaction follows. For the political life of France the line drops very low indeed, but by degrees it rises again, and when peace is restored in 1815 in France, and in 1688 in England—both countries are found to have attained a level much higher than they were on prior to their Revolutions.

After that, evolution is resumed: our line again begins to rise slowly: but, besides taking place on a very much higher level, the rising of the line will in nearly every case be also much more rapid than before the period of disturbance.

This is a law of human progress, and also a law of individual progress. The more recent history of France confirms this very law by showing how it was necessary to pass through the Commune to arrive at the Third Republic.

The work of the French Revolution is not confined merely to what it obtained and what was retained of it in France. It is to be found also in the principles bequeathed by it to the succeeding century—in the line of direction it marked out for the future.

A reform is always a compromise with the past, but the progress accomplished by revolution is always a promise of future progress. If the Great French Revolution was the summing up of a century's evolution, it also marked out in its turn the programme of evolution to be accomplished in the course of the nineteenth century.

It is a law in the world's history that the period of a hundred or a hundred and thirty years, more or less, which passes between two great revolutions, receives its character from the revolution in which this period began. The nations endeavour to realise in their institutions the inheritance bequeathed to them by the last revolution. All that this last could not yet put into practice, all the great thoughts which were thrown into circulation during the turmoil, and which the revolution either could not or did not know how to apply, all the attempts at sociological reconstruction, which were born during the revolution, will go to make up the substance of evolution during the epoch that follows the revolution, with the addition of those new ideas to which this evolution will give birth, when trying to put into practice the programme marked out by the last upheaval. Then, a new revolution will be brought about in some other nation, and this nation in its turn will set the problems for the following century. Such has hitherto been the trend of history.

Two great conquests, in fact, characterise the century which has passed since 1789–1793. Both owe their origin to the French Revolution, which had carried on the work of the English Revolution while enlarging and invigorating it with all the progress that had been made since the English middle classes beheaded their King and transferred his power to the Parliament. These two great triumphs are: the abolition of serfdom and the abolition of absolutism, by which personal liberties have been conferred upon the individual, undreamt of by the serf of the lord and the subject of the absolute king, while at the same time they have brought about the development of the middle classes and the capitalist *régime.*

These two achievements represent the principal work of the nineteenth century, begun in France in 1789 and slowly spread over Europe in the course of that century.

The work of enfranchisement, begun by the French peasants in 1789, was continued in Spain, Italy, Switzerland, Germany, and Austria by the armies of the *sans-culottes.* Unfortunately, this work hardly penetrated into Poland and did not reach Russia at all.

The abolition of serfdom in Europe would have been already completed in the first half of the nineteenth century if the French *bourgeoisie,* coming into power in 1794 over the dead bodies of Anarchists, Cordeliers, and Jacobins, had not checked the revolutionary impulse, restored monarchy, and handed over France to the imperial juggler, the first Napoleon. This ex-*sans-culotte,* now a general of the *sans-culottes,* speedily began to prop up aristocracy; but the impulsion had been given, the institution of serfdom had already received a mortal blow. It was abolished in Spain and Italy in spite of the temporary triumph of reaction. It was closely pressed in Germany after 1811, and disappeared in that country definitively in 1848. In 1861, Russia was compelled to emancipate her serfs, and the war of 1878 put an end to serfdom in the Balkan peninsula.

The cycle is now complete. The right of the lord over the person of the peasant no longer exists in Europe, even in those countries where the feudal dues have still to be redeemed.

This fact is not sufficiently appreciated by historians. Absorbed as they are in political questions, they do not perceive the importance of the abolition of serfdom, which is, however, the essential feature of the nineteenth century. The rivalries between nations and the wars resulting from them, the policies of the Great Powers which occupy so much of the historian's attention, have all sprung from that one great fact—the abolition of serfdom and the development of the wage-system which has taken its place.

The French peasant, in revolting a hundred and twenty years ago against the lord who made him beat the ponds lest croaking frogs should disturb his master's sleep, has thus freed the peasants of all Europe. In four years, by burning the documents which registered his subjection, by setting fire to the châteaux, and by executing the owners of them who refused to recognise his rights as a human being, the French peasant so stirred up all Europe that it is to-day altogether free from the degradation of serfdom.

On the other hand, the abolition of absolute power has also taken a little over a hundred years to make the tour of Europe. Attacked in England in 1648, and vanquished in France in 1789, royal authority based on divine right is no longer exercised save in Russia, but there, too, it is at its last gasp. Even the little Balkan States and Turkey have now their representative assemblies, and Russia is entering the same cycle.

In this respect the Revolution of 1789–1793 has also accomplished its work. Equality before the law and representative government have now their place in almost all the codes of Europe. In theory, at least, the law makes no distinctions between men, and every one has the right to participate, more or less, in the government.

The absolute monarch—master of his subjects—and the lord—master of the soil and the peasants, by right of birth—have both disappeared. The middle classes now govern Europe.

But at the same time the Great Revolution has bequeathed to us some other principles of an infinitely higher import; the principles of communism. We have seen how all through the Great Revolution the communist idea kept coming to the front, and how after the fall of the Girondins numerous attempts and sometimes great attempts were make in this direction. Fourierism descends in a direct line from L'Ange on one side and from Chalier on the other. Babeuf is the direct descendant of ideas which stirred the masses to enthusiasm in 1793; he, Buonarotti, and Sylvain Maréchal have only systematised them a little or even merely put them into literary form. But the secret societies organized by Babeuf and Buonarotti were the origin of the *communistes matérialistes* secret societies through which Blanqui and Barbès conspired under the *bourgeois* monarchy of Louis-Philippe. Later on, in 1866, the International Working Men's Association appeared in the direct line of descent from these societies. As to "socialism" we know now that this term came into vogue to avoid the term "communism," which at one time was dangerous because the secret communist societies became societies for action, and were rigorously suppressed by the *bourgeoisie* then in power.

There is, therefore, a direct filiation from the *Enragés* of 1793 and the Babeuf conspiracy of 1795 to the International Working Men's Association of 1866–1878.

There is also a direct descent of ideas. Up till now, modern socialism has added absolutely nothing to the ideas which were circulating among the French people between 1789 and 1794 and which it was tried to put into practice in the Year II. of the Republic. Modern socialism has only systematised those ideas and found arguments in their favour, either by turning against the middle-class economists certain of their own definitions, or by generalising certain facts noticed in the development of industrial capitalism, in the course of the nineteenth century.

But I permit myself to maintain also that, however vague it may have been, however little support it endeavoured to draw from arguments dressed in a scientific garb, and however little use it made of the pseudo-scientific slang of the middle-class economists, the popular communism of the first two years of the Republic saw clearer, and went much deeper in its analyses, than modern socialism.

First of all, it was communism in the consumption of the necessaries of life—not in production only; it was the communalisation and the nationalisation of what economists know as consumption—to which the stern republicans of 1793 turned, above all, their attention, when they tried to establish their stores of grain and provisions in every commune, when they set on foot a gigantic inquiry to find and fix the true value of the objects of prime and secondary necessity, and when they inspired Robespierre to declare that *only the superfluity of food stuffs should become articles of commerce, and that what was necessary belonged to all.*

Born out of the pressing necessities of those troublous years, the communism of 1793, with its affirmation of the right of all to sustenance and to the land for its production, its denial of the right of any one to hold more land than he and his family could cultivate—that is, more than a farm of 120 acres—and its attempt to communalise all trade and industry—this communism went straighter to the heart of things than all the minimum programmes of our own time, and even all the maximum preambles of such programmes.

In any case, what we learn to-day from the study of the Great Revolution is, that it was the source of origin of all the present communist, anarchist, and socialist conceptions. We have but badly understood our common mother, but now we have found her again in the midst of the *sans-culottes,* and we see what we have to learn from her.

Humanity advances by stages and these stages have been marked for several hundred years by great revolutions. After the Netherlands came England with her revolution in 1648–1657, and then it was the turn of France. Each great revolution has in it, besides, something special and original. England and France both abolished royal absolutism. But in doing so England was chiefly interested in the personal rights of the individual, particularly in matters of religion, as well as the local rights of every parish and every community. As to France, she turned her chief attention to the land question, and in striking a mortal blow at the feudal system she struck also at the great fortunes, and sent forth into the world the idea of nationalising the soil, and of socialising commerce and the chief industries.

Which of the nations will take upon herself the terrible but glorious task of the next great revolution? One may have thought for a time that it would be Russia. But if she should push her revolution further than the mere limitation of the imperial power; if she touches the land question in a revolutionary spirit —how far will she go? Will she know how to avoid the mistake made by the French Assemblies, and will she socialise the land and give it only to those who want to cultivate it with their own hands? We know not: any answer to this question would belong to the domain of prophecy.

The one thing certain is, that whatsoever nation enters on the path of revolution in our own day, it will be heir to all our forefathers have done in France. The blood they shed was shed for humanity—the sufferings they endured were borne for the entire human race; their struggles, the ideas they gave to the world, the shock of those ideas, are all included in the heritage of mankind. All have borne fruit and will bear more, still finer, as we advance towards those wide horizons opening out before us, where, like some great beacon to point the way, flame the words—LIBERTY, EQUALITY, FRATERNITY.

Citizens: A Chronicle of the French Revolution

Asked what he thought was the significance of the French Revolution, the Chinese Premier Zhou En-lai is reported to have answered, "It's too soon to tell." Two hundred years may still be too soon (or, possibly, too late) to tell.

Historians have been overconfident about the wisdom to be gained by distance, believing it somehow confers objectivity, one of those unattainable values in which they have placed so much faith. Perhaps there is something to be said for proximity. Lord Acton, who delivered the first, famous lectures on the French Revolution at Cambridge in the 1870s, was still able to hear firsthand, from a member of the Orléans dynasty, the man's recollection of "Dumouriez gibbering on the streets of London when hearing the news of Waterloo."

Suspicion that blind partisanship fatally damaged the great Romantic narratives of the first half of the nineteenth century dominated scholarly reaction during the second half. As historians institutionalized themselves into an academic profession, they came to believe conscientious research in the archives could confer dispassion: the prerequisite for winkling out the mysterious truths of cause and effect. The desired effect was to be scientific rather than poetic, impersonal rather than impassioned. And while, for some time, historical narratives remained preoccupied by the life cycle of the European nation-states—wars, treaties and dethronements—the magnetic pull of social science was such that "structures," both social and political, seemed to become the principal objects of inquiry.

In the case of the French Revolution this meant transferring attention away from the events and personalities that had dominated the epic chronicles of the 1830s and 1840s. De Tocqueville's luminous account, *The Old Regime and the Revolution,* the product of his own archival research, provided cool reason where before there had been the burning quarrels of partisanship. The Olympian quality of his insights reinforced (albeit from a liberal point of view) the Marxist-scientific claim that the significance of the Revolution was to be sought in some great change in the balance of social power. In both these views, the utterances of orators were little more than vaporous claptrap, unsuccessfully disguising their helplessness at the hands of impersonal historical forces. Likewise, the ebb and flow of events could only be made intelligible by being displayed to reveal the *essential*, primarily social, truths of the Revolution. At the core of those truths was an axiom, shared by liberals, socialists and for that matter nostalgic Christian royalists alike, that the Revolution had indeed been the crucible of modernity: the vessel in which all the characteristics of the modern social world, for good or ill, had been distilled.

By the same token, if the whole event was of this epochal significance, then the causes that generated it had necessarily to be of an equivalent magnitude. A phenomenon of such uncontrollable power that it apparently swept away an entire universe of traditional customs, mentalities and institutions could only have been produced by contradictions that lay embedded deep within the fabric of the "old regime." Accordingly, weighty volumes appeared, between the centennial of 1889 and the Second World War, documenting every aspect of those structural faults. Biographies of Danton and Mirabeau disappeared, at least from respectable scholarly presses, and were replaced by studies of price fluctuations in the grain market. At a later stage still, discrete social groups placed in articulated opposition to each other—the "bourgeoisie," "sansculottes,"—were defined and anatomized and their dialectical dance routines were made the exclusive choreography of revolutionary politics.

In the fifty years since the sesquicentennial, there has been a serious loss of confidence in this approach. The drastic social changes imputed to the Revolution seem less clear-cut or actually not apparent at all. The "bourgeoisie" said in the classic Marxist accounts to have been the authors and beneficiaries of the event have become social zombies, the product of historiographical obsessions rather than historical realities. Other alterations in the modernization of French society and institutions seem to have been anticipated by the reform of the "old regime." Continuities seem as marked as discontinuities.

Nor does the Revolution seem any longer to conform to a grand historical design, preordained by inexorable forces of social change. Instead it seems a thing of contingencies and unforeseen consequences (not least the summoning of the Estates-General itself). An abundance of fine provincial studies has shown that instead of a single Revolution imposed by Paris on the rest of a homogeneous France, it was as often determined by local passions and interests. Along with the revival of place as a conditioner have come people. For as the imperatives of "structure" have weakened, those of individual agency, and especially of revolutionary utterance, have become correspondingly more important.

... I have pressed one of the essential elements in de Tocqueville's argument—his understanding of the destabilizing effects of modernization *before* the Revolution—further than his account allows it to go. Relieved of the revolutionary coinage "old regime," with its heavy semantic freight of obsolescence, it may be possible to see French culture and society in the reign of Louis XVI as troubled more by its addiction to change than by resistance to it. Conversely, it seems to me that much of the anger firing revolutionary violence arose from hostility towards that modernization, rather than from impatience with the speed of its progress.

... [I attempt] to confront directly the painful problem of revolutionary violence. Anxious lest they give way to sensationalism or be confused with counter-revolutionary prosecutors, historians have erred on the side of squeamishness in dealing with this issue. I have returned it to the center of the story since it seems to me that it was not merely an unfortunate by-product of politics, or the disagreeable instrument by which other more virtuous ends were accomplished or vicious ones were thwarted. In some depressingly unavoidable sense, violence *was* the Revolution itself....

⋅◈⋅

The tenth to the twelfth of March [1793] saw the first stage in the uprising, when spontaneously assembled crowds in villages and *bourgs* attacked the offices and houses of mayors, *juges de paix, procureurs* and dangerously isolated units of the National Guard. The riot at Machecoul was repeated, with less murderous consequences, in Saint-Florent-le-Veil, Sainte-Pazanne, Saint-Hilaire-de-Chaléons and Clisson. The leaders who emerged from this first wave of violence were often, like the gamekeeper and ex-soldier Stofflet, men who had long been identified in their locality with resistance to the revolutionary authorities. Once they had evicted their enemies and taken their weapons, the crowds coalesced with each other, forming processions towards larger towns and snowballing in size as they traveled along the roads.

At this stage, the riots in the Vendée seemed no different from similar antirecruitment riots taking place in many other parts of France from the Calvados in Normandy to the Côte d'Or in Burgundy and the Puy in the southern Massif Central. Some of the worst upheavals occurred north of the Loire in Brittany. But there the government had been so obsessed by the possibility of counter-revolutionary plots, it had in place sufficient force to take rapid and decisive action against the centers of resistance. The Vendée, in contrast, was dangerously depleted of troops. At Challans, for example, there were just two hundred Patriot Guards who had to face more than a thousand insurgents on the twelfth of March. By the time that reinforcements could be provided, the several riots had already fused into a general insurrection. Moreover, even of the fifty thousand republican soldiers who were eventually concentrated in the Vendée by the third week of March, only a tiny proportion—perhaps fewer than two thousand—were veterans of the "line"—the old royal army. The remainder were unseasoned volunteers, badly fed and equipped and, more critically for the situation they faced, extremely apprehensive about the rebels. None of the armies of France in the spring and summer of 1793 showed such propensity to take to panic and break ranks as the *bleus* of the Vendée. Perhaps they feared the fate of the republicans of Machecoul. As it was, many of them were dispersed in small units of fifty or some hundreds, numerous enough to provide a target for the infuriated rebels but not substantial enough to overawe them.

By the time that the Republic understood the gravity of the situation, the rebels had already taken many of the larger centers, in particular Cholet, Chemillé and Fontenay-le-Comte. On the fourteenth of March, Stofflet joined his forces with those attached to another gamekeeper, Tonnelet, and men following the wagoner-vendor Cathelineau. After failing to persuade the republican troops, commanded by the citizen-marquis de Beauveau, to lay down their arms, the rebels overwhelmed the *bleus* in a great barrage of fire, mortally wounding de Beauveau. . . .

⋅◈⋅

The second half of March brought a steady drumbeat of calamity to republican France. Within the same week, the Convention heard of the defeat at Neer-winden, a further military collapse near Louvain, Custine's abrupt retreat in the Rhineland and the Vendéan uprising. Report after report described Repub-lican armies dissolving on contact with the enemy (especially in the Vendée); volunteers demoralized and disorderly, deserting or taking to their heels; the tricolor trampled in the mud. When Delacroix returned from the Belgian front, he brought with him a gloom as deep and as dark as the weeks be-fore Valmy. French troops had fallen back on Valenciennes, but if that fortress fell, he warned, there was nothing between the Allied armies and Paris. To many deputies, and not just those of the Mountain, there could be only one explanation for this sorry trail of disasters: conspiracy. The commissioners with General Marcé's defeated army in the Vendée accused him of either "the most cowardly ineptness" or, worse, "the most cowardly treason." His son; his second-in-command, Verteuil; and another Verteuil presumed to be *his* son (but in fact a distant relative) were all arrested for being "in treasonable contact with the enemy." . . .

Faced with this military landslide, the Convention, with very few excep-tions, acknowledged that it had to strengthen the powers of the state. Without an effective executive and a coherent chain of command, centrifugal forces would pull France apart. For the first time since the beginning of the Revolu-tion, the legislature set about creating strong organs of central authority au-thorized to do the Republic's work without endless reference to the "sovereign body." On March 6 it dispatched eighty of its own members (known, from April on, as "representatives on mission") to the departments to ensure compliance with the central government's will. They were, in effect, a revolutionary ver-sion of the old royal *intendants,* traveling embodiments of sovereignty. Much of their work was meant to concern itself with judicial and punitive matters. On March 11 a special Revolutionary Tribunal was established in Paris to try suspects accused of counter-revolutionary activities. On March 20, with the rebellions in the Vendée and Brittany in mind, the Convention adopted Cam-bacérès' proposal giving military courts jurisdiction over anyone who had been employed in public positions (including clergy and nobles) and who was found with the white royalist cockade or fomenting rebellion. If guilty, they were to be shot within twenty-four hours. A day later, every commune in the country was equipped with committees of surveillance and all citizens were encouraged to denounce anyone they suspected of uncertain loyalties. Predictably, the law rapidly became a charter for countless petty dramas of revenge.

Finally, on April 6, it was decided to replace the Committee of General Defense, set up in January as a body of twenty-five to coordinate the work of the several committees of the Convention. In its place was to be a much tighter committee of just nine members, to be known as the Committee of Public Safety....

On October 10 Saint-Just came before the Convention to issue a report in the name of the Committee of Public Safety on the "troubles affecting the state." He took the righteously self-scrutinizing line of declaring that the people had only one enemy, namely the government itself, infected as it was with all sorts of spineless, corrupt and compromised creatures of the old regime. The remedy was unremitting austerity of purpose, implacable punishment for the backsliders and the hypocrites. The charter of the Terror—the Law of Suspects, enacted on September 17, which gave the Committee and its representatives sweeping powers of arrest and punishment over extraordinarily broad categories of people defined as harboring counter-revolutionary designs—should be applied with the utmost rigor. "Between the people and their enemies there can be nothing in common but the sword; we must govern by iron those who cannot be governed by justice; we must oppress the tyrant.... It is impossible for revolutionary laws to be executed unless the government itself is truly revolutionary."...

⁕⊙⁕

The Terror went into action with impressive bureaucratic efficiency. House searches, usually made at night, were extensive and unsparing. All citizens were required to attach to their front doors a notice indicating all residents who lived inside. Entertaining anyone not on that list, even for a single night, was a serious crime. Denunciations poured into the Commission. People were accused of defaming Chalier, of attacking the liberty tree, secreting priests or émigrés, making speculative fortunes and—one of the standard crimes of the year II— writing or uttering *"merde à la république."* From early December the guillotine went into action at a much greater tempo. As in Paris, pride was taken in its mechanical efficiency. On the eleventh of Nivôse, according to the scrupulous accounts kept, thirty-two heads were severed in twenty-five minutes; a week later, twelve heads in just five minutes.

For the most eager Terrorists, though, this was still a messy and inconvenient way of disposing of the political garbage. Citizens in the Streets around the place des Terreaux, on the rue Lafont, for example, were complaining about the blood overflowing the drainage ditch that led from beneath the scaffold. A number of the condemned, then, were executed in mass shootings on the Plaine des Brotteaux—the field beside the Rhone where Montgolfier had made his ascent. Yet another ex-actor, Dorfeuille, presided over some of these *mitraillades,* in which as many as sixty prisoners were tied in a line by ropes and shot at with cannon. Those who were not killed outright by the fire were finished off with sabers, bayonets and rifles. On the fourth of December, Dorfeuille wrote to the President of the Convention that a hundred and thirteen inhabitants of "this new Sodom" had been executed on that single day and in those that followed he hoped another four to five hundred would "expiate their crimes with fire and shot."...

By the time that the killings in "Ville-Affranchie" had finished, one thousand nine hundred and five people had met their end....

•◦❀◦•

The violence did not stop, however, with the Terror. Richard Cobb has written eloquently of the waves of the Counter-Terror, especially brutal in the Midi and the Rhone Valley; of anarchic murder gangs picking off selected targets implicated in Jacobinism. Republican officials; army officers; members of departmental administrations; conspicuous militants of the popular societies; and, in the south, Protestant farmers and merchants—all became prey for the *sabreurs* of the year III. Corpses were dumped in front of cafés and inns in the Midi or thrown into the Rhone or Saône. In many areas, the Counter-Terrorists would gather together at an inn as if for a day's hunting, and go off in search of their quarry.

Considerable areas of the country—the Midi and Rhone Valley, Brittany and western Normandy—remained in a virtual state of civil war, though the violence now proceeded in a haphazard, hit-and-run fashion rather than by organized insurrection. The great engines of capitalist prosperity in late eighteenth-century France, the Atlantic and Mediterranean ports, had been broken by antifederalist repression and British naval blockade. When Samuel Romilly returned to Bordeaux during the peace of 1802, he was dismayed to find the docks silent and ghostly and grass growing tall between the flagstones of the quai des Chartrons. Marseille and Lyon only recovered as the Revolution receded and the reorientation of the Bonapartist state towards Italy offered new markets and trade routes....

What had the Revolution accomplished to balance these penalties? Its two great social alterations—the end of the seigneurial regime and the abolition of the guilds—both promised more than they delivered. Though many artisans were undoubtedly happy to be free of the hierarchy of the corporations that constrained their labor and reward, they were, if anything, even more nakedly exposed to the economic inequities that persisted between masters and journeymen. Likewise the abolition of feudalism was more in the way of a legal than a social change and merely completed the evolution from lords to landlords that had been well under way in the old regime. There is no question that peasants were thankful for the end of seigneurial exactions that had imposed a crushing burden of payments on static rural incomes. Equally certainly, they were determined at all costs to oppose their reimposition. But it is hard to say whether the mass of the rural population were measurably better off in 1799 than they had been in 1789. Though the redemption tariff for feudal dues had been abolished outright in 1793, landlords often compensated themselves by various rent strategies that deepened the indebtedness of share-cropping *métayers*. Moreover, the taxes demanded by the Republic—among them the single land tax, the *impot fôncier*—were certainly no lighter than those exacted by the King. Before long the Consulate and Empire would revert to indirect taxes on at least as onerous a scale as under the old regime. All that they were spared, fiscally, were extraordinary poll taxes, including the old *capitation* and the *vingtième*, but this relief was only a consequence of the ever-expanding military frontier. Taxes lifted from the shoulders of the French were now dropped on those of the Italians, Germans and Dutch. When that frontier suddenly retreated in 1814, back to the old limits of the hexagonal *patrie,* the French were stuck with the bill, which, just as in 1789, they adamantly refused to pay, thus sealing the Empire's fate.

Was the world of the village in 1799 so very different from what it had been ten years before? In particular regions of France where there had been heavy emigration and repression, rural life had indeed been emptied of noble dominance. But this obvious rupture disguises a continuity of some importance. It was exactly those sections of the population who had been gaining economically under the old regime that profited most from the sale of noble and church lands. Those sales were declared irreversible, so there was indeed a substantial transfer of wealth. But much of that transfer was *within* the landed classes—extending from well-to-do farmers up to "patriot" nobles who had managed to stay put and actually benefited from the confiscations. Fat cats got fatter.... There were, to be sure, many regions of France where the nobility as a group lost a considerable part of their fortune. But there were also others —in the west, the center and the south—where, as Jean Tulard has shown, lands that remained unsold could be recovered by families who returned in substantial numbers after 1796. Thus, while many of the leading figures in this history ended their lives on the guillotine, many others stayed put and reemerged as the leading notables of their department....

By contrast, the rural poor gained very little at all from the Revolution. Saint-Just's Ventôse laws remained a dead letter and it became harder than ever to pasture animals on common land or gather fuel from the open woods. In all these respects the Revolution was just an interlude in the inexorable modernization of property rights that had been well under way before 1789. No government—that of the Jacobins any more than that of the King—had really answered the cries for help that echoed through the rural *cahiers de doléances* in 1789....

Had the Revolution, at least, created state institutions which resolved the problems that brought down the monarchy? Here, too, as de Tocqueville emphasized, it is easier to discern continuities, especially of centralization, than any overwhelming change. In public finance, the creation of a paper currency came to be recognized as a catastrophe beside which the insolvencies of the old regime looked almost picayune. Eventually the Bonapartist Consultate (whose finances were administered overwhelmingly by surviving bureaucrats of the old regime) returned to a metallic system based on Calonne's important monetary reform of 1785 fixing the ratio of silver to gold. Fiscally, too, post-Jacobin France slid inexorably back to the former mixture of loans and indirect as well as direct taxes. The Republic and Empire did no better funding a large army and navy from these domestic sources than had the monarchy and depended crucially on institutionalized extortion from occupied countries to keep the military pump primed.

The Napoleonic prefects have always been recognized as the heirs of the royal *intendants* (and the revolutionary *représentants-en-mission*), brokering administration between central government priorities and the interest of the local notability. Without any question that notability had suffered a violent shock during the height of the Jacobin Terror, especially in the great provincial cities, where, after the federalist revolt, they were virtually exterminated. The constitution of the year III, however, with its reintroduction of tax qualifications for the electoral assemblies, returned authority to those who had, in many places, exercised it continuously between the mid-1780s and 1792. As we have seen, in some small towns, such as Calais, where adroit mayors paid lip service to passing regimes, there was unbroken continuity of office from 1789 through the Restoration.... For these men and countless others like them, the Revolution had been but a brutal though mercifully ephemeral interruption of their social and institutional power....

What killed the monarchy was its inability to create representative institutions through which the state could execute its program of reform. Had the Revolution done any better? On one level, the succession of elected legislatures, from the Estates-General to the National Convention, was one of the most impressive innovations of the Revolution. They took the intensive debate on the shape of governing institutions in France, which had been going on for at least half a century, into the arena of representation itself and articulated its principles with unparalleled eloquence. But for all their virtues as theaters of debate, none of the legislatures ever managed to solve the issue that had bedeviled the old regime: how to create a viable working partnership between the executive and the legislature? Once the Constituent had rejected Mounier and Mirabeau's "British" proposal of drawing ministers from the assembly, it regarded the executive not as the administration of the country, working in good faith, but as a fifth column bent on subverting national sovereignty. With this doomed beginning, the executive and legislative branches of the constitution of 1791 simply intensified the war with each other until their mutual destruction in 1792. The Terror effectively reversed matters by putting the Convention under the thrall of the committees, but still make it impossible to change governments except by violence.

The framers of the constitution of the year III (1795) obviously learned something from this unhappy experience. A two-chamber legislature was introduced, elected indirectly from colleges in which property was the criterion for membership. A governing council was in theory accountable to the legislature (as indeed the committees had been). In practice, however, the experiment remained darkened by the long shadow of the revolution itself, so that factions inevitably crystallized, not around specific issues of government but plans for the overthrow of the state, hatched either by royalists or neo-Jacobins. With the separate organs of the constitution in paralyzing conflict with each other, violence continued to determine the political direction of the state far more than did elections.

But the violence was, after the year III, no longer coming from the streets and *sections* but from the uniformed army. If one had to look for one indisputable story of transformation in the French Revolution, it would be the creation of the juridical entity of the citizen. But no sooner had this hypothetically free person been invented than his liberties were circumscribed by the police power of the state. This was always done in the name of republican patriotism, but the constraints were no less oppressive for that. Just as Maribeau —and the Robespierre of 1791—had feared, liberties were held hostage to the authority of the warrior state. Though this conclusion might be depressing, it should not really be all that surprising. The Revolution, after all, had begun as a response to a patriotism wounded by the humiliations of the Seven Years' War. It was Vergennes' decision to promote, at the same time, maritime imperialism and continental military power which generated the sense of fiscal panic that overcame the monarchy in its last days. A crucial element—perhaps, indeed, *the* crucial element—in the claim of the revolutionaries of 1789 was that they could better regenerate the *patrie* than could the appointees of the King. From the outset, then, the great continuing strand of militancy was patriotic. Militarized nationalism was not, in some accidental way, the unintended consequence of the French Revolution: it was its heart and soul. It was wholly logical that the multimillionaire inheritors of revolutionary power—the true "new class" of this period of French history—were not some *bourgeoisie conquérante* but *real* conquerors: the Napoleonic marshals, whose fortunes made even those of the surviving dynasts of the nobility look paltry by comparison.

For better or worse, the "modern men" who seemed poised to capture government under Louis XVI—engineers, noble industrialists, scientists, bureaucrats and generals—resumed their march to power once the irritations of revolutionary politics were brushed aside. "*La tragédie, maintenant, c'est la politique,*" claimed Napoleon, who, after the coup d'état that brought him to power in 1799, added his claim to that which had been made by so many optimistic governments before him, that "the Revolution is completed."

At other times, though, he was not so sure. For if he understood that one last achievement of the Revolution had been the creation of a military-technocratic state of immense power and emotional solidarity, he also realized that its *other* principal invention had been a political culture that perennially and directly challenged it. What occurred between 1789 and 1793 was an unprecedented explosion of politics—in speech, print, image and even music—that broke all the barriers that had traditionally circumscribed it. Initially, this had been the monarchy's own doing. For it was in the tens of thousands of little meetings convened to draft *cahiers* and elect deputies to the Estates-General that French men (and occasionally women) found their voice. In so doing, they became part of a process that tied the satisfaction of their immediate wants into the process of redefining sovereignty.

That was both the opportunity and the problem. Suddenly, subjects were told they had become Citizens; an aggregate of subjects held in place by injustice and intimidation had become a Nation. From this new thing, this Nation of Citizens, justice, freedom and plenty could be not only expected but required. By the same token, should it not materialize, only those who had spurned their citizenship, or who were by their birth or unrepentant beliefs incapable of exercising it, could be held responsible. Before the promise of 1789 could be realized, then, it was necessary to root out Uncitizens.

Thus began the cycle of violence which ended in the smoking obelisk and the forest of guillotines. However much the historian, in the year of celebration, may be tempted to see that violence as an unpleasant "aspect" of the Revolution which ought not to distract from its accomplishments, it would be jejune to do so. From the very beginning—from the summer of 1789—violence was the motor of the Revolution. The journalist Loustalot's knowing exploitation of the punitive murder and mutilation of Foulon and Bertier de Sauvigny conceded nothing in its calculated ferocity to the most extreme harangues of Marat and Hébert. *"Il faut du sang pour cimenter la révolution"* (There must be blood to cement revolution), said Mme Roland, who would herself perish by the logical application of her enthusiasm. While it would be grotesque to implicate the generation of 1789 in the kind of hideous atrocities perpetrated under the Terror, it would be equally naive not to recognize that the former made the latter possible. All the newspapers, the revolutionary festivals, the painted plates; the songs and street theater; the regiments of little boys waving their right arms in the air swearing patriotic oaths in piping voices—all these features of what historians have come to designate the "political culture of the Revolution"—were the products of the same morbid preoccupation with the just massacre and the heroic death.

Historians are also much given to distinguishing between "verbal" violence and the real thing. The assumption seems to be that such men as Javogues and Marat, who were given to screaming at people, calling for death, gloating at the spectacle of heads on pikes or processions of men with their hands tied behind their backs climbing the steps to the *rasoir national* were indulging only in brutal rhetoric. The screamers were not to be compared with such quiet bureaucrats of death as Fouquier-Tinville who did their jobs with stolid, silent efficiency. But the history of "Ville-Affranchie," of the Vendée-Vengé, or of the September massacres suggests in fact a direct connection between all that orchestrated or spontaneous screaming for blood and its copious shedding. It contributed greatly to the complete dehumanization of those who became victims. As "brigands" or the "Austrian whore" or "fanatics" they became nonentities in the Nation of Citizens and not only could but had to be eliminated if it was to survive. Humiliation and abuse, then, were not just Jacobin fun and games; they were the prologues to killing.

Why was the French Revolution like this? Why, from the beginning, was it powered by brutality? The question might seem to be circular since if, in fact, reform had been all that had been required, there would have been no Revolution in the first place. The question nonetheless remains important if we are ever to understand why successive generations of those who tried to stabilize its course—Mirabeau, Barnave, Danton—met with such failure. Was it just that French popular culture was already brutalized before the Revolution and responded to the spectacle of terrifying public punishments handed out by royal justice with its own forms of spontaneous sanguinary retribution? That all naive revolutionaries would do, would be to give the people the chance to exact such retribution and make it part of the regular conduct of politics? This may be part of the explanation, but even a cursory look beyond French borders, and especially over the Channel to Britain, makes it difficult to see France as uniquely damaged, either by a more dangerous distance between rich and poor or indeed by higher rates of crime and popular violence, than places which avoided violent revolution.

Popular revolutionary violence was not some sort of boiling subterranean lava that finally forced its way onto the surface of French politics and then proceeded to scald all those who stepped in its way. Perhaps it would be better to think of the revolutionary elite as rash geologists, themselves gouging open great holes in the crust of polite discourse and then feeding the angry matter through the pipes of their rhetoric out into the open. Volcanoes and steam holes do not seem inappropriate metaphors here, because contemporaries were themselves constantly invoking them. Many of those who were to sponsor or become caught up in violent change were fascinated by seismic violence, by the great primordial eruptions which geologists now said were not part of a single Creation, but which happened periodically in geological time. These events were, to borrow from Burke, both sublime and terrible. And it was perhaps Romanticism, with its addiction to the Absolute and the Ideal; its fondness for the vertiginous and the macabre; its concept of political energy, as, above all, electrical; its obsession with the heart; its preference for passion over reason, for virtue over peace, that supplied a crucial ingredient in the mentality of the revolutionary elite: its association of liberty with wildness. What began with Lafayette's infatuation with the hyena of the Gévaudan surely ended in the ceremonies of the pike-stuck heads.

There was another obsession which converged with this Romanticization of violence: the neoclassical fixation with the patriotic death. The annals of Rome (and occasionally the doomed battles of Athens and Sparta) were the mirrors into which revolutionaries constantly gazed in search of self-recognition. Their France would be Rome reborn, but purified by the benison of the feeling heart. It thus followed, surely, that for such a Nation to be born, many would necessarily die. And both the birth and death would be simultaneously beautiful.

POSTSCRIPT

Was the French Revolution Worth Its Human Costs?

In many ways, Schama's book was revolutionary and was considered so by his peers in the historical profession. Covering a subject dominated by a myriad of historical special interest groups, he returned to the domain of the historical narrative as his vehicle of expression, something that seemed passé to many of this generation's historians. Secondly, Schama's focus was "an unfashionable 'top-down' rather than 'bottom-up' approach" (*Citizens*, p. xvi). Finally, although a scholar of impeccable credentials, he was considered an outsider in the field of French Revolution historiography because he had not "been a lifetime toiler in the vineyards of the Revolution" (Allan Spitzer, "Narrative's Problems: The Case of Simon Schama," *Journal of Modern History* [March 1993, p. 176]). Clearly, personal factors can influence one's view of any historical subject.

The most controversial feature of the French Revolution was the infamous Reign of Terror, and it is a subject that all toilers in the garden of the Revolution have to explain. The horrors of the twentieth century (some committed in the name of revolution) demand that the Terror gets the fullest treatment possible. Only then can the question of whether or not the Revolution was worth its human costs be answered. If Kropotkin's work speaks to the spirit of the nineteenth century's age of democratic revolutions, Schama's does the same to the dreams deferred and lives lost to the twentieth century's failed revolutions.

Issue 4 in this volume contains an analysis of Japan's nineteenth-century Meiji Restoration and whether it was a revolution in the classical sense. To examine this question, we suggest a comparison of the Meiji movement with other revolutions (including the French) by using the model established by Crane Brinton in *The Anatomy of Revolution* (Random House, 1966). A comparison of the Meiji Japan and French revolutionary experiences would be a tool that could be used to learn about the nature of revolutions.

To list all of the major sources on the French Revolution is daunting, but two general accounts that are readable and perfect for the beginning student are William Doyle, *The Oxford History of the French Revolution* (Oxford University Press, 1989) and Donald M. G. Sutherland, *France, 1789–1815: Revolution and Counter-Revolution* (Oxford University Press, 1986).

Finally, two films that contain visuals that provide an understanding of the French Revolution are *La Nuit de Varennes,* for its study of the chaotic nature of French Revolutionary society before the Reign of Terror, and *Danton,* for the horror that the Terror would become.

ISSUE 3

Did British Policy Decisions Cause the Mass Emigration and Land Reforms That Followed the Irish Potato Famine?

YES: Christine Kinealy, from *This Great Calamity: The Irish Famine 1845–52* (Roberts Rinehart, 1995)

NO: Hasia R. Diner, from *Erin's Daughters in America: Irish Immigrant Women in the Nineteenth Century* (Johns Hopkins University Press, 1983)

ISSUE SUMMARY

YES: Christine Kinealy, fellow of the University of Liverpool, argues that the British government's response to the Irish potato famine was deliberately inadequate. The British government's "hidden agenda" of long-term economic, social, and agrarian reform was accelerated by the famine, and mass emigration was a consequence of these changes.

NO: Historian Hasia R. Diner documents large-scale emigration both before and after the Irish potato famine. Diner credits the Irish people with learning from their famine experiences that the reliance of the poor on the potato and the excessive subdivision of land within families were no longer in their own best interests.

Beginning in 1845 a fungal disease repeatedly struck the potato crop of Ireland and was not eradicated until the early 1850s. The failure of the potato harvest in a country with a population of eight million people caused the death of approximately one million and the emigration of another million. On the eve of the famine, two-thirds of the population earned their living by working the land—for the most part land that they did not own. Still, Ireland was able to feed its own people and also to export food to feed two million Britons. During these years, Ireland was part of the United Kingdom, which also included England and Scotland.

Initially the British government responded to the failure of the Irish potato crop by purchasing and storing Indian corn from America, which it later sold to those who could afford to buy it. Unwilling to offer handouts, the British government provided subsidy only to those who entered the workhouses. As the crisis deepened, the government undertook public works projects, such as road and pier construction, to offer the poor a means to earn money. Ultimately it set up a network of soup kitchens.

By 1847, however, the British government transferred responsibility for Ireland's poor to Ireland itself, insisting that outside aid would be available only after local resources were exhausted or if it could be demonstrated that without outside aid people would die. As the blight continued, British aid was provided to the manufacturing districts in the north of England, which were undergoing an economic slump, but not to the Irish.

Prosperous counties in Ireland were less dependent on the potato crop and resented being held exclusively responsible for the financial bailout of the poorest of their neighbors. If Ireland is truly part of the United Kingdom, they argued, all of the United Kingdom should be equally responsible for alleviating the suffering of any of its members.

However, prevailing stereotypes frequently contrasted the "deserving" poor—industrious factory workers in England's manufacturing centers—with the "undeserving" poor—notably the Irish, who were believed to be lazy and without ambition. How much of a role did these prejudices, which appeared regularly in cartoons and print descriptions, play in the neglect that allowed a million people to die and forced another million to emigrate?

Laissez-faire (literally, to leave alone) economic principles, pioneered by British philosopher Adam Smith and others, contend that government should stay out of the regulation of the economy. Without outside manipulation, this theory suggests, the "hidden hand" of economic forces, such as supply and demand, will regulate the economy efficiently. The prevalence of this theory and others concerning the "undeserving" status of the Irish gave the British government solid justification for withholding economic aid to Ireland.

Christine Kinealy faults British government policies for exploiting the chaos of the famine in order to implement what she calls a "hidden agenda." Seeing the failure of the potato crop as a golden opportunity to force conversion of the Irish economy to a more commercial system of agriculture, the British government, Kinealy explains, was able to rid itself of "non-productive elements." These included landless laborers and apathetic landlords. The million Irish who emigrated, along with the million who died, improved the demographics and facilitated modernization of the Irish economy—but at a terrible cost.

Hasia R. Diner sees more continuity than discontinuity in emigration patterns. While the famine may have accelerated this process, the Irish had been moving to other parts of the British Empire and to the United States in large numbers at least since the late eighteenth century. Calling the famine the "great convincer," Diner attributes changes in agricultural diversity, land inheritance patterns, and marriage practices to the Irish people themselves, acting on their own behalf as agents of historical change.

Christine Kinealy

 **YES**

This Great Calamity: The Irish Famine 1845–52

The Famine that affected Ireland from 1845 to 1852 has become an integral part of folk legend. In the popular imagination, the Famine is associated with nationwide suffering, initially triggered by the potato blight, compounded by years of misrule and consolidated by the inadequate response of the British government and Irish landlords alike. The resultant large-scale emigration took the tragedy of the Famine beyond the shores of Ireland to an international stage. Recent scholarly studies of the Famine have attempted to move away from this traditional view. In doing so, a sanitised alternative has emerged that has endeavoured to remove the patina of blame from the authorities involved in providing relief, while minimising the suffering of those who were most directly affected by the loss of the potato crop.

Several specific issues need to be addressed in order to evaluate the varying responses of those in power. At a broad level there are three questions. First, what relief measures were implemented? Second, what were the determinants of the measures that were introduced? Third, and most significantly, how effective were they?

These questions are fundamental to an understanding of the Famine. There is still a widespread view that the Famine relief measures were inadequate. Much of the blame is laid at the door of the British government, and to a lesser degree, Irish landlords. Is this an unfair assessment, especially when seen in the context of the perceived role of government in the middle of the nineteenth century?

Early in the nineteenth century, Ireland was widely regarded as a poor country, dominated by a stagnant subsistence agriculture based substantially upon the ubiquitous potato. On the eve of the Famine, the Irish economy supported a population in excess of eight million people which was large by European standards and represented a sizeable portion of the United Kingdom population as a whole—the population of England and Wales at the same period was approximately sixteen million, and of Scotland, under three million. On the eve of the Famine, the economy of Ireland supported its own population

From Christine Kinealy, *This Great Calamity: The Irish Famine 1845–52* (Roberts Rinehart, 1995). Copyright © 1995 by Christine Kinealy. Notes omitted.

and supplied food for a further two million mouths in Britain. Ireland, therefore, should have been a significant consideration in any social or economic policies that affected the United Kingdom as a whole.

The onset of the Famine was unexpected although partial crop failures and food shortages were not unusual. In 1845, therefore, the potato blight, regardless of the lack of understanding of either its origins or an antidote, was not regarded with undue alarm. Although approximately 50 per cent of the main subsistence crop failed in 1845–6, the consequence of the resultant shortages was not famine, nor did emigration or mortality increase substantially. The role played by the government, local landlords, clerics, and various relief officials was significant in achieving this outcome. The second, more widespread, blight of 1846 marked the real beginning of the Famine. Ominously, the impact of the shortages was apparent in the period immediately following the harvest. Inevitably also, the people undergoing a second year of shortages were far less resilient than they had been twelve months earlier. The government responded to this potentially more serious situation by reducing its involvement in the import of food into the country and by making relief more difficult to obtain.

The distress that followed the 1847 harvest was caused by a small crop and economic dislocation rather than the widespread appearance of blight. The government again changed its relief policy in an attempt to force local resources to support the starving poor within their district. The government professed a belief that this policy was necessary to ensure that a burden which it chose to regard as essentially local should not be forced upon the national finances. This policy underpinned the actions of the government for the remainder of the Famine. The relief of famine was regarded essentially as a local responsibility rather than a national one, let alone an imperial obligation. The special relationship between the constituent parts of the United Kingdom forged by the Act of Union appeared not to extend to periods of shortage and famine.

To what extent was a famine or other disaster inevitable when viewed within the context of the general, and some would say increasing, poverty of Ireland? This assumption of Irish poverty, which underpinned political prescription during the Famine, perhaps owed more to distantly derived dogmas than to the reality. For example, a number of recent studies have suggested that height is a reliable indicator of 'nutritional status' (that is, 'the balance of nutritional intake with growth, work, and the defeat of disease'). Surveys of nineteenth-century British military records indicate that Irish recruits were taller than recruits from the rest of the United Kingdom. This implies a sustained nutritional advantage within Ireland. Also, it is now widely accepted that Ireland's pre-Famine economy was more diverse, vibrant, dynamic and responsive to change than has traditionally been depicted. In contrast to this situation, recent quantitative studies of the British economy have reassessed the impact of industrialisation in the first half of the nineteenth century and concluded that, throughout this period, Britain's economic growth remained 'painfully slow'....

The slump of 1847 was a sharp reminder to the government of the problems on its own doorstep. During the autumn of 1847, news of Irish distress vied increasingly for column space in the English newspapers with stories of hardship, unemployment and bankruptcies in England, notably in Lancashire, the flagship of industrial Britain. Poverty and distress, therefore, were not confined to Ireland but were also evident in one of the wealthiest parts of the British Empire. The demands of the Irish poor were now in direct competition with the demands of the urban poor within Britain. An obvious comparison was drawn between the distress of the feckless Irish peasants and their irresponsible and greedy landlords, with the distress of the hard-working factory operatives and the enterprising entrepreneurs upon whom, it was believed, much of the success of the British Empire rested. Since the reign of Elizabeth I, Poor Law philosophy had drawn a distinction between the 'deserving' and the 'undeserving' poor. The English factory operatives, unemployed through no fault of their own, were regarded as deserving poor; it was apparent that the Irish peasants could be regarded with equal justification as falling into the latter category.

A hardening attitude to Irish distress was illustrated by the response to appeals for additional assistance as a third year of shortages became inevitable. An early indication of a resistant official response occurred in October 1847, when a group of Catholic bishops and archbishops appealed to the government for an increase in official aid. They were informed, in a widely published response, that such a request was unreasonable, particularly as it implied that:

> the means for this relief should be exacted by the government from classes
> all struggling with difficulties, and at a moment when in England trade
> and credit are disastrously low, with the immediate prospect of hundreds
> of thousands being thrown out of employment or being as destitute of the
> means of existence as the poorest peasant in Ireland.

An appeal for funds in the form of a second 'Queen's Letter' was also published in October 1847 and read out in all churches throughout England. It elicited more criticism than cash.

The government remained committed to the policy of forcing Ireland to depend on its own resources as far as possible, chiefly through the mechanism of the Poor Law. Within the domestic economy, however, the government did depart from its declared *laissez faire* policy and intervened to allow the terms of the 1844 Bank Charter Act to be relaxed in order to aid the industrial sector. By the end of 1847, the financial crisis in Britain was over and a period of prosperity was under way. The Great Exhibition of 1851 was a triumphant demonstration of Britain's international industrial and economic supremacy. In the same year, in a different part of the United Kingdom, the west of Ireland, a portion of the population was about to confront a seventh consecutive year of famine and shortages.

The contribution of outside charitable bodies was mostly confined to the early years of the Famine. By 1847, most of these sources had dried up or, as in the case of the Quakers, they had decided to use their remaining funds to concentrate on long-term improvements rather than immediate relief. Significantly, the Quakers' men on the ground who toured the west of Ireland in the winter of 1846–7 were critical both of absentee landlords and the policies pursued by the British government alike. The British Relief Association, which remained operative after 1847, allowed its funds to be allocated through the medium of the

Treasury. This was not without problems. Count Strzelecki, the Association's local agent, fought a hard battle with the Treasury to ensure that a successful scheme to feed schoolchildren was continued, regardless of the disapproval of [Charles] Trevelyan.

A fundamental policy position of government, enforced rigorously throughout the Famine, as noted earlier, was the determination to make local resources support local distress. The Irish landlords were singled out continually as a group that needed to be reminded of, and occasionally coerced into, undertaking their duties to the poor. Following the 1845 blight, however, the money contributed voluntarily by the landlords and other subscribers was the highest amount ever raised. Regardless of this achievement, the Irish contribution was represented as derisory and the landlords increasingly targeted as the object of public opprobrium. Irish landlords undoubtedly provided an easy and obvious scapegoat both as a cause of, and as contributors to, the Famine. This was a view taken both by their contemporaries and by some later historians....

To what extent, however, can any individual group, organisation or state body be blamed for the degree of suffering that resulted from successive years of potato blight? Would the outcome of the years of shortages and suffering have been different if the response of the authorities, various charitable organisations, and other key individuals to successive years of blight had been different?

There is no doubt that the part played by the government was pivotal within the whole relief endeavour. Was it, however, within the remit of the government—either ideologically or financially—to provide sufficient relief to keep suffering, emigration, and mortality to a minimum level? The policies of the government, and the way in which it perceived its role, are crucial to an understanding of the Famine years. The changing perceptions and strategies of the British government determined the type of relief provided and the methods and timing of its allocation. The role played by the Treasury, both in implementing the various relief policies and in advising the government, was critical. Charles Wood, the Chancellor of the Exchequer, together with his colleague, Charles Trevelyan, represented a school of economic orthodoxy which advocated both non-intervention and fiscal rectitude. A populist version of their views found a wider audience in the columns of *The Times* and the cartoons of *Punch*. It was also supported in the learned contributions to the *Edinburgh Review* and the fledgling *Economist*. In the wake of the financial and monetary crisis of 1847, the demand for retrenchment was also welcomed by a politically influential industrial middle class. The Treasury, in effect, became not only the guardian of the relief purse, but—mainly due to the energetic and prolonged involvement of Charles Trevelyan—was increasingly deferred to by members of the government as the oracle of all wisdom regarding Ireland. Although no one person can be blamed for the deficiencies of the relief policies, Trevelyan perhaps more than any other individual represented a system of response which increasingly was a mixture of minimal relief, punitive qualifying criteria, and social reform.

The Treasury's agenda for Irish relief went far beyond the mere allocation of government funds. Its imprint was evident throughout both the public and private sectors. Not only did it arbitrate on the crucial issue of who deserved to be given financial support and how much they should receive, but increasingly it attempted to control the day-to-day administration of relief. No other organisation played such a sustained role or showed such an obvious interest in the affairs of Ireland. The government, which was in the midst of a foreign crisis, an economic depression, and a year of revolutions and uprisings in Europe which extended both to Britain and Ireland, was no doubt glad to be able to allow the Treasury to shoulder such a large portion of the Irish relief burden. Also, despite evidence to the contrary, many officials, including even the well-informed Trevelyan, publicly declared the Famine to be over in 1848. The problems of Ireland, therefore, were necessarily a low priority to a government at the centre of a large and still expanding Empire. However, by allowing the Treasury to play such a pivotal role in the provision of relief, it was perhaps inevitable that the need to 'balance the books'—an excellent objective in Treasury terms—should at times overshadow the need to provide adequate relief. By using the Treasury in such a capacity, its role far exceeded that of guardian of the public purse and extended both to influencing public policy and, even more significantly, to final arbitrator in the provision of relief....

The Famine was a disaster of major proportions, even allowing for an inevitable statistical uncertainty on its estimated effect on mortality. Yet the Famine occurred in a country which, despite concurrent economic problems, was at the centre of a still-growing empire and was an integral part of the acknowledged workshop of the world. There can be no doubt that despite a short-term cyclical depression, the combined resources of the United Kingdom could either completely or much more substantially have removed the consequences of consecutive years of potato blight in Ireland. This remains true even if one accepts Trevelyan's proud assertion that no government had done more to support its poor than Britain had done during the Famine years. The statement implies that not only was enough done to help the suffering people in Ireland, but that it was accompanied by a generosity that patently is not borne out by the evidence. To have fed in excess of three million people in the summer of 1847 was a worthy and notable achievement. It also dispels the frequent assertion that the British government did not possess the administrative capability to feed such a large number of starving people. But if the measure of success is judged by the crudest yet most telling of all measures—that of mortality—the British government failed a large portion of the population in terms of humanitarian criteria.

In this context, Trevelyan's comment reveals the separateness of Ireland from the rest of the United Kingdom. His perception mocked the precepts of the Act of Union. It should not, however, be forgotten that the government and the Treasury had to provide a system of relief that would satisfy both parliamentary and public opinion. If measured by this criterion alone—accepting, however, the individual criticisms of the opposition party—the relief measures were undoubtedly regarded as successful, and to some, even over-generous.

The policies of the government increasingly specified criteria that disallowed external assistance until distress was considerable and evident. The leitmotif of relief provided by the central government throughout the course of the Famine was that assistance would be provided only when it—or, in fact, its agent, the Treasury—was satisfied that local resources were exhausted, or that if aid was not provided, the distressed people would die. By implementing a policy which insisted that local resources must be exhausted before an external agency would intervene, and pursuing this policy vigorously despite local advice to the contrary, the government made suffering an unavoidable consequence of the various relief systems which it introduced. The suffering was exacerbated by the frequent delays in the provision of relief even after it had been granted and by the small quantity of relief provided, which was also of low nutritional value. By treating the Famine as, in essence, a local problem requiring a local response, the government was, in fact, penalising those areas which had the fewest resources to meet the distress.

The government response to the Famine was cautious, measured and frequently parsimonious, both with regard to immediate need and in relation to the long-term welfare of that portion of the population whose livelihood had been wiped out by successive years of potato blight. Nor could the government pretend ignorance of the nature and extent of human tragedy that unfolded in Ireland following the appearance of blight. The Irish Executive and the Poor Law Commissioners sent regular, detailed reports of conditions within the localities and increasingly requested that even more extensive relief be provided. In addition, Trevelyan employed his own independent sources of information on local conditions, by-passing the existing official sources of the Lord Lieutenant. This information revealed the extent of deprivation caused by the Famine. It also showed the regional variations arising from the loss of the potato crop; and it exposed the inability of some areas to compensate for such losses from their own internal resources. There was no shortage of detailed and up-to-date information. What was crucial was the way in which the government used this information.

While it was evident that the government had to do something to help alleviate the suffering, the particular nature of the actual response, especially following 1846, suggests a more covert agenda and motivation. As the Famine progressed, it became apparent that the government was using its information not merely to help it formulate its relief policies but also as an opportunity to facilitate various long-desired changes within Ireland. These included population control and the consolidation of property through a variety of means, including emigration, the elimination of small holdings, and the sale of large but bankrupt estates. This was a pervasive and powerful 'hidden agenda'. The government measured the success of its relief policies by the changes which were brought about in Ireland rather than by the quality of relief provided *per se*. The public declaration of the Census Commissioners in the Report of the 1851 Census, which stated that Ireland had benefited from the changes brought about by the Famine, is a clear example of this....

The response of [Whig leader Lord John] Russell's government to the Famine combined opportunism, arrogance and cynicism, deployed in such a way as to facilitate the long-standing ambition to secure a reform of Ireland's economy. In the midst of dealing with a famine in Ireland, increasing reference was made to the need to restructure agriculture in Ireland from the top to the bottom. This had been the ambition of a succession of governments prior to

1845, but the Famine provided a real opportunity to bring about such a purpose both quickly and, most importantly, cheaply.

In the early decades of the nineteenth century, for example, state-sponsored emigration had been recommended by select committees, social theorists and government advisors alike, all of whom agreed that it would be beneficial to Ireland; but the government had refused to involve itself in the additional expenditure that an active pursuit of this policy would involve. The Famine, however, gave the impetus to emigration to flourish, without imposing an additional financial burden on the government. It, therefore, provided opportunities for change. The Whig administration, through legislation such as the Quarter-Acre Clause and the Encumbered Estates Acts, ensured that such opportunities were not wasted.

If the potato blight had been confined to 1845, its impact would have been insignificant and it would have been remembered only as one of the many intermittent subsistence crises which affected Ireland and all agricultural societies. Even though over half of the crop was lost through blight in 1845, the increase in excess mortality and emigration was insignificant. In 1845-6, as had so clearly been demonstrated in the subsistence crisis of 1782-4, if the political and social will existed, a subsistence crisis did not necessarily have to become a famine.

In the 1840s, the policy of the British government was shaped by a prevailing economic dogma, inspired by a particular interpretation of free market economics. The champions of this philosophy were Adam Smith and his successors such as Nassau Senior and Harriet Martineau. In the context of providing poor relief in Ireland, this influential philosophy decreed that ultimately such relief was damaging and that genuine improvements could be achieved only through self-help. In its more extreme form, the principles embodied in this dogma denied any government responsibility for the alleviation of distress. Proponents of such theories even managed to suggest that during periods of extraordinary distress it could be better for those affected not to have access to extraneous relief lest the self-righting mechanisms of the economic system—the allegedly ubiquitous yet truly imperceptible 'invisible hand'—became ensnared by unwarranted interference. The outcome of a slavish adherence to these self-adjusting mechanisms would inevitably be human suffering. Yet this appeared to be of little consequence to those who worshipped at the altar of *laissez faire.* Short-term suffering appeared to be a small price to be paid for long-term improvement, especially if the theoreticians did not have to participate directly in the experiment.

Despite the fashionable adherence to these theories at the time of the Famine, they were only one of the many influences upon political decision-making. It is clear that such theoretical dogma could be dismissed when prevailing pressures demanded: the intervention by the government in the autumn of 1847 to alleviate the impact of a slump in the manufacturing districts of England providing a concurrent example. The philosophy of non-interference was in practice employed selectively and pragmatically. Its content and application changed as the government considered necessary. Within the Whig government itself, there existed differences of opinion regarding the level of financial intervention in Ireland. Significantly, those who favoured a minimalist approach, spearheaded by the men at the Treasury, were in the ascendant. Nevertheless, during the crucial period in the provision of Famine relief, that is, after the complete devastation of the potato crop in 1846, there is no doubt that this economic theory had powerful public support and, more significantly, enjoyed a popular appeal among many of the ruling elite, particularly those most directly responsible for determining the extent and means of providing relief.

From the perspective of a political response to the Famine, the most substantial deviation from the purist theories of free market economics came about in Ireland itself. This deviation was motivated by the less than purist desire to seek a major reform of the Irish economy, especially in the 'potato economy' districts in the west. In these areas, the free market clearly had failed to deliver spontaneously the desired result, particularly in terms of larger, more efficient holdings, and the British government chose to use the Famine as a means of facilitating and imposing their own reforms. The Famine provided a unique opportunity to bring about long-term structural changes in Ireland's agrarian sector.

During the latter part of the Famine, notably following the transfer of relief to local responsibility through the mechanism of the Poor Law in the autumn of 1847, a 'hidden agenda' of reform is increasingly apparent. Much of this was covert. The government and its agents were not willing to admit openly that the suffering of many people in Ireland, and the consequent high levels of mortality and emigration, was being employed to achieve other purposes. The government was able to use the chaos caused by the Famine to facilitate a number of social and economic changes. In particular, it took the opportunity to bring about a more commercial system of farming within Ireland which no longer would offer refuge to a variety of non-productive elements—whether they were landless labourers or apathetic landlords. If, due to its ultimate aim, this policy could be judged as altruistic, its implementation, based on the prevailing view of the Irish, cannot be. Irish peasants, feckless and indolent as they were perceived to be, were judged less 'worthy' to receive relief than their counterparts in Britain. One consequence of this perception occurred in 1846 when Ireland was not allowed to receive imports of food until supplies had been delivered to Scotland first....

In conclusion, therefore, the response of the British government to the Famine was inadequate in terms of humanitarian criteria and, increasingly after 1847, systematically and deliberately so. The localised shortages that followed the blight of 1845 were adequately dealt with but, as the shortages became more widespread, the government retrenched. With the short-lived exception of the soup kitchens, access to relief—or even more importantly, access to food —became more restricted. That the response illustrated a view of Ireland and its people as distant and marginal is hard to deny. What, perhaps, is more surprising is that a group of officials and their non-elected advisors were able to dominate government policy to such a great extent. This relatively small group of people, taking advantage of a passive establishment, and public opinion which was opposed to further financial aid for Ireland, were able to manipulate a theory of free enterprise, thus allowing a massive social injustice to be perpetrated within a part of the United Kingdom. There was no shortage of resources to avoid the tragedy of a Famine. Within Ireland itself, there were substantial resources of food which, had the political will existed, could have been diverted, even as a short-term measure, to supply a starving people. Instead, the government pursued the objective of economic, social and agrarian reform as a long-term aim, although the price paid for this ultimately elusive goal was privation, disease, emigration, mortality and an enduring legacy of disenchantment.

Hasia R. Diner

Where They Came From

If poverty, persecution, and violence seem to have been eternal elements of Irish life, changes in the economic and social structure nonetheless did occur.... Historians love watersheds: dramatic incidents that set off one epoch from another; major upheavals that loom as signposts along the historic path. The Great Famine of the late 1840s has generally been considered the event in Irish history which sent shock waves throughout Irish society, whose reverberations could be felt around the world, in Boston, London, Toronto, Sydney, and Melbourne, and whose intensity lasted over a century. Nothing remained the same after the devastation of the Famine. The harrowing memory of the starvation, disease, and destruction that engulfed Ireland after the potato blights of 1845–49 altered all relationships; the footing between landlord and tenant changed, as did that between priest and parishioner. The ruler and the ruled shifted ground as they faced each other. Entire classes of people disappeared. The Famine signaled the demise of the Irish cottier class, that landless mass on the lowest stratum of the social structure.

Sheer numbers also confirm the brutal impact of the Famine. After the four years of continuous blight on the potato crop, the Irish staff of life, at least one million people had vanished. Some were felled by starvation, typhus, and dysentery. In the same year three million were reduced to charity. Others fled the Emerald Isle. The Famine's shadow seems to have left no one untouched. The memory of the starvation and what was considered the inaction of the British (some saw it as pure malice) would, over the course of the next century, become a major weapon of nationalist propaganda. Irish journalists, poets, novelists, and playwrights would constantly cull the maudlin scenes of those years for pathetic and gripping material. Father Theobald Matthew, who led Ireland's highly popular temperance movement in the 1870s, invoked such wrenching scenes in sermon after sermon:

> There, admist the chilling damp of a dismal hovel see yon famine-stricken fellow-creature; see him extended on his scanty bed of rotten straw; see his once manly frame, that labour had strengthened with vigour, shrunk to a skeleton; see his once ruddy complexion, the gift of temperance, changed by hunger and concomitant disease to a shallow ghastly hue. See him extend

From Hasia R. Diner, *Erin's Daughters in America: Irish Immigrant Women in the Nineteenth Century* (Johns Hopkins University Press, 1983). Copyright © 1983 by Johns Hopkins University Press. Reprinted by permission. Notes omitted.

his yellow withering arm for assistance; hear how he cries out in agony for food, for since yesterday he has not even moistened his lips!

Who could forget the vision of a strange and fearful sight like what we read of in beleaguered cities; its streets crowded with gaunt wanderers, sauntering to and from with hopeless air and hunger-struck look—a mob of starved, almost naked women around the poor-house clamoring for soup tickets.

People around the world gasped at the horrors of the Famine. Relief poured in. Generous Americans collected money to send food to Ireland's starving millions. American magazine readers were fed a constant diet of grim details about "a widow with two children who for a week had eaten nothing but cabbage.... Another woman with two children, and not far from being confined again, stated that during the last week they had existed upon two quarts of meal and two heads of cabbage... famine was written in the faces of this woman and her children."

Intimate relationships between men and women, husbands and wives, parents and children, brothers and sisters, were not exempted from this massive restructuring of life. The qualities of personal ties and social bonds were swept away by the Famine's blast. The 1851 Census of Ireland surveyed the ruin of the countryside and lamented that

> the closest ties of kinship were dissolved; the most ancient and long cher-
> ished usages of the people were disregarded; the once proverbial gaiety
> and lightheartedness of the peasant people seemed to have vanished com-
> pletely, and village merriment or marriage festival was no longer heard or
> seen throughout the regions desolated by the intensity and extent of the
> Famine....

The watershed approach does have its pitfalls. Few of the changes that occurred after the cataclysm were totally unrelated to the nature of the earlier society. The great upheaval merely accentuated trends that had begun earlier and accelerated forces unleashed in more tranquil and stable times. For example, the great upsurge in religiosity that occurred in post-Famine Ireland, the devotional revolution with its tremendous growth in both the number and the power of the clergy, swept a society that was religiously oriented to begin with. Religion had been a powerful political identity for a long time, and the priest, the *soggarth aroon,* had long held a cherished place in the hearts of the masses.

So, too, the trends in Irish demography—a constantly decreasing population with late and infrequent marriage and high rates of celibacy, a social environment of gender segregation and reluctant sexuality, the concomitant ethic of intense gender animosity—had roots that reached far back into Irish folk life and characterized some classes in the pre-Famine structure. Yet after the Famine these elements came to be synonymous with all of Irish culture and these trends became the norm of Irish behavior. Similarly, the Famine did not cause the massive emigrations. For one thing, the Famine of the late 1840s was not the first to ravage Ireland in modern times. In 1800, 1807, 1816, 1822, and 1839 massive crop failures and wide-ranging epidemics had shaken up the rural Irish. Immigration had in fact begun before the Famine and it continued well afterwards. At least seven hundred thousand people abandoned the thirty-two counties of Ireland between 1825 and 1844. As early as 1841 a half million Irish-born men and women had decided to settle permanently in England and Scotland, while in the same year over ten thousand new arrivals to the port of Boston listed Ireland as their birthplace. In the 1831–41 decade a half million Irish emigrated. Long after the Great Famine had become a memory and a closed chapter of Ireland's sorrowful history, twentieth-century Ireland continued to send its young men and women around the world, making people Ireland's chief export.

⚫

The legacy of the Famine as it shaped emigration to the United States, and particularly as it stimulated a massive female exodus, involved a demographic transition and an alteration in family relations much more subtle than millions of individuals merely fleeing their native land. Drawing upon older Irish traditions and social trends associated with the more stable classes in pre-Famine society, Ireland became a country that held out fewer and fewer attractions to women. By the last decades of the nineteenth century many young women had no reason to remain in the agricultural towns of Catholic Ireland. They had no realistic chances for marriage or employment. For Irish women to attain either, they had to turn their backs on the land of their birth.

Ireland became the Western world's most dramatic and stark example of a demographic pattern associated with the shift from traditional to modern societies. Ireland led the world by the 1870s as the nation with the latest age of marriage. Irish men and women decided more frequently than men and women elsewhere to eschew marriage and live out their lives in a single state. Ireland was, in fact, one of the only countries in Europe to enter the twentieth century unconcerned about overpopulation, because decades earlier it had achieved more than "zero population growth." This, however, had not always been the case. Before the Great Famine, more likely than not an Irish peasant or laborer married young. Until the decade of the Famine Irish population figures had risen with alarming rapidity. Ireland's mushrooming—perhaps, more appropriately, exploding—population had, in fact, provided Thomas Malthus with his gloomiest example of the improvidence of the poor and the inexorable cycle whereby population grew far out of proportion to resources.

A large and controversial body of demographic literature has attempted to explain how this happened. The issues in the analysis of Irish population trends are clouded by the difficulty of obtaining accurate statistics on just how many births and deaths occurred in any given year before 1864, when compulsory registration of nationwide vital statistics was enacted. The first official head count of any kind was made in 1821, and that of 1841 is considered the first that approached reliability. Generally, it is accepted by demographers and historians that the 1821 Census counted fewer people than actually existed, whereas the 1831 count overstated the number. Despite the technical problems of portraying

Irish demographic movement, scholars and commentators on the Irish scene have sought to come to terms with the ways in which the population changed and why. The impact of the Great Famine is central to this endeavor, and from it we can begin to discern the nature of women's lives in Irish society.

On the eve of the Famine, over eight million people inhabited Ireland. Fifty years later the same island had been home to fewer than three million. This tremendous growth occurred without any industrialization or increase in economic opportunities and without any influx of foreigners. In fact, this staggering proliferation occurred while emigration had already become an established part of life. Over four hundred thousand Irish-born men and women lived in Great Britain in 1841, whereas between 1780 and 1845 more than one million Irish had made their way to the United States and Canada. Thus, despite a continuous stream of Irish leaving Ireland in this same half century, the rate of population increase constituted a major demographic revolution.

One strand of analysis which attempts to explain Irish population dynamics focuses on diet—on the impact of the lowly potato on mortality and fertility trends. The potato culture, which gradually came to characterize all Ireland, triggered a constant and seemingly unending process by which the land was broken into smaller and smaller holdings. Widespread was "the general practice with farmers to divide their land into portions, which were given to their children as they got married. The last married frequently got his father's cabin along with his portion of the ground, and there the parents liked to stop feeling attached to the place where they spent their lives." The fleshy tuber could be grown anywhere, even on the most miniscule of plots, and contained just enough nutrients to sustain the life of the poor.

As the Irish had become potato-eaters by the end of the eighteenth century, they also had become early marriers. The poor, in particular, saw no reason not to marry spontaneously, that is, without protracted negotiations between families, and certainly without the aid of a matchmaker. Young men and women married when they wanted, and since they could always grow potatoes, a family of hungry mouths was not a burden. A priest from Mayo generalized to the Commission of Inquiry on the Irish Poor in 1836 that "small holders are induced to marry by feeling that their condition cannot be made worse, or rather, they know they can lose nothing, and they promise themselves some pleasure in the society of a wife." This testimony typified the statements that were offered by the clerics and laymen alike to the commission, to the Devon Commission, which met in 1841, and to other, similar bodies. One man in County Galway confessed in 1835, "if I had been a blanket to cover her, I would marry the woman I liked; and if I should get potatoes enough to put into my children's mouths, I would be as happy and content as any man." Similarly, very few Irish men and women did not marry. The nature of the economy and the social structure left very little room for the unattached adult. Within marriage, fertility was high. There was no incentive for, or seeming interest in, contraception of any kind as there was in France at the same time. Some scholars even argue that, by providing a cheap and easily cultivated source of nutrition, the potato improved the health of women and gradually led to heightened fertility.

Even before the Famine this pattern of early and improvident marriage characterized the depressed peasants—the cottiers and the poor laborers—much more than any other class. Townspeople, tradesmen, and farmers with more than a potato plot demonstrated greater reticence about marriage. For those with hope of economic stability and with aspirations for a more "middle-class" kind of existence improvident marriage could spell disaster. Marrying too young meant the expense of feeding and clothing a family too soon. Marrying too young was clearly associated with the reckless behavior of the poor, who inched closer and closer to doom as they subdivided and resubdivided their possessions.

A County Kilkenny observer noted that "those who are a grade above the cottier are more cautious as to marriage, and it is chiefly among small farmers that you will find bachelors." Similarly, in County Limerick one could have found "a greater proportionate number of unmarried men amongst the farmers and tradesmen than amongst the lowest classes of agricultural labourers." This same phenomenon could be plotted geographically. In the wealthier and more fertile East, which supported the cultivation of grains as well as potatoes, people generally married later than in the poverty-stricken West, which was home for the most destitute of laborers and cottiers. Thus, even in the early nineteenth-century, when Irish population grew rapidly, the growth was clustered in the bottom classes.

The late- and nonmarriers of "higher" social status in Irish society provided the link between the pre- and post-Famine eras of Irish history. They undermine the more dramatic interpretation that sees the Famine as the central and defining event in Ireland's development. It is in part because of these more prosperous farmers that the rapid population growth had actually begun to slacken by 1821, and the 1831 Census registered a marked increase in the number of nonmarried adults. What the Famine did accomplish was to dramatically universalize trends that were already in operation. This happened in a number of ways. In the first place, the Famine could claim grim responsibility for the almost total elimination of the cottier class. Second, the memory of the Famine impressed the British lawmakers enough in the succeeding decades to enact legislation that outlawed subdivision and other practices associated with pre-Famine agriculture, thus transforming most Irish men into holders of small, although viable, farms.

The Famine might also be seen as the great convincer. It demonstrated to all the folly of agrarian practices that defined a postage-stamp-size piece of land as enough just because it brought forth potatoes. Irish agriculture was going to have to become much more diversified, and though potatoes could remain a central dish on the Irish family's table, that same farm family would also have to produce a cash crop as well as butter, eggs, and other dairy products for markets. The Famine also demonstrated to Irish parents that no one prospered if they cut up their holdings into equal portions for all their sons. An inheritance came to be the entire holding or nothing. Similarly, the Famine also convinced Irish men and women that early marriage was reckless marriage; that nonmarriage was an option, too. As the Irish changed their marriage patterns, they basically adapted the behavior of the more economically stable elements in the society, convinced that the devastation and destruction of the late 1840s had in part been caused by irrational, carefree marriage and family practices that failed to treat conjugal life as a fundamentally economic enterprise.

⋅⟨◉⟩⋅

Whereas before the Famine commentators on Irish life—Catholic clergymen, economists, and British officials alike—lamented the reckless marriage patterns that seemed to accompany the Irish descent into poverty and destitution, after the Famine concern mounted that the Irish in Ireland were increasingly uninterested in remaining at home, marrying, and reproducing themselves. In 1902 one writer mourned, "In saying all this we are fully alive to the sadness of seeing a grand old race disappear as it were, off the face of the earth." Richard J. Kelly in 1904 shared this pessimism with readers of the *New Ireland Review* and chided the experts. "Economists, so-called, read lessons to us on our over-population and improvident early marriages and, as they said, consequent wretchedness. But they can no longer, with any regard for truth say so now, with a smaller population, lower marriage and a lower birth rate than most countries in Europe." Descriptions of Irish life in the last decades of the century all stressed the gloom of decay, the moribund quiet of a society in decline, although perhaps a decline accompanied by increasing prosperity. A magistrate of County Meath saw his home as

> one of the most melancholy counties I know. This grass grown road, over which seemingly little, if any, traffic passes, is a type of solitude everywhere found. Tillage there is none; but in its stead one vast expanse of pasture land extends. Human habitations are rarer than the bare walls of roofless cottages. Where once a population dwelt, and as consequence, see how lonely and untrodden are these roads.

Census figures painfully recorded the dwindling of Irish numbers. In the fifty years between 1841 and 1891, Ireland lost 3,470,374 residents, plummeting from the pre-Famine population of 8,175,124 in 1841 to 4,704,750 in 1891. Constant migration picked off many of these Irish men and women, but migration could not alone be blamed. The decline in Irish population stemmed most fundamentally from a change in family life and a major demographic shift. There were, to be sure, bad harvests in the last half of the nineteenth century which took their toll, somewhat reminiscent of the Famine, but they lacked the bite of the 1840s devastation.

The bulk of the late-nineteenth-century population decline occurred in the rural areas, siphoning off the residents of farm regions much more rapidly than residents of towns. Ireland was becoming somewhat less overwhelmingly rural in the last half of the century. In 1841 only 17 percent of the population was urban; by 1891 over one-quarter of all the Irish could be found in cities like Dublin and Cork. Even the urban population of the country slumped, however, falling from over a million city dwellers in 1841 to eight hundred thousand in 1891. Only Dublin grew in that same time period, but that growth was hardly dramatic and clearly indicated the stagnation of Irish population and the absence of any industrial development or commercial rejuvenation to draw discontented farm people into the cities. Ireland had basically become a nogrowth nation. It had no urban-industrial attractions to stimulate a massive internal movement. It had in fact become a nation characterized by late and reluctant marriage as well as by a massive voluntary exodus.

In the early 1840s, before the Famine shocked and convinced the Irish out of impoverished, although perhaps comfortable, ways, the rate of marriage was 7.0–8.0 per thousand per year. It bore a close resemblance to the rate of marriage throughout Europe. From 1868, four years after compulsory registration of vital statistics, to 1870 the rate of marriage spiraled down to 5.1 per thousand and then fell to 4.0 in the years 1881–90. Clearly, in any given year or span of years during the second half of the century fewer Irish men and women were setting up families than in years past. Many were merely deferring, that is, they were marrying later than they might have in earlier periods. In 1864, for example, 18.1 percent of all women who married were under twenty-one. In 1911 only 5.3 percent entered marriage by that age. Similarly, in 1864 71.1 percent of all wives in a first marriage were under twenty-five; in 1911 only 51.1 percent were similarly situated. But Ireland also came to be the home of large numbers of men and women who just chose not to marry or who were unable to. In 1861, 11 percent of all men in Ireland sixty-five or over were permanent bachelors; in 1926 that figure had risen to 26 percent. Again using 1841, or the last pre-Famine census, as the point of contrast, the percentage of women age twenty-five to thirty-four who were single in Ireland went from 28 percent to 39 percent in 1851. It did not change in 1891. Although fewer Irish women continued to be unmarried as they approached old age, among women forty-five to fifty-four the number of singles also increased from 12 percent in 1841 to 17 percent in 1891. Figures for men were significantly higher in both age categories, in all years. No longer did Irish society live under the specter of the impetuous young rushing off emotionally to marry and set up homes.

Not surprisingly, this matrimonial trend occurred in tandem with yet another development that characterized post-Famine Irish society. Parents increasingly became reluctant to subdivide their land among heirs, and Ireland as a whole came to have fewer and fewer holdings. In 1841, for example, there were 691,000 holdings in all of Ireland, the largest percentage being the smallest holdings, one to five acres. In 1861, 568,000 estates were primarily of the five- to fifteen-acre size, whereas in 1891 the number of holdings declined to 469,000, most of them over thirty acres. Evictions certainly help account for this trend toward land accretion. The poorest could no longer hold onto their tiny plots, and consolidation in Ireland became the basic trend. The cottiers were gone and increasingly the middling Irish farmer had control of a reasonably viable piece of land, which was to be used for pasture-farming, not for tillage.

These middling Irish farmers either had survived the Famine themselves or their parents had witnessed the harrowing devastation, commonly attributed to the wrath of God, or to the heartlessness of the Saxon ruler, or, importantly, to the impetuous romanticism of the poor. The middling Irish farmers were *not* going to err again. They were not going to find themselves in the same position as had the Irish in the 1840s. To ensure their continuous survival without want and destitution they finally sought to shake off the yoke of British rule. To ensure their continued survival with a degree of material comfort and security they sought to establish families that enhanced their economic needs. Land and the economic security it brought became obsessions with the Irish. A folk proverb suggested, "Let any man go down to hell and open an Irish man's heart... the first thing writ across it was land."

Whereas there is no agreement in sight for the lively and sparring scholarly debate over the cause of the pre-Famine population growth, there is unanimity as to the nature of post-Famine marriage: what it was and why it developed into a more discriminate and rationalized institution. Marriages were based now on economic calculation with parents figuring and weighing the financial benefits and liabilities of their children's marital futures. Land would not be divided. An estate would pass intact and undisturbed from one generation to another. Therefore, only one member of the family's younger generation could hope to inherit the land. No systematic or established pattern developed which designated that single heir. Primogeniture was not the rule, nor was the younger son the immediately designated heir. Who inherited the land became the decision of father and mother and they made that decision as late in their lives as possible. Parents held onto control of their fields until well into old age. (Interestingly, Ireland had among Europe's most impressive statistics on longevity.) At the same time they tenaciously held onto control of their children's futures.

POSTSCRIPT

Did British Policy Decisions Cause the Mass Emigration and Land Reforms That Followed the Irish Potato Famine?

Ireland's leading economist, Cormac O'Grada, studies famine folklore, the limitations of medical science, the selection of who would emigrate (many through landlord-funded programs) and who would not, and even the role of the weather in intensifying the famine in *Black '47 and Beyond: The Great Irish Famine in History, Economy, and Memory* (Princeton University Press, 1999). This interdisciplinary work looks at stories and songs that suggest what it was like to live during famine times, explores the impact of famine-related diseases on the city of Dublin, and follows one group of emigrants to New York City's Sixth Ward. *Emigrants and Exiles: Ireland and the Irish Exodus to North America* (Oxford University Press, 1985) by Kerby A. Miller documents both pre- and post-famine exoduses and explores the traditional Irish Catholic worldview that led the Irish to regard themselves as involuntary "exiles."

The Great Irish Famine, edited by Cathal Poirteir and produced in association with Irish Television (Radio Telefis Eireann), has an especially interesting essay by Peter Gray on "Ideology and the Famine," which explores anti-Irish prejudice, the influence of economic theories on British policy, and the reality of political considerations. Two television series have explored this topic: *The Great Famine*, produced by Arts & Entertainment Television Networks (A&E) and *Ireland: A History*, produced by the British Broadcasting Company and Radio Telefis Eireann (BBC/RTE). Accompanying the latter is a well-illustrated book of the same title by Robert Kee (Abacus, Little, Brown & Company, 2001). A similar "you are there" feeling is available in *Famine Diary* (Irish Academic Press, 1999) by Brendan O'Cathaoir, author of *The Irish Times* column of the same name. It features unabridged accounts from newspapers, official correspondence, and diaries.

The 150th anniversary of the beginning of the potato famine has sparked a scholarly reassessment of the traditional interpretation that focused on nationwide suffering, years of misrule, and inadequate responses from both the British government and Irish landlords. Revisionist interpretations have tended to minimize the degree of suffering and are reluctant to blame the authorities for the crisis. Works such as the Yes-side selection by Kinealy are, in part, a response to what can be viewed as a "sanitized" version of the potato famine that trivializes the catastrophe and fails to acknowledge its causes.

ISSUE 4

Did the Meiji Restoration Constitute a Revolution in Nineteenth-Century Japan?

YES: Thomas M. Huber, from *The Revolutionary Origins of Modern Japan* (Stanford University Press, 1981)

NO: W. G. Beasley, from *The Meiji Restoration* (Stanford University Press, 1972)

ISSUE SUMMARY

YES: Historian Thomas M. Huber states that the Meiji Restoration was responsible for the most dramatic change in Japan's history and deserves to be referred to as a revolution.

NO: Historian W. G. Beasley argues that when compared with other revolutions such as the French and Russian, the Meiji Restoration did not constitute a revolution in the classical sense.

In 1603 the Japanese closed themselves off from the rest of the world. Fearful of Western economic and religious influences, which could corrupt their traditions and mores, they banned foreign contacts and meted out severe punishments (including death) to any who violated the ban. Part of this process was the outlawing of Christianity as a recognized religion in Japan. This self-imposed exile was to last for more than 250 years.

The decision to isolate was made by the Tokugawa Shogunate (1603–1868), Japan's ruling power during that period. Since the feudal period of Japanese history, the country had been ruled by shoguns, who were hereditary leaders. Like dynastic rulers anywhere, their right to rule lasted as long as their ability to maintain control, and they could always be replaced by another leader who could then establish his family's rule over the country. Thus, for most of the second millennium, Japan was ruled by successive shogunates: Kamakura (1192–1333), Ashikaga (1335–1573), and Tokugawa (1603–1868). During this time civil wars became prevalent, as there was no shortage of ambitious men to test the waters of political supremacy.

The shoguns were assisted in their rule by *daimyo,* feudal lords who sometimes posed threats to their masters. The samurai, Japan's legendary warrior class, provided the power base for any shogun. (For more information on the samurai, see *Taking Sides: Clashing Views on Controversial Issues in World History, Volume 1,* Issue 12.) Under this system, the Japanese emperor, whose office dated back to the fifth century C.E., had been reduced to that of an isolated figurehead. With the modern world casting covetous eyes around the globe, many wondered how long Japan's self-imposed exile would last and whether it would end by outside force or national choice.

In 1853 United States commodore Matthew Perry arrived in Tokyo, seeking and receiving a treaty from the Japanese government. Although the treaty's terms were not seriously detrimental to Japanese hegemony, it did start a trend that resulted in similar treaties with other foreign nations. In Japan these actions had the dual effect of forcing the Japanese to consider what they could do to limit further Western intervention and causing the rise of nationalist sentiment against foreign elements. This resulted in an overthrow of the Tokugawa shogunate by an alliance of feudal lords and samurai in 1866, which returned the emperor to a position of authority in the new Japanese government. The new emperor took the name *Meiji* (enlightened government), and since that time the period in Japanese history from 1868 to 1912 had been known in the West as the Meiji Restoration. Thus began Japan's modern history.

The transformation of Japan seemed to be profound; no part of Japanese life escaped the winds of change. Although those who overthrew the Tokugawa government had no set plan—and many of them had diametrically opposed goals and objectives—change was the order of the day. Some of the most important results of Meiji rule were the growth of Japan's industrial and military power, presumably accomplished to counterbalance Western power in Asia. This was done under the aegis of a highly centralized government, which featured a "top down" power structure. Under such a system, a premium was placed on nationalism as a unifying force. Some of the Meiji-made decisions were to have a positive impact on Japan's modernization; others, such as imperialism, were to have drastic consequences for the nation and its people.

Some basic questions about the Meiji Restoration concerns the nature of the movement itself. How much and what type of change did it effect? Was it revolutionary? How does it compare to its French and Russian counterparts? A problem facing one who attempts to answer these questions lies in definition and, in this case, an accurate translation of words. The Japanese word to describe the Meiji movement is *Ishin,* which may be closer in meaning to *renovation* than the Western-translated *restoration.* Keep this in mind as we assess the revolutionary nature of the Meiji Restoration through the work of Thomas M. Huber and W. G. Beasley, who present complementary, yet differing, opinions on the subject. The former refers to the Meiji Restoration and its reforms as "the most dramatic event in Japan's modern history" and asserts that they merit the title of revolution. The latter agrees that the Meiji Restoration was revolutionary, but argues that it "lacked the avowed social purpose that gives the 'great' revolutions of history a certain common character."

Thomas M. Huber

 **YES**

The Revolutionary Origins
of Modern Japan

Introduction

The creation of the Meiji Restoration government in 1868, and the sweeping reforms that followed, constitute the most dramatic event in Japan's modern history. Within a decade Japanese leaders established a system of universal education, formed a modern army and navy, and recruited an efficient administrative bureaucracy, both nationally and locally. They developed a network of telegraph and rail communications, and laid the broad fiscal and financial foundations that were needed for rapid industrialization. The Restoration transformed Japan into a modern society by the standards of the day, and rescued her alone among her Asian neighbors from the bondage of colonialism, and from the feudal encumbrances of her own past. . . .

This [selection] will show that the Meiji transformation was accomplished only after a long and daring political insurgency, by men dedicated to reformist principles that were articulated in the 1850's and even earlier. It was over these principles, representing as they did the vision of a new society and the aspirations of a new social class, that the bitter struggles of the 1860's were waged, and for the sake of these principles that the Chōshū men and others put their lives at risk. The Chōshū leaders probably did not see themselves at first as being the foremost champions of these new values, but when fortune so decreed, they proved worthy of the task. In this [selection] the origins of the Meiji state are characterized as revolutionary. If the explanation offered here is correct, they were nothing less. . . .

Idealism and Revolution

. . . In the decade between 1868 and 1878, the newly constituted imperial government under the Chōshū leaders and their colleagues implemented national reforms at a rapid pace. A central administrative bureaucracy recruited solely on a basis of merit was established immediately. A national university was created in 1869, as if in belated response to Yoshida Shōin's repeated petitioning for one ten years before. An ambitious public educational system was founded in 1872 that would soon open tens of thousands of primary and secondary schools throughout the country. All of the gratuitous privileges of the samurai class were phased out in the 1870's, and official discrimination based on the old classes was completely abolished. Hundreds of semiautonomous feudal domains were legally reconstituted as homogeneous prefectures, and a solid fiscal basis for the new government was achieved by imposing a uniform tax on land. The new tax eliminated and displaced the heavy domainal dues on land that had been the main material foundation of the old aristocratic system. A modern army and navy patterned after Western models and open to talent were equipped and readied for service by 1876. Timely and imaginative reforms were carried out in the judiciary, foreign relations, banking, communications, and many other fields as well.

These sweeping changes altered the essential quality of public life. They brought a vitality and rationality that enlivened all spheres of public action. There soon followed unprecedented growth in crop yields, commerce, and industry. There arose a vigorous press and a healthy general clamor for democracy. Philosophy, literature, and the arts, nourished by foreign as well as native inspiration, flourished as never before. Famine was unknown, and modern medical knowledge spread across the land. In the end the reforms would rescue tens of millions of ordinary Japanese from ignorance, disease, and want. Their momentous impact makes the search for their origins a matter of utmost historiographical importance....

The Origins of the Meiji Reforms

The Restoration reforms were carried out swiftly after the "imperial army" entered Edo in 1868. These reforms went smoothly because the principles behind the programs, and even the programs themselves, were understood by many, long before 1868. The Meiji reforms of the 1870's grew out of reformist interests that were already being articulated by political thinkers in Chōshū in the 1850's and even earlier. This is a matter of crucial importance for any analysis of the Meiji Restoration, yet one that historians have tended to overlook.

Virtually all of the later Meiji reforms were guided by two broad principles used by Chōshū thinkers early in the 1850's to justify major departures from the institutional status quo. These were, first, the substitution of preferment by merit for preferment by birth and, second, the redirection of the realm's institutional energies to better meet the people's actual needs in the present and to eliminate lavish expenditure on the empty ritual practices of the past. These principles were developed by local reformers who were trying to overcome organizational contradictions that had long plagued the institutional life of their own domains, especially contradictions associated with university training. By the 1850's these same thinkers had come to realize that solutions that were desirable at the local level would be still more desirable if implemented nationally. [Commodore] Perry's [a United States naval officer] sudden appearance had made such a reconstruction seem not only more useful but also more likely of achievement. Moreover, as the years wore on, the reformers had reached an anguished understanding that the old society could not tolerate the kinds of changes they wanted. In order to stabilize their reforms, they would have to impose them everywhere in a manner that would change permanently the center of gravity of public life.

...Yoshida Shōin [a thinker and educator who plotted against the government] demanded rigorous merit recruitment for the Chōshū academy in 1848. Once Yoshida had developed his basic reformist concepts in the institutional microcosm of the Chōshū university, he was able to apply them rapidly to a broad spectrum of institutional practices that reached far beyond the walls of the local academy. By 1858 he was applying his reformist approaches to the larger task of reordering national institutions. Having reached this point, however, Yoshida was executed before he could take the next step, which was to apply his innovative ideas to the problem of radically reorganizing the apparatus of the central authority itself.

Kusaka Genzui converted his mentor's many discrete proposals into a plan for Restoration by taking this last step. In 1862 he recommended that the Bakufu in its national responsibilities be replaced altogether by a new merit bureaucracy centered on the court. Kusaka substantially described in 1862 the institutional pattern that would be realized by his closest friends and followers in 1868.

The Meiji reforms rested not only on twenty years of reformist articulation but also on ten years of actual experimentation within Chōshū. [Author and historian] W. G. Beasley has referred to these developments as a "Meiji Restoration in miniature." By the mid-1860's, Chōshū had already instituted a large degree of merit selection in government posts, the elimination of almost all rank considerations in favor of ability in han-sponsored education, the nucleus of a Western-style infantry and navy composed of commoners as well as samurai, and a significantly streamlined bureaucracy. This pattern of Chōshū as bellwether continued even after 1868. The abolition of autonomous han, announced in 1871, was piloted by the voluntary surrender of privileges to the Tokyo government by Chōshū and three other reformist han in 1869.

There is another instructive case of the reformers' tendency to use Chōshū as an experimental forerunner. On 12/2/68 Chōshū's activist-controlled government slashed samurai stipends of 1,000 koku or more by 90 percent, and even stipends between 100 and 1,000 koku were all reduced to 100. At the same time, stipends of less than 100 koku were left entirely untouched. Fiscally, this bold stroke was the end of the "men of large stipend" who had been the perennial target of Yoshida Shōin's complaints in the 1850's. This act was a prelude, of course, to the restorationists' abolition of these and other feudal privileges on a national scale several years later.

It is meaningful, then, to speak of the Meiji reforms of the 1870's as representing a well-developed version of the political goals sought by the Chōshū intelligentsia even before they became involved in the activism of the mid-1860's. Rationalizing reforms like those carried out in the 1870's had been the object of the Chōshū activists' study, petitioning, and experimentation for decades....

Modern Idealism and World Revolution

It has sometimes been claimed that the Meiji Restoration was sui generis, a type of revolutionary transformation unique to Japan. Although it is true that the Restoration does not resemble the familiar "bourgeois" and "proletarian" archetypes of revolutionary change, there are elements of similarity linking the Meiji experience with the "great" revolutions of the West. Consideration of such similarities may yield some interesting comparative insights. I will try to highlight some of these by applying to Western revolutions the Japanese paradigm . . . instead of the reverse approach that has been more common. I will sketch the paradigm, then apply it. I will argue that the utopian goals and ideal motives that distinguished the Chōshū restorationists have been present in most of the great revolutionary upheavals of recent history.

Late Tokugawa society represented a neofeudal or "absolutist" stage of development, characterized by sophisticated social organization and considerable surplus wealth. This was so especially in the vicinity of the country's national and regional metropolises. Much of this wealth went to the lavish support of a politically powerful but functionally noncontributive aristocracy. Coexisting with these privileged few was a more numerous service class, who held only minor aristocratic perquisites. These persons, literate and resourceful, actually managed and produced the growing social wealth, while absorbing little of it themselves.

This inequitable state of affairs was stable, because it was sanctioned by custom and tradition, and because confident aristocratic elements used their political power boldly to protect privilege, whereas the service strata lacked leverage, confidence, and traditional sanction.

This stable traditional pattern was shaken by the sudden intrusion of a formidable external threat: Commodore Perry. The traditional assumptions justifying aristocratic social organization were thus critically undermined causing a shift of the center of political gravity toward the service classes. Service elements enjoyed two advantages that allowed them to parlay this security crisis into a large-scale social reconstruction: ideological competence and paramilitary opportunity. The basic conceptual tools needed to plan and legitimize a new society had been forged a generation and more before Perry, and so were readily available to many when the moment came. In addition, the reformers were fortunate in being able to mobilize an effective army, relying on a combination of service-class loyalties and various forms of sentimental nationalism.

The restorationists' determined ideological activity, combined with their military power, enabled them in time to overwhelm the old order. They then appropriated the country's large aristocratic surpluses as planned and invested them in new forms of socially creative activity, including industrialization. The result was a new regime with startling advantages. The new society was more equitable, orderly, and provident for everyone.

Absolutist society is tormented by a paradox: its means have become modern, but its ends are still feudal. Its wealth is generated by firm, modern institutions, but gathered in by a small class of aristocratic grandees and financial notables. This leads to other paradoxes, namely, a tremendous artificial disparity between rich and poor in general, and the emergence of a disciplined service intelligentsia that selflessly creates and harvests all the growing wealth, but is nonetheless excluded, like the ordinary people, from its major benefits. Two other circumstances, if added to this milieu, will produce a revolutionary reconstruction: a widespread ideological preparation for change among the public, to which is added a national security crisis (or sense that the national interest is being compromised). This is what happened in the Japanese case.

Let us consider the origins of the innovative class that brought the Restoration about. It had arisen as a consequence of the increasingly sophisticated institutional growth that characterized much of the long Tokugawa era. Its ranks included scholars, administrators, physicians, clerics, military technicians, and even a few poets. Although it had come into existence gradually over the course of the preceding two centuries, this group already represented a substantial and active minority in the society of perhaps 10 to 15 percent of the population.

The Meiji Restoration can be understood as a revolution carried out by this modern social class, which found itself oppressed by the institutional configurations of the late feudal status quo. It bears a resemblance to one of the four social classes described by Max Weber [a German sociologist and political economist]. In the middle ground between small merchants and persons "privileged through property," Weber identified a social class that consisted of "propertyless intelligentsia," "specialists," and "civil servants." The intelligentsia, Weber maintained, was a major social category, essentially distinct, in both its social attributes and its political interests, from other social groups.

In other words, the Japanese intelligentsia was a modern social class that had emerged from a long process of institutional evolution. This modernizing evolutionary process is that described by Weber as "rationalization" and "bureaucratization." (It was in this connection that Weber once asserted that the Christian monk was the first modern man.) The restorationists were a class produced by this Weberian dynamic of institutional rationalization and increasing social efficiency, and who had an interest both in carrying that process further, and in terminating the lingering neofeudal (or "patrimonial") misappropriation of its hard-won benefits.

Although this group was obviously interested in a more equitable distribution of material rewards, ideal values must nevertheless be regarded as the key to the distinctive identity and conduct of this class. Their selfless dynamism, in both service and rebellion, is hard to explain without reference to ideal interests and rewards. The realm's disciplined new intelligentsia was prepared to give much yet take little because it was motivated not by simple quid pro quo advantages, but rather by "loyalty" (*chūkō*), or what Weber called "vocation." They were encouraged throughout to respond to ideal values, not material values. Thus the high social cost of service functions of modern quality was borne at first in such a way as not to undermine the premises of aristocratic social organization, by the remarkable expedient of paying for it with "ideal" rewards. (This pattern also dictated the necessity of extreme thrift as a value in the private lives of much of the service class, thus imparting a "puritanical" quality to the ethos of that class.) The immense advantages for an aristocratic elite that could perpetrate such an arrangement on its ablest servants are obvious. Yet it would not be proper to assume that the servants themselves were simply exploited by this. They, after all, had the highest gratification of all: doing right (or believing that they did).

The cultivated idealism of the intelligentsia by and by came to have a momentum of its own, however. The intellectual capabilities of the service classes and their idealist values eventually combined to yield utopian goals. It occurred to philosophers of the service echelon that the selfless rationality by which they gathered the new surplus wealth might also be applied to the allocation of that wealth in such a way as to create a more dynamic society and general enrichment. The loyalties of the service class eventually shifted, from the transitional absolutist institutions that had brought them into being, toward the more modern forms that were still only imagined. A satisfying utopian program, a strong ideal interest in the well-being of all, and consequently a very high tolerance for personal risk, are the essential characteristics of modernizing intelligentsia-based revolution that distinguish it from political agitation on the part of other interest groups. Modern idealism is the hallmark of service revolution.

Recent work by the Japanese scholar Ueyama Shumpei suggests that the phenomenon of service revolution was not unique to Bakumatsu Japan, and that elements of it can be found in the French Revolution. Ueyama observed close institutional similarities between the minor royal officials and priests who made up the revolutionary majority in France's Estates General in 1789 and the "lower-class samuari" who brought about the Meiji Restoration. He found close parallels in the language of the revolutionary ideologist Abbé Sieyès and the Mito scholar Fujita Tōko regarding the unsatisfactory relationship between public service echelons and the privileged minority.

Ueyama's analysis is directly supported by the work of Alfred Cobban, John McManners, and others. In his *Myth of the French Revolution,* Cobban pointed out that the "bourgeois" revolution in 1789 is hard to find, and suggested that the essence of the revolutionary phenomenon in France may have been something very different, namely, a rebellion of "minor officials." The militant leaders and followers of the Third Estate, whether from the church, the military, or the royal administration, fell overwhelmingly into this category. In Cobban's words, "a class of officials and professional men moved up from the minor to the major posts in government and dispossessed the minions of an effete Court: this was what the bourgeois revolution meant."

There were, of course, enormous differences in the respective ideologies and forms of violence that emerged in the Meiji Restoration and in the French Revolution. Nevertheless, the French case, like the Japanese case, sprang from many decades of growing awareness among the nation's leading thinkers that a better world was possible. From the days of Montesquieu and Voltaire on, Enlightenment philosophers began with growing excitement to hammer out among themselves what liberty and equality could really mean. Ideas were everywhere for reconstructing every conceivable institutional practice.

When in 1789 only a courageous stand was needed to bring these ideas into reality, thousands stood up for revolution without looking back. In the

French Revolution as in the Japanese Restoration, privileges relating solely to birth were aggressively eliminated, and in both cases, thousands of career opportunities were suddenly opened to "talent." Both cases involved sudden and conscious institutional reform in the direction of radical bureaucratization, and other structural ameliorations that would lead quickly to a phenomenal increase in general welfare and prosperity.

The European revolution most explicitly associated with intelligentsia activity is the Russian Revolution of 1917. Ideologies and forms of violence once again differed markedly from other cases. Still, the leadership role of the intelligentsia was unmistakable. Beginning with Alexander Herzen on the institutional side and [Mikhail] Bakunin and [Peter] Kropotkin on the theoretical side, Russian thinkers were embarked for much of the nineteenth century on a quest for new utopian values and needed structural reforms. Although even discussing these matters involved great risk, many proponents of a new Russia were soon going beyond this to sacrifice themselves in lone terrorist assaults on the living symbols of old regime authority. These thinkers and activists were the *raznochintsy,* and their ranks were filled primarily by "clergy" and "the minor professional and bureaucratic classes." Martin Malia has seen the Russian intelligentsia as a "class" with its own autonomous interests. The boundaries of that class, as in the French and Japanese cases, were defined institutionally, that is, by university experience and institutional condition.

The upheaval of 1917 led to a "rational" restructuring of Russian society leading among other things to large-scale industrial development. Thousands of careers were suddenly open to talent, while aristocratic privileges, material and political, were swept away. The intelligentsia itself did benefit from this, but the Russian masses were perhaps the greatest beneficiaries, and there is no doubt that many of the revolutionaries shared idealistic motives.

A few years ago, Michael Walzer published a well-received study entitled *Revolution of the Saints.* Walzer argued that England's seventeenth-century revolution against monarchical authority was carried out by a "Puritan intelligentsia." These men had the kind of Calvinist calling described by Weber, but it was not directed at economic activity. Rather it was aimed at political activity, such that in the evolutionary course of things they had as a group finally come to wield more power in the state than the prince and the peerage. Moreover, they achieved success by engaging in a disciplined form of "radical politics," leading Walzer to characterize puritanical "radicalism" as a "general historical phenomenon." He has suggested the need for a "systematic comparison of Puritans, Jacobins, and Bolsheviks."

The utopian dimension was prominent in the English Revolution. Francis Bacon in his *New Atlantis* of 1626 had described a perfect land in the Americas where philosophers in the House of Solomon would assure the health and welfare of the people. Many Puritan intellectuals in Bacon's day believed that with God's inspiration they could remake society and create a paradise on earth. (The contemporaneous rise of modern science was one consequence of this attitude.) This was an exhilarating prospect for them, and in the political upheaval and Great Migration to North America that followed, many of the institutional reforms they envisioned came true.

Service revolution deriving from a Weberian evolutionary dynamic may be more than a Japanese idiosyncrasy. Rebellion of the service intelligentsia for its own reasons may have been a powerful or even decisive factor in each of the great revolutions of Europe. In Japan as in Europe, and now in new nations as ideologically diverse as Vietnam and Israel, the Weberian, or organizational, transformation has preceded the large-scale industrial, or Marxist, transformation. In each case, the transformational upheaval has generally been carried out by service elements, often with minor aristocratic perquisites of their own, operating in the name of utopian values against a powerful aristocratic (or colonial) stratum, in circumstances of a widely perceived external threat to the national welfare.

In the typical Third World case, impoverished proletarians are nowhere to be seen. Rather, students, professors, clergymen, technicians, teachers, young officers, and the like join to demand reform in the name of transcendent social values. Despite great risk, they strive relentlessly against a small class of estate-holders and financial grandees who are thought to enjoy close ties with foreign interests. The reformers' insurgency has often been focused on a monarch figure who derives lavish personal income from public functions owned by himself, and who serves as the absolutist guarantor of a larger system of social privilege. Signs of this dynamic have been apparent in recent years in Nicaragua, Ethiopia, Iran, and elsewhere. The insurgent group may seek to organize ordinary people for paramilitary activity, and always fashions a judicious combination of traditional folk belief and modern social philosophy such as will accommodate both the demands of sentimental nationalism and the insurgents' program of social rationalization. This kind of pattern conforms closely to the assumptions of service revolution.

In both European and non-European cases, the dynamics of idealist service revolution have gone largely unnoticed in the past, because so little attention has been paid to developing the theoretical paradigms against which they could be perceived. Careful scrutiny of the Meiji Restoration, where the dynamic of service revolution is so clearly present, may provide the essential contours of such a paradigm.

W. G. Beasley

 **NO**

The Meiji Restoration

Introduction

During the middle decades of the nineteenth century China and Japan both faced pressure from an intrusive, expanding West. This entailed, first, a political and military danger, manifested in two Anglo-Chinese wars and in the use of force on many other occasions, threatening their independence; and second, a challenge to their traditional culture from one that was alien in many of its fundamental concepts, as well as superior in technology and science. Emotionally and intellectually, Chinese and Japanese reacted to the threat in similar ways: with simple hostility, with manifestations of cultural chauvinism, with a grudging recognition of their own inferiority in "wealth and power." Yet they differed greatly in the kind of actions that this response induced. In China, the Confucian order proved strong enough to inhibit change, whether in polity or ideas, thereby bringing about a union of conservatism at home with concession abroad that led eventually to dynastic decline and an age of revolutions. In Japan, men succeeded in "using the barbarian to control the barbarian" so as to initiate policies that produced a "modern" state, powerful enough in the end to meet the West on equal terms. Hence Japan, unlike China, moved to empire and industry, not poverty and civil war.

The Meiji Restoration is at the heart of this contrast, since it was the process by which Japan acquired a leadership committed to reform and able to enforce it. For Japan, therefore, the Restoration has something of the significance that the English Revolution has for England or the French Revolution for France; it is the point from which modern history can be said to begin. For this reason it has been much studied. Equally, it has been the subject of enduring controversy, for its significance—and thus the way in which it is to be explained —has changed with every change of attitude toward the society that it brought into being....

Conclusions

The history of the Meiji Restoration... is relevant to a number of themes that are important not only for Japan. In part it was a response to the nineteenth-century expansion of the West in Asia. Hence studying it raises questions about the nature of imperialism and nationalism and of their relationship to change in the modern world. Equally, the Restoration was at least in some respects a revolution. One must therefore ask, what kind of revolution was it? How does it compare with other great political upheavals in other parts of the world at other times? And are the features that mark it off from them idiosyncratically Japanese, or do they arise from the fact and nature of the West's involvement? Finally, since the Restoration is the historical starting point for the modernization of Japan, a process that is highly significant for theories of economic growth, it poses yet another question, to wit: How far is a radical restructuring of society a necessary condition—and not merely a consequence—of the transformation of a pre-modern into a modern economy.

Clearly, though the example of Japan is an element in the discussion of all these matters, it is not necessarily a decisive one. Therefore a [selection] like this, which approaches the Restoration from inside, as it were, that is, as a part of Japanese history, ought not to offer itself as providing answers that are universally valid. What it *can* do, what these closing remarks are intended to do, is to present its conclusions in such a way that others might be able to use them to these ends. As a preliminary to this, it might be helpful to recapitulate the story in a rather more generalized form than was possible when setting out the detailed narrative.

❦

Under the Tokugawa, Japanese society was gradually modified by economic change in such a way as to bring about by the nineteenth century a disjunction between contemporary reality and the inherited ideal. This was manifested in a number of phenomena for which the traditional order had no place: samurai whose debts turned them into ambitious office-holders or impoverished umbrella-makers; farmers abandoning subsistence agriculture to become commercial producers and rural entrepreneurs or laborers and quasi-tenants; and city merchants enjoying feudal patronage in a kind of symbiosis with authority or escaping into an urban subculture of their own.

Because these things happened at different speeds in different areas, they disturbed the balance of power between the Bakufu [or "tent government" because soldiers lived in tents] and the domains, which had depended originally on a carefully calculated distribution of land. Because they happened at all, they produced social upheaval: a blurring of status distinctions, stimulating samurai unrest; and economic disruption, provoking peasant revolt. These were reflected in turn in a "what-is-wrong-with-the-world" literature and attempts at "reform," the latter seeking either to reconstitute an ideal past (a restoration of feudal authority and its agrarian base) or to exploit commercial growth for the benefit of the ruling class (if at some cost to its ethos). One result was to give more samurai a degree of participation in active politics than hitherto. Another was to make the concept of "reform" familiar and to prompt a feeling that society was in danger of destruction from within.

Yet the country's social and political institutions proved to be remarkably durable: eroded but far from demolished, they did not seem in 1850 to be on the point of being swept away. Not least, this was because the system of institutional checks and balances coupled with deliberate regional fragmentation that had been devised to restrain the anticipated disaffection of samurai and feudal lords proved capable also of imposing controls on the new "men of substance" who might have challenged the established order from outside the samurai class. Accordingly, most of these men sought their opportunities of advancement through conformity, not revolution, acquiring status by purchase or marriage, but remaining politically passive.

It was into this situation that there were injected the West's demand for trade relations in the years 1853–58, leading to "unequal" treaties. The manner in which the treaties were obtained, that is, by gunboat diplomacy, was as important as their content, for it helped to produce in Japan an upsurge of emotion greater than any that had been aroused by domestic issues. Its importance was not merely that the blow to Japanese pride led to a call for "action" (not necessarily of any specific kind); it was also that this was a "national" dishonor in the sense that it could be felt in all areas and at all levels in Japanese society. It thereby helped to break down the regional and social fragmentation that had been one of the foundations of Tokugawa power.

Moreover, the humiliation at the hands of the West precipitated struggle and controversy. The struggle arose when men questioned the efficiency of the country's leaders, especially their ability to defend Japan; and it brought to the surface many of the latent divisions in the national polity by asking, if only implicitly, who their replacements should be in case they failed. The controversy concerned both short-term diplomatic issues and long-term cultural ones, but it had a single, central thread: the extent to which Japan must abandon custom in order to save herself, first in the context of technology, or particular institutional devices to serve particular ends, and then, more generally, in the context of radical changes in society, such as industrialization had induced in the countries of the West. . . .

History offers many different examples of the kind of motivating force that is capable of overcoming inertia and the bonds of tradition: imperial ambition, religious faith, the pursuit of social justice, the aspirations of a newly emergent class. For Japan in the nineteenth century, nationalism had this function. Again and again in the documents of the years we have been considering there are phrases that put policy of every kind—economic and political, as well as diplomatic—into the context of the "national" interest, justifying proposals on the grounds that they would "restore our national strength" or "make the imperial dignity resound beyond the seas." What is more, most of the major political crises centered on the question of Japan's relations with the outside world: that of 1858, when the signing of the treaties became linked with the question of the Tokugawa succession; that of 1863–64, when the fate of the "men of spirit" was decided against a background of foreign bombardment; that of 1873, when the debate about Korea brought into the open a struggle about priorities at home. Throughout, Japanese opinion was moving from a consciousness of foreign threat to an awareness of national identity, expressed in demands for unity and independence.

The contrast with China underlines the extraordinary speed and thoroughness of Japan's response. Despite widespread anti-foreign feeling among gentry and officials, Chinese continued to behave, at least until the end of the nineteenth century, as a people defending a civilization that was threatened, not a nation defending a country that was under attack. Long before then, the Japanese, subscribing to a more articulate and sophisticated version of the Restoration's search for "wealth and strength," had found in nationalism a means of reconciling the conflict between cultural tradition and imperative circumstance.

The "liberal" constitutional movement was heavily influenced by that new-found nationalism. "The one object of my life is to extend Japan's national power," Fukuzawa Yukichi wrote in 1882. "Compared with considerations of the country's strength, the matter of internal government and into whose hands it falls is of no importance at all. Even if the government be autocratic in name and form, I shall be satisfied with it if it is strong enough to strengthen the country." This is Fukuzawa the nationalist overcoming Fukuzawa the liberal, if only temporarily.

Taking a wider framework, the newspaper *Nihon* celebrated the announcement of the Meiji Constitution in 1889 by urging that a limit be set to the adoption of foreign ways. It had no desire "to revive a narrow xenophobia," *Nihon* declared, for "we recognise the excellence of Western civilisation. We value the Western theories of rights, liberty and equality.... Above all, we esteem Western science, economics and industry." Nevertheless, it continued, these things "ought not to be adopted simply because they are Western; they ought to be adopted only if they can contribute to Japan's welfare." In Tokyo in 1889 this was a conservative warning not to go too fast or too far. In contemporary Peking it would have been reformist.

One is bound to ask, why did Japan evolve in a generation a nationalism that in China came much more slowly and with much less effect, given that both countries had long traditions of political and cultural unity? Difference of size was a factor, of course. In Japan, which was smaller and had a very long coastline, the presence of the foreigners and their ships was evident to a higher percentage of the population, making the danger from them easier to believe and act on. China was not only larger, but more varied—in spoken language, social patterns, types of crop—so that there were great practical obstacles to imposing administrative and economic unity in the nationalist sense, just as there were in India and the Ottoman Empire, for example. China did not lend herself very readily to being made into a "country," Japan did.

In addition to all this, however, there are historical differences between the two that have a particular relevance to the study of the Meiji Restoration. One is Japan's relative freedom of cultural choice: she was less bound than China to a single view of her society and her place in the world. Japan had already imported elements of Chinese civilization, which coexisted with others that were her own; thus to adopt a part of Europe's civilization was not to damage an entity that was whole and unique, but to add a third possibility to an existing two, one of which was in any case "foreign." For instance, medicine was a Chinese science in pre-modern Japan, using many Chinese drugs, hence accepting a Western alternative was not so very shocking. Warfare, the samurai's trade, was studied in a Chinese classic text (albeit embodied in a thoroughly Japanese mystique) and was conducted with the help of a seventeenth-century "Dutch" technology. There was nothing in this to inhibit following alien models. As Rutherford Alcock noted of the Japanese when he first became acquainted with them, "they have little of the stupid conceit of the Chinese, which leads them to ignore or deny the superiority of foreign things."

It was the same with political institutions. No educated Japanese of the Tokugawa period could fail to be aware that the political structure of his country differed from that of China, which the philosophers he read upheld as an ideal. His country had a Shogun as well as an Emperor; it was administered through a feudal system, not a bureaucratic one. This helped to heighten his sense of Japaneseness, which was an element in nationalism, but it also made him aware that substantial variations could exist within the limits of what was known and acceptable.

In other words, in abolishing the Bakufu, reasserting the Emperor's authority, and instituting a centralized bureaucratic state, the Japanese could see themselves as making a fresh set of choices among the variables that their history already contained, however much they reinterpreted them. Hence renovation (ishin) could be coupled with restoration (fukko) in a manner that causes the least offense. This was especially so because of the nature and ethos of the ruling class. In China, civil officials held office by virtue of being Confucian, that is, as exemplars of a structure of belief on which their whole society was founded. To tamper with part of that structure was to undermine the whole, weakening their power. This was not so in Japan. The samurai, it is true, had accepted the Confucian ethic and some of the bureaucratic habits that went with it. He did not depend on these, however, to validate his rule. As a feudal lord or retainer, his position rested on birth, on inheritable status received as a reward for past military prowess. His code, Bushidō, though it coexisted with Confucianism, emphasized different virtues, the specifically military ones. Accordingly, he did not feel a need to accept or reject Confucianism as a whole. He could employ it—as Meiji society did—in the context of personal and family behavior while turning to other concepts for his political and economic life: nationalist ones, which could be given a Shintō coloring; or Western ones, explaining the new phenomena of industry and commerce. And the fact that the new amalgam was not a conspicuously logical one worried him less because of the equal irrationality of the old.

Finally, one must note the significance of Japan's having entered this phase of her history, unlike China, under a *military* ruling class. This relates to nationalism to the extent that soldiers were more inclined to think of defending a territory than defending a system of ideas, more of defending country than culture. It also relates to modernization, since it contributed to the identification of agreed priorities, where individuals had a multiplicity of views. Indeed, it may well be that a military habit of mind, variously applied, was the samurai's most important contribution to Meiji society—and hence, to the making of the modern Japanese state.

What has been said [earlier] amounts to an assertion that nationalism had a double function in Japan in the twenty years after 1853: first, that it provided a motive compelling men to act; second, that it shaped their aims and priorities. Unhappily, this pleasingly simple explanation of what took place is incomplete. Side by side with the story of nationalism and the foreign threat, there is another, that of social change; and in turning to it, we move from a discussion of men's purposes to a discussion of the circumstance in which they found themselves. It was from the interaction of the two that history was made.

... [H]ow, then, are we to set political struggle and social change in relation to each other? I would suggest, as follows:

1. The class composition of the politically active minority in late-Tokugawa Japan already reflected the results of economic change in that it did not accord with the *formal* allocation of authority in society: a few daimyo, a few upper samurai, a good many middle samurai, a much larger number of lower samurai and "men of substance" from outside the samurai class. Proportionately, this corresponds fairly well with the number of men within each of these groups. Yet no Japanese of the time would have been prepared to argue that participation in decision-making should be proportional to numbers in this way; traditionally, it should have been almost entirely the prerogative of lords and senior retainers. Departure from traditional norms in this respect therefore suggests that at the *beginning* of the period with which we have dealt, the outlines of a new ruling class were emerging from within the old. It was *within* this class that most of the crucial debates took place.

2. In the various proposals for curing the country's ills after the conclusion of the treaties, there was usually an element of class or group interest, though not necessarily a dominant one. Bakufu and feudal lords, despite their rivalries, both sought to defend Japan without much disturbing its society; by promoting "men of talent," the middle samurai meant principally themselves; and the "men of spirit," despite an inability for the most part to get away from feudal terminology, clearly envisaged that the success of their plans would bring them a status they did not already have. Thus the defeat of kōbu-gattai, "unity of Court and Bakufu," and of kinnō, "serving the Emperor," were defeats for socially conservative and politically radical formulations of reform, respectively, as well as for particular ideas about how Japan could best be defended from the foreigner.

3. The men who emerged as leaders in succession to the reforming lords and dissident samurai, mostly after 1864, were realists, pragmatists, bureaucrat-politicians whose social origins matched their role: that is, they were nearly all middle or lower samurai, not high enough in the feudal hierarchy to be bent on preserving it, nor excluded from it to

the point of wanting above all to break it down. Moreover, they were convinced that national defense required national unity. Accordingly, they believed as much in conciliation as reform, and so began to bring together the components of what was a social, as well as a political, alliance. Edo intransigents and rebellious peasants they would not tolerate, because both were obstacles to order and unity in their different ways. But the rest could all find a place: Court nobles, feudal lords, samurai, landlords, influential merchants, even servants of the Shogun in the end. To belong, one needed only to subscribe to the national objectives, as the inner group defined them.

4. Victory over the Tokugawa made these men responsible for government, that is, for implementing on a national scale the policies that would bring Japan "wealth and strength." In much of what they then did they acted still as samurai-bureaucrats trained in Confucian ideas: manipulating the Emperor as they had their lords; caring for the people's welfare, subject to the tax needs of the state; framing an education system that contributed to good order and to the citizen's skills. Concepts of government and its functions did not change as much from Tokugawa to Meiji as the emphasis on modernization sometimes makes us think. Yet some of the differences were vital. Since feudalism contributed nothing to efficiency and was an obstacle to military strength, it had to go. Equally, since land tax was an essential resource and defining it involved the recognition of what had happened in the village, landlords got confirmation of their landed rights. Indirectly, they also obtained an extension of their economic opportunities. In fact, though the purpose of it all was not to change society, but rather to identify the least degree of social adjustment that would make possible fukoku-kyōhei—a militarily strong Japan rich enough to sustain a position of independence in the world—the application of these policies produced something very different from the Japan of twenty years before. For the minimal change, once identified, proved to be substantial. Consciously, there was an attack on samurai privilege; but consequentially this made possible the emergence into a position of influence of a new class, the well-to-do commoners whose power had until then been only latent.

5. Several factors came together to ensure that the society which emerged at the end of these years would be a capitalist one. Some of the long-term trends in the Tokugawa period were already moving in that direction, providing a basis on which to build. They were given a stimulus by contact with the capitalist West, initially through the effects of foreign trade, then because of the nature of the advice Japan received and the models she studied; the Western solutions that were applied to Japanese problems were inevitably those of the contemporary industrial state. Development was also given a particular direction by the nature of the policies that were devised for the promotion of national strength—the encouragement of industrial and commercial growth, coupled with an unusual degree of government intervention in the country's economy—so that Japan's transition from the "centralized

feudalism" of Tokugawa days was to a similarly centralized form of capitalism. This resolved one Tokugawa anomaly, that of merchant wealth, by bringing the entrepreneur, like the landlord, into the dominant class and giving him a means to fulfill his aspirations legally. It left another, that of peasant unrest, aside. In the short term the second issue was settled by force; but as the pressures on the cultivator increased with the growth of industry it re-emerged to become a problem of the twentieth century in a different form.

Does all this amount to a revolution? Perhaps to ask the question is to invite an argument about the meaning of words, since the reader is likely to have and to apply criteria of his own in finding an answer. Nevertheless, there are a number of points that can be made by way of a final gloss on what has been said [earlier]. For example, the Bakufu had some of the classic characteristics of an ancien régime; it had grave financial problems; it tried unsuccessfully to effect reform; it was indecisive and ineffective at the end in suppressing opposition; and for a variety of reasons it lost the confidence of a considerable segment of the ruling class. Also, those who overthrew it included men of many social origins (but not the lowest); they were generally of some respectability and experience; and they produced what might well be called "a dictatorship in commission." One could even argue that Restoration politics moved through appropriate stages of moderation and extremism before eventually bringing about, not "a brand-new ruling class," but "a kind of amalgamation, in which the enterprising, adaptable or lucky individuals of the old privileged classes [were] for most practical purposes tied up with those individuals of the old submerged classes, who, probably through the same gifts, were able to rise."

There are other tests, too. There was a considerable shift in the locus of political power, which was downwards by pre-Restoration standards. Broadly speaking, there was—if one takes a long enough time base—a change from feudalism to capitalism as the organizing principle of Japanese society. There was even an application of force to politics to bring about these things, or at least to bring about some of the specific decisions that went to make them up.

Yet despite it all, I am reluctant to call the Restoration a revolution in the full meaning of the term. In part, this is because what happened in Japan lacked the avowed social purpose that gives the "great" revolutions of history a certain common character. But it is also because of the nature of the society to which the Restoration gave rise, in which "feudal" and "capitalist" elements worked together in a symbiosis dedicated to acquiring national strength. The political movement that brought this society into being cannot properly be called "bourgeois" in view of the dominant role samurai played in it and the power they retained when it was done. It was certainly not "peasant," given the fate of peasant revolt. Nor was it "absolutist" or "rightist," if that is to imply that the primary stimulus was a fear of popular unrest. What then is left, when none of these standard categories satisfactorily apply? Only to call it a nationalist revolution, perhaps, thereby giving recognition to the nature of the emotions that above all brought it about.

POSTSCRIPT

Did the Meiji Restoration Constitute a Revolution in Nineteenth-Century Japan?

An interesting question raised by this issue is the nature and meaning of the term *revolution*. The criteria used would have an impact on the debate. A good starting point to begin this issue would be a brief exploration of the term *revolution,* with comparisons made with other noted world revolutions. In *The Anatomy of Revolution*, rev. ed. (Random House, 1966), Crane Brinton (1898–1966) presents an interesting model for studying the nature of revolutions and uses the English, American, French, and Russian revolutions as case studies. From his data Brinton drew the following conclusions regarding the revolutionary process:

1. The countries were generally prosperous prior to the revolution, however, government machinery was clearly inefficient. Discontent was strongly felt by those wealthy citizens who felt restrained by the titled aristocracy who contributed little to the country's well-being. The intellectuals eventually transferred their loyalty from the ruling monarchy to the discontents.
2. The revolutions generally passed through three phases: (a) the moderate stage in which reformers who overthrew the monarchy and now controlled the government worked to gradually solve the country's problems in a moderate, nonviolent way; they were opposed by the extremists who argued for immediate change, if necessary, through violent means, (b) the radical phase in which the extremists took control of the government, got rid of the moderates, and began a radical restructuring of society; they were assisted by the people who demanded a strong central government to bring stability at home and to provide the military forces to deal with foreign countries that opposed their revolution, (c) the counter-revolutionary phase in which the tyranny of the extremists was overthrown by a coalition of forces that desired an end to the violence and a return to a peaceful, secure society.
3. Results: while the revolution brought many changes to the country, it ended with a government that was similar to the one in place before the revolution.

How does Japan's Meiji Restoration compare to Brinton's model?

Sources of modern Japanese history abound. A general reference work is Marius B. Jansen, ed., *The Cambridge History of Japan, vol. 5: The Nineteenth*

Century (Cambridge University Press, 1989). W. G. Beasley's *The Rise of Modern Japan* (St. Martin's Press, 1995) is a readable volume, written by one who has contributed much to an enlightened understanding of Japan and its history. Some specific sources on the Meiji era include Carol Gluck, *Japan's Modern Myths: Ideology in the Late Meiji Period* (Princeton University Press, 1985); Kenneth B. Pyle, *The New Generation in Meiji Japan, 1885–1895* (Stanford University Press, 1969); and two works by Beasley, *The Meiji Restoration* (Stanford University Press, 1972) and *Japanese Imperalism, 1894–1945* (Oxford University Press, 1987), which concentrates on late Meiji diplomacy and its influence on Japan's future twentieth-century course. A specialized study is Marius Jansen and Gilbert Rozman, eds., *Japan in Transition: From Tokugawa to Meiji* (Princeton University Press, 1986), which contains scholarly essays on related aspects of Japanese history during this important time period.

ISSUE 5

Were Economic Factors Primarily Responsible for British Imperialism?

YES: Lance E. Davis and Robert A. Huttenback, from *Mammon and the Pursuit of Empire: The Economics of British Imperialism*, abridged ed. (Cambridge University Press, 1988)

NO: John M. MacKenzie, from *The Partition of Africa, 1880–1900: And European Imperialism in the Nineteenth Century* (Methuen & Co., 1983)

ISSUE SUMMARY

YES: Professor Lance E. Davis and Robert A. Huttenback state that, although statistics prove that British imperialism was not a profitable venture, it was supported by an economic elite that was able to promote and derive profits from it.

NO: Professor John M. MacKenzie argues that the motivation for British imperialism was multicausal and that most of the causes can be found in the general anxiety crisis permeating British society in the late nineteenth century.

From the earliest stages of history, civilizations have extended beyond their boundaries to conquer neighboring peoples. Historians use the term *empire* to describe this process of domination and what results from it. It is easy to chronicle human history as a series of eras in which one or more civilizations display dominance and maintain it until they are conquered by a more powerful force. With the development of nation-states in the early modern period, the nation replaced the civilization. But the process of conquest and dominance continued; perhaps there were more players in the game, but things didn't change very much.

The term *imperial* is used to characterize this empire building. Derived from the Latin *imperium* (command), it denotes the process by which a group of people extend their control over a larger area. For example, when the small Roman republic extended its control over vast territories, it assumed the title *Imperium Romanum*.

The last half of the nineteenth century is considered to be imperialism's apex. During that era European nations (and ultimately the United States) began to extend their influence over the non-Western world. The results were swift and decisive; within a generation there were few areas in Asia and Africa that were free from European intrusion. The mad scramble for colonies had begun.

Why did Western nations begin this process of domination? Historians have offered many reasons, among them the development of global capitalism, nationalistic imperialism, religious missionary zeal, reflections and demands of popular culture, strategic protection for national interests, and new technology. Despite the fact that modern imperialism is little more than a century old, it has received much attention from historians due to its far-reaching consequences.

Because nineteenth-century imperialism accompanied the rapid rise and development of capitalism, historians first saw the two as symbiotic. The West expanded to procure raw materials, establish foreign markets for domestically produced goods, and provide additional sources for investment capital. In 1902 Englishman John A. Hobson was the first to state this viewpoint. Russian Vladimir Lenin took the argument one step further. Borrowing Karl Marx's idea that capitalism must expand to survive, Lenin saw imperialism as capitalism's last spasm before the Communist revolution would bring it to an end.

This economic interpretation of imperialism held sway for many years until newer examinations began to uncover other possibilities. The national rivalries that led to World War I caused some historians to see imperialism as an example of nationalism gone mad, with Western nations using the acquisition of colonies as manifestations of national pride. Other historians saw strategic territories as an excuse for the acquisition of overseas territories. Once some were acquired, others were needed to protect and defend them. Heaven forbid that a rival nation be in a position to endanger one's colonial possessions!

In recent years historians have developed several new theses for the growth of nineteenth-century imperialism. Some point out the effect of the masses on its development, offering countless examples from popular culture as proof. Others show how the cultural images of non-Western peoples in Western literature and music (which are usually untrue and condescending) have created a "white man's burden" mentality that has both promoted and justified imperialism. Finally, there are those who stress the role of the military and diplomatic corps that led businesspeople, missionaries, and others down the primrose path of imperial conquest.

In the following selections, Lance E. Davis and Robert A. Huttenback investigate the profitability of nineteenth-century imperialism. They contend that, while on the whole the system did not pay for itself, an elite group did profit immeasurably and used its influence to promote it. Therefore, the authors propose an up-to-date use of economics as a factor in imperialist development. While not disagreeing with them, John M. MacKenzie finds all of the many causes of nineteenth-century imperialism rooted in a Europe strongly influenced by a crisis/anxiety mentality.

**Lance E. Davis and
Robert A. Huttenback**

Imperium Economicum: In Retrospect

M. K. Gandhi, an unlikely imperialist, once wrote, "Though Empires have gone and fallen, this Empire perhaps may be an exception." That opinion was based on the conviction that the British Empire was "not founded on material but on spiritual foundations." The future Mahatma was no more correct than the rhetoricians who saw the Empire as the expression of Britannia's divine mission. "Wherever her [Britain's] sovereignty has gone," one writer averred, "two blades of grass have grown where one grew before. Her flag wherever it has advanced has benefited the country over which it floats; and has carried with it civilization, the Christian religion, order, justice and prosperity." Other observers were not so certain. In response to Betsy Prig's comment, "... ain't it lovely to see 'ow Britannia improved her position, since Benjy picked up the dropt threads of England's imperial tradition." Clio, less sure, in an 1878 issue of *Punch* replied: "Fine phrases and flatulent figures (sez she) are the charlatan's tools."

This book is essentially about the "flatulent figures" and the often eloquent message they carried. However difficult it may be to disentangle figures and messages, it is possible to measure one aspect of the Empire: its costs and its revenue. Even [Benjamin] Disraeli, the great avatar of Britain's conquering might, in a brief incarnation as Chancellor of the Exchequer, referred to "Those wretched colonies..." as "a mill stone around our neck." A few years later, Karl Marx, an observer of a different political stripe, filed a supportive brief in the *New York Daily Tribune* in which he wondered whether "this dominion [India] does not threaten to cost quite as much as it can ever to expected to come to."

For whatever reason, Empire to many Britons seemed not only politically desirable but hypnotically alluring. Disraeli, despite his earlier reservations, thundered: "... no Minister in this country will do his duty who neglects the opportunity of reconstructing as much as possible of our colonial empire...." So potent was the message that the ordinarily archliberal [William] Gladstone was forced to dissemble and to protest: "... Gentlemen, while we are opposed to imperialism we are devoted to empire." While he proclaimed that "nothing will induce me to submit to these colonial annexations," he nevertheless ordered the bombardment of Alexandria and the virtual annexation of Egypt. To conclude that Disraeli had suddenly discovered that Empire was costless is wrong. He merely felt that other considerations were of greater importance than cost effectiveness. Even in the Crystal Palace Speech, he admitted that: " ... It has been proved to us that we have lost money on our colonies. It has been shown with precise, with mathematical demonstration, that there never was a jewel in the Crown of England that was so costly as the possession of India." ...

No one can sanely argue that there were not British politicians dedicated to maintaining and expanding the Empire, nor that there were not business-men who recognized that such policies might redound to their profit. It may well have been that both groups increased in size after the mid-1880s as in-creasing political and economic competition from the continental powers and the United States exacerbated the rising protectionist sentiment both in the newly competitive nations and in the Dominions. [Joseph] Chamberlain, him-self, bought Canadian Pacific Railroad bonds and lost £50,000 in an ill-fated attempt to grow sisal in the Bahamas. Nevertheless, Lenin went too far when he concluded that, "leading British bourgeois politicians fully appreciated the con-nection between what might be called purely economic and the political–social roots of imperialism."

Few of the nineteenth-century proponents and critics of Empire thought that the enterprise was without expense. Adderley had railed against the colonies' refusal to pay their just share of expenses; and Marx doubted that the Empire would ever carry its own financial weight. Disraeli, even as he proposed further imperial expansions, acknowledged that the Empire was costly and that India was a particularly expensive undertaking. Chamberlain, although he looked at imperial expenditures as potentially profitable investments, admitted that they required money; and Hicks-Beach at the Treasury had threatened his resignation when presented with the estimated expenses of one of the Colonial Secretary's development schemes. For those, like Chamberlain, who argued that the Empire was good business for the British, imperial costs had still to be offset against private profits in any calculation of social gain: a point Marx had recognized as early as 1858. Even if the claim was only that the Empire was good for a few but not for the many, the question still remains: How much did it cost the many to enrich the few?

Both Marx and Adderley emphasized the major, but not the only, element in the British subsidy to the imperial investor. The former, in reference to In-dia, had pointed to "the military and naval expenses made by the people of England on Indian account," and the latter, speaking of a British colony, to the exemption "in purse and person from the cost of its own defense." Despite the widespread recognition of the absurdity of the situation—an appreciation that had already in 1861 led to the creation of a Parliamentary select committee—there is no evidence that circumstances were significantly better in 1914 than they had been in that earlier year. ...

The failure of a long succession of governments to distribute the defense burden between home and Empire in some more equitable fashion lay rooted in history, in the law, in the bureaucratic mire, and in the pressing nature of defense requirements. The colonies with responsible government argued that they did not have to contribute, the dependent Empire said that it could not afford to pay, and hence who but the British taxpayer was left to redress the balance?...

Nor was the peculiar inequity in the distribution of the burden a figment in the minds of British politicians. The expenditure figures suggest that, if anything, the magnitude of the problem was understated. On average, in the late nineteenth and early twentieth centuries, the cost of British defense was about two and a half times as great as that borne by the citizens of a typical developed country and almost twice that of the French and Germans. The denizens of the colonies with responsible government meanwhile assumed a fiscal responsibility only a quarter that of the resident of a foreign developed country; and in the dependent colonies, the impost was less than one-quarter of that demanded from inhabitants of underdeveloped nations....

Although defense was the largest single component in the total imperial subsidy, it was by no means the only one. De facto and de jure guarantees made it possible for Empire governments to borrow at rates much below those available to non-Empire nations. The gains were not spread evenly over the Empire but, given the actual level of borrowing, the differentials meant that the residents of the colonies with responsible government saved about 10 percent of their tax bill and those of the dependent Empire about one-half that amount.

The British government also provided regular administrative subsidies to the dependent colonies and a substantial additional amount of direct support on an irregular basis. At times, those latter awards were relatively small. (Newfoundland, for example, received a grant of £260 in 1906 to help offset the effects of a severe depression in the fishing industry.) At other times, however, they were not. The Gold Coast received more than £400,000 in 1900, and the Ugandan railroad cost the British taxpayer almost £9 million between 1896 and 1914.

The fact that the sun never set on the Empire may well have provided vicarious pleasure to many inhabitants of the home islands; however, the global dispersion of Dominions and colonies did present serious problems of administration and control. To help provide the links necessary to hold the Empire together, the government found it necessary to subsidize both telegraphs and steamship lines. The British, for example, paid a quarter of a million pounds to help finance a cable connection between Australia and Canada; and, even in the 1860s, Empire shipping subsidies were running over a million pounds a year.

Finally, the British government founded and underwrote the operations of the Crown Agents. This organization acted as the marketing agency for the sale of colonial securities and as the purchasing agent for colonial supplies. Acting as an effective monopolist in the market for colonial issues and as an monopsonist in the market for the supplies bought by those colonial governments, the Agents obtained very fortuitous marketing arrangements for bond issues and equally favorable prices for the goods and services destined for their colonial customers.

It is difficult to measure precisely the total cost to the British of the non-defense component of the imperial subsidy, but it appears unlikely to have been less than one-fifth of the defense subsidy and it may have been twice that. Although the actual amount of Empire investment is unknown, the best estimates indicate that it amounted on average to about £17–8 per capita in prices of 1913. As has been noted, the defense subsidy alone amounted to at least 10 shillings and 10 pence per year for every British man, woman, and child and it could have been as high as 12 shillings and 10 pence, more than 20 percent of national savings. The minimum figure suggests that private Empire returns would have to have been reduced by more than 3 percent to provide a true estimate of the social returns, even if the nondefense components of the subsidy were zero. At the other extreme, assuming the larger defense figure and a very generous £.20 for the nondefense component, the adjustment would be almost 5 percent. Even the lower charge is sufficient to reduce Empire returns below levels that could have been earned at home or in the foreign sector after the mid-1880s.

The British as a whole certainly did not benefit economically from the Empire. On the other hand, individual investors did. In the Empire itself, the level of benefits depended upon whom one asked and how one calculated. For the colonies of white settlement the answer is unambiguous: They paid for little and received a great deal. In the dependent Empire the white settlers, such as there were, almost certainly gained as well. As far as the indigenous population was concerned, while they received a market basket of government commodities at truly wholesale prices, there is no evidence to suggest that, had they been given a free choice, they would have bought the particular commodities offered, even at the bargain-basement rates.

It is clear that imperial exactions placed on the British taxpayer enabled the colonists and residents of the Dominions and the dependent Empire to pay fewer taxes and to devote a substantial proportion of the taxes they did pay to a variety of projects that did not include defense. The Empire was a political system, and it should have been possible to align the pattern of colonial expenditures so as to increase the level of support for business and to guarantee that the revenues required to command those resources were charged not to those businesses but to the taxpayers at large.

The potential for government subsidization is vast, and such subsidies can take as many forms as Joseph's coat had colors. Some, involving nothing but the manipulation of political decisions, are difficult to discover even at the time and probably impossible to uncover a century later. Many subsidies, however, involve government expenditures, and for those, the government budget provides a paper trail that can be followed. It is possible to measure the impact of government policy on expenditures on law and justice (costs incurred in part at least to maintain property rights and enforce contracts), public works (the real capital component of social overhead investment), science and human capital (the nontraditional component), and direct business support.

Whether it is the total package or its individual components that is analyzed, the pattern is the same. Great Britain spent somewhat more than other developed countries, but hardly more than that nation's advanced state of development would suggest. The same is not true for the colonies whether dependent or blessed with responsible government. On average the latter group of colonies spent at levels about twice those prevailing in Britain. The former spent at rates not much different from those at home; but that figure is remarkable given the fraction of a colony's total expenditures that were involved, the relative state of development of the colonies in question, and the amounts spent by countries in the underdeveloped world....

In general, the colonial Empire provides strong evidence for the belief that government was attuned to the interest of business and willing to divert resources to ends that the business community would have found profitable. That behavior is, however, not necessarily evidence that the British used the political process to distort the allocation of governmental resources. Expenditures that benefited business were greatest in the colonies with responsible government, where even the British government, let alone British businessmen, had almost no influence. They were next highest in the dependent colonies, where the British did have a very substantial voice in policy making but not a total monopoly. Moreover, within that set, expenditures tended to be larger in those colonies with some local participation in political decision making and smaller in those with little or no consultation. Finally, expenditures were lowest in India, where British influence was strongest and where there were no representative institutions at the national level.

Perhaps the explanation for this ordering lies not with the British but with the local business community. Those merchants and manufacturers may have been quite willing and able to bend the structure of government expenditures to their own benefit. If that is correct, except in India, where financial crisis and the threat of famine overrode all other considerations, they appear to have been successful. It cannot be denied, however, that the policies adopted, perhaps under local business pressure, served the interest of the British investor as well as his colonial cousin.

In the late nineteenth century the London capital market acted as a conduit for the greatest international movement of private capital in the history of the world. Nevertheless, most of the flow of funds that passed through the stock exchange was not destined for the Empire. Of the almost £5-billion total, less than 70 percent passed out of Britain and almost two-thirds of that amount went to Europe and other parts of the world not pledging fealty to the House of Hanover. The largest single recipient was the United States, but a not-insubstantial portion (more than a quarter) was directed to the underdeveloped but politically independent countries of South America. In fact these Latin countries received substantially more than all the funds destined for the dependent Empire. Although the Empire as a whole absorbed nearly a quarter of the total, two-thirds of that amount went to the colonies of white settlement; and those colonies were, at least in matters economic, not likely objects for British exploitation. They were colonies that, since the middle of the nineteenth century, had begun pursuing a strongly protectionist policy—one aimed explicitly at British manufacturers and traders.

If Britain itself absorbed 30 percent of the total, if the nations over which the British exercised no political control drew an additional 45, and if the colonies over which its control was, at best, limited took an additional 16: Less than £1 in 10 remained for all of India and for colonies such as St. Kitts, the Bahamas, the Falklands, the Gold Coast, Malta, and Hong Kong, which had few representative institutions. Certainly, the amount of finance that was directed to the dependent Empire was substantial enough (it averaged more than £8 million per year) to ensure that some Englishmen could have become rich, but it appears doubtful (unless the "exploitative" profit rate was higher than even Lenin dreamed) that the total was sufficient—even if there were no offsetting social costs—to make the "average" British subject substantially better off.

Perhaps profits were very high, or possibly the dependent Empire was good business for the few but not for the many. In either case, financial flows were not evenly distributed across the world or across the industrial map. Of the £415 million received by India and the colonies of the dependent Empire, Asia received 65 percent (India alone, 56) and Africa an additional 19 percent. In India that investment was largely associated with railroads and, to a lesser extent, government finance. In the dependent colonies the relative concentrations of British investment were in the agriculture and extractive industries, in finance (the financial, land, and development companies) and in government. Just how profitable were these investments?

Although the measure of "the" rate of return is only approximate, the general outlines confirm the individual industry comparisons. Questions of timing and level are still open, but it would take a massive reversal of the evidence to alter the general conclusions. If the standard is domestic earnings, it appears that in the years before 1885 Empire returns were substantially higher. While some of the observed differences may reflect the small size of the sample and the mix of firms included in the study, it would be very difficult to argue that colonial profits were any less than domestic, and they were almost certainly substantially higher. In the case of the returns on manufacturing and commercial investments, for example, Empire returns through 1880 were one and one-quarter of domestic—and that measure is the most favorable for the home economy. Over time, the advantage eroded, and for the last half of the period Empire returns were substantially below those available at home. There was, however, some recovery in Empire earnings after the turn of the century, and in the last decade before the War they may well have equaled domestic.

As Marx had predicted, profits were falling; however, they were declining more rapidly in the Empire than in the foreign sector and faster there than in the domestic. It is, of course, not the trend but the home–Empire differential that is important for the Hobson–Lenin argument [This argument, created by John A. Hobson and Vladmir Lenin, states that capitalism by nature must expand to survive. Imperialism is necessary to ensure this expansion.] In the same way that it is difficult to deny that the Empire was *relatively* very profitable in the earlier years, it is even more difficult to conclude that profits in the colonies were substantially above those at home in the later ones.

The explanation of the trends in relative returns can in large measure be traced to two phenomena. First, early entrants into new markets and regions had distinct advantages. To the extent that property rights were well defined and enforced they may have been able to acquire the potentially most profitable lands at bargain prices. Secondly, they frequently had an initial monopoly position that allowed them to exploit those new opportunities until, in [Joseph] Schumpeter's terms, the "herd like movement" of the imitative entrepreneurs undercut their profits. . . .

While some stockholders clearly benefited from the imperial connection, the evidence indicates that probably at no time, and certainly not after the 1870s, were Empire profits sufficient to underwrite *British* prosperity. However, for the shareholders in the agricultural and extractive and the public utility sectors (and perhaps others as well), where competition was blunted or enforced property rights pushed potential competitors onto inferior lands, the Empire was important, and it was profitable. One can readily conclude that there should have been some economic imperialists. How many and who they were is a different matter. . . .

A separation of investors into businessmen and elites (peers, gentlemen, financiers, and the like) indicates that, place of residence aside, businessmen were less likely to invest in foreign securities than were their elite counterparts. Moreover, they were *far* less inclined to invest in Empire than foreign enterprise; and among all businessmen, only merchants displayed any significant willingness to invest beyond the seas. In the Empire the elites were most willing to invest in commercial banks; in financial, land, and development companies; in iron, coal, and steel firms; and in the public utilities. To the extent that they entrusted their resources to the Empire at all, businessmen tended to put their funds to work in the private sector—competitive and less in need of government charters or licenses—industries, in short, much less dependent on political control.

The geographic distribution of shareholder "tastes" indicates that there were two very different groups of investors: those who lived in London, and others, who made their homes in the provinces. A typical Londoner's portfolio was composed of about one-quarter domestic, one-third foreign, and two-fifths Empire shares. Outside the metropolis, the portfolio was more than one-half domestic and contained less than one-quarter each of foreign and Empire shares. Within London, those who gave the City as their address preferred Empire to domestic securities, but much preferred foreign to Empire. Beyond the Wall, however, London investors appeared largely indifferent between home and foreign issues, but displayed a very strong preference for Empire over both. The London connection was particularly well illustrated in the case of South African gold mines, and even [Cecil] Rhodes turned to metropolitan investors when he needed further capital.

Further exploration of the "two-England" hypothesis indicates that Empire investors in London were drawn from a different socioeconomic background than were the Empire investors who lived outside the capital. While London elites do not appear to have behaved substantially differently than their provincial counterparts, London businessmen acted very differently than their confreres residing elsewhere. London merchants, manufacturers, professionals, and managers all invested far less frequently in home and far more frequently in Empire activities. On average, London businessmen were only one-fifth as likely to invest in domestic securities as those businessmen who lived in places like Sheffield or Manchester, but they were half again as inclined to put their resources to work in the Empire.

Overall, Empire investors tended to be drawn from two groups: elites, wherever they lived, and businessmen (particularly, in terms of numbers, merchants) who resided in London. The attractiveness of the Empire seemed to decline almost exponentially the farther one traveled north from the City. In terms of the socioeconomic background of its participants, the British capital market was clearly two markets, and it is from one of those segments, the segment populated by elites and London businessmen, that the most strident Empire support could have been expected to come.

Finally, to the extent that the Empire investments were less profitable than home and foreign alternatives, it would have been expected that the elites, while continuing to rally political support for the Empire, would gradually have attempted to divest themselves of those securities and to reinvest their assets in other more viable enterprises. Although the data do not permit an exact test of this hypothesis, they do allow a less precise examination. If the firm sample is split at 1890 and the two parts compared, the ratio of elite to business investors is substantially lower in the second period. The decline, however, is not related to a rise in business holdings (in fact, they fell as well), but to an increase in the Other owners—including women, children, and retirees....

If the residents of the dependent Empire spent little on taxes, the British, as we have already seen, spent a great deal. Even the citizens of the colonies with responsible government, who chose to tax themselves more heavily than they might have, were largely freed of defense costs and thus able to devote the vast bulk of their resources to more directly productive ends. In the United Kingdom, however, the real tax level increased by about two-thirds over the half-century in question, and as a fraction of per capita national income it rose by about one-sixth. In England the tax structure historically had depended very heavily on consumption taxes, and it was certainly regressive. As the second half of the century wore on, however, regressivity declined as customs and excises were replaced by increases in the income and inheritance taxes. The latter sources together had produced only about one-quarter of the total when Disraeli first became prime minister but had risen to account for more than £2 in 5 by the election of 1911. Over the same period, consumption taxes had declined from more than three-fifths to less than one-half of all the imposts. Over Gladstone's protests, the income tax had "lost its terrifying character" and by the mid-1890s, again despite Gladstone's reservations, death duties had begun to bite.

Even with the very regressive tax structure of the 1860s, between three-fifths and two-thirds of British taxes were paid by the middle and upper classes. Given the increasing reliance on income and inheritance taxes, it seems reasonable to conclude that this proportion did not decline and may have risen as the century wore on. Of more direct interest, the fraction that fell on the middle class was probably close to two and a half times the amount paid by the upper class. It is hardly surprising that the Gladstonian Liberals opposed higher taxes while the upper classes found that, if the resources gained by tax increases could be used for "productive purposes," they would not only countenance but support such levies. The middle class bore far more than its share of the imperial subsidy and, as is so apparent in an enumeration of their investments, they did not share equally in its benefits. The profits of Empire accrued largely to the upper class.

When it came to the formulation and execution of official policy toward the Empire, the responsibility, of course, rested fundamentally with Parliament and particularly the House of Commons. It was a quintessentially patrician legislative body, dominated by the elite classes, business, and the professions. The members had attended the ancient universities and the major public schools and they were "club men" with a vengeance. It is this homogeneity that makes it difficult to explain individual political behavior. In general, on imperial issues Liberals deviated more from established party positions than Conservatives and university-educated Liberals were particularly anti-imperial. The safeness of a member's seat, his club memberships, his profession, his level of education, and the district from which he was elected seem to provide very little help in explaining his voting behavior. On the fundamental question of the degree to which economic self-interest affected a House member's voting behavior on imperial issues, no intimate connection appears to exist between the two, although further research may prove otherwise.

Parliament, much as any other democratic legislative body, was subject to considerable outside pressure. Individual companies, the chambers of commerce, the trade associations, and a fluctuating array of usually short-lived commercial coalitions all tried to influence the course of events. Although not usually successful in the foreign arena, in the colonies with responsible government, and in the dependent colonies, because of long-established British disinclination to interfere on behalf of private businessmen, they were more effective in the case of India—the cotton tariffs being a case in point. Tariffs in the self-governing colonies attracted considerable attention from the various pressure groups, but constitutional inhibitions and lack of Parliamentary sympathy precluded the implementation of the desired policy. Even in the dependent colonies, the Crown Agents actively sought foreign bids when they felt domestic ones were excessive.

Much, no doubt, remains to be said concerning the relationship between Empire and economics. But perhaps, when all is said and done, Cecil Rhodes came closest to summing the whole thing up when he said, not totally in jest, that imperialism was nothing more than philanthropy plus 5 percent! But philanthropy for whom? It appears that imperialism can best be viewed as a mechanism for transferring income from the middle to the upper classes. Because of the technology of the imperial machine, the process involved some transfer of those resources to the colonies; however, it is not obvious that either India or the dependent colonies would have chosen to accept that imperial subsidy had they been given the opportunity to object. The Elites and the colonies with responsible government were clear winners; the middle class, certainly, and the dependent Empire, probably, were losers. A strange kind of philanthropy—socialism for the rich, capitalism for the poor.

NO

John M. MacKenzie

The Partition of Africa: 1880–1900

We have been witnesses of one of the most remarkable episodes in the history of the world.

So wrote Sir John Scott Keltie in the opening sentence of his book *The Partition of Africa,* published in 1893. Keltie and his contemporaries were enthralled by the statistics of that 'most remarkable episode'. More than 10 million square miles of African territory and over 100 million African people had fallen to European rule in the space of little more than a decade. The concluding acts of the Partition were yet to come in the late 1890s and in the years immediately preceding the first world war, but in Keltie's time the map of Africa was already beginning to look like its modern counterpart. In the middle of the century the European cartographer saw Africa as a continent of blank spaces where the principal physical features—rivers, lakes, mountains—were gradually being filled in by European exploration. In the late 1880s and early 1890s maps of Africa in school atlases were revised every year, for political boundaries and various colourings for the different empires were now the rage.

Since the publication of Keltie's book, writers and historians have conducted an energetic debate on the causes of the Partition of Africa, culminating in a veritable flood of books and articles in the last twenty years. This enduring interest is perhaps not surprising. The Scramble for Africa (as the Partition is sometimes more luridly known) was the most dramatic instance of the partition of the world by Europe and America in the late nineteenth century. It inaugurated a great revolution in the relationship between European and African peoples, and it sent out political, economic and social shock-waves, which continue to be felt in Africa to this day. Africans naturally find the Partition a distasteful event, yet they are prepared to defend the artificial boundaries established by it to the point of war if necessary. The modern challenge to Africa remains the struggle to consolidate and develop the national and economic units carved out by Europeans in the Partition period, and so knowledge of the Partition is fundamental to an understanding of contemporary Africa.

This [selection] is concerned, however, with one great problem. What were the causes of the Partition of Africa and why did it occur when it did? Why was it that, after several centuries of nibbling at the edges of Africa, Europeans suddenly rushed in to establish direct military and political control over almost the entire continent? Why did European politicians who had traditionally resisted the extension of empire in Africa become caught up in a hectic demarcation of territory? . . .

Interpretation

. . . [T]he Partition was not a sudden and wholly unpremeditated affair. 'Creeping partition' had been going on in Africa for some time. The French had already conceived grand designs in the 1870s, and commercial pressures had been exerted on the British from the same period. Nevertheless, the speed with which the Partition was finally accomplished, after more than 300 years of European coastal activity, and the comprehensiveness of the land grab do suggest that this was a new and dramatic phase. Historians have elaborated and debated many different theories to explain the events of the 1880s and 1890s.

These interpretations have overlaid each other, and it is perhaps helpful to divide them into categories to bring some order to a very complex process of theorizing. It has become customary to divide explanations into metropolitan and peripheral, economic and non-economic. Metropolitan interpretations are those which seek to explain the Scramble in terms of developments in Europe, while peripheral ones look to events in Africa itself. The economic–non-economic categories cut across the metropolitan–peripheral ones, so that there are some metropolitan and some peripheral explanations which are also economic and some which are not.

Metropolitan

Capitalist Imperialism

The first explanation offered for the Partition in the early years of this century saw the European grab for Africa as arising from an inherent problem in capitalism. To maintain their capacity for growth capitalist economies had repeatedly to find new outlets for investment. In the late nineteenth century, the capitalist economies entered upon a particularly difficult period. Rates of return on capital invested at home were falling, and so capitalists believed that surplus capital had to be exported. Further, this interpretation suggests that the power to dispose of capital was falling into fewer hands, particularly large banking interests. Those who disposed of such capital desired that it should be protected, and imperialism was therefore the policy of a small, highly influential capitalist group.

Certainly this was a period of considerable capital exports from Europe, and such exports played an important role in the development of Europe's relationship with the world as a whole, but this explanation seems to offer little help for the Partition of Africa. Significant amounts of capital were exported to South Africa, but Africa generally remained the continent receiving less investment than any other right up to the first world war. Moreover, the development of great capitalist combines and concentrated banking interests did not occur until after the Partition had been accomplished.

Markets

The second metropolitan explanation is also economic. This suggests that European capitalist economies had encountered not so much a crisis of excess capital as a crisis of excess competition and production. Germany and the United States were industrializing rapidly, and France and Italy were also attempting to produce their industrial response. The British experience showed that industrialism necessarily involved global specialization. The industrial state had to maintain itself through an exchange of foodstuffs and raw materials for industrial goods. No industrial state could be self-sufficient, and to survive it had to export. New industrial states had to find new markets or encroach on those of existing exporters. Colonies could offer assured markets, particularly if the European state's relationship with them was protected by tariffs which would keep competitors out.

In addition, the capitalist economies seemed to have moved into a period of depression between the 1870s and 1890s. There were downturns in trading activity in the decade preceding the Scramble and again in the 1880s and 1890s when the Scramble was at its height. These difficulties caused alarm to industrialists and merchants throughout Europe. Italy, Germany and France responded with new tariffs in 1878, 1879 and 1881 respectively, and that compounded alarm in Britain, where the Government was still wedded to free trade. It is true that protectionist policies did not come fully to fruition until the 1890s, but the anxiety was there at the earlier period. Some indication of the alarm in Britain can be secured from the Royal Commission appointed to enquire into the Depression of Trade and Industry in 1885-6. Chambers of Commerce and Trades Societies, representing both employers and labour, were circularized as to the reasons for the depression, and their suggestions for the measures that could be taken to alleviate it. Many commented on foreign competition and tariffs, and several urged the opening of new markets, for example in Africa, and the consolidation of trading relations with colonies.

Again this market explanation, though much used at the time as an argument that colonial expansion should be undertaken, is limited in the African case. Africa's population was small, and the opportunities for marketing industrial goods were slight. But hopes are invariably more potent than reality.

Raw Materials

If markets are one end of the industrial chain, raw materials are the other. The early phase of the industrial revolution depended on iron and coal which were available in Europe, and on cotton which had to be supplied by the United States and later by India and Egypt. But by the late nineteenth century other raw materials were beginning to be important. Vegetable oils were used in the manufacture of soaps and industrial lubricants. The large firm of Lever Brothers on Merseyside built its power mainly on west African palm oil, and Liverpool was the port most closely connected with the west African trade. Rubber had become important for insulation of the new electrical and telegraph wires and for tyres. Until the rubber plantations were developed in Malaya at the beginning of this century, rubber was only collected in the wild in South America and in Africa....

It was recognized too that the new industrial age would emphasize base metals like copper. Copper deposits were well known in Africa, for Africans had exploited them for hundreds of years, and in many places had used copper as a currency. If base metals were to become more important, gold retained the fascination it had held for Europeans for many centuries. All industrial states had placed their currencies on the gold standard in the nineteenth century in order to stabilize them, and were building up reserves of gold to underpin these currencies. Gold had therefore become, even more than before, a source of power and stability for the western economic system. Some of the older sources of gold were beginning to decline in significance, so no state could allow a vital source of gold like the Transvaal to fall into the hands of a protectionist rival.

There was, therefore, much discussion of Africa as a source of raw materials, and the continent was likely to be more significant as a supplier than as a market. But raw materials had been extracted from Africa for many years without the need for political controls. The mere existence of raw materials does not fully explain why Europe felt it necessary to partition the continent, although there can be no doubt that the pace was quickening, and the fears and hopes were intensifying at this period.

Statesmen's Imperialism

This political and diplomatic explanation sees the Partition as part of European statesmen's power-play. Statesmen used overseas territories as bargaining counters in a global game of diplomacy, as a safety valve for European nationalist tensions. This idea has always been suggested most forcibly with reference to Bismarck, who has been seen by some as actually precipitating the Scramble in order to secure his diplomatic ends in Europe, namely the isolation of France. It is a view which is no longer fashionable, for it smacks too much of the influence of 'great men' upon history, and the forces at work in Africa were much too powerful and complex to be controlled or manipulated by single political figures. Even before Leopold and Bismarck took a hand, some form of Partition was gathering momentum.

However, the last acts of the Partition in north Africa do seem to have rather more diplomatic content. Britain had the most considerable economic interests in Morocco, but she allowed France to have a free run there. Even so France did not declare a protectorate over Morocco (partitioning it with Spain) until threatened by Germany in the Moroccan crises of 1905 and 1911.

Imperialism and Nationalism

This is the argument that the Partition of Africa occurred as a by-product of the friction created by new aggressive nationalisms in Europe rubbing against old-established centralized states and imperial powers. Both Germany and Italy were newly united states in this period. Both had to satisfy strongly nationalist demands within them; both sought to use colonial policies to reconcile internal tensions. Italy was already dreaming of recreating the Roman empire in the

1870s and turned her attention to Tunis, the historic Carthage. Both Germany and Italy made grabs for territory in 1884 and 1885. Neither seemed to base its claim on strong existing commercial rights. In both countries there were powerful colonial propaganda groups at work looking to empire as a means whereby the new nation states could come of age. Moreover in Germany, with its liberal franchise, a colonial policy seemed to be a popular one. It has even been said that Bismarck staged his colonial advances on several fronts in 1884 as an electioneering stunt for the election that took place in Germany late that year.

If Germany and Italy represented the aggressive force of new nationalisms, Britain and France represented the defensiveness of the old. For France after all, the German empire had been proclaimed in the aftermath of the humiliation of the Franco-Prussian War of 1870–1, in which France lost Alsace-Lorraine. A forward French policy dated from the 1870s. Defeat forced France to look outwards. Colonies, it has been suggested, were a balm for French wounded pride. The British on the other hand had been accustomed to secure their commercial ends without competition from other powers. Sometimes they had been forced to annex territory in the mid-nineteenth century, but generally they had avoided it. The British had preferred to work through informal empire, and British politicians were reluctant to translate that into formal control unless some very important national interest demanded it. From 1880 the British were forced to do so repeatedly to protect their interests from the new aggressive nationalisms and the revived imperial vision of France.

Popular Imperialism

It has also been argued that the new nationalisms were not just a matter for statesmen and colonial pressure groups; they also satisfied popular psychological needs. European peoples (and no state was immune from this) developed an aggressive xenophobia in order to define sharply their national identity and national ambition. In Britain this came to be known as jingoism, a term significantly coined from a music-hall song at the time of the Congress of Berlin of 1878, an international conference which had an important bearing on the Partition. Popular culture, as expressed in the theatre and popular songs, took on a strongly nationalist and patriotic tone, and this inevitably became bound up with at least the protection, if not the extension of empire. Indeed, it became a great age of propaganda. The expansion of education led to a considerable increase in literacy, and this was exploited by colonial pressure groups, the army, the navy and above all the missions.

The missions were very important in propagating imperial ideas. Mission societies, which had appeared in all denominations and in all European countries in the nineteenth century, became convinced of their divine mission to convert the world, to save other people from what they saw to be 'barbarism' and 'savagery'. To achieve this, they required both money and recruits, and they set about opening people's pockets and minds through every publicity technique available to them. Notable missionaries became heroes, and books by them or about them became best-sellers. These and other popular works propagated racial ideas which seemed at one and the same time both to explain and to justify European technical and military superiority in the world.

It has sometimes been objected that 'popular imperialism' was a result of the Partition and other imperial advances of the age, not a cause. But popular imperialism does seem to have its roots in the 1870s and imperial events did raise popular outcries.... Thus popular opinion certainly seems to have been significant by the 1890s when politicians were confirming the more tentative moves (the chartering of companies, for example) of the 1880s. These are all British examples, but 'jingoism' was just as evident in the rest of Europe.

Electoral behaviour is of course the best index of popular opinion. We have already seen that Bismarck may well have been responding to electoral pressures in 1884. In Britain, there can be no doubt that colonial discontents contributed to the fall of Gladstone in 1885, and when he formed his fourth ministry in 1892 the Liberal Party had developed a strongly imperialist complexion. His successor, Rosebery, was almost indistinguishable from any Conservative imperialist. Even the Labour movement had imperial elements within it: some Labour leaders accepted the idea that the possession of empire was important to the interests of the working classes, or that it was an inevitable obligation which had to be fulfilled in as ethical a manner as was possible. To attack the possession of colonies seemed to be unpatriotic, and therefore electorally dangerous.

Feudal Atavism

Another social explanation is one that sees imperialism as the policy of the surviving feudal elements of European society, military castes which sought new employment and the continuation of their influence. In France, imperial attitudes were largely forged in the military establishments of Algeria. Both the German and Italian empires had a strongly military flavour, administrators being usually military men rather than civilians. Empire provided them with a source of power removed from domestic politics. Even in the British empire, where the principle of civilian rule was firmly established, the army found an opportunity for employment, and an excuse for growth. In all the empires, colonial revenues could be used to pay for a proportion of the army, a technique long used by the British in India.

Technology

Another explanation, at least for the timing of the Partition, is one which highlights the importance of technology. This suggests that railways, steamships, the telegraph, and medical advances were crucial to the Partition, which could not have been achieved without them....

Clearly, such technical advances did not create imperialism in Africa, but they did produce the vital conditions that rendered its extension more readily possible. Moreover, such technical achievements seemed to emphasize the cultural gap between Europe and Africa which was important in the popular thinking of the period.

Peripheral

Strategic and Egyptocentric

Perhaps the first and most influential peripheral explanation is that which relates the entire Partition to the crisis in Egypt and the two routes to India.... The British invaded Egypt in 1882. The French, having apparently lost their former influence in Egypt, now looked for compensation elsewhere and this provoked Anglo-French rivalries in west Africa.

The vital point about this interpretation is that the British went into Egypt not to protect the bondholders, but for strategic reasons, to protect the Suez Canal and the crucial route to India. Similarly, British interest in the Cape was strategic, to protect the Cape route to the East and the important Royal Navy base at Simon's Bay. The British could not permit any other power to achieve an interior preponderance which might threaten the Cape, and it was this that drew them into the interior. The Partition in east Africa was bound up with the strategic concern with the Nile. The British believed that their position in Egypt was only secure if they commanded the entire Nile system. To keep the French from the upper Nile they needed a convenient route from the east coast. It was this consideration that lay behind the retention of Uganda and the decision to build the east African railway. According to this view, the Partition of Africa is no more than a giant footnote to the British Indian empire. This interpretation had great influence for some time, but it can now be discounted. French advances were not necessarily related to Egypt. The complex interaction of peripheral and metropolitan forces, for example in south Africa, renders such a single-cause interpretation untenable....

The General Crisis

Finally, there is an interpretation which we can perhaps describe as 'global'. It seems to combine aspects of several of the interpretations.... This suggests that there was a 'general crisis' in the relations between European and non-European peoples at this time, a general crisis induced by the European efforts to create a fully integrated world economy. Industrial Europe required a highly specialized world, in which some areas would produce food for its industrial proletariat, others would produce raw materials for the industrial process, and the entire world would constitute a market for industrial goods. But to achieve this Europe needed to recast the world in its own image, to create the same infrastructures and similar institutions that would permit resources to be exploited and trade to be conducted. By the end of the nineteenth century it was apparent that Europe required a greater degree of coercion to press forward this process, coercion that could only be effected by direct imperial rule. In some areas people were resisting the new dispensation, and in consequence new military and political techniques were required to supplement the purely economic relationship.

This explanation is attractive because it appears to subsume metropolitan and peripheral elements, social and military strains, the widening of the technological gap, and the heightened tensions of the period under one umbrella thesis associated with a particular stage of economic development in the world.

But there are some problems with it too. There were crises in some areas of the world, notably China, Siam, Persia and the Gulf, which did not lead to the imposition of direct political controls. But even more significantly from our point of view, there were large areas of Africa, on the face of it much less important economically than the Asian regions just mentioned, where no immediate crisis seemed to have occurred, and yet where political controls were established.

Conclusion

We must now attempt to draw from this complex set of explanations some answers to the question posed at the beginning of the [selection]. Why did the European powers cease their long-standing process of nibbling at Africa and suddenly seize huge chunks of the continent?

There are a number of theses that we can reject straightaway. It seems to have had little to do with the export of capital. The 'great man' explanation simply will not do, for statesmen were largely reacting to the growing pressures and a climate of opinion which they found difficult to oppose. Napoleon III may have had ambitions in the 1850s; Leopold II had personal pretensions by the 1870s; individual Germans like Nachtigal and Peters hoped that Germany would institute an imperial policy; Mackinnon, Goldie and Rhodes all developed, to varying degrees, a passionate interest in the extension of British rule. But none of these was able to achieve his ambitions until the necessary forces came together. Finally, the Egyptocentric and strategic thesis is no longer convincing except as a powerful expression of one motivation of one European country. French decisions to advance in west Africa were made ahead of the British invasion of Egypt. French and Italian rivalries in north Africa, for example over Tunisia, and new German ambitions cannot be related to it. And in southern Africa developments were much too complex to be linked solely to the route to India.

Other 'explanations' are not really explanations at all. Public opinion, technology and African initiatives cannot explain the Partition, but they can demonstrate that the convergence of forces was now such that a partition was more likely to take place. Indeed, one of the remarkable things about the 1870s and 1880s was that so many developments in the realm of ideas, in missionary activity, in propaganda, in the technical and military gap between Europe and the rest of the world did seem to converge. A set of background conditions made the partition much easier to accomplish.

Why then were the crucial decisions made against the background of these conditions? One thing does now seem to be clear, and that is that we cannot be satisfied with an explanation which is wholly European or solely peripheral. Very important lines of force were developed from the periphery, but the thinking of people in Europe was also vital. Despite the creeping imperialism of the British and the French in west Africa, or the creeping partition of southern Africa by Dutch and English settlers, wholesale extensions of territory were resisted for a time. Both Goldie and Mackinnon had their pleas for a recognition of their concessions and the provision of charters rejected at first. Yet a few years later they were accepted. This is not to say that they simply went into cold storage until statesmen decided to use them. It is to say that the tensions, anxieties and pressures had not yet reached the necessary pitch. If there was a convergence of background conditions, there also had to be a conjunction of economic, social and political tensions between metropolis and periphery.

The Scramble for Africa seems to have emerged from a combination of exaggerated hope and over-heated anxiety. The economic conditions of the day, the trough between the first industrial revolution of coal, cotton and iron, and the second of electricity, copper, steel; the appearance of new industrial states protecting themselves with tariffs; the decline in some commodity prices; and the heightened commercial competition everywhere produced all the alarms associated with the transition from one economic system to another. At the same time there were many publicists concerned to argue that Africa was a tropical treasure house, capable of producing plantation crops, base and precious metals, as well as other valuable commodities like rubber and ivory. Verney Lovett Cameron, who had been sent to find Livingstone, published just such an ecstatic account in his *Across Africa* in 1877. Many others wrote in similar vein. The growth in the palm oil trade, the buoyant prices of rubber and ivory, the discovery of diamonds and then of gold, all seemed to confirm this view. Africa could solve some of the problems of the age. A state which missed out on these opportunities might be imperilled in the future. These hopes and anxieties took some time to foment fully, but by the mid-1880s they were ready to blow the lid off the politicians' restraint. Politicians do not so much act as react to the forces round about them.

An influential generation was seized by this combination of exaggerated fear and overpowering ambition. Although it is difficult to see a small group of finance capitalists influencing governments to do their bidding, there was nevertheless a rather more extensive and powerful élite at work. In London, Paris and Berlin, commercial, shipping, geographical, intellectual and official figures did come together to press for imperial advance. Although politicians, particularly in Britain, liked to claim that no official actions were taken to further the interests of individual investors and economic concerns, in fact they were. The London élite was closely connected by ties of education, social life and marriage. Some officials in the Foreign and Colonial Offices developed close connections with the capitalist concerns and furthered their ends from a growing conviction of the need for British expansion. Ex-ministers joined the boards of companies, and colonial administrators were often rewarded with directorships of companies whose ends they had furthered when in office. This was not a conspiracy; it was merely the normal operations of such an élite group converted to a dominant idea.

There was, moreover, something irrational about the Partition—as reflected in the grandiose ambitions of figures like Leopold, Rhodes, Peters, even Mackinnon—which deeply disturbed the rational minds of politicians like Salisbury and Bismarck. In many respects the Scramble was not so much a reaction to events that had already taken place as to events it was feared might take place. It was less the result of a 'general crisis' than a symptom of the anxieties that a general crisis was on the way.

There was much that was chimerical about the Partition, and in many parts of Africa it produced disappointing results. South Africa remained the world's most important source of gold, yet by 1910 the British had abdicated political control there. Central Africa was to be one of the western world's most important sources of copper, but this was not fully exploited until the years before the second world war. In some places European coercion upon Africans to produce agricultural raw materials or to go out to work produced large-scale revolts. Railway lines often failed to pay, and administrations invariably required subsidies from the mother countries. Some of the resources of Africa, such as the oil of Nigeria, were scarcely even discovered during the imperial period.

In retrospect, Keltie's opening sentence takes on a new significance. Not only was the speed of Europe's grab for Africa a most remarkable episode, so was the speed of Europe's withdrawal. Many Africans were born before the Partition occurred, and were still alive when Europe departed in the early 1960s. By that time Africa had perhaps been recast in Europe's image, with recognizable national boundaries, an infrastructure of sorts, and relatively similar institutions. But was that what the original Scramblers really intended?

POSTSCRIPT

Were Economic Factors Primarily Responsible for British Imperialism?

No historian who has researched nineteenth-century imperialism will discount any of the factors—economic, political, social, strategic, religious, cultural—that influenced its development. Rather, their work concentrates on discovering which ingredients were either more or less important than others. History seldom provides monocausal explanations for events and movements.

Because nineteenth-century imperialism had such far-reaching consequences, ties can be made between it and several issues in this volume. Issue 7 deals with China's Boxer Rebellion, which some have seen as a manifestation of anti-imperialism. Issue 15 explores the causes of modern Africa's problems, some of which can be attributed to imperialism. Less directly it can be related to Issue 14, which deals with the growth of Islamic revivalism.

Works related to modern imperialism have been numerous and significant. Two important studies of economic factors and imperialism are John A. Hobson, *Imperialism: A Study* (1902) and Vladimir Lenin (Ulyanov), *Imperialism: The Highest Stage of Capitalism* (1916).

A seminal book in the study of nineteenth-century imperialism is Ronald Robinson, John Gallagher, and Alice Denny, *Africa and the Victorians: The Climax of Imperialism* (Doubleday, 1968), which argues that British imperialism's main impetus came from national security and diplomatic rivalry sources. A work of ancillary value is Daniel R. Headrick, *Tools of Empire: Technology and European Imperialism* (Oxford University Press, 1981), which relates technology to the entire process of imperialism.

Exploring the relationship between culture and imperialism has been a timely topic, and the work in this field has been dominated by Edward Said. His *Culture and Imperialism* (Alfred A. Knopf, 1993) shows how nineteenth-century Western misperceptions of non-Westerners in cultural venues such as literature and grand opera played a role in imperialism's development. On a lighter side (culturally speaking), MacKenzie's edited volume *Imperialism and Popular Culture* (St. Martin's Press, 1989) relates the fascination of the masses with exotic people and places and sees it as a motivating factor in imperialism's maturation.

Because many of the world's contemporary problems can be traced to the effects of imperialism on indigenous peoples, it would be remiss not to include some sources that deal with this subject. Eric Wolf's *Europe and the People Without History* (University of California Press, 1997) explores the topic as does David S. Landes's *The Wealth and Poverty of Nations: Why Some Are So Rich and Some So Poor* (W. W. Norton, 1998), which has provoked interesting responses from its reviewers.

ISSUE 6

Were Indigenous Sex Workers in the British Empire Always Powerless?

YES: Denis Judd, from *Empire: The British Imperial Experience, From 1765 to the Present* (BasicBooks, 1996)

NO: Luise White, from "Prostitution, Differentiation, and the World Economy: Nairobi 1899–1939," in Marilyn J. Boxer and Jean H. Quataert, eds., *Connecting Spheres: Women in the Western World, 1500 to the Present* (Oxford University Press, 1987)

ISSUE SUMMARY

YES: British historian Denis Judd finds that throughout the British Empire sexual contact with "native" women was one of the perks of the imperial system. He documents the abuse and exploitation of indigenous sex workers, or prostitutes, calling it part of a pattern of conquest wherever the British flag was raised.

NO: Historian of African history Luise White interviewed indigenous sex workers in Nairobi, Kenya, and concluded that rather than being passive victims, these women acted as historical agents, doing through prostitution what in better times they would have done through marriage—stock their fathers' herds and keep livestock values competitive.

Sex workers, or prostitutes, have traditionally been thought of as victims, forced to sell their bodies under unsafe and degrading conditions. They have also been viewed as passive and as lacking alternatives. Typically, the transaction between male customer and female provider is thought of as signifying his power and her powerlessness. The question to consider in this issue is whether or not this assessment is valid. Focusing on the British Empire, the colonial experience should be examined from the differing perspectives of colonizing males and indigenous women.

In his selection, Denis Judd analyzes the 1903 suicide of Sir Hector Mac-Donald, the commander-in-chief of British forces in Ceylon (a posting chosen to avoid facing a court-martial for homosexual activity with young boys), in the wider context of sex and the British Empire. The experience of the colonial empire provided British men with opportunities for sexual expression, which would not likely have been available at home. The men who served in the armed forces or as administrators or traders usually were not accompanied by British women (at least not at first). For sexual release and satisfaction, they turned to indigenous women, asserts Judd. As holders of status and privilege, British men made the decisions. In Judd's view they were the powerful ones; women, although sometimes appreciated and even valued, were powerless.

Using interviews with 170 women who had been sex workers in Nairobi, Kenya, and 26 men who had visited prostitutes, Luise White concludes that sexuality can be shaped by forces other than personal desire. She discovers motivations rooted in family considerations as well as larger forces, such as cattle disease and drought. White states that prostitution is neither a marginal nor an aberrant activity; instead, it can be seen as economically rational behavior. During the early 1900s White's subjects turned to prostitution in response to a sudden decline in fortune experienced by their wealthy agricultural families. A devastating series of cattle epidemics, accompanied by drought and smallpox, had left a generation of wealthy men in central Kenya without the means to continue their way of life. Particularly at risk were those men who had several wives and many daughters. Marriage, the traditional method of exchanging and solidifying wealth in cattle, had suddenly become inoperative.

By the early years of the twentieth century, the daughters of these men became temporary sex workers, not for personal survival but to purchase the cattle that would maintain their family's position of wealth and status. Cattle that would ordinarily have come to the family by way of a bride price (paid by the husband's family) were, instead, supplied through the resourcefulness of the daughters. After the daughters accomplished this objective, they retired from the trade and returned home. During World War I another group of Kenyan sex workers sought out British and South African troops in pursuit of extra money. They saved the cash they earned or used it to buy urban real estate. It is important to note that pimping was not practiced; whatever money a woman earned by controlling and regulating sexual access to her body was hers to keep.

White argues that the daughters of wealthy families understood that permanent sexual access to them (through marriage) had an exchange value; by coming to Nairobi for a time and engaging in sex work, they merely controlled the exchange in such a way that repeated access to many men yielded the cattle that allowed the family to retain its status and wealth. Far from being powerless, these women understood very well how to use their power, concludes White.

Sex and the British Empire

Just as explorers, missionaries, traders, administrators, soldiers and settlers could make their fortunes, enhance their reputations or indeed, fail miserably, as a result of their activities within the [British] Empire, so they could follow, indulge, or even discover their sexual needs. [The] Empire provided countless men, and even some women, with the opportunity to express their sexuality in ways which would have been difficult, if not downright impossible, at home. In a variety of ways, the British Empire acted as a liberating agent, allowing British libidos unrestrained fulfilment overseas.

There were several obvious reasons why this should have been the case. To begin with, over the decades, millions of British men either served in the armed forces which conquered and controlled the Empire, pushed forward the frontiers of settlement or became administrators and traders within the imperial system. Far more often than not, they were not accompanied, at least initially, by British women. As a result, sexual release and satisfaction could be found in the arms of prostitutes or the women of indigenous cultures....

Within the Empire there were manifold opportunities to act out hetero-sexual inclinations in contact with indigenous societies whose attitude towards a wide range of sexual needs and tastes was far more relaxed and compliant than those officially upheld with such puritanical rigour at home. In addition, the vast majority of British men living or serving within the British Empire held positions of power and authority, whether based on their official status, their wealth, or their positions as landowners, merchants, explorers, mission-aries and the like. It has often been remarked that political power is one of the most potent of aphrodisiacs. So, too, was the power—official, personal and financial—wielded by plantation overseer, chain-gang leader, prosperous trader, the wearer of a military uniform, or even the possessor of a white skin.

There is no question that sexual relations between individuals or groups of people are frequently based on, or largely manifest themselves in, struggles for power or financial reward. Within the Empire there was, for the most part, no doubt where power lay. This is not to say that sexual relationships between rulers and ruled were invariably exercises in power and control. The history of the British Empire is littered with examples of loving and tender contact and of fond, long-term relationships between the British and their subject peoples, as well as between countless individuals of different colour, ethnicity and national identity. Although there is considerable evidence that the British abused their power in a variety of ways within the Empire, and mostly at the expense of local women, who were raped, abducted, forced into unwelcome liaisons or simply seduced, there were also many examples of permanent or semi-permanent relationships; these included marriage or long-term concubinage (as it was rather quaintly called by contemporaries), in the negotiating of which local forms and customs were often followed scrupulously. Lonely British administrators in the African bush, or in the rainforests of South-East Asia, quite frequently went through the formalities of paying the 'bride-price' for the women with whom they formed partnerships and liaisons.

Nor is there a great deal to choose between the undoubted power exercised by British men over the women of indigenous cultures and the way in which such females were subjected to the authority and control of their own menfolk. In a material sense, and perhaps also in terms of the respect and attention paid to her, a 'native' woman might well be better treated by a European male than by a husband or partner from her own tribe or race. The wholesale subordination of women, and indeed children of both sexes, to the needs and desires of indigenous males was unmistakable throughout the history of the British Empire, and is plainly discernible today throughout much of the world. This fact does not, of course, excuse or modify the British imperial male's exploitation of power and position in regard to sexual satisfaction, but it does at least put it into some sort of perspective.

It has often been argued that within the great sweep of territories that comprised the British Empire, men—and they are overwhelmingly men, not women—were also able to find sublimation or release in a variety of activities, from the demands of military campaigning to exploration, from administrative triumphs to the founding of new colonies. On this analysis, the 'asexual' male was able to 'sublimate' his sexual feelings in the undertaking of satisfying and constructive work, or in the completion of noble, or indeed ignoble, missions. Thus men described by their contemporaries as 'misogynists' or 'women-haters' . . . found fulfilment and, often obliquely, the satisfaction of their erotic needs in deeds of Empire.

. . . What the Empire provided for those British citizens who emigrated to it, served in it, or ruled it, was a wider, more complex, more varied, and often more compliant environment in which to fulfil their sexual needs than at home. It was often waggishly remarked during the heyday of British imperialism that 'the sun never set upon the Empire' because the Almighty was unable to trust what the British would get up to in the dark. It is now clear that at least some of what the British got up to in the dark was sexual and erotic in nature.

Even when this was not the case, a variety of perverse tastes could more easily be satisfied in the Empire's service. It was, for example, almost inevitable that service overseas involved British officials and officers in the handing out of punishment to both indigenous people and British subjects in the colonies. To those with a love of blood-letting, or simply with the desire to terrify and dominate their victims, the Empire was rich in opportunity.

This temptation to indulge sadistic inclinations could be found at the highest level. The activities of Lord Curzon, Viceroy of India between 1898 and 1905, are instructive in this respect. It is evident that Curzon was easily hurt, and also enjoyed hurting others. He was cruel to his exotic mistress, Elinor Glyn—of 'tiger skin' fame; he bullied his subordinates so constantly that when he left India it was said that there was not a single administrator of any standing whom he had not personally insulted; he routinely humiliated Indians, even the princes he affected to admire; he dismissed whole nations out of hand—Greeks, Bengalis, Egyptians and Turks.

But Curzon was not just a sadistic tormentor—a trait which perhaps sprang from what he claimed was a tyrannical fathering, and perhaps from homosexual harassment at Eton—he was also a masochist. He suffered for most of his life from the agonies—as he described it—of a permanently injured back. He reacted to political and administrative frustration with self-pitying disbelief. As Balfour shrewdly told him: 'You seem to think you are injured whenever you do not get exactly your own way!' His bitter quarrel with Kitchener [of Khartoum] over whether the latter—as Commander-in-Chief of the Indian Army—or the Military Member of the Viceroy's Council should have control of military policy and spending left him so broken and humiliated that he resigned his office in a tantrum. Almost his last great reform in India was the highly controversial partition of Bengal; this can be seen as both an act of cruel viceregal butchery and a Samson-like display of self-destruction, in that it ruined at a stroke his proclaimed strategy of convincing the Indian people that British rule was benevolent and superior to the rule of their own leaders.

It should not be supposed, however, that nineteenth- or early-twentieth-century Britain was a bastion of morality, peopled either by a race of rigidly controlled puritans or by individuals with uncomplicated, unwavering heterosexual tastes. The caricature of Victorian society as one of almost universal sexual repression and restraint is exactly that—a caricature. Despite the fact that the age of marriage among men was unusually high compared with that throughout much of the African and Asian countries of the Empire—averaging twenty-nine for males at the middle of the nineteenth century; despite the fact that upper- and middle-class opinion-makers and moralists insisted that children had no interest in sex and that 'respectable' women found little or no pleasure in sexual intercourse; despite the conspiracy of silence over sexual matters that descended all too often upon the home and almost completely upon the school classroom; despite the tendency to deny—or vehemently condemn—illegitimacy, prostitution and 'fornication', the Victorians were at least as sexually active within the United Kingdom as the generations that came before and after them.

For males from the upper and middle classes, heterosexual opportunities were almost limitless. By the 1880s the servant population, which was overwhelmingly female, numbered nearly 1,500,000, many of whom 'lived in'. Chambermaids and assistant cooks often carried out the 'off-duty' work of initiating young male members of the household into sexual knowledge and techniques. Nor did exile to boarding school mean the end of sexual experience. The public school system not merely taught Greek and Latin, the games ethic and various forms of muscular Christianity to its pupils, but also provided a flourishing venue for extra-curricular activities such as buggery and bullying.

For those older public school boys who preferred it, heterosexual sex was readily and cheaply available, often only a short walk from their seats of learning. Prostitution was one of the major industries of Victorian Britain. Although, unfortunately, it could do nothing to reduce the annual deficit in commodity trading, Victorian prostitution was an established fact of life throughout the country. Naturally enough, prostitutes worked mostly in the cities and towns of Britain: by the mid-nineteenth century it has been estimated that some 80,000 operated in London, with proportional amounts scattered throughout other cities and towns. The widespread use of prostitutes—particularly by men from the middle and upper classes—at least kept the ideals of the virgin bride and the chaste wife intact. A considerable number of female prostitutes were juveniles, perhaps not surprisingly in an age when so many families lived in poverty and when the age of consent for girls remained at twelve until 1875, when it was raised to thirteen.

The age of consent did not apply to boys at all, which may well have accounted for the considerable number of youthful male prostitutes who not merely worked in brothels but also hung around the London parks and railway stations, and were to be found in other major urban areas.

To all of this must be added the widespread accessibility and prevalence of pornography. The British Vice Society confiscated over 250,000 pornographic photographs between 1868 and 1880, and London was recognised towards the end of the century as the capital, not only of the British Empire, but of a booming international trade in erotic pictures and pornographic writing.

The poverty, and the overcrowded and brutal living conditions, which far too often characterised the life of the urban poor were doubtless important contributory factors to what Victorian moralists denounced as 'vice'. A considerable number of working-class marriages—perhaps as many as a third—took place with the woman already pregnant. As if all of this was not bad enough for the moralists, the level of venereal disease, and the difficulty in curing it, gave rise to widespread concern. The embarrassing discovery at the outset of the Boer War in 1899 that a very substantial number of working-class volunteers were unfit for military service merely confirmed in a dramatic fashion the various forms of ill-health that were endemic among an alarming proportion of the population.

All of this accorded ill with the late-Victorian and Edwardian need to see Britain as a nation fit to triumph in the struggle between rival imperial systems and economies. It also coincided with, and partly provoked, the increasingly widely expressed anxieties over national degeneracy and decline, anxieties that became linked in the minds of many individuals and groups with the perils of masturbation and licentious living. Lord Rosebery asserted in 1900 that 'An Empire such as ours requires as its first condition an Imperial race—a race vigorous and industrious and intrepid. Health of mind and body exalt a nation in the competition of the universe. The survival of the fittest is an absolute truth in the conditions of the modern world.'

This rising tide of anxiety and self-criticism not merely encouraged the social reforms of the Edwardian era, but had already helped to launch a vigorous and frequently intolerant 'Purity Campaign' towards the end of the nineteenth century. Although it is difficult to estimate the impact of the Purity Campaign upon sexual activities of all kinds, there is no doubt that it led many leading figures in British society to pursue their sexual inclinations with far more prudence than before. It was in juxtaposition to this trend that the trial and prosecution of Oscar Wilde in 1895 became such a *cause célèbre,* not least because Wilde was perceived as hurling an obscene challenge at the purity campaigners through the ostentation with which he flaunted his homosexuality.

As a result of all this, by the turn of the century it had become virtually impossible to discuss sexual matters in public, and almost as difficult to speak of them in private. Rather than face condemnation, disgrace and ridicule, the overwhelming majority of British people, especially those from the upper and middle classes, refrained from mentioning sexual matters and as a consequence failed to address, either in public or in private, sexual problems and difficulties.

Within the British Empire, however, it was far easier to lead relatively uninhibited sexual lives. There is overwhelming evidence that throughout the imperial system white men continued to liaise with, abuse and exploit the women of indigenous societies wherever the British flag was raised. Sexual contact with 'native' women became a perk of the imperial system, something to be anticipated and enjoyed rather than avoided and disguised. Indeed, many Victorian men glorified in the sexual opportunities thus vouchsafed them, and recorded their pleasures unashamedly:

> [Native women] understand in perfection all of the arts and wiles of love, are capable of gratifying any tastes, and in face and figure they are unsurpassed by any women in the world.... It is impossible to describe the enjoyment I experience in the arms of such syrens.

The dancing girls of South India, the Chinese women of Malaya, girls from Nigeria, the exotic maidens of the South Seas, and the mixed-race females of the West Indies were all praised for their sexual skills and their passion, as well as for their availability.

The sexual services of local boys and men were also widely available throughout the Empire, nearly always on the basis of payment, or at least material reward. Despite the moral indignation that evidence of such 'free-market' sodomy provoked among the purity campaigners and many others, the economic imperatives of Empire, particularly manifested in the shipping of tens of thousands of indentured labourers to man plantations, build railways or work the mines, made homosexual activity in the workers' compounds an inevitable part of the process. The moral outcry that accompanied the campaign in Britain against the system of 'Chinese slavery' in the gold mines of the Transvaal after the Boer War owed at least part of its intensity to the belief that homosexual activity was commonplace within the mining compounds.

Indentured labourers and miners locked up in their dormitories at night could at least protest that they were being denied access to women. For their part, many British men who engaged in sexual relationships with 'native females' also tended to claim that they acted as they did chiefly because they were unable to find enough European women to meet their needs. For much of the history of the British Empire, service overseas often did indeed mean a solitary lifestyle or living within an all-male environment. Despite the disapproval of purity campaigners, it was generally recognised that sexual activity brought emotional release and some degree of private satisfaction to individual lives.

It was thus possible to construct a plausible argument that sexual relationships with African and Asian women, and, at a pinch, with local males, fulfilled an important imperial function. If the energies and activities of traders, military personnel, administrators and emigrants—among others—made the wheels of Empire turn, the complex machinery was at least partially lubricated by the sexual activities of the British overseas.

In India during the eighteenth century, British servants of the East India Company had been positively encouraged to enter into liaisons with, or even to marry, Indian females. No doubt such contacts helped to improve and consolidate the commercial and political relationships between Europeans and the indigenous people. By the end of the eighteenth century, however, official policy stamped out the hitherto cosmopolitan and inter-racial character of the British presence in the sub-continent. Not merely were Indians prohibited from holding military and civil office under the East India Company, but Anglo-Indians—the products of inter-racial marriage and intercourse—were denied office and barred from official functions. By the beginning of the nineteenth century intermarriage between British and Indians had virtually ceased.

Later, by the mid-Victorian period, the improved and speedier communications between Britain and India, as well as the need to stabilise and consolidate British control in the post-Mutiny period, had led to the arrival of large numbers of British women in the sub-continent. As the memsahibs grew in number, social contacts between British males and Indians, whether male or female, dwindled. The presence of the memsahibs also made British men more sensitive to the perceived dangers of Indian men finding British females sexually attractive. The end-product of all of this was a deepening of distrust and an increase in intolerance.

There was another price to pay for British imperial expansion. This was, quite simply, a substantial increase in overseas prostitution, and the concomitant increase in venereal disease amongst British men serving in the Empire. In order to keep some control of the situation, the British authorities in India sanctioned the introduction of regulated prostitution. During the post-Mutiny period, until the late 1880s, seventy-five cantonments were designated as centres of regulated prostitution, complete with medical examination, systematic registration, and the hospital facilities to treat prostitutes suffering from venereal disease. The introduction of the system had more to do with maintaining the good health of the troops and, as a consequence, military efficiency, than with demonstrating liberal enlightenment.

It was, nonetheless, an effective arrangement. Between 1880 and 1888, when these practical arrangements were officially suspended as a result of the objections of the moral purity campaigners, the incidence of syphilis in the army in India was running at a rate below that recorded among soldiers serving in the British Army at home. But after 1888 there was a dramatic increase in the occurrence of syphilis in the Indian Army, peaking at over 250 per thousand troops in 1895. So bad had the situation become that by 1897 new regulations were introduced which had the effect once more of dramatically reducing the incidence of syphilis in the Indian Army, which had fallen to a new low by 1908.

During the twentieth century, and particularly after the First World War, the elaborate prostitution networks which had characterised the latter part of the nineteenth century, as well as the incidence of venereal disease among British men serving overseas, diminished. Among the factors that contributed to this were the improvements in the employment prospects of women, particularly in Europe, the greater availability of the condom for the male, improved standards of personal hygiene and somewhat more open attitudes towards sexual identity and sexual problems. . . .

It would be a pointless exercise to attempt to evaluate what nearly four centuries of contact between the British and the indigenous people of their colonies amounted to. It has been argued that, on balance, 'Sexual interaction between the British and non-Europeans probably did more long-term good than harm to race relations.' Whether anybody can arrive at a more concrete and confident judgement is extremely doubtful.

As in the lives of individuals and communities throughout the world, sexual contacts within the British Empire were characterised by joyful discovery, mutual esteem, exploitation, abuse, violence, compromise and accommodation. Although whites were overwhelmingly in control of the interaction, they were not universally so, and some at least, like the suicidal Hector MacDonald [the Commander-in-Chief of British forces in Ceylon (now Sri Lanka)], paid a terrible price.

In one area, moreover, the potential for sexual interaction between the races was almost always damaging and destructive. This was when black or brown men made advances to, were perceived to desire, or even had sexual relationships with, white females. On these rare occasions, the cause of race relations was certainly not advanced, and violent and deep-seated hatreds of black or brown men, who were perceived—consciously or unconsciously—as representing the primitive, atavistic 'other', became common currency.

Finally it must be remembered that very large numbers of British men overseas refrained, for a whole variety of reasons, from sexual relationships with indigenous females. Although Empire was almost always about economic profitability and political power, it would be wrong to assume that the ruthless and unbridled sexual exploitation of the black and brown subjects of imperial rule was an inevitable part of the power structure—a perk of office like a handsome pension or a solar topee.

At the same time, it is perhaps too much to claim that 'There are, at least in the pre-AIDS era, worse sins in running an empire, as in life, than the sexual ones.' The use of one individual by another solely for the purpose of self-gratification, however, is rarely an edifying spectacle, as even the briefest assessment of late-twentieth-century prostitution, particularly of the growth of 'sexual tourism' to economically needy states like Thailand or the Philippines, will reveal. In this regard the British Empire can claim no special dispensation. The imagery of imperial control reeked of sexuality: continents were 'penetrated', tribes 'subdued', districts 'ravished', territories 'mastered', local potentates 'seduced', countries 'raped'. It was small wonder that uncountable numbers of indigenous people suffered similar fates.

Prostitution, Differentiation, and the World Economy: Nairobi 1899–1939

The Era of the Interventionist State...

We tend to think that sexual relations are personal and private matters. While we may read dozens of books advising us on how to achieve intimacy, we generally believe that decisions about who sleeps with whom, where, for how long, and under what kinds of encouragement are the results of passions so personal that they cannot be studied systematically. We believe this partly because we see matters such as sexual attraction and choosing a partner as timeless qualities, where choice is personal, so personal as to make any serious inquiry difficult, if not pointless. But how do we know what is personal and what is not? Perhaps if we look at those sexual relations that are the most furtive—conducted in alleys and doorways not because either party likes it better that way, but because those are the only spaces available for such acts—we can see people brought together by forces other than their personal desires. Perhaps we can begin to observe people who occasionally sleep together because of cattle diseases, falling food crop prices, and increased cash crop production.

In this [selection] I want to look at two forms of prostitution that developed in Nairobi, Kenya between 1899 and 1939. Both forms, or ways for women to conduct the sale of sexual access to themselves, emphasized brief sexual relations with customers rather than night-long fictions of matrimonial bliss, and both forms were known for the aggressiveness with which women sought their customers. All the labor forms, in Nairobi and presumably elsewhere, were determined by specific crises in rural society and the women's relationship to housing in the town. In Kenya there is no evidence, oral or written, of anything that could be even vaguely construed as pimping: when women prostitute themselves, they retain all their earnings. How a woman prostitutes herself —with which form—indicates the urgency with which she requires money. In Kenya the women who walked the streets (*watembezi* in Swahili, widely spoken in Nairobi) were precisely those women who took the pennies from sex conducted in doorways back to the stunted agricultural economies of East Africa, and enabled their families to recoup some of the losses the world economy had forced upon them. It was the women who quietly waited in their rooms for men to come to them (*malaya* in Swahili), the ones who provided the widest range of domestic services, including cooked food and bath water, and had the most discreet and circumspect of relationships, who accumulated capital for themselves, and most definitely not for their families.

Nairobi was founded in 1899 at the foot of the fertile highlands that were to be taken over by white settlers. Built around a swamp where no one had lived before, everyone who came there, black or white, female or male, was a migrant of some sort. Europeans came to settle because Kenya offered more opportunities than they might otherwise inherit in their homes; African men came because their inheritance was substantially delayed (by the untimely combination of natural disaster and European conquest), and because they were forced to do so. From 1902, a tax was levied on married men, payable in coin that could most easily be obtained by working for Europeans. Young African men were observed to work to pay their fathers' taxes (polygamous men had higher tax rates), and then work to enhance their own inheritance. They left the wage labor force once they married, and to secure a still larger supply of male laborers, in 1910 a tax was introduced on all males over 16.

Why did women come to Nairobi, and why did they become prostitutes? We know that they became prostitutes because there were simply no jobs for women then or in the next forty years. Some came to set themselves up as independent heads of households. "In those days," said one widow, "I didn't get another husband; there was another way to make a living then." Another woman said, "At home, what could I do? Grow crops for my husband and my father. In Nairobi, I could earn my own money, for myself." But most women came to help their families. By the end of the nineteenth century those families were primarily agriculturalists already differentiated into rich and poor and everything in between. In almost all those families women and livestock were the traditional elements of wealth, exchange, reproduction, and, of course, status. They could be exchanged for each other and they could reproduce more like themselves. They were integral elements in the cycle of family formation and they were at the same time investments. Thus, men with many wives could produce more daughters and grain with which to exchange for livestock, and young men would work for their fathers so that they would eventually be given the livestock with which to wed. The most valuable livestock was cattle, then sheep, then goats.

In the 1890s, a devastating series of cattle epidemics swept through Eastern Africa. By 1897, central Kenya was struck by drought, famine, and smallpox. It had the effect of turning the world (and its values) inside out—with as many as 60 percent of all the local cattle dead, famine devalued the remaining cattle and, indeed, everything but foodstuffs. Agriculturalists dominated, and men with many wives could find no one to marry their daughters and thus replenish their herds. Virtually an entire generation of wealthy men faced an end to their way of life. All the available evidence points to the fact that these men's dwindling status and wealth was restored and restocked by their daughters' prostitution. These women already knew that permanent sexual access to them had an exchange value; they simply transformed the location and control of the work so that they sold repeated sexual access to themselves to many men. Thus, as early as 1899 daughters of the "loose women" in Kenya's rudimentary townships, and by 1909 some 300 Masai *watembezi* prostitutes were arrested in Nairobi.

How do we know that these women were the daughters of wealthy fathers? How do we know they were not impoverished young women who sought through prostitution to better their own lives? First of all, we know that in the years before World War I, prostitutes earned roughly between four and eight times what male wage-earners did (partly due to the low value of the currency at that time), so that any rapid gains accruing to the older generation would almost have to have come from prostitutes' earnings. Secondly, we know because these women, the *watembezi,* left prostitution once the requisite number of livestock were acquired. Those women who came from impoverished households also came to Nairobi, and the best evidence I have indicates they and they alone became *malaya* prostitutes.

The pre–World War I interaction of the colonial state, the Masai, and other pastoral peoples provides an excellent example of a sequence of destocking, prostitution, and livestock acquisition. Masai herds were decimated in the epidemics of the 1890s and their economy seriously undermined; Masai women seem to have been active in prostitution even before Nairobi was established, and in the early years of this century they were said to dominate Nairobi prostitution. Meanwhile, pastoral peoples in western Kenya, an area largely unaffected by the cattle epidemics, raided British installations. The British led Masai soldiers in punitive expeditions against the Kipsigis and Nandi, and by 1905 it was estimated that 55 percent of Nandi cattle had been taken to Nairobi. The Masai soldiers were paid in goats that they parlayed into cattle (at rates of about fifteen goats per cow), just as prostitutes' profits were invested in livestock. In 1911, when Masai herds were said to approach their nineteenth-century levels, there was a noticeable Masai retreat from prostitution and wage labor. By 1907, however, colonial officials began to observe an increasing number of Kipsigis and Nandi women entering prostitution, replacing the Masai women and accosting men on settlers' farms and on the streets of Nairobi. These women, too, were said to buy livestock with their earnings, at rates that were at least double what the Masai had paid, as white settlements brought about a demand for meat that slowly began to raise the value of cattle. According to contemporary male authors, by 1909 Nandi women were "notorious" throughout Kenya and by 1913 "the most enlightened" Nandi were those prostitutes who had returned home after a few years in Nairobi—presumably they knew the most English and belonged to the wealthiest families.

What were these women doing? They were doing through prostitution what in better times they would have done through marriage: stock their fathers' herd and keep livestock values competitive. They had to restore their fathers' property—cattle, not daughters—to its earlier level of prestige. That they were doing this in the streets, in alleys, loudly, aggressively, testifies to the urgency with which monies were required. For despite how disrespectful the *watembezi* form looked, despite its emphasis on brief sexual encounters in less than sensual surroundings, the means of accumulation was anything but disorderly: it was aggressive and swift by design; it matched high risks with high profits. It would then seem that anything more than occasional *watembezi* prostitution was not caused by dire poverty; it was the response of relatively wealthy families to a sudden decrease in their wealth. Young women became streetwalkers not as a survival strategy, but to help their families maintain previous levels of differentiation—and most of these women did not just survive, they prospered.

During World War I prostitution in Nairobi changed. The *watembezi* form still dominated, indeed it took on a revitalized dimension in pursuit of British and South African troops during the war, but its practitioners tended to be long-term residents of Nairobi, not immigrants from newly impoverished societies. "It was extra money, we went to pick beans and had a man in secret; sometimes a woman would go... just for the men," said a teenage woman who had been born in Nairobi. World War I *watembezi* were on the whole older than the young women who had sought men on the streets and back alleys of the prewar city. Wartime *watembezi* earned large sums, but they saved their cash or bought urban real estate. They could not have bought cattle with their earnings had they wanted to, so successfully had pastoralist fathers and daughters managed to reconstruct and reestablish the value of their herds.

Unlike pastoralists, many East African cultivators prospered from the events of the 1890s and the coming of colonial rule. Not only were they able to sell grain at exceptionally high rates of exchange to other Africans, they fed the European expansion into East Africa as well. Until World War I, African agriculturalists dominated local and export markets, and many of the Kikuyu farmers in central Kenya became wealthy. Until the ravages of military conscription during World War I and the rapidly increased white settlement after the war, the Kikuyu had sent relatively few sons into wage labor and fewer daughters into prostitution. The combined weight of white farmers' land-grabbing, and legislation introduced to prevent further white farmers' labor shortages, reduced many Kikuyu farmers to resident laborer status on European farms. Nevertheless, many Kikuyu "squatters" and cultivators on their own farms were able to produce and sell surplus crops. By the mid-1920s the increased production of maize and rice in other parts of the country began to erode the profits Kikuyu farmers could get for potatoes and millet in Nairobi. The price of potatoes, for example, had increased by 57 percent between 1924 and 1928 and the prices of other Kikuyu crops had risen as well: fewer people bought them. By 1928, both Kikuyu chiefs and *malaya* prostitutes in Nairobi complained about married Kikuyu women coming to town as if they were selling vegetables, but prostituting themselves with workingmen in the alleys of the African areas, and returning to their homes before dark. It seems very likely that these Kikuyu *watembezi* were not acting out of any immorality or personal insecurities; they were engaging in prostitution so that they could maintain the standard of living that only a few years before they had obtained solely through the sale of their farm produce. This *watembezi* prostitution was not about any preference for sex conducted in doorways and bushes, but about keeping a standard of living buoyant in the face of declining food profits.

Cattle diseases and state-sponsored destocking do not qualify as an incursion of the world economy into peoples' private lives. Rising crop prices are facts of life for farmers all over the world, and are not a unique characteristic of colonized peoples. To see how the world economy influences what we think of as intimate behavior, we have to look at those crops introduced specifically by colonial powers for the specific reason of making their colonies pay off: cash crops. Coffee, tea, cotton, sugar, and tobacco are a few examples. Among critics of imperialism, cash crops have an importance almost unmatched by any other colonial introduction: they are almost never edible crops; they take up arable land that might be better used for food crops; they are often produced on plantations and concentrate local labor in such a way as to remove people from food production. They are often produced at gunpoint. This list could go on for pages, but the most significant thing about cash crops is that they draw producers into a worldwide system of supply and profit and loss that is determined by conditions far outside the country producing the coffee, tea, or sugar. Unlike mining—the wholesale extraction of a country's wealth—cash crop production pits various countries' producers against each other. Coffee growers in Kenya do not compete with each other, they compete with coffee growers in Brazil and Colombia and Sumatra. The amount they pay their workers in each of these countries has nothing to do with how hard these men and women work; it has to do with the competitive value of their coffee crop relative to that of coffees produced thousands of miles away under different conditions. The only real influence local producers have on profit is quantity, but this can backfire when demand drops. In most colonies it was a crime for Africans to uproot their cash crops when prices were low and plant food crops instead. Some scholars have argued that cash crop production enabled Africans to resist the depredations of wage labor, but this argument fails to tell us what happens when the cash crop is not wanted, or is overproduced, or is deemed obsolete by the production of synthetics. The introduction of cash crops made African cultivators as dependent on the health and stability of world markets as they were on the rainfall.

It is this kind of dependence that determines not only who becomes a prostitute, but the duration of the services prostitutes provide. The process does not happen overnight, but it does happen with great clarity. In 1903 the German colonizers of what was to become Tanganyika (when it was handed over to the British at the end of World War I) introduced coffee to the Haya people on the western shore of Lake Victoria, a thousand kilometers (600 miles) from the sea. They did not concentrate coffee in plantations, but gave some to every large farm. Before the War, coffee did well in the fertile hills of Bukoba, but it was not until the worldwide boom of the 1920s that Haya producers began to see spectacular profits. By the mid-1920s the wealthier Haya were almost heady with success; they hired laborers from the neighboring Belgian colonies to come pick their coffee and "squat" on their land, and as Christians they ceased exchanging their daughters for livestock and requested and received a cash bride-price, which by about 1927 was the equivalent of $175 or more. Unlike many African peoples, the Haya permitted divorce, and fathers returned the bride-price in full. Thus, in 1930 when the world price of coffee dropped a staggering 90 percent, Haya producers were in trouble; it was not even worth their while to ship their produce to the coast, but they had laborers living on their farms who demanded payment nonetheless. Although the problem lay in cash crop production, the solution was found in women. Young wives were divorced and fathers repaid the bride-price, shifting the problem back on themselves—a generation of fathers now had to come up with cash to repay their own increasing debts and refurbish the foundations of a sagging cash crop economy. How the decision to solve this problem was made within individual households is not known, but within two or three years Haya women in their early twenties appeared in large numbers on the streets of Kampala (Uganda), Dar es Salaam (Tanganyika), and Nairobi.

Haya women did not walk in the streets in these towns; instead they rented rooms in the African areas and sat outside their houses and solicited men from there. This was called the *Wazi-Wazi* form, from a slang term for Haya common in Nairobi. Haya women scandalized the more sedate and circumspect prostitutes of these areas, who saw such open solicitation and aggressive behavior as a threat to their respectability and their profits. Haya women were known for shouting out their prices to men, and they took these men into the four-by-eight foot rooms they shared with other Haya immigrants for brief sexual encounters, for which they received just about 17 percent of the world price of raw coffee beans. Between 1930 and 1935 the world price for a thirty-five-pound bag of coffee beans varied between three and seven shillings. In those same years, *Wazi-Wazi* prostitutes in Nairobi charged fifty cents—one half of one shilling—for sexual intercourse. *Malaya* women were justifiably upset since this had the overall effect of lowering the price for brief sexual relations for all prostitutes, at a time when most *malaya* prostitutes earned perhaps a third more than male laborers did. *Wazi-Wazi* prostitutes were also said to fight with the men who refused to pay them and call on their neighbors for help —practices unheard of by both *malaya* and *watembezi* women in 1930s Nairobi. An old woman born near Nairobi in about 1900 said that the biggest change she observed in her lifetime was that after the mid-1930s "women beat up men." According to a younger *malaya* woman, cash was so important to a Haya woman that she "would risk her blood to get her money." Indeed, it was so important to Haya women that they were reputed to send money home each week or month, and if a Haya woman died in Nairobi her friends would take her body and her money the hundreds of miles back to Bukoba. Why did Haya do all this? Clearly because the advantages and opportunities of being a daughter of a well-to-do coffee-growing family outweighed the disadvantages of being a prostitute in Nairobi.

How did the colonial state respond to streetwalkers and *Wazi-Wazi* women? While it was not in the interests of public order that women be allowed to call out a price to men as they returned from work, there were few arrests of *watembezi* prostitutes in colonial Nairobi, and none of Haya women. More than any other kind of political entity, colonial states do not act with one voice, let alone motivation; they mediate between different and competing interests—the government at home, the settlers it must protect, the African leaders who make ruling easier, and the Africans who must be made to work in colonial enterprises, but in ways that do not antagonize any of the groups above. Although we might think that no state encourages prostitution, these particular interest groups had nothing against it. In Nairobi and other cities, the presence of prostitutes and the amenities and cooked food they sometimes offered, made the task of getting urban Africans back to work day after day somewhat easier. It also reduced African wages just enough to keep them at work a few months longer than they otherwise would have stayed. Moreover, the colonial police were busy with the Africans the state made into criminals, those Africans who broke the law by spending more than a month looking for work in Nairobi, or leaving an employer before their labor contract had expired. The state knew about Haya and *watembezi* women, but found them more of a service than an offense. The values of accumulation and entrepreneurship subsidized solid, Christian, patriarchal households on the western shore of Lake Victoria and helped extend the laboring time of hundreds of badly needed unskilled African workers in Nairobi.

No new forms of prostitution emerged after 1939. While the *watembezi* form dominated World War II prostitution, it did so under special circumstances, only some of which could be identified as young women's family labor. That no new forms emerged after the mid-1930s is especially significant, and may well mark a point of transition in East African agricultural history. The biggest change in African colonial history has nothing to do with barbarism and civilization, nothing to do with tribe and nation. It has to do with a transition around the issue of Africans' participation in wage labor. In most of Africa in the era before World War II, wage labor was a means by which Africans could supplement their farm production. It was not something they relied on solely for their subsistence. The monies earned working enhanced farming, however unwillingly and hesitantly that labor was originally undertaken. By World War II, in those areas where most men were migrant laborers, wage labor became the means by which most people subsisted, and farming itself was dependent on the cash migrant laborers brought home. So atrophied were the agricultural systems of these parts of Africa that women farmers could not plant maize or cotton or beans unless their husbands, working on tea estates in Kenya or the docks of East Africa, sent them the money to buy seeds—even subsistence required an assist from wage labor. These areas also sent a steady stream of prostitutes to towns, but they went as independent accumulators, not as daughters bailing their families out of trouble. Elsewhere, African agriculture took off in ways that colonialists had not full expected—and in fact were to complain about—and these families did not have daughters who became prostitutes. That no new forms of prostitution emerged after 1939 testifies to the impoverishment of the poorest peasant households; they continued to have crises, but they no longer attempted to solve them—if they could be solved at all—from within the family.

POSTSCRIPT

Were Indigenous Sex Workers in the British Empire Always Powerless?

A good source for consideration of the subject of prostitution, or sex work, is Judith R. Walkowitz, *Prostitution and Victorian Society: Women, Class, and the State* (Cambridge University Press, 1980). Placed in the context of moral reform and, specifically, of the Contagious Diseases Acts of 1864, 1866, and 1869, Walkowitz's study examines the complex net of social attitudes and relationships in late-nineteenth-century Victorian England within which women became prostitutes. Prostitution still represented a choice even if that choice was among undesirable alternatives. And, Walkowitz found, the trade was largely organized by women who established a strong female subculture; they were not victims but agents of change for their own lives.

Margaret Strobel explores the experience of British women in "Gender, Race, and Empire in Nineteenth- and Twentieth-Century Africa and Asia," in Renate Bridenthal, Susan Mosher Stuard, and Merry E. Weisner, eds., *Becoming Visible: Women in European History,* 3rd ed. (Houghton Mifflin, 1998). As wives of colonial administrators, domestic servants, missionaries, ethnographers, and anthropologists, British women were sometimes also reformers. Critical of indigenous practices, they were, however, unwilling or unable to critique imperialism itself.

Patricia W. Romero has edited *Women's Voices on Africa: A Century of Travel Writings* (Markus Wiener Publishing, 1992). Spanning the century from 1853 to 1954, this collection ranges from Nigeria and the Gold Coast in West Africa, through Capetown and Durban in southern Africa, to Kenya and Ethiopia in East Africa. The book includes the voices of missionaries, colonial wives, and travelers. Many of these women are interested in and comment on the African women they meet, sometimes critically, often maternalistically.

Ruth Rosen's *The Lost Sisterhood: Prostitution in America, 1900–1918* (Johns Hopkins University Press, 1982) examines prostitution as both a cultural symbol and a social institution that women used as a means of survival. Many reformers saw in prostitution proof of the sexual and economic exploitation of women in a patriarchal society; for sex workers, it may have been simply a form of work, better than some, worse than others. Chapter 9 of Christine Stansell's *City of Women: Sex and Class in New York, 1789–1860* (University of Illinois Press, 1987) draws a similar conclusion. Titled "Women on the Town," the chapter deals with the movement of prostitution out of the bawdy houses and into public spaces like Broadway, observing that prostitution was neither a tragic fate (as the moralists believed) nor an act of defiance, but rather it was a way of "getting by."

121

On the Internet . . . DUSHKIN ONLINE

The Boxer Rebellion of 1900

The Boxer Rebellion of 1900 Web site contains a lengthy essay on the rebellion, including causes and results; it also has other visual and print materials.

http://mebn.org/bxr.html

German Responsibility for the Outbreak of the War

Despite its title, German Responsibility for the Outbreak of the War, the author of this lengthy, essay-based Web site finds plenty of blame to go around. The scope extends beyond the war to include its effect on the postwar decades.

http://www.colby.edu/personal/r/rmscheck/GermanyC1.html

Marxist Writers: Alexandra Kollontai (1872–1952)

Marxist Writers: Alexandra Kollontai (1872–1952) is a Web site devoted to one of the early Soviet Union's most powerful women.

http://www.marxists.org/archive/kollonta/

Holocaust Learning Center

The Holocaust Learning Center Web site is the creation of the Washington-based United States Holocaust Memorial Museum and provides multilinked connections on the subject.

http://www.ushmm.org/topics/themes.htm

The American Experience: General Douglas MacArthur (1880–1964)

The American Experience: General Douglas MacArthur (1880–1964) is a PBS Web site that covers the life of the man who governed Japan during the immediate postwar years and decided that Emperor Hirohito would not be held responsible for World War II.

http://www.pbs.org/wgbh/amex/macarthur/peopleevents/pandeAMEX96.html

Cold War International History Project

The Cold War International History Project Web site contains a document library of materials related to all aspects of the cold war.

http://cwihp.si.edu/cwihplib.nsf?OpenDatabase&Start=1&Count=30&Expand=1

PART 2

The Early Twentieth Century

*T*his section covers the first half of the creative, chaotic twentieth century, which was marked by great technological improvements and two disastrous world wars. The events of the twentieth century prove that societies in every century face the same problems. However, as the world becomes more technologically sophisticated, the stakes seem to get higher.

- Were Environmental Factors and Their Psychological Effect on Chinese Society Responsible for the Boxer Rebellion?

- Were German Militarism and Diplomacy Responsible for World War I?

- Did the Bolshevik Revolution Improve the Lives of Soviet Women?

- Was German "Eliminationist Antisemitism" Responsible for the Holocaust?

- Should Emperor Hirohito Have Been Held Responsible for Japan's World War II Actions?

- Was Stalin Responsible for the Cold War?

ISSUE 7

Were Environmental Factors and Their Psychological Effect on Chinese Society Responsible for the Boxer Rebellion?

YES: Paul A. Cohen, from *History in Three Keys: The Boxers as Event, Experience, and Myth* (Columbia University Press, 1997)

NO: Henrietta Harrison, from "Justice on Behalf of Heaven: The Boxer Movement," *History Today* (September 2000)

ISSUE SUMMARY

YES: Professor Paul A. Cohen contends that while antiforeign and anti-Christian attitudes played a role in the start of the Boxer rebellion, a more immediate cause was a severe drought and its impact on Chinese society.

NO: Historian Henrietta Harrison concedes that while the Boxers were motivated by more than a single factor, opposition to Christian missionary activity was at the core of their rebellion.

Issue 5 of this volume examines the causes of imperialism, by which the West attempted to extend its influence over the peoples of the non-Western world. This issue provides a case study of the opposition that resulted from imperialism in China: the Boxer rebellion (1898–1900).

Western domination of Asia and Africa took different forms. The establishment of colonialism, which brought direct Western rule to much of Asia and Africa, was the most prevalent. In China, however, geographic size and a large population made this impossible. European nations established "spheres of influence," recognized zones of China that were controlled and exploited by various Western nations. In these areas, China's rule was in name only.

Accompanying those coming to Asia for economic gains were missionaries who came to gain converts for evangelical Christianity. In China, with so many souls to save, this missionary zeal was a powerful force, and to many Chinese, a particularly odious one.

What made this domination of China possible was the weakened nature of the Chinese government. The Manchu dynasty and its Empress Dowager Tsu

Hsi appeared to be powerless to stop this Western tidal wave sweeping over the country. When the Chinese did fight back, they were soundly defeated.

During the late 1830s the Chinese government made an attempt control the Western commerce within its borders, especially the opium traded by the British. The latter went to war to guarantee their right to sell the drug in China and won. As a result, the Chinese were forced to grant trade concessions, and a pattern of subservience was established. Any Western nation interested in trade with China would now demand the same deal the British received. In 1857 Britain and France went to war to force China to grant further diplomatic and commercial concessions, and once again the Chinese government was made to accede to their demands.

By the turn of the century, a seemingly intolerable situation became worse, made so by more Western nations becoming involved in Chinese affairs, their increasing demands for further concessions from the Chinese, and the large number of Christian missionaries who had entered China since 1860. These conditions were exacerbated by the Sino-Japanese War (1894–1895), which China lost. The war resulted in the signing of another humiliating treaty. The Chinese government not only seemed powerless to stop Western encroachment; it could not stop the encroachment of one of its Asian neighbors. If China's government was powerless, it was reasoned, perhaps some of China's citizens would have to fight to win back control of their country and bring an end to Western imperialism within its borders. The Boxers were a product of such conditions and concerns.

The Boxer rebellion had its roots in the economically depressed Shandong province, made so by a devastating drought that not only caused massive starvation but brought its people to a psychological breaking point. Many young people turned to secret societies to vent their anger and disillusionment. Eventually they coalesced into a group known as the "Fists of Righteous Harmony." Because its members practiced martial arts, the term *Boxer* was applied to the movement by Westerners. It is a misnomer, which has endured to this day.

The movement began with sporadic attacks in the countryside, aimed primarily at Western missionaries and Chinese converts to Christianity. As the movement grew and its influence spread to some of China's urban centers, many wondered what Tsu Hsi would do. She was under intense pressure from Western officials to suppress the insurrection. But she also recognized in the Boxers a useful tool in fighting against Western influences and restoring Manchu hegemony in China. After a period of fence-straddling, she decided to openly support the Boxer cause. Thus, when the rebellion was suppressed by Western forces, she had to bear responsibility for their actions.

What motivated the Boxers to act as they did seems a simple enough question to answer—they were fighting to rid their country of the "foreign devils" who were causing it irreparable damage. However, some recent scholarship on the subject points to the severe drought and its psychological impact on Chinese society as an overriding factor. In the following selections, Paul A. Cohen stresses the latter, while Henrietta Harrison emphasizes the former.

Paul A. Cohen

Drought and the Foreign Presence

Drought, Anxiety, and the Spread of the Boxer Movement

Prayer,... even when offered up by the most powerful people in the realm, does not always work. And, as a drought continues and people become more and more desperate, restlessness, anxiety, and ultimately panic easily set in. To imagine how profound the panic can be among impoverished farmers and poor city folk living in a society with little in the way of a "safety net," it is illuminating to look at the reactions of the newly unemployed in California in the early stages of the recession that began in the latter half of 1990. "The hardest thing," observed the part owner of a small marketing company in Huntington Beach that had recently gone out of business, "is to see how panicked people are.... Right now, I don't have a dime. I'm worried about buying things like sugar. I'm that close to losing my home. Now is when the nerve systems are really going." A young film editor from Hollywood, noting the "prevailing air of uncertainty," expressed a lack of confidence "about the future."

Uncertainty about the future governs virtually all phases of human experience. But it does not always produce anxiety. For anxiety to result, the uncertainty must bear on an aspect of life that is of vital importance: a child's safety, one's performance in a play or a sporting event, the fate of a loved one engaged in combat, the time frame of one's own mortality, the security and dependability of one's livelihood. It was the last-named area of uncertainty that was shared by Californians in 1990 and Chinese farmers in North China almost a century earlier. Different societies, however, are differentially susceptible to the effects of natural or social disasters, and in the case of the drought of 1899–1900 in China (or that of 1899 in western India), because of the absence of a well-functioning crisis support system, it was much more a matter of life and death.

A wide range of sources, including gazetteers, diaries, official memorials, oral history accounts, and the reports of foreigners, indicate a direct link between the spread and intensification of the Boxer movement, beginning in late 1899, and growing popular nervousness, anxiety, unemployment, and hunger occasioned by drought. As early as October 1899, Luella Miner [American Board of Commissioners for Foreign Missions] (ABCFM) identified drought as one cause of growing Boxer-related unrest in northwestern Shandong. In the Beijing area, where for many months very little rain had fallen and the wheat seedlings had completely withered, popular feeling was described as unsettled and volatile, owing to drought-induced hunger, and from late April 1900 contagious diseases began to break out with increasing frequency and seriousness. In other parts of Zhili it was much the same. American legation secretary W. E. Bainbridge, noting that during the preceding year "there had been insufficient rain" and that "the entire province was on the verge of famine," concluded that conditions were "peculiarly favorable to its [the Boxer uprising's] friendly reception.... As Spring advanced and early Summer approached with no rains to aid the crops, the excitement... reached a fever heat." From Zhuozhou, just southwest of Beijing, apprehensions were expressed in early June that, if it did not rain soon, it would become increasingly difficult to control the thousands of Boxers who had gathered in the area. A gentry manager of a *baojia* [local level mutual security system] bureau just west of Tianjin reported that in the spring of 1900 young farmers idled by the drought often took up boxing because they had nothing else to do with their time. The relationship among drought, idleness, and augmented Boxer activity found blunt corroboration in the testimony of a former Boxer from the Tianjin area: "*Gengzi* [1900] was a drought year and there was nothing to do, so we began to practice Yihe Boxing."...

Drought conditions in large areas of Shanxi had by summer 1900 become, if anything, even worse than in Zhili. In many places there had been no rain at all since winter. Farmers were without work. The prices of wheat and rice had shot up. Hunger was widespread and popular anxiety at a high pitch. A missionary report stated that the "organization of the Boxer societies spread rapidly throughout the province when so many were idle because of the drouth." The gazetteers of Qinyuan, Quwo, Lin, Jie, Linjin, Xiangning, and Yuci counties all connected the first emergence of the Boxers in mid- or late June to the protracted drought in their areas. Moreover, it was alleged that famine victims regularly joined in when the Boxers stirred up trouble.

I do not at all want to suggest that the expansion of the Boxer movement in the spring and summer of 1900 was due to drought alone. Within a given area, the official stance toward the Boxers, pro (as in Shanxi) or con (as in Shandong), played a role of perhaps equivalent weight. Nevertheless, drought —and the range of emotions associated with it—was a factor of crucial importance. It is significant, in this connection, that in a number of instances when rain fell to interrupt the drought and possibly bring it to an end, Boxers (as well as Big Sword Society members) dropped everything and returned to their fields. Esherick observes that when "a substantial penetrating rain" fell in early April along the Zhili-Shandong border, peasants went home to plant their spring crops, "quieting things down considerably." After being defeated by the foreign forces in Tianjin during a torrential downpour on July 4, fleeing Boxers are reported to have said to one another: "It's raining. We can return home and till the soil. What use is it for us to suffer like this?" The following day, accordingly, most of them dispersed.

Oral history accounts from Shandong tell a similar story. In late June 1900, during the drought in the western part of the province, a Big Sword Society leader from Zhili named Han Guniang (Miss Han) was invited to a Big Sword gathering at the hemp market at Longgu, just west of the Juye county seat. Rumored to be a Red Lantern with extraordinary magical powers—it was said that, in addition to being able to withstand swords and spears, "when she mounted a bench it turned into a horse, when she straddled a piece of rope it turned into a dragon, and when she sat on a mat it turned into a cloud on which she could fly"—Han Guniang took charge of food distribution. Within a short time, upwards of a thousand people joined her Big Swords. The grain she handed out had been seized from the supplies of rich families. "After two or three days," one account continues, "there was a big downpour. The next day there were no Big Swords anywhere in sight. They were all gone. The reason these people had come in the first place was to get something to eat. As soon as it rained, they all went back to tend their crops."

Lin Dunkui, who has made a special study of the role of natural disasters in the history of the Boxers, concludes that "from the time of the first outbreak of the Big Sword Society right up to the high tide of the Boxer movement, a sizable number of peasants were prompted to take part in these movements mainly by the weather." . . .

The Boxer Construction of the Drought

What is fascinating is the degree to which contemporary Chinese—non-Boxers as well as Boxers—also viewed everything that happened in the world, including whether it rained or not, as being in the control of Heaven or "the gods." Indeed, although the Chinese construction of reality differed greatly in specifics from that of the missionaries, in a number of broad respects it formed almost a mirror image of the missionaries' construction. Where the missionaries saw themselves as representatives of the Lord, sometimes describing themselves as "God's soldiers" and often believing quite literally that they had been called by Jesus Christ to go to China to labor for that country's salvation, in jingles repeated and notices circulated throughout North China in 1900 the Boxers were often portrayed, in comparably salvific (as well as martial) terms, as "spirit soldiers" (*shenbing*) sent down from Heaven to carry out a divine mission or, which amounted to the same thing, as mortals whose bodies had been possessed by spirits (thereby rendering them divine) for the identical purpose.

Again, where the missionaries constructed the Boxer movement as a satanic force, whose capacity for evil knew no bounds, the Boxers (and, one presumes, millions of Chinese who were not active participants in the movement) saw the missionaries, and by extension all other foreigners (as well, of course, as Chinese Christians and other Chinese who in one way or another had been tainted by foreign contact), as the root source of evil in their world, the immediate reason for the anger of the gods. The explanation of the drought found in Boxer notices was embedded in a full-blown religious structuring of reality; the notices also provided participants in the movement with a clear program of action designed to mollify the gods and restore the cosmic balance.

Such notices began to be widely circulated at least as early as the beginning of 1900. (It is doubtful that one would encounter drought-related notices much before this date, as it was probably not until the late months of 1899 that people in North China began to experience the protracted dry weather as a "drought.") In February of this year the Tianjin agent of the American Bible Society reported the following text to have been "posted everywhere" in North China: "On account of the Protestant and Catholic religions the Buddhist gods are oppressed, and our sages thrust into the background. The Law of Buddha is no longer respected, and the Five Relationships are disregarded. The anger of Heaven and Earth has been aroused and the timely rain has consequently been withheld from us. But Heaven is now sending down eight millions of spiritual soldiers to extirpate these foreign religions, and when this has been done there will be a timely rain." . . .

Boxer Motives: Anti-Imperialism, Antiforeignism, or Anxiety Over Drought?

The crisis remedy proposed by the Boxers in 1900 reveals a close kinship to that described by [Norman] Cohn for the millenarian movement of 1420. In one placard after another, the Chinese people are enjoined to kill off all foreigners and native Chinese contaminated by foreigners or foreign influence. Only after this process of physical elimination of every trace of the foreign from China has been completed will the gods be appeased and permit the rains once again to fall.

What is peculiar here and needs somehow to be accounted for is why at this particular moment in Chinese history there was such an extreme response to the foreign presence. Chinese had often shown a tendency, during times of military or cultural threat, to lapse into a form of racial thinking that categorized outsiders as fundamentally different and called for their expulsion, and this tendency had been greatly magnified in the nineteenth century with the appearance of "physically discontinuous" Westerners, who also happened to be carriers of a symbolic universe that diverged radically from the Chinese and, directly and indirectly, challenged the validity of the Chinese cultural world. From the early 1800s, people who had had contacts of any sort with Westerners were regularly referred to as "Chinese traitors" (*Hanjian*). More specifically, there had been efforts prior to the Boxer era to link natural disasters (as well as the failure of Chinese prayers to relieve them) with the presence of Christians. And of course there had been no end of anti-Christian and antiforeign incidents in China in the decades leading up to 1900. Never before, however, had there been a movement like the Boxers, uncompromisingly dedicated to the stamping out of foreign influence and backed, all the evidence indicates, by the broadest popular support. How do we explain this?

The reasons are without doubt very complex. Chinese historians, insisting upon the "anti-imperialist and patriotic" (*fandi aiguo*) character of the Boxer movement, tend to assign primary responsibility to the intensification of foreign imperialism in the last years of the nineteenth century. My own view is that the vocabulary of anti-imperialism is so deeply colored by twentieth-century Chinese political concerns and agendas that it gets in the way of the search for a more accurate, credible reading of the Boxer experience. This is not to deny that imperialism was a fact of life in China at the turn of the century or that it formed an important part of the setting within which the Boxer movement unfolded. It was only one causal agency among several, however, and its gravity relative to other causal forces varied considerably from place to place and over time. Furthermore, action taken against the more tangible reflections of imperialism—missionaries and Chinese Christians, railways, telegraphs, foreign armies, and the rest—could, when it occurred, derive from a range of possible motives; it need not have been inspired by either "patriotism" or "anti-imperialism." To superimpose this vocabulary on the Boxer movement, therefore, is to risk radical oversimplification of the complicated and diverse motives impelling the Boxers to behave as they did.

... We have hundreds of samples of Boxer writing—handbills, wall notices, charms, slogans, jingles, and the like. And even though most if not all of these may be assumed to have been composed by Boxer leaders or elite Chinese sympathetic to the Boxer cause rather than by rank-and-file participants in the movement, there is, as argued earlier, little doubt that they incorporate values and beliefs widely shared among the Boxers in general, not to mention millions of Chinese who witnessed and often supported, but were not directly engaged in, the activities of the Boxer movement. Still, as crucially important as these materials are in establishing the mindset of the Boxers, they fall well short of supplying the kind of intimate tracking of experience that we get, say, from the memoir literature of participants in the Cultural Revolution or the heresy trial testimony of the sixteenth-century Italian miller Menocchio or the letters, journals, and even poems composed by British soldiers in the trenches in World War I. In fact, it was not until after 1949 that elderly survivors of the Boxer uprising, mainly in western Shandong and Tianjin and other parts of Hebei (Zhili) province, were finally given a chance to describe more or less in their own words their experiences at the turn of the century. As useful as these oral history materials can sometimes be, however, their value is circumscribed by the advanced age of the respondents, the remoteness in time of the events under discussion, the political and ideological constraints built into the environment within which the interviewing was conducted, the specific questions the interviewers posed, and the editorial process by which the resulting responses were structured.

Consequently, in attempting to get at the range of motives that impelled the Boxers to attack foreigners, foreign-made objects, and foreign-influenced Chinese, we are regularly faced with the necessity of inferring these motives from Boxer actions, of reading back, as it were, from behavior to intent. This is one of the more dangerous kinds of business in which historians must unfortunately all too often engage, as it presents us with an open invitation to discern in the experience of the past the values, thought patterns, and psychological orientations that make the greatest sense to us in our own day.

Although on a macrohistorical level we hear much of the intensification of foreign imperialism that took place in China in the years following the

Sino-Japanese War of 1894, it is arguable that, unlike drought, a conspicuously growing foreign presence was not, in 1899–1900, the common experience of the vast majority of Chinese inhabiting the North China plain. Whether we train our sights on expanded communities of native Christians or the growth in strength of the Catholic and Protestant missionary bodies or the construction of railways and telegraphs or the intrusion of foreign armies, the experience of direct confrontation with the foreign or foreign-influenced remained, for those living away from large urban centers, a sporadic and highly localized one in these years. Despite a substantial increase in the numbers of Protestant and Catholic converts in China as a whole in the 1890s—from approximately 37,000 Protestants in 1889 to 85,000 in 1900, and from about 500,000 to over 700,000 Catholics between 1890 and 1900—there were still, in 1899–1900, large stretches of North China that had Christian communities of negligible size or none at all. Similarly, in the case of both the Catholic and Protestant missionary efforts in the empire, although impressive growth occurred in the last decade of the century, this growth was far more in evidence in certain areas—the greatly expanded Catholic presence in southern Shandong, for example—than in others. Again, as of 1899–1900, the only railway lines that had been completed in North China were the Beijing-Baoding line, the Beijing-Tianjin line, and the line extending northeastward from Tianjin, through Tangshan, into Manchuria. And, leaving out the military activities of the Russians in Manchuria, foreign troop movements in the Boxer summer were largely confined to Tianjin and Beijing, their immediately surrounding areas, and the corridor connecting these two cities (although in the months following the lifting of the siege of the legations, . . . punitive expeditions were carried out in other parts of Zhili and in eastern Shanxi).

In other words, despite an overall expansion in the opportunities for direct contact with foreigners, foreign-influenced Chinese, and foreign technology in the last years of the century, these opportunities were not evenly distributed throughout North China. Furthermore, there is the curious circumstance—curious, at least, if one interprets the behavior of the Boxers as having been guided in significant measure by anti-imperialist impulses—that the areas where the impact of imperialism was greatest often did not coincide with those areas in which the Boxers were most active. This was especially true in Shandong, where the arenas of greatest foreign economic activity—the eastern and southern coasts—were conspicuously free of Boxer involvement and where approximately half of the missionized areas also were left untouched by the Boxers. Mark Elvin, who includes southern Zhili as well as Shandong within his purview, is so struck by the weakness of the link between "Boxerism and the religious and foreign irritant usually supposed to have caused it" that he questions whether it can serve as "a convincing sufficient explanation" of the movement's origins.

I am not particularly concerned here with the origins of the Boxer movement. I do, however, believe that there is room for a fresh understanding of the range of motives that lay behind what was perhaps the Boxers' most distinctive and defining characteristic: their antiforeignism. The reality of Boxer antiforeignism—and the antiforeignism of many millions of Boxer supporters and sympathizers—is not at issue. What is at issue is the underlying meaning of this antiforeignism. Was it a reflection of simple hatred of foreigners owing to their foreignness? Or did it result from anger over specific foreign actions? Or did it spring from fear and anxiety and the need for a credible explanation for the problems—above all, drought—occasioning this fear and anxiety?

My own view is that antiforeignism, in the sense of fear and hatred of outsiders, was there all along in China in latent form, but that it needed some disturbance in the external environment, a rearrangement of the over-all balance of forces within a community or a geographical area, to become activated. Chinese antiforeignism thus functioned in much the same way as fear of witchcraft in late seventeenth-century Salem or anti-Semitism in 1930s Germany. In each of these instances outsiders—Westerners in China, people accused of being witches in Salem, Jews in Germany—lived more or less un-eventfully within their respective communities when times were "normal." But when something happened to create an "abnormal" situation—economic insecurity in Germany, apprehension concerning the enormous economic and social forces transforming New England in the late 1600s, anxiety over drought in turn-of-the-century North China—and people sought in desperation to ad-dress their grievances and allay their insecurities, outsiders became especially vulnerable.

The specific circumstances favoring outbreaks of antiforeignism in North China in 1899–1900 varied from place to place. In Shandong, escalating Boxer anti-Christian activity in late 1899 resulted (under foreign pressure) in the re-placement as governor of Yuxian, who had followed a policy of leniency toward the Boxers, with Yuan Shikai, who, after the killing of the British missionary S. M. Brooks on December 31, pursued an increasingly strong policy of sup-pression. In Zhili province, especially in the Beijing and Tianjin areas and the corridor connecting the two, there was a relatively high level of expo-sure to the full range of foreign influences and, from the winter of 1899–1900, to rapidly growing numbers of Boxers. In Shanxi, where there were no sig-nificant manifestations of foreign influence apart from the missionaries and native Christians, there was a governor (Yuxian having been transferred there in March) who was deeply antiforeign and pro-Boxer.

Although the precise mix of factors was thus variable, the drought was shared in common throughout the North China plain. It was this factor, more than any other, in my judgment, that accounted for the explosive growth both of the Boxer movement and of popular support for it in the spring and summer months of 1900. Missionary reports and oral history accounts occasionally used the term "famine" to describe conditions in North China at the time. This was, for the most part, a loose usage; severe famine did not appear until the early months of 1901, mainly in Shanxi and Shaanxi. The evidence is overwhelm-ing, on the other hand, that *fear* of famine, with all its attendant bewilderment and terror, was extremely widespread. As has often been the case in other agri-cultural societies, moreover, the uncertainty, anxiety, and increasingly serious food deprivation accompanying the Chinese drought—the *delírio de fome* or "madness of hunger," in the arresting formulation of Nancy Scheper-Hughes —seem to have inclined people to be receptive to extreme explanations and to act in extreme ways. The year 1900 was not a normal one in China. The menace of inopportune death was everywhere. And, as can be seen in the periodic eruptions of mass hysteria and the apparent readiness of many members of society to give credence to the most spectacular religious and magical claims of the Boxers, there was a strong disposition on the part of the population to depart from normal patterns of behavior.

Justice on Behalf of Heaven

On the fifth day of the seventh month of the twenty-sixth year of the Guangxu Emperor, Liu Dapeng, a tutor and diarist, stood at the door of his family home in the village of Chiqiao in Shanxi province and watched an army of a thousand Boxers pass through. Liu was a brave man; some forty years later during the Second World War he was to stand on the roof of that same house watching the bombs falling from Japanese planes on his neighbours' houses. When the Boxers passed through, most of the other villagers had fled to the hills or were hiding behind the locked doors of their houses in fear that the Boxer forces would loot and extort money and goods. Liu himself had taken leave from his job as a private tutor in a grand house some twenty or thirty miles away and come home to look after his mother, wife and children because of the crisis. At the head of the Boxers came a young man known as Third Prince, who Liu guessed was less than twenty years old. Two banners before him proclaimed 'Bring justice on behalf of Heaven!' and 'Support the Qing! Destroy the foreign!' Then came rank after rank of men marching down the narrow street that ran through the centre of the village. There were men of all ages, but Liu reckoned that at least two-thirds were not yet adults. All of them wore red belts and red cloths tied around their heads. They marched in an orderly fashion, divided into companies and brigades, and did not, after all, do any damage in the village.

Liu's attitude to the Boxers was divided. On the one hand he approved of their loyalty to the Qing dynasty and their opposition to the expansion of foreign power in China. He was particularly supportive of their campaign against the local Catholics, whom he perceived as having sold out to the foreigners. On the other hand, he was dubious about the movement's religious elements and particularly concerned about the threat they posed to law and order. While he approved of the provincial governor's efforts to force Catholics to renounce their religion, he found it hard to condone the murder of travellers suspected of poisoning wells, let alone pitched battles between Catholic villages and Boxer forces. Liu's feelings, in this respect, were typical of the time and were shared across a wide social spectrum. Indeed, it was just such conflicting attitudes at court that allowed the Boxer movement to spread on such a wide scale. Although events in the northern coastal province of Shandong where the

Boxer movement originated are better known, some of the worst violence in the uprising took place in the adjoining Shanxi province, witnessed by Liu.

The Boxers' opposition in the foreign powers and especially to Christianity struck a chord with many Chinese and drew widespread support. China's defeat by Japan in the war over Korea in 1894 was a turning point in perceptions of the foreign threat. The country's perception of itself as the Middle Kingdom, a central realm of civilisation surrounded by tributary states, and by savages and barbarians beyond that, had been affirmed by Korea, which had conducted an elaborate tributary relationship with China. The loss of Korea, moreover, brought with it humiliating defeat by the Japanese, hitherto often dismissively referred to as 'dwarf pirates'. In the Treaty of Shimonoseki, which concluded the war, China not only agreed to Korean independence, but ceded Taiwan to Japan and gave the Japanese the same treaty rights as those of Westerners. These were the events that roused Sun Yat-sen, later China's first President, to plan his first revolutionary uprising. But it was not only members of China's tiny reformist elite who were concerned at this outcome. The news was carried across the country and was talked about by the farmers in Chiqiao village, all of whom, Liu reported, opposed the terms of the treaty. Li Hongzhang, who had been the chief negotiator on the Chinese side, became extremely unpopular, with rumours circulating in the countryside that he had married his son to the daughter of the Japanese emperor, and satirical rhymes attacking him for selling his country. It is important to remember that, though often condemned as ignorant, superstitious and xenophobic, the Boxers were acting in an environment where China's changing international situation was widely known and resented.

Popular opposition to foreign power was confirmed in Shanxi when news came through in the summer of 1900 that the government had declared war on the foreign powers. Liu heard that governors had been ordered to kill collaborators, that is to say Christians, and to arrest any foreigners and execute them if they planned to make trouble or plotted with the Christians. Shanxi's governor, Yu Xian, was said to be delighted at the news and immediately sent soldiers to round up those foreigners residing in the province and bring them to the provincial capital. Less than a month later some forty unfortunate foreigners were formally executed outside the provincial government building. The Chinese leaders of the Catholic community were ordered to renounce their faith and one who refused was executed. It was thus clear that the government declaration of war on the foreign powers included not only foreign civilians but also Catholic villagers. When the Boxers marched through the countryside carrying banners that said 'Restore the Qing! Destroy the foreign!' their claims that they were loyal forces obeying the orders of the dynasty were hard to deny.

Catholics were seen as potential collaborators in a war with the foreign powers because Christianity had been introduced into China by foreign missionaries. Indeed the right for Christian missionaries to reside in the interior had repeatedly been the object of treaty negotiations between the Qing dynasty and the foreign powers. In Shanxi, the Protestant missionaries had only a handful of converts, but Catholicism was firmly rooted in many rural areas and had been widespread since the eighteenth century. The heart of the problem lay in the contradictions between Christianity and the belief system that underlay the structures of the state. In the villages—where the Boxers operated —the problems of integrating Christianity in the imperial state were focused around the issue of temple festivals and opera performances. Temple festivals were funded by contributions from all members of the local community. In addition to a market they included sacrifices to the deity in whose honour the festival was held and often theatrical performances on a stage facing the temple. Wealthy villages would hire a travelling opera company who would perform for three to five days. Poorer villages might only have a puppet theatre for a single day. The festival performances were intended for the deity but were also a source of entertainment. Friends and relations came from miles around to see the operas, meet and chat, while the market drew large crowds. The funds raised to pay for the opera, meanwhile, also provided a working budget for such village level local government as existed. They might, for example, be used to pay for the dredging of dikes for a communal irrigation system or a law suit against a neighbouring village. Christians, however, refused to pay the levies on the grounds that they would be used to support idolatrous practices.

By refusing to contribute to the festivals, Shanxi Catholics were excluding themselves from the local community. At the same time locals were aware that allowing Christians to opt out of paying taxes made Christianity, which was generally seen as a heterodox religion, a financially advantageous option for the poor, who often turned out to enjoy the festivities even if they had not helped to pay for them. As a result, the 1890s saw an increasing number of legal cases being brought by village leaders against recalcitrant Catholics. The Catholics were able to fight these suits because the foreign consuls, backed by the threat of arms, negotiated with the central government for the right of Christians not to pay for religious practices in which they did not believe. Both the village leaders and the magistrates, however, saw the cases as resting on matters of loyalty and obedience to the state rather than on religious toleration. An extract (translated by Roger Thompson) from one magistrate's interrogation of a Catholic named Yang accused of refusing to pay village levies gives a sense of the way in which Christians were seen as alienating themselves from the state:

Magistrate: You are a person of what country?

Yang: I am a person of the Qing.

Magistrate: If you are a person of the Qing dynasty then why are you following the foreign devils and their seditious religion? You didn't pay your opera money when requested by the village and you were beaten. But how can you dare to bring a suit? Don't you know why Zuo Zongtang went to Beijing? In order to kill—to exterminate—the foreign devils. You certainly ought to pay the opera subscription. If you don't you won't be allowed to live in the land of the Qing. You'll have to leave for a foreign country.

Liu Dapeng, watching the Boxers pass his front door on their way to join an attack on Catholic villages, shared this view. In his opinion:

> When the foreign barbarians preach their religion, they say they are urging men to do good, but in fact they are disrupting our government, creating turmoil in our system, destroying our customs, and deceiving our people; that is to say that they want to turn the people of China into barbarians.

The issue of Catholic refusal to participate in the religious practices of the local community became particularly powerful and problematic in the summer of 1900 because of the fear of drought. Drought was a constant threat to the North China Plain, where farmers rely on rain falling at precisely the right times of year. In Shanxi many remembered with fear the great famine of the 1870s when in Chiqiao one in ten of the population died, and in parts of the south of the province the death toll was worse still. Drought like this was widely seen as divine punishment for immorality and people reacted with ritual and prayer. In Chiqiao men went with bare heads and bare feet to a spring high up in the mountains to pray for rain. The villages through which they passed set up altars in front of their homes laid out with candles, cakes, branches of willow and dragons' heads carved from gourds. As the procession passed through the village the men would repeat the words 'Amitabha Buddha' and the onlookers knelt and used the willow branches to scatter water on them. For three days the men stayed at the temple beside the spring, eating only thin gruel and praying constantly for rain. Such rituals were commonplace throughout northern China in times of drought and were believed to require the sincere participation of the whole community in order to be effective. Catholic refusal to participate in the rituals needed to save the local community from famine accentuated an already problematic relationship.

The conflict between Catholics and villagers meant that the Boxers could be seen as representing and embodying the community even as they attacked and burned their neighbours' homes. With their banners 'Bring justice on behalf of Heaven!' and 'Support the Qing! Destroy the foreign!', they claimed to uphold the moral and social order where the dynasty, because of foreign pressure, was unable to do so. As Liu Dapeng put it, 'the court could not kill the Christians and the officials dared not kill them, so the Boxers killed them.'

However, the people of Chiqiao village, which had no Catholic families at all, nevertheless fled in panic when they heard the Boxers were approaching the village. Doubts lingered about the beliefs and rituals of the Boxers, and about their violence. People expected that boxing, or martial arts, techniques would be learned from a teacher over many years, but these were mostly young boys with hardly any training. Liu Dapeng went to see them practising at a large temple near Chiqiao. They set up sticks of incense and kowtowed to them. Then they stood facing southeast, put their hands in a certain position and recited an invocation to several deities. Immediately they fell on the floor, as if asleep. Then, as the crowds of spectators gathered, their hands and feet began to move and slowly they stood up and began a kind of dance sometimes with weapons, all the time keeping their eyes closed. Although their expressions were terrifying, they somehow looked as if they were drunk. After keeping up these strange movements for a while they fell to the ground again, and eventually awoke. Later they said that they did not remember what they had done while they were in the trance. When one of the onlookers asked what would happen if they had to face guns, they replied that Heaven was angry and had sent them as soldiers to warn the people. This was the 'spirit possession' that was central to the Boxer movement. Spirit possession by semi-professional mediums is a feature of Chinese folk-religious practice, but mass spirit possession of this sort was, as Liu commented, very strange indeed.

But the strangeness of Boxer claims was not limited to spirit possession. As at other times when drought threatened, bizarre rumours were rife. In Shanxi it was said that the wives of the foreign missionaries stood naked on the roofs of their houses fanning back the winds that would have brought rain. Other rumours concerned the Catholics, who were said to be poisoning village water supplies. Western power, and particularly science, was considered to border on black magic in the eyes of much of the population. The same black magic was also attributed to the Chinese Catholics. Rumours spread through Shanxi that Catholics had painted blood on doorways, and where they had done this the entire family would go mad within seven days. The Boxers claimed to have the power to oppose this Catholic magic and Liu saw people washing the blood off their doors with urine as the Boxers instructed. Strange stories told of full-scale battles between the Catholic and the Boxer magic. In a large town near Chiqiao there was a panic one night that the Catholics had come and many of the townspeople went to guard the city walls. When they were there they heard a huge noise like tens of thousands of people attacking and then suddenly a green hand as big as a cartwheel appeared in the air. The local Boxer leader pointed at it and there was a crash of thunder and rain began to fall. He explained that the green hand had been a form of Catholic magic and he had destroyed it. Outside the city wall the villagers saw the lights, heard strange noises and fled from their homes in panic to hide in the fields. It is clear that such stories were widely believed at the time, and yet there was always an underlying distrust. The next morning, when the villagers cautiously emerged from their hiding places, they realised that there had been no Catholic army and no battle. The fear of drought inevitably gave rise to rumours, but many, including Liu, were not wholly convinced by the magical claims of the Boxers.

Distrust of the Boxers' spiritual powers was increased by a growing realisation of the threat they posed to law and order. This began with the murder of people accused of poisoning wells. Most of these were not even Catholics, but were accused of being in their pay. Magistrates, unsure of how to respond to the movement, failed to investigate the crimes and Boxer confidence grew. Large groups of men assembled and began to fight their Catholic neighbours. The army of men that Liu saw marching through his village had gone out to a nearby village which had a sizable Catholic population. The Catholics had hired men from another province to protect them and had withdrawn to their solidly-built stone church. The Boxers besieged the church and the battle lasted for six days. More than thirty of the mercenaries were killed before the church fell. A few of the Catholics survived the seige and escaped, but the rest were massacred and the church burned.

Magistrates' failure to act in the face of such disorder was due to the weakness and indecision of the central government, which vacillated between support for the Boxers and fear of the foreign powers. For more than fifty years the foreign threat had been at the centre of factional divisions within the court. At the heart of this debate was the question of whether a modern, well-equipped army or popular feeling should be more important in withstanding the foreign powers. The leaders of the bureaucracy were examined and trained in Confucian thought and for many of them it was an article of faith that victory in battle would be the result of the people's support. On the other side stood a faction, many of whom were drawn from the Manchu ruling ethnic group, who had accepted the strength of the European powers and believed that it was necessary to approach them cautiously until such time as China had built up the technical expertise to face them. The radical Confucians saw the growth of the Boxer movement as a sign that the people were at last aroused to fight the foreigners. Putting their trust in this, they were prepared to overlook the folk-religious aspects of the movement, which were clearly at odds with Confucian rationalism, and also the inevitable threat to law and order that would arise if the people were allowed to bear arms outside state control. With the support of the ruling Empress Dowager the court declared war on the foreign powers. However, the more cautious modernisers, many of whom had power bases in the southern provinces, believed that China was still unable to defeat the foreign powers; the governors general of the southern provinces refused to enter the war. Instead they drew up private agreements with the foreign powers, giving protection to foreigners and Christians in return for a promise that the foreigners would not invade. Although the Confucian radicals had won at court the central government was not strong enough to control the regions. The result was indecision and a series of conflicting orders. The Qing army never really engaged with the foreign troops, but country magistrates dared not arrest the Boxers, and thus appeared to be encouraging the movement to spread.

The debate over whether the Boxers should be seen as loyal and patriotic enforcers of the moral order or superstitious and xenophobic peasants has remained at the heart of Chinese perceptions of the uprising. In the early years of the twentieth century the modernisers, who had added a desire for the adoption of Western culture to their Qing predecessors' perception of the need for Western technology, continued to criticise the movement. Indeed, for this group in the 1910s and 20s, the failure of the uprising to solve China's problems by driving out the foreigners was symbolic of the failure of China's encounters with the West. The Boxers embodied what the modernisers saw as the very national characteristics that had led to China's international weakness. They were depicted as ignorant and conservative, a group whose folly and credulous belief that they could be saved from bullets by reciting magic rhymes had ultimately led to the imposition of the huge Boxer Indemnity that sunk the nation in the burden of debt.

However, from the 1920s onwards, a new generation of historians and politicians began to rewrite history in terms of China's resistance to Western imperialism, rather than of its development towards modernity. The events of 1900 came to be known, as they are in China today, not as the Boxer Uprising but as the invasion of the Eight Allied Armies, thus shifting the focus from the Boxers themselves to the foreign response. In addition, the Communists took over the mantle of the radical Confucians in their belief in the centrality of mass popular movements as the foundation of resistance to foreign powers. During the Cultural Revolution in the 1960s the Boxers were depicted as heroic, anti-imperialist fighters while the threat they posed to law and order was reconstructed as rebellious opposition to the forces of feudalism. The mass spirit possession and other elements of folk religion at the centre of the movement were completely ignored. The story of the Boxers was rewritten as one of peasant rebellion against foreign imperialism.

Since the 1980s there has been renewed interest in the Boxers. Chinese social historians are beginning to integrate popular folk religion and mass spirit possession into their interpretations of the movement. However, the ambivalence between interpretations of the Boxers as patriots or a superstitious and disorderly rabble has continued to form the framework of the argument. The ambivalence of contemporaries who observed the Boxers and which in many ways created the movement as a national phenomenon has continued to inform Chinese interpretations of the uprising.

POSTSCRIPT

Were Environmental Factors and Their Psychological Effect on Chinese Society Responsible for the Boxer Rebellion?

Many problems arise when current interpretations of the Boxer uprising as a historical movement are attempted. One concerns motivation, the subject covered in this issue. Another concerns how the Boxers themselves should be viewed. Were they, as Harrison expresses it, "loyal and patriotic enforcers of the moral order or superstitious and xenophobic peasants"? Finally, as Cohen points out, an important question is, How do we separate Boxer myth from Boxer reality? All of these questions form the basis of all historical inquiry and answers to them must be sought.

Complicating matters is China's status today as a communist nation, adhering to a strict Marxist interpretation of history. There is strong pressure in such a society to fit historical events into this predetermined historical theory, and sometimes the truth can be lost within that process. But even as China's needs change, so does its history. According to Harrison, during the cultural revolution of the 1960s, "The story of the Boxers was rewritten as one of peasant rebellion against foreign imperialism," different from previous Chinese interpretations of the movement. See Hu Sheng's *From the Opium War to the May Fourth Movement*, 2 vols. (Foreign Language Press, 1991) for an analysis of the major events in Chinese history from 1840 to 1920 from a Marxist perspective.

Joseph W. Eshrick's *The Origins of the Boxer Uprising* (University of California Press, 1987) was an important modern work that encouraged others to pursue the Boxers-as-history movement. Cohen's *History in Three Keys: The Boxers as Event, Experience, and Myth* (Columbia University Press, 1997) is an interesting companion, and when combined with Sheng's work mentioned earlier, provides the reader with three different points of view on the Boxer uprising.

The centenary anniversary of the Boxer uprising has produced a number of interesting articles on the subject. R. G. Tiedemann's "Baptism of Fire: China's Christians and the Boxer Uprising of 1900," *International Bulletin of Missionary Research* (January 2000) views the rebellion as a "tragic anomaly" in China's relationship with Christian missionaries. Robert Bickers, in "Chinese Burns Britain in China, 1842–1900," *History Today* (August 2000), places the blame for the Boxer rebellion squarely on the shoulders of British and European imperialism.

Finally, for a more popularly written account of the Boxer uprising, see Diane Preston, *The Boxer Rebellion: The Dramatic Story of China's War on Foreigners That Shook the World in the Summer of 1900* (Walker & Company, 2000).

ISSUE 8

Were German Militarism and Diplomacy Responsible for World War I?

YES: V. R. Berghahn, from *Imperial Germany, 1871–1914: Economy, Society, Culture, and Politics* (Berghahn Books, 1994)

NO: Samuel R. Williamson, Jr., from "The Origins of the War," in Hew Strachan, ed., *The Oxford Illustrated History of the First World War* (Oxford University Press, 1998)

ISSUE SUMMARY

YES: History professor V. R. Berghahn states that, although all of Europe's major powers played a part in the onset of World War I, recent evidence still indicates that Germany's role in the process was the main factor responsible for the conflict.

NO: History professor Samuel R. Williamson, Jr., argues that the factors and conditions that led to the First World War were a shared responsibility and that no one nation can be blamed for its genesis.

One could argue that the First World War was the twentieth century's most cataclysmic event. It was responsible for the destruction of four major empires (Turkish, Russian, Austrian, and German), was tied inexorably to the rise of fascism and communism, and caused more death and carnage than any event up to that time. It also created an age of anxiety and alienation that shook the foundations of the Western artistic, musical, philosophical, and literary worlds. No wonder it has attracted the attention of countless historians, who have scrutinized every aspect in search of lessons that can be derived from it.

The major historical questions to answer are why it occurred and who was responsible for it—a daunting task yet an important one if we are to learn any lessons from the mistakes of the past. Historians have identified four major long-range causes of the war: nationalism, militarism, imperialism, and the alliance system. But these causes only partly answer why in August 1914, after a Serbian nationalist assassinated Archduke Franz Ferdinand of Austria-Hungary, Europe divided into two armed camps—the Allied Governments (England, France, and Russia, and later, Italy) and the Central Powers (Germany,

Austria-Hungary, and the Ottoman Empire)—and engaged in a conflict that would involve most European countries and spread to the rest of the world.

Important as these factors are, they fail to include the human factor in the equation. To what extent were the aims and policies of the major powers, which were formulated by individuals acting on behalf of national states, responsible for the war? Is there enough culpability to go around? Or was one nation and its policymakers responsible for the onset of the Great War? Of course, the Treaty of Versailles, which brought an end to the war, answered the question of responsibility. In the now-famous Article 231, Germany and her allies were held accountable for the war and all concomitant damages since the war was imposed on the Allied and Associated Governments "by the aggression of Germany and her Allies." Little or no historical investigation went into making this decision; it was simply a case of winners dictating terms to losers.

The first to write of the war were the diplomats, politicians, and military leaders who tried to distance themselves from responsibility for what they allowed to happen and offered explanations for their actions suited to their country's needs and interests. Historian Sidney Bradshaw Fay was the first to offer an unbiased interpretation of the war's onset. In a monumental two-volume work, *Before Sarajevo: The Origins of the World War* and *After Sarajevo: The Origins of the World War* (The Macmillan Company, 1928), he states that liability has to be shared by all involved parties. To find Germany and her allies solely responsible for it, "in view of the evidence now available, is historically unsound" (vol. 2, p. 558).

Unfortunately, the influence of Fay's work was minimized by the effects of the worldwide economic depression and the fast-approaching Second World War. The historiography of the First World War was temporarily put on hold. It was reopened after 1945 with some surprising results.

In 1961 German historian Fritz Fischer's *Germany's Aims in the First World War* (W. W. Norton, 1967) ignited the debate. While believing that no nation involved in the war was blameless, Fischer found primary culpability in the expansionist, militarist policies of the German government. The book sparked a national controversy that later moved into the international arena. Thus, two works published more than 30 years apart established the framework of the debate.

Recent historical scholarship seems to balance both sides of the World War I historical pendulum. V. R. Berghahn, working within the framework of Germany's economy, society, culture, and politics from 1871 to 1914, holds Germany primarily responsible for the war. Samuel R. Williamson, Jr., sees the onset of World War I as a condition of joint responsibility.

The Crisis of July 1914 and Conclusions

In the afternoon of August 1, 1914, when the German ultimatum to Russia to revoke the Tsarist mobilization order of the previous day had expired, Wilhelm II telephoned [Chief of the General Staff Helmuth von] Moltke, [Reich Chancellor Theobald von] Bethmann Hollweg, [Admiral Alfred von] Tirpitz, and Prussian War Minister Erich von Falkenhayn to come without delay to the Imperial Palace to witness the Kaiser's signing of the German mobilization order that was to activate the Schlieffen Plan and the German invasion of Luxemburg, Belgium, and France. It was a decision that made a world war inevitable.

The meeting took place at 5 p.m. When the monarch had signed the fateful document, he shook Falkenhayn's hand and tears came to both men's eyes. However, the group had barely dispersed when it was unexpectedly recalled. According to the later report of the Prussian War Minister, "a strange telegram had just been received from Ambassador Lichnowsky" in London, announcing that he had been mandated by the British government "to ask whether we would pledge not to enter French territory if England guaranteed France's neutrality in our conflict with Russia." A bitter dispute apparently ensued between Bethmann Hollweg, who wanted to explore this offer, and Moltke, whose only concern by then was not to upset the meticulously prepared timetable for mobilization. The Chief of the General Staff lost the argument for the moment. The Kaiser ordered Foreign Secretary Gottlieb von Jagow to draft a reply to Lichnowsky, while Moltke telephoned the Army Command at Trier ordering the Sixteenth Division to stop its advance into Luxemburg. As Falkenhayn recorded the scene, Moltke was by now "a broken man" because to him the Kaiser's decision was yet another proof that the monarch "continued to hope for peace." Moltke was so distraught that Falkenhayn had to comfort him, while the latter did not believe for one moment "that the telegram [would] change anything about the horrendous drama that began at 5 p.m." Lichnowsky's reply arrived shortly before midnight, detailing the British condition that Belgium's border must remain untouched by the Germans. Knowing that German strategic planning made this impossible, Moltke now pressed Wilhelm II to order the occupation of Luxemburg as a first step to the German invasion of Belgium and France. This time he won; World War I had definitely begun.

From V. R. Berghahn, *Imperial Germany, 1871–1914: Economy, Society, Culture, and Politics* (Berghahn Books, 1994). Copyright © 1994 by Volker R. Berghahn. Reprinted by permission of Berghahn Books. Notes omitted.

After many years of dispute among historians about who was responsible for the outbreak of war in August 1914 in which German scholars either blamed the Triple Entente for what had happened or argued that all powers had simultaneously slithered into the abyss, the . . . Fischer controversy [a controversy involving historian Frite Fischer's theory of the origin of World War I] produced a result that is now widely accepted in the international community of experts on the immediate origins of the war—it was the men gathered at the Imperial Palace in Berlin who pushed Europe over the brink. These men during the week prior to August 1 had, together with the "hawks" in Vienna, deliberately exacerbated the crisis, although they were in the best position to de-escalate and defuse it. There is also a broad consensus that during that crucial week major conflicts occurred between the civilian leadership in Berlin around Bethmann Hollweg, who was still looking for diplomatic ways out of the impasse, and the military leadership around Moltke, who now pushed for a violent settling of accounts with the Triple Entente. In the end Bethmann lost, and his defeat opened the door to the issuing of the German mobilization order on August 1.

In pursuing this course, the German decision-makers knew that the earlier Russian mobilization order did not have the same significance as the German one. Thus the Reich Chancellor informed the Prussian War Ministry on July 30, that "although the Russian mobilization has been declared, her mobilization measures cannot be compared with those of the states of Western Europe." He added that St. Petersburg did not "intend to wage war, but has only been forced to take these measures because of Austria" and her mobilization. These insights did not prevent the German leadership from using the Russian moves for their purposes by creating a defensive mood in the German public without which the proposed mobilization of the German armed forces might well have come to grief. The population was in no mood to support an aggressive war. On the contrary, there had been peace demonstrations in various cities when, following the Austrian ultimatum to Serbia on 23 July, suspicions arose that Berlin and Vienna were preparing for a war on the Balkans. The Reich government responded to this threat by calling on several leaders on the right wing of the SPD [Social Democratic Party] executive and confidentially apprising them of Russia's allegedly aggressive intentions. Convinced of the entirely defensive nature of Germany's policy, the leaders of the working-class movement quickly reversed their line: the demonstrations stopped and the socialist press began to write about the Russian danger.

It is against the background of these domestic factors that a remark by Bethmann may be better understood. "I need," the Reich Chancellor is reported to have said to Albert Ballin, the Hamburg shipping magnate, "my declaration of war for reasons of internal politics." What he meant by this is further elucidated by other surviving comments. Thus Admiral von Müller, the Chief of the Naval Cabinet, noted in his diary as early as July 27 that "the tenor of our policy [is] to remain calm to allow Russia to put herself in the wrong, but then not to shrink from war if it [is] inevitable." On the same day, the Reich Chancellor told the Kaiser that "at all events Russia must ruthlessly be put in the wrong." Moltke explained the meaning of this statement to his Austro-Hungarian counterpart,

Franz Conrad von Hoetzendorff, on July 30: "War [must] not be declared on Russia, but [we must] wait for Russia to attack." And when a day later this turned out to be the sequence of events, Müller was full of praise. "The morning papers," he recorded in his diary on August 1, "reprint the speeches made by the Kaiser and the Reich Chancellor to an enthusiastic crowd in front of the Schloss and the Chancellor's palace. Brilliant mood. The government has succeeded very well in making us appear as the attacked."

While there is little doubt about the last days of peace and about who ended them, scholarly debate has continued over the motives of the Kaiser and his advisors. In order to clarify these, we have to move back in time to the beginning of July 1914. Fritz Fischer has argued in his *Griff nach der Weltmacht* and in *War of Illusions* that the Reich government seized the assassination of Archduke Ferdinand and his wife at Sarajevo on June 28 as the opportunity to bring about a major war. He asserted that Bethmann, in unison with the military leadership hoped to achieve by force the breakthrough to world power status which German diplomacy had failed to obtain by peaceful means in previous years. However, today most experts would accept another interpretation that was put forward by Konrad Jarausch and others and captured by a chapter heading in Jarausch's biography of Bethmann: "The Illusion of Limited War." In this interpretation, Berlin was originally motivated by more modest objectives than those inferred by Fischer. Worried by the volatile situation on the Balkans and anxious to stabilize the deteriorating position of the multinational Austro-Hungarian Empire (Germany's only reliable ally, then under the strong centrifugal pressure of Slav independence movements), Berlin pushed for a strategy of local war in order to help the Habsburgs in the southeast. Initially, Vienna was not even sure whether to exploit, in order to stabilize its position in power politics, the assassination crisis and the sympathies that the death of the heir to the throne had generated internationally. Emperor Franz Joseph and his civilian advisors wanted to wait for the outcome of a government investigation to see how far Serbia was behind the Sarajevo murders before deciding on a possible punitive move against Belgrade. Only the Chief of the General Staff Conrad advocated an immediate strike against the Serbs at this point. Uncertain of Berlin's response, Franz Joseph sent Count Alexander von Hoyos to see the German Kaiser, who then issued his notorious "blank check." With it the Reich government gave its unconditional support to whatever action Vienna would decide to take against Belgrade.

What did Wilhelm II and his advisors expect to be the consequences of such an action? Was it merely the pretext for starting a major war? Or did Berlin hope that the conflict between Austria-Hungary and Serbia would remain limited? The trouble with answering this question is that we do not possess a first-hand account of the Kaiser's "blank check" meeting with Hoyos and of the monarch's words and assumptions on that occasion. Jarausch and others have developed the view that Bethmann persuaded Wilhelm II and the German military to adopt a limited war strategy which later turned out to be illusory. They have based their argument to a considerable extent on the diaries of Kurt Riezler, Bethmann's private secretary, who was in close contact with his superior during the crucial July days. As he recorded on July 11, it was the Reich Chancellor's plan to obtain "a quick fait accompli" in the Balkans. Thereafter he proposed to make "friendly overtures toward the Entente Powers" in the hope that in this way "the shock" to the international system could be absorbed. Two days earlier Bethmann had expressed the view that "in case of warlike complications between Austria and Serbia, he and Jagow believed that it would be possible to localize the conflagration." But according to Riezler the Reich Chancellor also realized that "an action against Serbia [could] result in a world war." To this extent, his strategy was a "leap into the dark" which he nevertheless considered it as his "gravest duty" to take in light of the desperate situation of the two Central European monarchies.

A localization of the conflict since the risks of a major war seemed remote —this is how Bethmann Hollweg appears to have approached the post-Sarajevo situation. It was only in subsequent weeks, when Vienna took much longer than anticipated to mobilize against Serbia—and above all when it became clear that the other great powers and Russia in particular would not condone a humiliation of Belgrade—that the Reich Chancellor and his advisors became quite frantic and unsure of their ability to manage the unfolding conflict. In its panic, the German Foreign Ministry proposed all sorts of hopelessly unrealistic moves and otherwise tried to cling to its original design. Thus on 16 July, Bethmann wrote to Count Siegfried von Roedern that "in case of an Austro-Serbian conflict the main question is to isolate this dispute." On the following day the Saxon chargé d'affaires to Berlin was informed that "one expects a localization of the conflict since England is absolutely peaceable and France as well as Russia likewise do not feel inclined toward war." On 18 July, Jagow reiterated that "we wish to localize [a] potential conflict between Austria and Serbia." And another three days later the Reich Chancellor instructed his ambassadors in St. Petersburg, Paris, and London that "we urgently desire a localization of the conflict; any intervention by another power will, in view of the divergent alliance commitments, lead to incalculable consequences."

The problem with Bethmann's limited war concept was that by this time it had become more doubtful than ever that it could be sustained. Another problem is that Jarausch's main source, the Riezler diaries, have come under a cloud since the Berlin historian Bernd Sösemann discovered that, for the July days, they were written on different paper and attached to the diary as a loose-leaf collection. This has led Sösemann to believe that Riezler "reworked" his original notes after World War I. Without going into the details of these charges and the defense and explanations that Karl Dietrich Erdmann, the editor of the diaries, has provided, their doubtful authenticity would seem to preclude continued reliance on this source unless other documents from early July corroborate the localization hypothesis. This would seem to indicate at the same time that the strategy was not just discussed and adopted in the Bethmann Circle, but by the entire German leadership, including the Kaiser and the military. Several such sources have survived. Thus on July 5, the Kaiser's adjutant general, Count Hans von Plessen, entered in his diary that he had been ordered to come to the New Palace at Potsdam in the late afternoon of that day to be told about the Hoyos mission and Francis Joseph's letter to Wilhelm II. Falkenhayn, Bethmann, and the Chief of the Military Cabinet Moritz von Lyncker were also present. According to Plessen, the view predominated that "the sooner the Austrians move against Serbia the better and that the Russians—though Serbia's friends—would not come in. H.M.'s departure on his Norwegian cruise is supposed to go ahead undisturbed."

Falkenhayn's report about the same meeting to Moltke, who was on vacation, had a similar tone. Neither of the two letters which the Kaiser had received from Vienna, both of which painted "a very gloomy picture of the general situation of a Dual Monarchy as a result of Pan-Slav agitations," spoke "of the need for war"; "rather both expound 'energetic' political action such as conclusion of a treaty with Bulgaria, for which they would like to be certain of the support of the Germain Reich." Falkenhayn added that Bethmann "appears to have as little faith as I do that the Austrian government is really in earnest, even though the language is undeniably more resolute than in the past." Consequently he expected it to be "a long time before the treaty with Bulgaria is concluded." Moltke's "stay at Spa will therefore scarcely need to be curtailed," although Falkenhayn thought it "advisable to inform you of the gravity of the situation so that anything untoward which could, after all, occur at any time, should not find you wholly unprepared."

Another account of the "blank check" meeting on July 5 comes from Captain Albert Hopman of the Reich Navy Office. On the following day he reported to Tirpitz, who was vacationing in Switzerland, that Admiral Eduard von Capelle, Tirpitz's deputy, was "ordered this morning to go to the New Palace at Potsdam" where Wilhelm II briefed him on the previous day's events. Again the Kaiser said that he had backed Vienna in its demand "for the most far-reaching satisfaction" and, should this not be granted, for military action against Serbia. Hopman's report continued: "H.M. does not consider an intervention by Russia to back up Serbia likely, because the Tsar would not wish to support the regicides and because Russia is at the moment totally unprepared militarily and financially. The same applied to France, especially with respect to finance. H.M. did not mention Britain." Accordingly, he had "let Emperor Franz Joseph know that he could rely on him." The Kaiser believed "that the situation would clear up again after a week owing to Serbia's backing down, but he nevertheless considers it necessary to be prepared for a different outcome." With this in mind, Wilhelm II had "had a word yesterday with the Reich Chancellor, the Chief of the General Staff, the War Minister, and the Deputy Chief of the Admiralty Staff" although "measures which are likely to arouse political attention or to cause special expenditures are to be avoided for the time being." Hopman concluded by saying that "H.M., who, as Excellency von Capelle says, made a perfectly calm, determined impression on him, has left for Kiel this morning to go aboard his yacht for his Scandinavian cruise." That Moltke, clearly a key player in any German planning, had also correctly understood the message that he had received from Berlin and approved of the localization strategy is evidenced by his comment: "Austria must beat the Serbs and then make peace quickly, demanding an Austro-Serbian alliance as the sole condition. Just as Prussia did with Austria in 1866."

If, in the face of this evidence, we accept that Berlin adopted a limited war strategy at the beginning of July which turned out later on to have been badly miscalculated, the next question to be answered is: Why did the Kaiser and his advisors fall for "the illusion of limited war"? To understand this and the pressures on them to take action, we must consider the deep pessimism by which they had become affected and which also pervades the Riezler diaries.

In his account of the origins of World War I, James Joll, after a comprehensive survey of various interpretations, ultimately identified "the mood of 1914" as the crucial factor behind Europe's descent into catastrophe. Although he admits that this mood can "only be assessed approximately and impressionistically" and that it "differed from country to country or from class to class," he nevertheless comes to the conclusion that "at each level there was a willingness to risk or to accept war as a solution to a whole range of problems, political, social, international, to say nothing of war as apparently the only way of resisting a direct physical threat." In his view, it is therefore "in an investigation of the mentalities of the rulers of Europe and their subjects that the explanation of the causes of the war will ultimately lie." There is much substance in this perspective on the origins of the war, but it may require further sociological differentiation with regard to the supposedly pervasive pessimistic sense that a cataclysm was inevitable. As in other countries, there were also many groups in German society that were not affected by the gloomsters and, indeed, had hopes and expectations of a better future. They adhered to the view that things could be transformed and improved. After all, over the past two decades the country had seen a period of unprecedented growth and prosperity. German technology, science, and education, as well as the welfare and health care systems, were studied and copied in other parts of the world. There was a vibrant cultural life at all levels, and even large parts of the working-class movement, notwithstanding the hardships and inequalities to which it was exposed, shared a sense of achievement that spurred many of its members to do even better. As the urbanization, industrialization, and secularization of society unfolded, German society, according to the optimists, had become more diverse, modern, colorful, complex, and sophisticated.

However, these attitudes were not universally held. There were other groups that had meanwhile been overcome by a growing feeling that the *Kaiserreich* was on a slippery downhill slope. Some intellectuals, as we have seen, spoke of the fragmentation and disintegration of the well-ordered bourgeois world of the nineteenth century. Their artistic productions reflected a deep cultural pessimism, a mood that was distinctly postmodern. Some of them even went so far as to view war as the only way of the malaise into which modern civilization was said to have maneuvered itself. Only a "bath of steel," they believed, would produce the necessary and comprehensive rejuvenation. If these views had been those of no more than a few fringe groups, their diagnoses of decadence and decline would have remained of little significance. The point is that they were shared, albeit with different arguments, by influential elite groups who were active in the realm of politics. The latter may have had no more than an inkling of the artistic discourse that was pushing beyond modernism, but they, too, assumed that things were on the verge of collapse, especially in the sphere of politics. Here nothing seemed to be working anymore.

The sense of crisis in the final years was most tangible in the field of foreign policy. The monarch and his civilian and military advisors along with many others felt encircled by the Triple Entente. Over the years and certainly after the conclusion of the Franco-British Entente Cordiale in 1904 and the Anglo-Russian accord of 1907 they had convinced themselves that Britain, France, and Russia were bent on throttling the two Central Powers. While the Anglo-German naval arms race had gone into reverse due to Tirpitz's inability to sustain it financially, the military competition on land reached new heights in 1913 after the ratification of massive army bills in Germany, France, and Russia.

However, by then tensions on the European continent were fueled by more than political and military rivalries. [I]n the early 1890s Germany finally abandoned Bismarck's attempts to separate traditional diplomacy from commercial policy. Reich Chancellor Caprivi had aligned the two before Bülow expanded the use of trade as an instrument of German foreign policy following the Tsarist defeat in the Far East at the hands of the Japanese in 1904 and the subsequent revolution of 1905. By 1913 a dramatic change of fortunes had taken place. Russian agriculture had been hit hard by Bülow's protectionism after 1902, and now it looked as if St. Petersburg was about to turn the tables on Berlin. As the correspondent of *Kölnische Zeitung* reported from Russia on March 2, 1914, by the fall of 1917 the country's economic difficulties would be overcome, thanks in no small degree to further French loans. With Germany's commercial treaties coming up for renewal in 1916, the Tsar was expected to do to the Reich what Bülow had done to the Romanov Empire in earlier years. Accordingly an article published in April 1914 in Deutscher Aussenhandel warned that "it hardly requires any mention that in view of the high-grade political tension between the two countries any conflict in the field of commercial policy implies a serious test of peace."

What, in the eyes of Germany's leadership, made the specter of a Russo-German trade war around 1916 so terrifying was that this was also the time when the French and Russian rearmament programs would be completed. Not surprisingly, this realization added the powerful Army leadership to the ranks of German pessimists. Given the precarious strategic position of the two Central European monarchies, the thought that the Tsarist army was to reach its greatest strength in 1916 triggered bouts of depression, especially in Moltke, the Chief of the General Staff, and Conrad, his Austro-Hungarian counterpart. By March 1914 the latter's worries had become so great that he wondered aloud to the head of his Operations Department, Colonel Joseph Metzger, "if one should wait until France and Russia [are] prepared to invade us jointly or if it [is] more desirable to settle the inevitable conflict at an earlier date. Moreover, the Slav question [is] becoming more and more difficult and dangerous for us."

A few weeks later Conrad met with Moltke at Karlsbad, where they shared their general sense of despair and confirmed each other in the view that time was running out. Moltke added that "to wait any longer [means] a diminishing of our chances; [for] as far as manpower is concerned, one cannot enter into a competition with Russia." Back in Berlin, Moltke spoke to Jagow about his meeting at Karlsbad, with the latter recording that the Chief of the General Staff was "seriously worried" about "the prospects of the future." Russia would have "completed her armaments in two or three years time," and "the military superiority of our enemies would be so great then that he did not know how we might cope with them." Accordingly Moltke felt that "there was no alternative to waging a preventive war in order to defeat the enemy as long as we could still more or less pass the test." He left it to Jagow "to gear our policy to an early unleashing of war." That Russia had become something of an obsession not just for the generals, but also for the civilian leadership, can be gauged from a remark by Bethmann, as he cast his eyes across his estate northeast of Berlin. It would not be worth it, he is reported to have said, to plant trees there when in a few years' time the Russians would be coming anyway.

However serious Germany's international situation may have been, the Reich Chancellor and his colleagues were no less aware of the simultaneous difficulties on the domestic front. Surveying the state of the Prusso-German political system in early 1914, it was impossible to avoid the impression that it was out of joint. The Kaiser's prestige was rapidly evaporating.... The government was unable to forge lasting alliances and compromises with the parties of the Right and the center—the only political forces that a monarchical Reich Chancellor could contemplate as potential partners for the passage of legislation. Meanwhile the "revolutionary" Social Democrats were on the rise and had become the largest party in the Reichstag. The next statutory elections were to be held in 1916/17 and no one knew how large the leftist parties would then become. Faced with these problems and fearful of a repetition of the 1913 tax compromise between the parties of the center and the SPD, Bethmann had virtually given up governing. The state machinery was kept going by executive decrees that did not require legislative approval. At the same time the debt crisis continued. Worse, since 1910 there had been massive strike movements, first against the Prussian three-class voting system and later for better wages and working conditions. While the integration of minorities ran into growing trouble, reflecting problems of alienation among larger sections of the population who felt left behind and were now looking for convenient scapegoats, the working class became increasingly critical of the monarchy's incapacity to reform itself. Even parts of the women's movement had begun to refuse the place they had been assigned in the traditional order. So the situation appeared to be one of increasing polarization, and the major compromises that were needed to resolve accumulating problems at home and abroad were nowhere in sight. Even increased police repression and censorship was no longer viable.

Even if it is argued, with the benefit of hindsight, that all this did not in effect amount to a serious crisis, in the minds of many loyal monarchists and their leaders it certainly had begun to look like one. Perceptions are important here because they shaped the determination for future action and compelled those who held the levers of power to act "before it was too late." With the possibilities of compromise seemingly exhausted and the Kaiser and his advisors running out of options that were not checkmated by other political forces, there was merely one arena left in which they still had unrestricted freedom of action. It is also the arena where the broad structural picture that has been offered in previous chapters links up with the more finely textured analysis put forward in the present one. [T]he Reich Constitution gave the monarch and his advisors the exclusive right to decide whether the country would go to war or stay at peace. It was this prerogative that was now to be used in the expectation that a war would result in a restabilization of Germany's and Austria-Hungary's international and domestic situation. The question was, what kind of war would achieve this objective? From all we know and have said about the early response to the assassinations of Sarajevo, this was not the moment to unleash a world war with its incalculable risks. The conservatives in Berlin and Vienna were not that extremist. They expected that war would lead to a major breakthrough in the Balkans and would stabilize the Austria-Hungarian Empire against Serb nationalism. If Moltke's above-mentioned reference to Prussia's victory over Austria in 1866 is any guide, memories of that war may indeed have played a role in German calculations. After all, the Prusso-Austrian had been a limited war in Central Europe, and it had the added benefit of solving the stalemate in Prussian domestic politics, in the wake of the constitutional conflict. Bismarck's "splendid" victory not only produced, after a snap election, a conservative majority in the Prussian Diet that enabled him to overcome the legislative deadlock that had existed since 1862, but it also "proved" that such "shocks" to the international system could be absorbed without further crisis.

And so the Kaiser and his advisors encouraged Vienna to launch a limited war in the Balkans. Their expectations that the war would remain limited turned out to be completely wrong. The Kaiser and his entourage, who under the Reich Constitution at that brief moment held the fate of millions in their hands, were not prepared to beat a retreat and to avoid a world war. The consequences of that total war and the turmoil it caused in all spheres of life were enormous. The world had been turned upside down.

The Origins of the War

Sarajevo

Košutnjak Park, Belgrade, mid-May 1914: Gavrilo Princip fires his revolver at an oak tree, training for his part in the plot. Those practice rounds were the first shots of what would become the First World War. Princip, a Bosnian Serb student, wanted to murder Archduke Franz Ferdinand, heir to the Habsburg throne, when the latter visited the Bosnian capital of Sarajevo. Princip had become involved with a Serbian terrorist group—the Black Hand. Directed by the head of Serbian military intelligence, Colonel Dragutin Dimitrijević (nicknamed Apis, 'the Bull'), the Black Hand advocated violence in the creation of a Greater Serbia. For Princip and Apis, this meant ending Austria-Hungary's rule over Bosnia-Hercegovina through any means possible.

Princip proved an apt pupil. If his co-conspirators flinched or failed on Sunday, 28 June 1914, he did not. Thanks to confusion in the archduke's entourage after an initial bomb attack, the young Bosnian Serb discovered the official touring car stopped within 6 feet of his location. Princip fired two quick shots. Within minutes the archduke and his wife Sophie were dead in Sarajevo.

Exactly one month later, on 28 July, Austria-Hungary declared war on Serbia. What began as the third Balkan war would, within a week, become the First World War. Why did the murders unleash first a local and then a wider war? What were the longer-term, the mid-range, and the tactical issues that brought Europe into conflict? What follows is a summary of current historical thinking about the July crisis, while also suggesting some different perspectives on the much studied origins of the First World War....

Vienna's Response to the Assassination

The Serbian terrorist plot had succeeded. But that very success also threatened [Serbian Prime Minister Nikolai] Pašić's civilian government. Already at odds with Apis and his Black Hand associates, Pašić now found himself compromised by his own earlier failure to investigate allegations about the secret society. In early June 1914, the minister had heard vague rumours of an assassination plot.

From Samuel R. Williamson, Jr., "The Origins of the War," in Hew Strachan, ed., *The Oxford Illustrated History of the First World War* (Oxford University Press, 1998). Copyright © 1998 by Oxford University Press, Inc. Reprinted by permission.

He even sought to make inquiries, only to have Apis stonewall him about details. Whether Belgrade actually sought to alert Vienna about the plot remains uncertain. In any event, once the murders occurred, the premier could not admit his prior knowledge nor allow any Austro-Hungarian action that might unravel the details of the conspiracy. Not only would any compromise threaten his political position, it could lead Apis and his army associates to attempt a coup or worse.

After 28 June Pašić tried, without much success, to moderate the Serbian press's glee over the archduke's death. He also sought to appear conciliatory and gracious towards Vienna. But he knew that the Habsburg authorities believed that Princip had ties to Belgrade. He only hoped that the Habsburg investigators could not make a direct, incontrovertible connection to Apis and others.

Pašić resolved early, moreover, that he would not allow any Habsburg infringement of Serbian sovereignty or any commission that would implicate him or the military authorities. If he made any concession, his political opponents would attack and he might expose himself and the other civilian ministers to unacceptable personal risks. Thus Serbia's policy throughout the July crisis would be apparently conciliatory, deftly evasive, and ultimately intractable. It did not require, as the inter-war historians believed, the Russian government to stiffen the Serbian position. Once confronted with the fact of Sarajevo, the Serbian leadership charted its own course, one which guaranteed a definitive confrontation with Vienna.

The deaths of Franz Ferdinand and Sophie stunned the Habsburg leadership. While there were only modest public shows of sympathy, limited by the court's calculation to play down the funeral, all of the senior leaders wanted some action against Belgrade. None doubted that Serbia bore responsibility for the attacks. The 84-year-old emperor, Franz Joseph, returned hurriedly to Vienna from his hunting lodge at Bad Ischl. Over the next six days to 4 July 1914, all of the Habsburg leaders met in pairs and threes to discuss the monarchy's reaction to the deaths and to assess the extensive political unrest in Bosnia-Hercegovina in the wake of the assassinations. Nor could the discussions ignore the earlier tensions of 1912 and 1913 when the monarchy had three times nearly gone to war with Serbia and/or Montenegro. Each time militant diplomacy had prevailed and each time Russia had accepted the outcome.

The most aggressive of the Habsburg leaders, indeed the single individual probably most responsible for the war in 1914, was General Franz Conrad von Hötzendorf, chief of the Austro-Hungarian general staff. In the previous crises he had called for war against Serbia more than fifty times. He constantly lamented that the monarchy had not attacked Serbia in 1908 when the odds would have been far better. In the July crisis Conrad would argue vehemently and repeatedly that the time for a final reckoning had come. His cries for war in 1912 and 1913 had been checked by Archduke Franz Ferdinand and the foreign minister, Leopold Berchtold. Now, with the archduke gone and Berchtold converted to a policy of action, all of the civilian leaders, except the Hungarian prime minister István Tisza, wanted to resolve the Serbian issue. To retain international credibility the monarchy had to show that there were limits beyond which the south Slav movement could not go without repercussions.

The Habsburg resolve intensified with reports from Sarajevo that indicated that the trail of conspiracy did indeed lead back to at least one minor Serbian official in Belgrade. While the evidence in 1914 never constituted a 'smoking gun', the officials correctly surmised that the Serbian government must have tolerated and possibly assisted in the planning of the deed. Given this evidence, the Habsburg leaders soon focused on three options: a severe diplomatic humiliation of Serbia; quick, decisive military action against Serbia; or a diplomatic ultimatum that, if rejected, would be followed by military action. Pressed by Conrad and the military leadership, by 3 July even Franz Joseph had agreed on the need for stern action, including the possibility of war. Only one leader resisted a military solution: István Tisza. Yet his consent was absolutely required for any military action. Tisza preferred the diplomatic option and wanted assurances of German support before the government made a final decision. His resistance to any quick military action effectively foreclosed that option, leaving either the diplomatic one or the diplomatic/military combination. Not surprisingly, those anxious for military action shifted to the latter alternative.

The Austro-Hungarian foreign minister, Berchtold, made the next move on 4 July, sending his belligerent subordinate Alexander Hoyos to Berlin to seek a pledge of German support. Armed with a personal letter from Franz Joseph to Wilhelm II and a long memorandum on the need for resolute action against Serbia, Hoyos got a cordial reception. The Germans fully understood Vienna's intentions: the Habsburg leadership wanted a military reckoning with Belgrade. The German leadership (for reasons to be explored later) agreed to the Habsburg request, fully realizing that it might mean a general war with Russia as Serbia's protector.

With assurances of German support, the leaders in Vienna met on 7 July to formulate their plan. General Conrad gave confident assessments of military success and the civilian ministers attempted to persuade Tisza to accept a belligerent approach. At the same time the preliminary diplomatic manoeuvres were planned. Finally on 13–14 July Hungarian Prime Minister Tisza accepted strong action and possible war with Serbia. He did so largely because of new fears that a possible Serbian-Romanian alignment would threaten Magyar overlordship of the 3 million Romanians living in Transylvania. Drafts of the ultimatum, meanwhile, were prepared in Vienna. Deception tactics to lull the rest of Europe were arranged and some military leaves were cancelled.

But there remained a major problem: when to deliver the ultimatum? The long-scheduled French state visit to Russia of President Raymond Poincaré and Premier René Viviani from 20 July to 23 July thoroughly complicated the delivery of the ultimatum. Berchtold, understandably, did not want to hand over the demands while the French leaders were still in St Petersburg. Yet to avoid that possibility meant a further delay until late afternoon, 23 July. At that point the forty-eight-hour ultimatum, with its demands that clearly could not be met, would be delivered in Belgrade.

Germany's decision of 5–6 July to assure full support to Vienna ranks among the most discussed issues in modern European history. A strong, belligerent German response came as no surprise. After all, Wilhelm II and Franz

Ferdinand had just visited each other, were close ideologically, and had since 1900 developed a strong personal friendship. Chancellor Theobald von Bethmann Hollweg, moreover, believed that Berlin must show Vienna that Germany supported its most loyal ally. Far more controversial is whether the civilian leaders in Berlin, pressured by the German military, viewed the Sarajevo murders as a 'heaven-sent' opportunity to launch a preventive war against Russia. This interpretation points to increasing German apprehension about a Russian military colossus, allegedly to achieve peak strength in 1917. And Russo-German military relations were in early 1914 certainly at their worst in decades. Nor did Kaiser Wilhelm II's military advisers urge any modicum of restraint on Vienna, unlike previous Balkans episodes. An increasingly competitive European military environment now spilled over into the July crisis.

However explained, the German leadership reached a rare degree of consensus: it would support Vienna in a showdown with Serbia. Thus the German kaiser and chancellor gave formal assurances (the so-called 'blank cheque') to Vienna. From that moment, Austria-Hungary proceeded to exploit this decision and to march toward war with Serbia. Berlin would find itself—for better or worse—at the mercy of its reliable ally as the next stages of the crisis unfolded.

The Austrian Ultimatum to Serbia

For two weeks and more Berlin waited, first for the Habsburg leadership to make its final decisions and then for their implementation. During this time the German kaiser sailed in the North Sea and the German military and naval high command, confident of their own arrangements, took leaves at various German spas. Bethmann Hollweg, meanwhile, fretted over the lengthy delays in Vienna. He also began to fear the consequences of the 'calculated risk' and his 'leap into the dark' for German foreign policy. But his moody retrospection brought no changes in his determination to back Vienna; he only wished the Habsburg monarchy would act soon and decisively.

By Monday 20 July, Europe buzzed with rumours of a pending Habsburg *démarche* in Belgrade. While the Irish Question continued to dominate British political concerns and the French public focused on the Caillaux murder trial, Vienna moved to act against Belgrade. Remarkably, no Triple Entente power directly challenged Berchtold before 23 July, and the foreign minister for his part remained inconspicuous. Then, as instructed, at 6 p.m. on 23 July Wladimir Giesl, the Habsburg minister in Belgrade, delivered the ultimatum to the Serbian foreign ministry. Sir Edward Grey, the British foreign secretary, would immediately brand it as 'the most formidable document ever addressed by one State to another that was independent'.

With its forty-eight-hour deadline, the ultimatum demanded a series of Serbian concessions and a commission to investigate the plot. Pašić, away from Belgrade on an election campaign tour, returned to draft the response. This reply conceded some points but was wholly unyielding on Vienna's key demand, which would have allowed the Austrians to discover Pašić's and his government's general complicity in the murders.

News of the Habsburg ultimatum struck Europe with as much force as the Sarajevo murders. If the public did not immediately recognize the dangers to the peace, the European diplomats (and their military and naval associates) did. The most significant, immediate, and dangerous response came not from the Germans, but from the Russians. Upon learning of the ultimatum, Foreign Minister Serge Sazonov declared war inevitable. His actions thereafter did much to ensure a general European war.

At a meeting of the Council of State on 24 July, even before the Serbians responded, Sazonov and others pressed for strong Russian support for Serbia. Fearful of losing Russian leadership of the pan-Slavic movement, he urged resolute behaviour. His senior military leaders backed this view, even though Russia's military reforms were still incomplete. The recently concluded French state visit had given the Russians new confidence that Paris would support Russia if war came.

At Sazonov's urgings, the Council agreed, with the tsar approving the next day, to initiate various military measures preparing for partial or full mobilization. The Council agreed further to partial mobilization as a possible deterrent to stop Austria-Hungary from attacking the Serbs. These Russian military measures were among the very first of the entire July crisis; their impact would be profound. The measures were not only extensive, they abutted German as well as Austrian territory. Not surprisingly, the Russian actions would be interpreted by German military intelligence as tantamount to some form of mobilization. No other actions in the crisis, beyond Vienna's resolute determination for war, were so provocative or disturbing as Russia's preliminary steps of enhanced border security and the recall of certain troops.

Elsewhere, Sir Edward Grey sought desperately to repeat his 1912 role as peacemaker in the Balkans. He failed. He could not get Vienna to extend the forty-eight-hour deadline. Thus at 6 p.m. on 25 July, Giesl glanced at the Serbian reply, deemed it insufficient, broke diplomatic relations, and left immediately for nearby Habsburg territory. The crisis had escalated to a new, more dangerous level.

Grey did not, however, desist in his efforts for peace. He now tried to initiate a set of four-power discussions to ease the mounting crisis. Yet he could never get St Petersburg or Berlin to accept the same proposal for some type of mediation or diplomatic discussions. A partial reason for his failure came from Berlin's two continuing assumptions: that Britain might ultimately stand aside and that Russia would eventually be deterred by Germany's strong, unequivocal support of Vienna.

Each of Grey's international efforts, ironically, alarmed Berchtold. He now became determined to press for a declaration of war, thus thwarting any intervention in the local conflict. In fact, the Habsburg foreign minister had trouble getting General Conrad's reluctant agreement to a declaration of war on Tuesday 28 July. This declaration, followed by some desultory gunfire between Serbian and Austro-Hungarian troops that night, would thoroughly inflame the situation. The Serbs naturally magnified the gunfire incident into a larger Austrian attack. This in turn meant that the Russians would use the casual shooting to justify still stronger support for Serbia and to initiate still more far-reaching military measures of their own.

By 28 July every European state had taken some military and/or naval precautions. The French recalled some frontier troops, the Germans did the same, and the Austro-Hungarians began their mobilization against the Serbs. In Britain, Winston Churchill, First Lord of the Admiralty, secured cabinet approval to keep the British fleet intact after it had completed manoeuvres. Then on the night of 29 July he ordered the naval vessels to proceed through the English Channel to their North Sea battle stations. It could be argued that thanks to Churchill Britain became the first power prepared to protect its vital interests in a European war.

Grey still searched for a solution. But his efforts were severely hampered by the continuing impact of the Irish Question and the deep divisions within the cabinet over any policy that appeared to align Britain too closely with France. Throughout the last week of July, Grey tried repeatedly to gain cabinet consent to threaten Germany with British intervention. The radicals in the cabinet refused. They wanted no British participation in a continental war.

Grey now turned his attention to the possible fate of Belgium and Britain's venerable treaty commitments to protect Belgian neutrality. As he did so, the German diplomats committed a massive blunder by attempting to win British neutrality with an assurance that Belgium and France would revert to the status quo ante after a war. Not only did Grey brusquely reject this crude bribery, he turned it back against Berlin. On 31 July, with cabinet approval, Grey asked Paris and Berlin to guarantee Belgium's status. France did so at once; the Germans did not. Grey had scored an important moral and tactical victory.

In St Petersburg, meanwhile, decisions were taken, rescinded, then taken again that assured that the peace would not be kept. By 28 July Sazonov had concluded that a partial mobilization against Austria-Hungary would never deter Vienna. Indeed his own generals argued that a partial step would complicate a general mobilization. Sazonov therefore got the generals' support for full mobilization. He then won the tsar's approval only to see Nicholas II hesitate after receiving a message from his cousin, Kaiser Wilhelm II. The co-called 'Willy-Nicky' telegrams came to nothing, however. On 30 July the tsar ordered general mobilization, with a clear recognition that Germany would probably respond and that a German attack would be aimed at Russia's French ally.

The Russian general mobilization resolved a number of problems for the German high command. First, it meant that no negotiations, including the proposal for an Austrian 'Halt in Belgrade', would come to anything. Second, it allowed Berlin to declare a 'defensive war' of protection against an aggressive Russia, a tactic that immeasurably aided Bethmann Hollweg's efforts to achieve domestic consensus. And, third, it meant that the chancellor could no longer resist General Helmuth von Moltke's demands for German mobilization and the implementation of German war plans. Alone of the great powers, mobilization for Germany equalled war; Bethmann Hollweg realized this. Yet once the German mobilization began, the chancellor lost effective control of the situation.

At 7 p.m. on Saturday, 1 August 1914, Germany declared war on Russia. The next day German forces invaded Luxembourg. Later that night Germany demanded that Belgium allow German troops to march through the neutral state on their way to France. The Belgian cabinet met and concluded that it would resist the German attack.

In France general mobilization began. But the French government, ever anxious to secure British intervention, kept French forces 6 miles away from the French border. In London Paul Cambon, the French ambassador, importuned the British government to uphold the unwritten moral and military obligations of the Anglo-French *entente*. Still, even on Saturday 1 August, the British cabinet refused to agree to any commitment to France. Then on Sunday 2 August, Grey finally won cabinet approval for two significant steps: Britain would protect France's northern coasts against any German naval attack and London would demand that Germany renounce any intention of attacking Belgium. Britain had edged closer to war.

On Monday 3 August, the British cabinet reviewed the outline of Grey's speech to parliament that afternoon. His peroration, remarkable for its candour and its disingenuousness about the secret Anglo-French military and naval arrangements, left no doubt that London would intervene to preserve the balance of power against Germany; that it would defend Belgium and France; and that it would go to war if Germany failed to stop the offensive in the west. This last demand, sent from London to Berlin on 4 August, would be rejected. At 11 p.m. (GMT) on 4 August 1914 Britain and Germany were at war.

With the declarations of war the focus shifted to the elaborate pre-arranged mobilization plans of the great powers. For the naval forces the issues were relatively straightforward: prepare for the great naval battle, impose or thwart a policy of naval blockade, protect your coast lines, and keep the shipping lanes open. For the continental armies, the stakes were far greater. If an army were defeated, the war might well be over. Committed to offensive strategies, dependent on the hope that any war would be short, and reliant on the implementation of their carefully developed plans, the general staffs believed they had prepared for almost every possible contingency.

In each country the war plans contained elaborate mobilization schedules which the generals wanted to put into action at the earliest possible moment. While mobilization raised the risks of war, in only two cases did it absolutely guarantee a generalized engagement: (1) if Russia mobilized, Germany would do so and move at once to attack Belgium and France; (2) if Germany mobilized without Russian provocation, the results were the same. Any full Russian mobilization would trigger a complete German response and, for Germany, mobilization meant war. Very few, if any, civilian leaders fully comprehended these fateful interconnections and even the military planners were uncertain about them.

The German war plans in 1914 were simple, dangerous, and exceptionally mechanical. To overcome the threat of being trapped in a two-front war between France and Russia, Germany would attack first in the west, violating Belgian neutrality in a massive sweeping movement that would envelop and then crush the French forces. Once the French were defeated, the Germans would redeploy their main forces against Russia and with Austro-Hungarian help conclude the war. The Russian war plans sought to provide immediate assistance to France and thereby disrupt the expected German attack in the west. The Russians would attack German troops in East Prussia, while other Russian forces moved southward into Galicia against the Habsburg armies. But to achieve their goals the Russians had to mobilize immediately, hence their escalatory decisions early in the crisis, with fateful consequences for the peace of Europe.

The Italians, it should be noted, took some preliminary measures in August 1914 but deferred general mobilization until later. Otherwise Rome took no further action to intervene. Rather the Italian government soon became involved in an elaborate bargaining game over its entry into the fray. Not until April 1915 would this last of the major pre-war allies enter into the fighting, not on the side of their former allies but in opposition with the Triple Entente.

The Process of Escalation

By 10 August 1914 Europe was at war. What had started as the third Balkan war had rapidly become the First World War. How can one assess responsibility for these events? Who caused it? What could have been done differently to have prevented it? Such questions have troubled generations of historians since 1914. There are no clear answers. But the following observations may put the questions into context. The alliance/*entente* system created linking mechanisms that allowed the control of a state's strategic destiny to pass into a broader arena, one which the individual government could manage but not always totally control. Most specifically, this meant that any Russo-German quarrel would see France involved because of the very nature of Germany's offensive war plans. Until 1914 the alliance/*entente* partners had disagreed just enough among themselves to conceal the true impact of the alliance arrangements.

The legacy of Germany's bombastic behaviour, so characteristic of much of German *Weltpolitik* and *Europolitik* after 1898, also meant that Berlin was thoroughly mistrusted. Its behaviour created a tone, indeed an edginess, that introduced fear into the international system, since only for Germany did mobilization equal war. Ironically, and not all historians agree, the German policy in 1914 may have been less provocative than earlier. But that summer Berlin paid the price for its earlier aggressiveness.

Serbia allowed a terrorist act to proceed, then sought to evade the consequences of its action. It would gain, after 1918, the most from the war with the creation of the Yugoslav state. Paradoxically, however, the very ethnic rivalries that brought Austria-Hungary to collapse would also plague the new state and its post-1945 successor.

Austria-Hungary feared the threat posed by the emergence of the south Slavs as a political force. But the Dual Monarchy could not reform itself sufficiently to blunt the challenge. With the death of the Archduke Franz Ferdinand, who had always favoured peace, the monarchy lost the one person who could check the ambitions of General Conrad and mute the fears of the civilians.

While harsh, Ottokar Czernin's epitaph has a certain truth to it: 'We were compelled to die; we could only choose the manner of our death and we have chosen the most terrible.'

Germany believed that it must support its Danubian ally. This in turn influenced Berlin's position towards Russia and France. Without German backing, Vienna would probably have hesitated to been more conciliatory toward Belgrade. But, anxious to support Vienna and possibly to detach Russia from the Triple Entente, Berlin would risk a continental war to achieve its short- and long-term objectives. Berlin and Vienna bear more responsibility for starting the crisis and then making it very hard to control.

Nevertheless, the Russians must also share some significant responsibility for the final outcome. St Petersburg's unwavering support of Serbia, its unwillingness to negotiate with Berlin and Vienna, and then its precipitate preparatory military measures escalated the crisis beyond control. Russia's general mobilization on 30 July guaranteed disaster.

Those Russian decisions would in turn confront the French with the full ramifications of their alliance with Russia. Despite French expectations, the alliance with Russia had in fact become less salvation for Paris and more assuredly doom. France became the victim in the Russo-German fight. Throughout the crisis French leaders could only hope to convince Russia to be careful and simultaneously work to ensure that Britain came to their assistance. Paris failed in the first requirement and succeeded in the second.

The decisions of August 1914 did not come easily for the British government. Grey could not rush the sharply divided cabinet. The decade-old *entente* ties to the French were vague and unwritten and had a history of deception and deviousness. Nor did the vicious political atmosphere created by Ireland help. Grey desperately hoped that the threat of British intervention would deter Germany; it did not. Could Grey have done more? Probably not, given the British political system and the precarious hold the Liberal Party had on power. Only a large standing British army would have deterred Germany, and that prospect, despite some recent assertions, simply did not exist.

In July 1914 one or two key decisions taken differently might well have seen the war averted. As it was, the July crisis became a model of escalation and inadvertent consequences. The expectation of a short war, the ideology of offensive warfare, and continuing faith in war as an instrument of policy: all would soon prove illusory and wishful. The cold, hard, unyielding reality of modern warfare soon replaced the romantic, dashing legends of the popular press. The élite decision-makers (monarchs, civilian ministers, admirals, and generals) had started the war; the larger public would die in it and, ultimately, finish it.

POSTSCRIPT

Were German Militarism and Diplomacy Responsible for World War I?

Recent events in the former Yugoslavia may have spurred interest in World War I—the first time that the Balkan powder keg exploded into the world's consciousness. Yugoslavia was created after that war, and some see its recent problems as a failure of the Versailles settlement.

Regardless of the truth of this assumption, it is certainly true that the last decade has seen the publication (and republication) of a number of important works on the Great War, including books by both authors in this issue: Berghahn's *Germany and the Approach of War in 1914* (St. Martin's Press, 1993) and Williamson's *Austria-Hungary and the Origins of the First World War* (St. Martin's Press, 1991). David G. Hermann's *The Arming of Europe and the Making of World War I* (Princeton University Press, 1996) concentrates on the size and strength of land armies and their role in the genesis of the war, a subject that has been neglected by historians who have emphasized naval buildup.

Many recent books on World War I have either been written by English historians or have concentrated on England's role in the war. Edward E. McCullough's *How the First World War Began: The Triple Entente and the Coming of the Great War of 1914-1918* (Black Rose Books, 1999) is a revisionist work that sees the creation of the Triple Entente as a prime force in the causes of the First World War. Comparing the condition of Germany today to England, France, and Russia, McCullough questions not only the folly of the war but notes its counterproductive results.

In *The Pity of War* (Basic Books, 1999), Scottish historian Niall Ferguson takes the revisionist viewpoint to a higher level. Arguing that the First World War was not inevitable, he asserts that the British declaration of war turned a continental conflict into a world war. He further argues that not only was Britain's participation in the war a colossal error, but it was counterproductive to the interests of the British nation and its people. He finds proof in the causes and results of World War II and the present condition of Great Britain.

Eminent English military historian John Keegan's *The First World War* (Alfred A. Knopf, 1999) may well prove to be one of the most widely read and influential volumes on the Great War. A general work written with skill, scholarship, and readability, it is strongly recommended. *World War I: A History* (Oxford University Press, 1998), edited by Hew Strachan, contains 23 chapters, each written by a different historian, that cover the war from origins to memory and everything in between. William Jannen's *The Lions of July: Prelude to War, 1914* (Presidio Press, 1997) is an extremely readable account of Europe's last month of peace as its statesmen and military men blundered into war.

ISSUE 9

Did the Bolshevik Revolution Improve the Lives of Soviet Women?

YES: Richard Stites, from "Women and the Revolutionary Process in Russia," in Renate Bridenthal, Claudia Koonz, and Susan M. Stuard, eds., *Becoming Visible: Women in European History*, 2d ed. (Houghton Mifflin, 1987)

NO: Françoise Navailh, from "The Soviet Model," in Françoise Thébaud, ed., *A History of Women in the West, vol. 5: Toward a Cultural Identity in the Twentieth Century* (Belknap Press, 1994)

ISSUE SUMMARY

YES: History professor Richard Stites argues that in the early years of the Bolshevik Revolution, the Zhenotdel, or Women's Department, helped many working women take the first steps toward emancipation.

NO: Film historian Françoise Navailh contends that the Zhenotdel had limited political influence and could do little to improve the lives of Soviet women in the unstable period following the revolution.

Compared with life under the czars, life for women after the Bolshevik Revolution was characterized by greater variety and freedom. The Romanov dynasty had ruled Russia for 300 years, and the Orthodox Church had been entrenched for a much longer period. Both had reinforced a world of patriarchal authority, class structure, and patterns of deference. Although the revolution overthrew the power of both church and monarch, the new communist state had a power and authority of its own. Between 1917 and 1920 Soviet women received equal rights in education and marriage, including the choice to change or keep their own names and the opportunity to own property; the rights to vote and to hold public office; access to no-fault divorce, common-law marriage, and maternity benefits; workplace protection; and access to unrestricted abortion. They were the first women to gain these rights—ahead of women in France, England, and the United States—but the question is whether or not these legal rights translated into improvements in their day-to-day lives.

A feminist movement had developed in urban areas as early as the 1905 workers' revolution, and women joined men in leading strikes and protest demonstrations. By the time of the Bolshevik Revolution in 1917, however, the goals of the leadership were primarily economic, and feminism was dismissed as bourgeois or middle class. In a workers' revolution, women and men were to be equal. Housework and child care were to be provided collectively, and the family, like the monarchy, was to be replaced with something new. In theory, women would become workers and gain access to economic independence, which would provide them the basis for equality within marriage.

The German philosopher Karl Marx had argued that the family reflects the economic system in society. Under capitalism, the bourgeois family exists to reproduce workers and consumers; it exploits women by unfairly burdening them with full responsibility for housework and child care. If similarly exploited workers—what Marx called the proletariat—overthrew the capitalist system that allowed factory owners to grow rich from their workers' labor, Marx believed that the family would undergo an equally dramatic transformation. In this scenario, no one would be "owned" by anyone else and people would be free to marry for love or sexual attraction rather than for economic considerations.

V. I. Lenin, who emerged as the leader and architect of the new order, was committed to women's rights. First and foremost, however, he was committed to a socialist revolution. When the struggle to make abstract legal changes "real" in women's lives came into conflict with the goals of the revolution, there was no question in Lenin's mind about which would have to be sacrificed. In this early period, a fascinating group of women briefly held highly visible leadership positions and had the chance to put their ideas into practice, at least during the first decade. Alexandra Kollontai was one of the most articulate and effective leaders of the Zhenotdel, or Women's Department, of the Communist Party, whose purpose between 1919 and 1930 was to educate and mobilize the women of the Soviet state to participate fully in the revolution.

In the following selections, Richard Stites focuses on what he calls the "idealistic foreground" of the Revolution—the part that is so often overlooked. Although poverty, cynicism, bureaucratic resistance, rural superstition, and urban blight ultimately thwarted many early dreams of reformers such as Kollontai, bold efforts undertaken by the Zhenotdel and experiments in sexual equality raised the consciousness of women and men. A brief glimpse of what might be possible in a stable society kept the dreams and experiments alive—at least for a time, Stites concludes.

Françoise Navailh, in contrast, examines the failure of the revolutionary dreams. She agrees with Stites that Kollontai's ideas were pathbreaking and imaginative, but sees Kollontai as marginalized and ignored by most of her comrades in the party hierarchy. Although Soviet women were granted unprecedented legal rights, almost without a struggle, the real task was to translate these rights into a new way of life. Zhenotdel raised the consciousness of women, but equality brought them the double shift—full responsibilities as workers and as mothers.

Women and the Revolutionary Process in Russia

Before the Revolution

Russian society before 1917 was a world of patriarchal power, deferential ritual, clear authority patterns, and visible hierarchy with stratified social classes or estates. At the pinnacle of the state, the tsar-emperor (called *batyushka* or little father by the common folk), considered Russia as a family estate or patrimony and his subjects as children—virtuous, obedient, and loyal. The imperial bureaucratic order of ranks, chanceries, uniforms, and rigidly ordered parades constituted a visual celebration of authoritarianism. To subjects of all classes of the empire, every official building—with its geography of guarded entrances, pass booths, waiting areas, office gates—represented authority, inequality, and the demand for deference. Far from the capital and the towns, in the vastness of rural Russia, a simpler absolutism prevailed in the village cabins where the male head of household wielded domestic power that contrasted sharply with the more or less egalitarian land distribution customs of the village community. The Russian Orthodox Church reinforced values of obedience and subordination at every level in its liturgical idiom, its symbols, its organization, and its political ethos of support for a conservative order. The women dwelling within this ancient authoritarian world felt the additional weight of male power and suffered from the sexual division of labor and open inequality between the sexes. . . .

Women who chose not to challenge the regime and its entire patriarchal structure but who nonetheless wished to improve the lot of women organized the Russian feminist movement (ca. 1860–1917). Feminist women shared the class background (largely gentry) of the nihilists and radicals, but did not call for the destruction of the existing social system. They worked for women's rights—not for the rights of peasants or workers, and not on behalf of a socialist vision. In the four decades or so after 1860 feminists agitated, with considerable success, for permission to form legal societies, engage in charity work, and open university level and medical courses for women. These courses produced impressive numbers of physicians, teachers, lawyers, and engineers. At the dawn of the twentieth century, feminists turned their attention to the national suffrage issue and continued to press for and win reforms in the status of women in the realm of property rights, divorce, freedom of movement, and other matters that primarily affected women of the gentry and the professional classes of Russia. From 1905 to 1917, no fewer than four feminist parties struggled unsuccessfully in the political arena. Thus all women (and millions of men) remained without representation in the central government. Russian feminism, in the words of its most eloquent historian, was "a movement for women's civil and political equality, whose supporters trusted that a better world could be created without resort to violence, and a constitutional solution be found to Russia's ills." . . .

Political Parties

The political parties of the late imperial Russia reacted to the question of women's rights in much the same way as their counterparts in Western Europe—their views on this issue being a litmus test for their outlook on social change and mass interests. Those on the right displayed outright hostility to any kind of feminist platform, identifying legitimate politics with the male sex and proclaiming as their program Faith, Tsar, and Fatherland. The liberal parties in the center—the Kadets, or Constitutional Democrats, most prominent among them—initially wavered on the question of votes for women in the Duma but by 1906 supported the more moderate of the feminist parties. The socialists—like the Populists earlier and like their counterparts in Western Europe—proclaimed support for women's equality, including political equality, maternity protection, and equal economic rights.

The socialist parties also included women activists at many levels, some of whom would become prominent political figures during the Revolution of 1917. Of the three major socialist parties—Socialist Revolutionary, Social Democrat-Menshevik, and Social Democrat-Bolshevik—the first eventually became the largest and most variegated. Heirs to the Populist tradition of the nineteenth century, the Socialist Revolutionaries continued to focus on peasant agrarian socialism and an alliance of the "social trinity": peasant, worker, and intelligentsia. Loose in organization and weak in theory, the Socialist Revolutionary party periodically fell back upon terror as its main weapon. Its best-known women were Ekaterina Breshko-Breshkovskaya (1844–1934), a veteran Populist of the 1870s who tried in the 1905 period to promote a theory of "agrarian terror" that included assaults on landlords in the countryside; and Maria Spiridonova (1886–?), a young schoolteacher who achieved fame first by her assassination of a general in 1906 and then in 1917 as the leader of the Left Socialist Revolutionary party. The Socialist Revolutionaries—like the Anarchist groups—could deploy a large number of female terrorists, but women played a minimal role in the organizational and theoretical work of the party.

The Marxists (Social Democrats) had split into Mensheviks and Bolsheviks in 1903. Both enrolled large numbers of women but in neither did many women rise to leadership positions. Among the Mensheviks, Vera Zasulich was the best-known woman (her fame arose from an attempted assassination she had performed in the 1870s) but her political influence remained strictly secondary. The most important activist women among the Bolsheviks—Roza Zemlyachka and Elena Stasova—were tough organizers, but not leaders or theoreticians. In all the socialist parties the leadership remained in the hands of men, men who spent most of the years from 1905 to 1917 in the émigré centers of Western Europe. Two of the best-known Bolshevik women, Nadezhda Krupskaya (Lenin's wife) and Inessa Armand (their friend), made their mark as loyal assistants of the party leader, Lenin, in the emigration years.

The presence of women in the major socialist parties did not advance the cause of women's rights in Russia. Less than ten percent of the delegates to Socialist Revolutionary conferences in the peak years from 1905 to 1908 were women; the percentages were even lower in Marxist and Social Democratic parties. Even if more women had risen to the top of these organizations, however, the picture would not have changed. Women constituted one-third of the Executive Committee of the People's Will of the 1870s, for example, yet those women displayed almost no interest in the issue of women's rights as such. The same mood prevailed in the generation of 1905; revolutionary women put what they called the "common cause" above what they saw as lesser issues. Vera Zasulich, when asked to help in forming a women workers' club, refused.

The most notable exception, Alexandra Kollontai, had to fight on many fronts when she set about combining the advocacy of women's rights with socialism: against her feminist competitors, against indifference in her own party (she was at first a Menshevik and later a Bolshevik), and against the prevailing opinion of the conservative society. Kollontai, a general's daughter, had come to a feminist consciousness through personal experience—the conflict of work and family. Like many European socialist women, particularly Clara Zetkin, Kollontai believed that women had special problems that Marxist programs did not sufficiently address. She opposed the feminists as bourgeois; she believed that women workers should rally to the proletarian banner; but she also insisted that working women needed their own self-awareness—as workers and as women. Out of this set of beliefs arose the Proletarian Women's Movement.

In the years from 1905 to 1908 Kollontai fought to create a socialist-feminist movement in order to win away proletarian women of St. Petersburg from the feminists who were trying to organize them into an "all-women's" movement. For three years, Kollontai and a few associates agitated among the factory women, taught them Marxism, and attempted to show them that their principal enemy was the bourgeoisie, not men. In this struggle, Kollontai opposed the bourgeois (as she perceived it) program of the feminists with her own vision of socialist feminism—a combination of gender and class awareness, a recognition of the double exploitation of working-class women (as workers and as women), and an honest facing of the issue of abusive proletarian husbands and insensitive socialist males. Although Kollontai exaggerated the selfish class character of Russian feminists, she did in fact go beyond them and beyond her own comrades in the socialist movement in trying to draw attention to these issues. Police harassment in 1908 forced her to leave the country, and during her years in Western Europe Kollontai deepened her understanding of the woman question through study and personal experience.

The Eve of Revolution

On the eve of war and revolution, the woman question in tsarist society remained a public issue. Thousands of women graduates of universities had entered professional life; hundreds languished in jail or in Siberia for their chosen profession as revolutionaries. The female terrorist was the Russian counterpart to the British suffragette—but far more violent. Organized feminists continued to agitate for important reforms in the status of women and won considerable legislative victories in legal, educational, and property rights—though mainly for women of the middle and upper classes. The female work force continued to grow and to feel the rigors of industrial life and of relative neglect by the rest of society. With the revival of the militant labor movement around 1912, Mensheviks and Bolsheviks alike reactivated their efforts to organize women workers. International Women's Day, established in Europe in 1910, was celebrated by adherents of both factions for the first time on Russian soil in 1913, and a newspaper, *The Woman Worker,* was established in 1914. During World War I much of the machinery for organizing women workers was smashed by the authorities and many leaders were arrested before the monarchy itself fell a victim to the same war.

The Revolutionary Era

After three winters of bitter fighting, bloody losses, and patent mismanagement of the war, widespread discontent and hatred of the regime found a focus. In February 1917, cold and hungry women of the capital (renamed Petrograd) rioted, beginning an uprising that led to the collapse of the Romanov dynasty within a week. With the men at the front and the women left behind as workers, breadwinners, and heads of households, the women of the lower classes perceived food shortages and related deprivations as a menace to their very existence and to their roles as women. They struck, demonstrated, rioted, and appealed to the class solidarity of garrison troops to persuade the troops not to fire upon them. When the tsar abdicated, the revolutionary parties linked up with the masses of women. A band of energetic Bolshevik women organizers—including Kollontai—created a network of agitation that was effective in spite of tactical squabbles and the enormous problems of communication in the midst of a major revolt. This network produced mass female demonstrations on behalf of Bolshevik issues, organized women in factories, and enlisted others in political, paramedical, and paramilitary work. Bolshevik leadership and dynamism in this arena proved vastly superior to that of the other radical parties, and Bolshevik hostility to the now-revived feminist movement was active and unambiguous. Out of this year of struggle and organization in many cities emerged the symbolically important "presence" of women in the October Revolution as well as the foundations of a postrevolutionary women's movement.

The Bolsheviks took power on October 25 (November 7 in the modern calendar), 1917, and established a Soviet socialist regime; in 1918 they moved the capital to Moscow, issued a constitution that was the framework for the world's first socialist state, and made peace with Germany. The first years of the new regime were marked by ruthless political struggle on all sides, a bloody and cruel civil war, intervention in that war by foreign troops on behalf of the anti-Bolshevik forces, and a deepening of the extraordinary economic hardship set off by war and revolution and made inevitable by the very backwardness of the country.

How, in this time of dreadful calamity, did the Bolshevik regime perceive the issue—historically always seen as marginal by all governments—of the emancipation of women? What did they do about it? The answers are very complicated; any assessment of their response depends upon how one views revolution in general and the Bolshevik Revolution in particular, and upon one's expectations from an insurgent, culture-changing government that sets out to remake the face of one of the largest countries in the world.

The men and women in the Bolshevik party displayed the contradictions inherent in all forceful agents of social and cultural change: practicality combined with vision, the imperatives of survival combined with the dream of transformation. The party's leader, V. I. Lenin, as both a Marxist and a Russian revolutionary, committed himself and his party to the educational, economic, legal, and political liberation of women; to the interchangeability of gender roles in a future under communism; and to special protection for woman as childbearer and nurturing mother. In addition, Lenin possessed an almost compulsive hatred of the domestic enslavement of women to mindless household work which he called "barbarously unproductive, petty, nerve-wracking, stultifying and crushing drudgery." Lenin's male and female colleagues shared his opinions on these major issues and framed their laws and policies accordingly. Most important, they endorsed the creation of a special women's organization to oversee the realization of these programs in Soviet society. Women did not play a major role in the upper reaches of the party hierarchy; and indeed hostility toward the expenditure of time on women's issues persisted in the party at various levels. This was an inheritance of the twenty years of underground life of party struggle, of the military mentality of Bolshevism that hardened during the Civil War, and of the upsurge within the party of people holding "traditional" patriarchal views of the female sex. In spite of these obvious weaknesses, it is astonishing what the Bolshevik regime proclaimed and actually carried out in the early years of Soviet power.

In a series of decrees, codes, electoral laws, and land reforms, the Bolsheviks proclaimed an across-the-board equality of the sexes—the first regime in history ever to do so. All institutions of learning were opened to women and girls. Women attained equal status in marriage—including the right to change or retain their own names—divorce, family, and inheritance and equal rights in litigation and the ownership of property. By separating church and state, the Bolsheviks legally invalidated all canonical and theological restrictions on the role of women in modern life—a sweeping and drastic measure in a land wrapped in the constraining meshes of traditional faiths, particularly Russian Orthodoxy and Islam. In 1920 the Bolsheviks legalized abortion. On the other hand, prostitution (legally licensed under the old regime) was made illegal. Taken together, these measures offered a structure for equality between the sexes unprecedented in history. The Bolsheviks offered a process as well: the organizations that helped overthrow the old order would help to erect the new one; art, culture, symbol, and mythic vision would reinforce the values of sexual equality.

The organizational form of women's liberation in the first decade of the Bolshevik (now renamed Communist) regime was the Women's Department of the Communist Party (1919–1930), known by its Russian abbreviation Zhenotdel. Founded as an arm of the party rather than as an independent feminist organization, Zhenotdel—led by Inessa Armand and Alexandra Kollontai in the early years—worked to transform the new revolutionary laws into reality through education, mobilization, and social work. Understaffed and hampered by a small budget, Zhenotdel went into the factory neighborhoods, the villages, and the remote provinces of the new Soviet state to bring the message of the Revolution to the female population. Instructors and trainees from among workers and peasant women addressed the practical concerns of women. In the towns they monitored factory conditions and fought against female unemployment and prostitution. In the countryside they opened literacy classes and explained the new laws. In the Muslim regions they opposed humiliating customs and attitudes. Everywhere they counselled women about divorce and women's rights—and tied all such lessons to political instruction about the values and aims of the regime. Activated by Zhenotdel, women virtually untouched by political culture entered into the local administrative process. Most crucial of all, the activists of Zhenotdel learned the rudiments of organizing and modernizing and taught themselves the meaning of social revolution.

Bolshevism contained vision as well as social policy. In societies wracked by poverty and dislocation, social vision—utopian or otherwise—plays a key role in capturing the sentiment of people, particularly the literate and the already engaged. Speculation about the future of sexual relations often helped to reinforce the process of working for improving such relations in the present. The most active and articulate Bolshevik woman activist, Kollontai, gave special attention to a program of communist sexual relations and communal "family" life. In regard to the first, Kollontai vigorously defended woman's need for independence and a separate income. This in turn would give her the dignity and strength needed for an equal and open love-sex relationship and would enhance the pleasure and quality of sexual intercourse. As to the second, she believed in a "marriage" unfettered by economic dependence or responsibility for children. The latter were to be cared for in communal facilities to which parents had easy access. Kollontai believed in parenthood—her ideal in fact for all humans—and in regular contact between parents and children. The material life of the children, however, was to be the responsibility of the local "collective" of work or residence. Housekeeping was to be no more than an "industrial" task like any other, handled by specialists—never the domain of a wife (or husband) alone.

Some of the more daring aspects of Kollontai's sexual theories fell victim to misinterpretation in the 1920s. Hers was an overall vision of equality in life, work, and love that matched the utopian visions of the science fiction writers and revolutionary town planners and architects who were the major futuristic thinkers in this decade of experiment. In the 1920s about 200 science fiction titles appeared, many of them outlining a future world of perfection characterized by social justice and ultramodern technology. Such utopian pictures almost invariably revealed a unified, urbanized globe bathed in peace, harmony, and affluent communist civilization inhabited by a near-androgynous population with genderless names and unisex costumes. Sexual tensions no longer tormented the human race, women worked as equals to men in a machine-run economy of universal participation and communist distribution, and healthy children thrived in colonies.

Architects and town planners of the 1920s and early 1930s designed living spaces as "social condensers"—communal buildings that would shape the collective consciousness of their inhabitants. Although the projects varied in scope, size, and density, almost all of the architectural planning of that period provided for private rooms for single persons and couples, easy divorce by changing rooms, communal care for children, communal cooking and dining, and an environment of male-female cooperation in household tasks. Some of these communal homes actually were built; others remained in the blueprint stage. As a whole, visionary architecture and town planning of that period attested to the central importance of woman's new role as an independent and equal member of society.

The ultimate experiments in sexual equality—the rural and urban communes of the 1920s—put communalism (the complete and equal sharing of lives, partly inspired by [Nicholas] Chernyshevsky) into practice wherever space could be found. Thousands in the countryside and hundreds in the cities joined to share goods, money, books, land, and property of every sort. Members of these collectives rotated work, apportioned income equally, and pooled all resources. Sexual equality worked better in the workers' and student communes of the cities than in the countryside, where the sexual division of labor often prevailed: women took over the big communal kitchens while men labored together in the fields. In the town communes, students and workers made sexual equality a mandatory condition. In these "living utopias," males learned how to cook and iron and wash floors under the guidance of women so that all could take their turns at housework on a strictly rotational basis. In some of the more rigorous communes, love and friendship were declared indivisible—cliques and romantic pairing were outlawed as violations of the collective principle. Tensions and flaring tempers beset many of these communes all through the 1920s; but they persisted as "laboratories of revolution" where communism could be practiced and lived day to day.

This part of the picture of women's liberation—the idealistic foreground—deserves emphasis because it is so often overlooked in assessments of the Revolution. Endemic misery and material poverty hampered these experiments, and cynicism and indifference made mockeries of the dreams, but the experiments and dreams persisted. Life for women—and men—was very difficult in the early years after the Revolution. The rural world presented a vast terrain of disease and superstition, suspicious peasants, archaic tools, and ancient agronomical technique. Towns were filled with unemployed women, deserted and abandoned children, criminals and organized gangs, and conspicuously wealthy businessmen. These last comprised a class created by the introduction of Lenin's New Economic Policy in 1921, which allowed a mixed economy, a limited arena of capitalism and hired labor with enclaves of privileged specialists, government leaders, and foreigners. Women were hit very hard by all of this. About 70 percent of the initial job cutbacks that occurred periodically during this period affected women. Between 70,000 and 100,000 women in *de facto* marriages with men possessed none of the financial security or legal protection that might have vouchsafed them with registered marriage.

Françoise Navailh

 **NO**

The Soviet Model

T he Russian Empire that preceded the Soviet Union was an autocracy. Although serfdom was not abolished until 1861 and the first elections were not held until 1906, the opposition quickly grew radical, and the "woman question" was incorporated into a broad revolutionary program. From the beginning large numbers of women joined the revolutionary movement, accounting for between 15 and 20 percent of the active membership of the revolutionary parties. In urban areas an independent feminist movement was especially active between 1905 and 1908. It concentrated its efforts chiefly on obtaining the right to vote, but in vain. On the eve of World War I Russian society consisted of a very small cultivated and westernized elite, a bourgeoisie still in embryo, and a backward peasantry that made up the remaining 80 percent of the population. People belonging to these different strata of society generally kept to themselves and knew little of other groups. This ignorance would prove a major impediment later on.

World War I broke out on August 1, 1914. Between 1914 and 1917 more than ten million men were mobilized, mostly peasants. Conditions in the countryside, already wretched, grew even worse. Many women were pressed into farm work, so many that women ultimately accounted for 72 percent of the rural workforce. They also replaced men in industrial jobs: the proportion of women in the workforce rose from 33 percent in 1914 to nearly 50 percent in 1917. From 1915 on, women found employment in new branches of industry and joined the government bureaucracy in large numbers. Their wages were lower than men's, however, at a time when prices were soaring. After 1916, the effort to keep food flowing to the cities and to the troops collapsed. The war, always unpopular, seemed hopeless, with no end in sight. For more than a year the country had been afflicted with bread riots and hunger strikes in which women played leading roles. Tension mounted. The regime began to crumble. The honor of initiating the revolution fell to women.

On February 23, 1917 (according to the Julian calendar, or March 8, according to our calendar), working women took their children out into the streets of Petrograd and staged a demonstration. Since the socialists had been unable to agree on a theme for the demonstration, the women improvised, calling for peace and bread. On the following day their ranks were swelled by an influx of male demonstrators, and the scope of the turmoil grew rapidly. On March 2 the czar abdicated. A provisional government was formed, and on July 20 it granted women the rights to vote and hold office (rights not granted in England until 1918 and the United States until 1920). Feminists, having achieved their goal, disappeared as an autonomous force. Liberal women lost control of events. When the Winter Palace was seized by the Bolsheviks on the night of October 25–26, it was defended by a women's contingent composed of intellectuals along with women of the bourgeoisie, aristocracy, and working class. The revolution now erupted into a bloody civil war whose outcome hung for a long time in the balance.

A Decade of Contradiction

Though surrounded by Whites, forces of the Allied powers, and nationalists, the Bolsheviks sallied forth from Moscow and Petrograd (later Leningrad) to regain control of nearly all of the territory that had constituted the old Russian Empire. They lost no time adopting a host of new laws concerning women. A decree of December 19, 1917, stipulated that in case of mutual consent divorce was to be granted automatically by the courts or the Registry offices (ZAGS); the principle according to which one party must be assigned blame was abolished, and the divorce decree no longer had to be publicized. Russia was the first country in the world to adopt such a liberal divorce policy. A decree of December 20, 1917, abolished religious marriage and standardized and simplified the civil marriage procedure. All children, legitimate or not, enjoyed the same legal rights. These two measures were extended by the Family Code of December 16, 1918—the most liberal in Europe at the time. The ZAGS became the chief agency for dealing with family matters. A man could no longer force his wife to accept his name, residence, or nationality. Husband and wife enjoyed absolute equality even with respect to the children. Maternity leave and workplace protection were guaranteed. The Family Code adopted a narrow definition of the family: direct ancestors and descendants together with brothers and sisters. A spouse enjoyed the same status as kin and collaterals, with no special privileges or prerogatives. The new family proved less stable than the old. Bonds between individuals were loosened: inheritance was outlawed in April 1918 (and only partially restored in 1923). Unrestricted abortion was legalized on November 20, 1920.

The Code of November 19, 1926, confirmed these earlier changes and took yet another step, abolishing all differences between marriages legally recorded by the ZAGS and *de facto* (common-law) marriages. Divorce could henceforth be obtained on the written request of either party: "postcard divorce" was now legal. Love was freer, but mutual obligations were more onerous owing to new alimony and child support requirements. The new Family Code was intended to liberate men, women, and children from the coercive regulations of another era. The past was to be completely effaced. People were urged to change their family names in March 1918 and their first names in 1924: suggestions for new names included Marlen (short for Marxism-Leninism), Engelsine, and Octobrine. Though intended to be an instrument of liberation, the code was also an instrument of coercion that could be used to strike at conservative segments of the society, particularly peasants and Muslims. In fact, the Communist Party, composed of a handful of urban intellectuals, deliberately ignored the views of those whom it sped along the road to a better tomorrow. Although lawmakers occasionally reversed themselves, their actions were always guided by two principles: to destroy czarism and build socialism....

Kollontai: A Reluctant Feminist

Alexandra Kollontai (1872–1952) was a pivotal figure in debates on women and the family during the first Soviet decade. She epitomizes all the contradictions of the period. Her biography is typical of her generation. Aristocratic by birth, she enjoyed a luxury-filled, dreamy childhood. After marrying at age nineteen to escape her family and milieu, she left her husband at age twenty-six and went to school in Zurich, then a Mecca for Russian intellectuals, where she became involved in politics, took increasingly radical positions, and eventually became a professional revolutionary. Her record was brilliant: as the first woman elected to the Central Committee in 1917, she voted in favor of the October insurrection. She then became the first woman to serve in the government, as people's commissar for health, and took an active part in drafting the Family Code of 1918. As an active member of the Workers' Opposition in 1920–1921, she sought to limit the vast powers of the Communist Party. In 1922 she became the first woman ambassador in the world. Her diplomatic career abroad kept her away from Moscow until 1945, yet her name is inseparable from the controversies of the 1920s, whose passions she fueled with countless articles, pamphlets, and brochures that were widely criticized, distorted, and even caricatured. She also wrote a number of theoretical tomes *(The Social Bases of the Woman Question,* 1909; *The Family and the Communist State,* 1918; *The New Morality and the Working Class,* 1918), as well as six works of fiction, all published in 1923. Although certain aspects of her work now seem dated, much of it remains remarkably up to date.

Kollontai proposed a synthesis of Marxism with a feminism she never avowed (and in fact always combated). Marxism, combined with a touch of Fourierist utopianism, would facilitate the realization of feminist goals. Like Marx and Engels, Kollontai believed that the bourgeois family had fallen apart and that revolution would lead to the regeneration of family life. She also drew extensively on the work of Bebel, particularly his idea that oppression tends to create unity among women. But she tried to go beyond these general arguments. Aware that the revolution was merely a starting point, she argued that to change the essence of marriage required changing people's attitudes and behavior. Therein lay her originality. She stressed the reifying tendency of the masculine will and noted the alienation of women who prefer any kind of marriage to solitude and are thus driven to wager everything on love. So Kollontai taught that love could be a kind of sport: if tender erotic friendship were based on mutual respect, jealousy and the possessive instinct might be eliminated. The "new woman," one of her recurrent subjects, was energetic and self-assertive. She let men know what she wanted; she refused to be dependent either materially or emotionally; she rebelled against socioeconomic obstacles, hypocritical morals, and "amorous captivity." Autonomous and active, she was free to explore "serial monogamy." In "Make Room for Wingèd Eros," an article published in 1923, Kollontai analyzed love's many facets: friendship, passion, maternal affection, spiritual affinity, habit, and so on. "Wingless Eros," or purely physical attraction, was to make room for "wingèd Eros," wherein physical gratification was combined with a sense of collective duty, that indispensable attribute in the era of transition to socialism. Finally, once socialist society had been established, there would be room for "Eros transfigured," or marriage based on healthy, free, and natural sexual attraction. To allow couples to develop, "kitchens must be separated from homes": in other words, society must build cafeterias, day-care centers, and dispensaries in order to relieve women of certain of their traditional responsibilities. Last but not least, motherhood was cast in a new light: it was "no longer a private affair but a social duty." Women must have children for the sake of the community. Kollontai considered abortion to be a temporary evil, to be tolerated only until the consciousness of working women had been raised to the point where it was no longer necessary. She denounced the refusal to bear children as petty-bourgeois selfishness. Nevertheless, she did not advocate the collectivization of child-rearing: parents should decide whether children were to be raised in a nursery school or at home.

As a spiritual value, however, love in general—and sex—should take precedence over the maternal instinct: "The workers' state needs a new type of relation between the sexes. A mother's narrow, exclusive love for her own child must broaden to embrace all the children of the great proletarian family. In the place of indissoluble marriage, based on the servitude of women, we look forward to the birth of free matrimony, an institution made strong by the mutual love and respect of two members of the brotherhood of Labor, equals in rights as well as obligations. In place of the individualistic, egoistic family will arise the great universal family of working people, in which everyone, men and women alike, will be first and foremost brothers and comrades." Kollontai called upon women to defend, propagate, and internalize the idea that they had value as human beings in their own right.

To be sure, Kollontai's argument was framed in terms of classical Marxism, to which the economy is primary, but she also insisted on the qualitative aspect of interpersonal relations: men and women should be attentive to each other's needs and playful toward one another. Ethics mattered to her as much as politics. Well before Wilhelm Reich, she was among the first to link sexuality with class struggle: "Why is it that we are so unforgivably indifferent to one of the essential tasks of the working class? How are we to explain the hypocritical relegation of the sexual problem to the realm of 'family affairs' not requiring collective effort? As if sexual relations and the morals governing them have not been a constant factor in social struggle throughout history."

Few people shared Kollontai's ideas in the Soviet Union of the 1920s. Her comrades looked upon her ideas as frivolous and ill-timed. Her views presupposed a yet-to-be-achieved social and economic infrastructure, and they came in for vehement criticism in a 1923 article by the Bolshevik P. Vinogradskaya, who had worked with Kollontai on the Women's Department of the Central Committee Secretariat (*Zhenotdel*) in 1920. Vinogradskaya attacked her opponent for confusing priorities, neglecting the class struggle, and encouraging sexual anarchy in an irresponsible way, since disorder in private life could lead to counterrevolutionary agitation. The task of the moment was to protect wives and children and to champion the cause of women without attacking men. Marx and Engels had already said everything there was to be said on the question, and it was pointless to indulge in "George-Sandism."

Lenin, for his part, related everything to the economy and opted in favor of monogamous marriage, egalitarian, earnest, and devoted to the cause, like his own tranquil union with Nadezhda Krupskaya. When Ines Armand saw poetry in free love, Lenin responded that what she mistook for poetry was nothing but bourgeois immorality. He borrowed his ideal from Nikolai Chernysbevski's austere novel *What Is to Be Done?* (1863), which, as he said, "bowled him over." Indeed, he thought so highly of the book that he used its title for his own theoretical work of 1902. His conversations with Clara Zetkin, which took place in 1920 but were not published until 1925, after Lenin's death, accurately reflected his rejection of lack of discipline in love and sexual matters. Lenin saw such lack of discipline as a sign of decadence and a danger to young people's health, hence to the revolution itself. He attacked the "anti-Marxist" theory according to which "in Communist society the satisfaction of sexual desires is as simple and soothing as drinking a glass of water." Lenin had nobody particular in mind. He was not attacking Kollontai, for his remarks preceded the polemic of 1923, but later Kollontai's adversaries used his wrath against her: "Of course thirst must be satisfied! But would a normal man, under normal conditions, prostrate himself in the street to drink from a filthy puddle? Or even from a glass previously soiled by dozens of other lips?" Here, purity is restored as an absolute value, and the underlying idea is that having more than one sexual partner is in itself immoral. Lenin's credo was a negative one: "No to the monk, no to the Don Juan, and no to that supposed happy medium, the German philistine." To be sure, he denounced the slavery of housework: "Woman is stifled, strangled, stupefied, and humiliated by the trivial occupations of domestic life, which chain her to the kitchen and nursery and sap her strength for work that is as unproductive, difficult, and exhausting as one can imagine." But he said nothing about the new family.

For orthodox Marxists, children did not figure in the conjugal scheme. They were to be taken care of either by certain designated women or by all the women of the community collectively—at the outset the choice is not clear. Fathers certainly play no role in the new system of child-rearing. The community supports, envelops, permeates, and transcends the reduced couple, in which man and woman are strict equals. The woman, like her husband, is a worker; traditional femininity is disparaged as a product of old bourgeois social relations. Equality in fact means identity of the sexes. The new industrious humanity consists of male and female twins, identical insofar as both are workers. "Economically and politically, which also means physiologically, the modern proletarian woman can and must become more and more like the modern proletarian man," wrote Marxist psychoneurologist Aaron Zalkind in 1924. Sexual relations, we are told, will not be a matter of great importance for such indistinguishable twins. One can interpret this claim in two ways. If sex is merely a physiological need, then the number of partners is unimportant: this is the attitude of the youth Zhenya in Kollontai's short story, "Three Generations of Love." The other interpretation leads to Leninist asceticism. In either case love must be restrained; it is a disruptive force. All of this was merely speculative, however. During the 1920s the private sphere remained intact, and various norms of sexual behavior coexisted.

A New Russia

In order to enforce the law, achieve economic equality, bring uniformity to a very disparate country, and accelerate the integration of women into the society, the Party in 1919 created the Zhenotdel, or Women's Department of the Central Committee Secretariat, with equivalents at every echelon of the hierarchy. Five women in succession led this Department during its existence, among them Ines Armand in 1919–20 and Alexandra Kollontai from 1920 to 1922. The Zhenotdel offered advice and assistance, settled labor and domestic conflicts, proposed laws and suggested amendments to Central Committee edicts, joined in actions such as the campaigns to eradicate illiteracy and abolish prostitution, coordinated the work of various agencies, oversaw the application of quotas that favored women in hiring and admission to soviets, dealt with problems of supply, housing, and sanitation, and inspected schools and orphanages. In addition to the Zhenotdel there was also a system of female delegates: women workers and peasants elected by their colleagues to participate in year-long training and indoctrination courses, after which they spent two months working with the soviets or the courts before returning to work. This system trained women to become "Soviet citizens." More than ten million of them signed up during the 1920s. Dasha, the heroine of Fedor Gladkov's novel *Cement* (1925), is a perfect example of the liberated woman. A militant delegate, she so completely threw off her old bonds that she sacrificed her marriage, her home, and even her little daughter, who died in an orphanage. There is no doubt that the Zhenotdel, together with the delegate system, had an impact on the consciousness of women. Its political influence remained negligible, however, and all too often it served only to convey the wishes of the hierarchy to the rank and file. In 1923 it was accused of "feminist deviationism," a fatal sin. . . .

Freedom and Disorder

. . . In one sense, women were granted all they could have hoped for right at the outset, without a struggle. But the most difficult part of the task remained: they had to learn how to make use of their newly won rights to forge a new way of life. But given the sociohistorical context and the gaps in the codes of 1918 and 1926, new freedoms gave rise to unintended consequences.

Two signs of the times were marital instability and a widespread reluctance to have children. The number of abortions rose, the birthrate declined precipitously, and newborn babies were frequently abandoned. Orphanages, overwhelmed by new admissions, became veritable charnel houses. Infanticide and wife-murder increased. In effect, women and children were the first victims of the new order. The condition of women clearly became more dire, especially in the cities. Men abandoned their families, leaving their wives without resources. The availability of divorce merely on application by either party led to cynical abuses. The government allowed common-law marriages in order to protect women from seduction and abandonment (and also to protect any children that might result from fleeting affairs); men were required to provide for the women they left behind, and thus to assume a burden that the government itself was unable to bear. But women had to prove that an affair had taken place, and the law failed to specify what constituted proof. The courts improvised. Lengthy and often fruitless paternity suits poisoned relations between the sexes and became a recurrent theme of contemporary fiction. The laws governing alimony were just as vague, and the courts were obliged to fix amounts on a case-by-case basis. Often it was set at one-third or one-fourth of the man's monthly wage, which sometimes created insurmountable difficulties. How was a man to survive if ten rubles were deducted from his wage of forty rubles? How was he to support a child born out of wedlock when he already had four "legitimate" children to take care of? Few men earned enough to cover alimony, and many refused to pay up. Rulings of the court went unenforced in more than half the cases.

There were practical problems as well. Allocation of housing was a state monopoly, and waiting lists were extremely long. Divorced couples were therefore obliged in some cases to go on living together. Abram Room's film *Bed and Sofa* (1927) is a marvelous depiction of conditions under the NEP [New Economic Policy]. It offers a new perspective on the eternal triangle, portraying a husband, wife, and lover forced to share a single room. After the seduction, moreover, the two men take a nonchalant attitude toward the situation and join in a macho alliance against the woman, the wife of one and mistress of the other.

Many women who wanted children were nevertheless forced to seek abortions because of the scarcity of housing, low wages, short supplies, and/or lack of a man. In a survey conducted in Moscow in 1927, 71 percent of women seeking abortions cited "living conditions" as the reason and 22 percent mentioned unstable love lives." Only 6 percent rejected motherhood on principle.

Although intellectuals and quasi-intellectuals in the cities went on leading bohemian lives, some segments of the population resisted any change in traditional mores. In 1928, 77.8 percent of the population still consisted of peasants, compared with only 17.6 percent blue- and white-collar workers. The Code of 1926 triggered a huge controversy that illustrates the continuing influence of the peasantry. Since accurate news was hard to come by despite innumerable published articles, brochures, and meetings, peasants were liable to be affected by unsubstantiated rumors, and many were convinced that the new code was going to make the sharing of women compulsory. The most controversial provision of the law concerned the treatment of de facto marriage as completely equivalent to lawful matrimony. The Agrarian Code of 1922 reinforced the communal organization of the village, or *mir,* and retained the undivided family property, or *dvor.* If a couple sharing in the *dvor* divorced and payment "of alimony led to division of the property, the farm might cease to be viable. Wary after years of ceaseless combat (1914–1921), the peasantry, fearful of novelty, drew back and clung to its traditional values.

It was an ambiguous image of woman that emerged from all the articles, brochures, pamphlets, investigations, speeches, novels, and films of the day: sometimes she was portrayed as a member of the vanguard of the working class, wearing an earnest look, work clothes, and a red scarf; at other times she was the backward peasant with her white kerchief pulled down over her eyes; or the mannish girl of the Komsomol (Young Communists), shockingly liberated in her ways; or the pert, flirtatious typist. Woman simultaneously embodied the past and the future. Conviction vied with confusion in the minds of the masses. Novels of the late 1920s are filled with restless, confused, unhappy heroines. Urban immorality and rural conservatism were matters of concern to both rulers and ruled. Women wanted stability, men declined responsibility, and the Party wanted to keep its program on course. By 1926 it was clear that, like it or not, the family would survive. Certain sectors of light industry were sacrificed in the name of economic progress. Home and children once again became the concern of women. The woman question was held to have been resolved once and for all, and in 1929 the Zhenotdel was abolished. . . .

A Contestable and Contested Model

By 1923 the die was cast. Although there was progress at the grass roots, there was stalemate at the top. The masses were enlisted in the struggle, but the once competent, combative, and cultivated elite was supplanted by squadrons of colorless yes-men. Strong personalities such as Alexandra Kollontai were removed or liquidated.

In the end Kollontai's fears were justified. Without a redefinition of sex roles economic emancipation proved to be a trap, for women were obliged to conform to a male model without being relieved of their burden as women. It may be that a comparable danger exists in any developing industrial society. A century of European evolution was compressed into two decades in the Soviet Union: the sexual revolution of the 1920s broke down the old family unit, while the Stalinist reaction of the 1930s reshaped the family in order to impose breakneck industrialization on a backward peasant society. The gap between the idealistic slogans and everyday reality was enormous.

The one-party state was not solely responsible for these developments, however. As in other countries, the role of women was ambiguous. Whether responding by instinct to ensure their own survival and that of their children or acting out of alienation, women accepted and internalized the rules of the Soviet game to a greater extent than men—and much to men's annoyance. Sober, long-suffering, conscientious, and disciplined, woman was one of the pillars of the regime: she did the washing, stood in line to buy food, cooked meals, took care of the children, worked in factories and offices and on collective farms, and did whatever she had to do. But to what end? Equality only added to her burden.

POSTSCRIPT

Did the Bolshevik Revolution Improve the Lives of Soviet Women?

It is one of history's ironies that, with the stroke of a pen, Soviet women were granted all the legal and political rights that women in Britain and the United States were struggling to achieve. Having won the rights to vote and hold public office, Soviet women struggled to translate those paper rights into improved lives for themselves and their children. It has been a conviction of Western feminism that legal and political equality pave the way for full emancipation of women. The Soviet case raises interesting questions about the confusion that arises when there are conflicting revolutions. Real political power belongs to those who can ensure that the goals of their revolution receive first priority. It was the socialist revolution, not women's emancipation, that the party leadership worked to achieve.

Popular accounts of the Russian Revolution may be found in John Reed, *Ten Days That Shook the World* (Penguin, 1977) and Louise Bryant, *Mirrors of Moscow* (Hyperion Press, 1973). The story of Reed and Bryant, two Americans who find themselves eyewitnesses to the Bolshevik Revolution, is captured in the film *Reds*. Another film covering the same period is *Doctor Zhivago,* which is based on the book of the same title by Boris Pasternak (1958). For Lenin's views on women, one of the best sources is his book *The Emancipation of Women* (International Publishers, 1972). *The Unknown Lenin: From the Secret Archives,* edited by the eminent Russian historian Richard Pipes (Yale University Press, 1996), dips into the secret archives and brands Lenin a ruthless and manipulative leader. Robert McNeal's *Bride of the Revolution* (University of Michigan Press, 1972) focuses on the fascinating marriage and revolutionary relationship between Lenin and Bolshevik propagandist Nadezhda Krupskaya. And Sheila Fitzpatrick, in *The Russian Revolution* (Oxford University Press, 1982), surveys the critical 1917–1932 period with special emphasis on the work of Zhenotdel. For essays on the lives of women during this period, students may want to see *Women in Soviet Society,* edited by Gail Lapidus (University of California Press, 1978), and *Women in Russia,* edited by D. Atkinson, A. Dallin, G. Lapidus (Stanford University Press, 1977), which grew out of a 1975 conference that was held at Stanford University titled "Women in Russia." The fascinating character Alexandra Kollontai, who died at 80, may be explored through her own writings in *Selected Writings* (W. W. Norton, 1972); *The Autobiography of a Sexually Emancipated Communist Woman* (Schocken Books, 1975); *Red Love* (Hyperion Press, 1990); and *Love of Worker Bees* (Academy of Chicago Press, 1978). Books about Kollontai include *Bolshevik Feminist* by Barbara Clements (Indiana University Press, 1979).

ISSUE 10

Was German "Eliminationist Antisemitism" Responsible for the Holocaust?

YES: Daniel Jonah Goldhagen, from *Hitler's Willing Executioners: Ordinary Germans and the Holocaust* (Alfred A. Knopf, 1996)

NO: Christopher R. Browning, from "Ordinary Germans or Ordinary Men? A Reply to the Critics," in Michael Berenbaum and Abraham J. Peck, eds., *The Holocaust and History: The Known, the Unknown, the Disputed, and the Reexamined* (Indiana University Press, 1998)

ISSUE SUMMARY

YES: Professor of political science Daniel Jonah Goldhagen states that due to the nature of German society in the twentieth century—with its endemic, virulent antisemitism—thousands of ordinary German citizens became willing participants in the implementation of Holocaust horrors.

NO: Holocaust historian Christopher R. Browning argues that Goldhagen's thesis is too simplistic and that a multicausal approach must be used to determine why ordinary German citizens willingly participated in the Holocaust.

Few historical events engender stronger emotional responses than the Nazi-directed Holocaust of World War II, in which millions of Jews were systematically exterminated as part of a ghastly plan for a diabolical new world order. Since its occurrence, many scholarly works have been written in an attempt to answer the questions that this "crime against humanity" has raised: What historical factors were responsible for it? How did people and nations allow it to roll toward its final destructive consequences? What lessons did it teach us about human nature? Could something like this happen again? Who bears the responsibility for it?

Much of Holocaust scholarship has concentrated on European anti-semitism as a major factor in the cause of the event itself and as a major reason why little was done to stop it. Some scholars have emphasized the schizophrenic nature of post–World War I politics, which they say allowed demagogic madmen to weave their magic web around an unsuspecting public. Others have stressed the violent nature of the twentieth-century world (especially after the Great War), which created an immunity-against-brutality temperament that made the Holocaust possible. And, of course, the major blame has been placed on Adolf Hitler and his Nazi henchmen for the initiation, design, and implementation of the Holocaust.

But just how unsuspecting was this public? Most people have long ago dismissed (as did the Nuremberg War Crimes Tribunal) the "I was only following orders" argument that so many who actively participated in Holocaust horrors have used. Others who were not directly involved have cited the hopelessness of opposition and the fear of reprisal to explain their acquiescence. But as we have been made witness to countless trials for war crimes in the last 50 years, some have wondered whether or not a larger segment of the population in those Nazi-controlled countries was involved in the Holocaust's worst aspects.

Daniel Jonah Goldhagen was not the first scholar to investigate this subject, but his 1996 book *Hitler's Willing Executioners: Ordinary Germans and the Holocaust*, which is excerpted in the following selection, has raised the issue to a new level and has created a maelstrom of controversy within the historical profession. Using recently discovered sources of information and tools of analysis newly available to social scientists, Goldhagen takes a fresh look at why and how the Holocaust occurred through an analysis of three related subjects: "the perpetrators of the Holocaust, German antisemitism, and the nature of German society during the Nazi period." Central to his thesis is the concept of *eliminationist antisemitism* (his own phrase), which turned "ordinary Germans" into "Hitler's willing executioners." Goldhagen's conclusions are a stinging indictment of large numbers of average German citizens, who he asserts willingly participated in the Holocaust's worst aspects, including police battalion killing squads, work camps, and death marches.

Goldhagen's work has received much public praise, including a National Book Critics nomination for nonfiction book of the year. But it has also had its share of critics, many of them Holocaust scholars. Some have found his work to be one-sided, inflammatory, and too narrow in its focus. One of Goldhagen's most persistent critics has been Christopher R. Browning. In the second selection, Browning states that antisemitism may have been widespread in pre-Nazi Germany, but it was not the major ideology of most German citizens. According to Browning, there are a variety of factors that were responsible for making ordinary Germans into willing killers. Goldhagen is critical of Browning's conclusions, and his critique can be found in "The Evil of Banality," *The New Republic* (July 13 & 20, 1992). Browning published a rejoinder to Goldhagen's critique as an afterword to the second edition of *Ordinary Men: Reserve Police Battalion 101 and the Final Solution in Poland* (Harper Perennial, 1998).

A proverbial hornet's nest has been stirred up by *Hitler's Willing Executioners*, and its reverberations are not likely to subside anytime in the near future. Regardless of opinions of the book, any future works on the Holocaust will have to at least consider the questions that it has raised.

Daniel Jonah Goldhagen

 **YES**

Reconceiving Central Aspects of the Holocaust

During the Holocaust, Germans extinguished the lives of six million Jews and, had Germany not been defeated, would have annihilated millions more. The Holocaust was also the defining feature of German politics and political culture during the Nazi period, the most shocking event of the twentieth century, and the most difficult event to understand in all of German history. The Germans' persecution of the Jews culminating in the Holocaust is thus the central feature of Germany during the Nazi period. It is so not because we are retrospectively shocked by the most shocking event of the century, but because of what it meant to Germans at the time and why so many of them contributed to it. It marked their departure from the community of "civilized peoples." This departure needs to be explained.

Explaining the Holocaust is the central intellectual problem for understanding Germany during the Nazi period. All the other problems combined are comparatively simple. How the Nazis came to power, how they suppressed the left, how they revived the economy, how the state was structured and functioned, how they made and waged war are all more or less ordinary, "normal" events, easily enough understood. But the Holocaust and the change in sensibilities that it involved "defies" explanation. There is no comparable event in the twentieth century, indeed in modern European history. Whatever the remaining debates, every other major event of nineteenth- and twentieth-century German history and political development is, in comparison to the Holocaust, transparently clear in its genesis. Explaining how the Holocaust happened is a daunting task empirically and even more so theoretically, so much so that some have argued, in my view erroneously, that it is "inexplicable." The theoretical difficulty is shown by its utterly new nature, by the inability of social theory (or what passed for common sense) preceding it to provide a hint not only that it would happen but also that it was even possible. Retrospective theory has not done much better, shedding but modest light in the darkness.

The overall objective of this [selection] is to explain why the Holocaust occurred, to explain how it could occur. The success of this enterprise depends upon a number of subsidiary tasks, which consist fundamentally of reconceiving three subjects: the perpetrators of the Holocaust, German antisemitism, and the nature of German society during the Nazi period.

❧

Foremost among the three subjects that must be reconceived are the perpetrators of the Holocaust. Few readers of this [selection] will have failed to give some thought to the question of what impelled the perpetrators of the Holocaust to kill. Few have neglected to provide for themselves an answer to the question, an answer that necessarily derives usually not from any intimate knowledge of the perpetrators and their deeds, but greatly from the individual's conception of human nature and social life. Few would probably disagree with the notion that the perpetrators should be studied.

Yet until now the perpetrators, the most important group of people responsible for the slaughter of European Jewry, excepting the Nazi leadership itself, have received little concerted attention in the literature that describes the events and purports to explain them. Surprisingly, the vast literature on the Holocaust contains little on the people who were its executors. Little is known of who the perpetrators were, the details of their actions, the circumstances of many of their deeds, let alone their motivations. A decent estimate of how many people contributed to the genocide, of how many perpetrators there were, has never been made. Certain institutions of killing and the people who manned them have been hardly treated or not at all. As a consequence of this general lack of knowledge, all kinds of misunderstandings and myths about the perpetrators abound. These misconceptions, moreover, have broader implications for the way in which the Holocaust and Germany during the Nazi period are conceived and understood.

We must therefore refocus our attention, our intellectual energy, which has overwhelmingly been devoted elsewhere, onto the perpetrators, namely the men and women who in some intimate way knowingly contributed to the slaughter of Jews. We must investigate their deeds in detail and explain their actions. It is not sufficient to treat the institutions of killing collectively or singly as internally uncomplicated instruments of the Nazi leadership's will, as well-lubricated machines that the regime activated, as if by the flick of a switch, to do its bidding, whatever it might have been. The study of the men and women who collectively gave life to the inert institutional forms, who peopled the institutions of genocidal killing must be set at the focus of scholarship on the Holocaust and become as central to investigations of the genocide as they were to its commission.

These people were overwhelmingly and most importantly Germans. While members of other national groups aided the Germans in their slaughter of Jews, the commission of the Holocaust was primarily a German undertaking. Non-Germans were not essential to the perpetration of the genocide, and they did not supply the drive and initiative that pushed it forward. To be sure, had the Germans not found European (especially, eastern European) helpers, then the Holocaust would have unfolded somewhat differently, and the Germans would likely not have succeeded in killing as many Jews. Still, this was above all a German enterprise; the decisions, plans, organizational resources, and the majority of its executors were German. Comprehension and explanation of the perpetration of the Holocaust therefore requires an explanation of the *Germans'* drive to kill Jews. Because what can be said about the Germans cannot be said about any other nationality or about all of the other nationalities combined —namely no Germans, no Holocaust—the focus here is appropriately on the German perpetrators.

The first task in restoring the perpetrators to the center of our understanding of the Holocaust is to restore to them their identities, grammatically by using not the passive but the active voice in order to ensure that they, the actors, are not absent from their own deeds (as in, "five hundred Jews were killed in city X on date Y"), and by eschewing convenient, yet often inappropriate and obfuscating labels, like "Nazis" and "SS men," and calling them what they were, "Germans." The most appropriate, indeed the only appropriate *general* proper name for the Germans who perpetrated the Holocaust is "Germans." They were Germans acting in the name of Germany and its highly popular leader, Adolf Hitler. Some were "Nazis," either by reason of Nazi Party membership or according to ideological conviction; some were not. Some were SS men; some were not. The perpetrators killed and made their other genocidal contributions under the auspices of many institutions other than the SS. Their chief common denominator was that they were all Germans pursuing German national political goals—in this case, the genocidal killing of Jews. To be sure, it is sometimes appropriate to use institutional or occupational names or roles and the generic terms "perpetrators" or "killers" to describe the perpetrators, yet this must be done only in the understood context that these men and women were Germans first, and SS men, policemen, or camp guards second.

A second and related task is to reveal something of the perpetrators' backgrounds, to convey the character and quality of their lives as genocidal killers, to bring to life their *Lebenswelt*. What *exactly* did they do when they were killing? What did they do during their time as members of institutions of killing, while they were not undertaking killing operations? Until a great deal is known about the details of their actions and lives, neither they nor the perpetration of their crimes can be understood. The unearthing of the perpetrators' lives, the presentation of a "thick," rather than the customary paper-thin, description of their actions, as important and necessary as it is for its own sake, lays the foundation for the main task of this [selection's] consideration of them, namely to explain their actions.

It is my contention that this cannot be done unless such an analysis is embedded in an understanding of German society before and during its Nazi period, particularly of the political culture that produced the perpetrators and their actions. This has been notably absent from attempts to explain the perpetrators' actions, and has doomed these attempts to providing situational explanations, ones that focus almost exclusively on institutional and immediate social psychological influences, often conceived of as irresistible pressures. The men and women who became the Holocaust's perpetrators were shaped by and operated in a particular social and historical setting. They brought with them prior elaborate conceptions of the world, ones that were common to their society, the investigation of which is necessary for explaining their actions. This entails, most fundamentally, a reexamination of the character and development of antisemitism in Germany during its Nazi period and before, which in turn requires a theoretical reconsideration of the character of antisemitism itself.

Studies of the Holocaust have been marred by a poor understanding and an under-theorizing of antisemitism. Antisemitism is a broad, typically imprecisely used term, encompassing a wide variety of phenomena. This naturally poses enormous obstacles for explaining the perpetration of the Holocaust because a central task of any such attempt is to evaluate whether and how antisemitism produced and influenced its many aspects. In my view, our understanding of antisemitism and of the relationship of antisemitism to the (mal)treatment of Jews is deficient. We must begin considering these subjects anew and develop a conceptual apparatus that is descriptively powerful and analytically useful for addressing the ideational causes of social action....

The study of the perpetrators further demands a reconsideration, indeed a reconceiving, of the character of German society during its Nazi period and before. The Holocaust was the defining aspect of Nazism, but not only of Nazism. It was also the defining feature of German society during its Nazi period. No significant aspect of German society was untouched by anti-Jewish policy; from the economy, to society, to politics, to culture, from cattle farmers, to merchants, to the organization of small towns, to lawyers, doctors, physicists, and professors. No analysis of German society, no understanding or characterization of it, can be made without placing the persecution and extermination of the Jews at its center. The program's first parts, namely the systematic exclusion of Jews from German economic and social life, were carried out in the open, under approving eyes, and with the complicity of virtually all sectors of German society, from the legal, medical, and teaching professions, to the churches, both Catholic and Protestant, to the gamut of economic, social, and cultural groups and associations. Hundreds of thousands of Germans contributed to the genocide and the still larger system of subjugation that was the vast concentration camp system. Despite the regime's half-hearted attempts to keep the genocide beyond the view of most Germans, millions knew of the mass slaughters. Hitler announced many times, emphatically, that the war would end in the extermination of the Jews. The killings met with general understanding, if not approval. No other policy (of similar or greater scope) was carried out with more persistence and zeal, and with fewer difficulties, than the genocide, except perhaps the war itself. The Holocaust defines not only the history of Jews during the middle of the twentieth century but also the history of Germans. While the Holocaust changed Jewry and Jews irrevocably, its commission was possible, I argue, because Germans had *already* been changed. The fate of the Jews may have been a direct, which does not, however, mean an inexorable, outgrowth of a worldview shared by the vast majority of the German people.

Each of these reconceivings—of the perpetrators, of German antisemitism, and of German society during the Nazi period—is complex, requires difficult theoretical work and the marshaling of considerable empirical material, and, ultimately, is deserving of a separate book in its own right. While the undertaking of each one is justifiable on its own theoretical and empirical grounds, each, in my view, is also strengthened by the others, for they are interrelated tasks. Together the three suggest that we must substantially rethink important aspects of German history, the nature of Germany during the Nazi period, and the perpetration of the Holocaust. This rethinking requires, on a number of subjects, the turning of conventional wisdom on its head, and the adoption of a new and substantially different view of essential aspects of this period, aspects which have generally been considered settled. Explaining why the Holocaust occurred requires a radical revision of what has until now been written....

This revision calls for us to acknowledge what has for so long been generally denied or obscured by academic and non-academic interpreters alike: Germans' antisemitic beliefs about Jews were the central causal agent of the Holocaust. They were the central causal agent not only of Hitler's decision to annihilate European Jewry (which is accepted by many) but also of the perpetrators' willingness to kill and to brutalize Jews. The conclusion of this [selection] is that antisemitism moved many thousands of "ordinary" Germans—and would have moved millions more, had they been appropriately positioned—to slaughter Jews. Not economic hardship, not the coercive means of a totalitarian state, not social psychological pressure, not invariable psychological propensities, but ideas about Jews that were pervasive in Germany, and had been for decades, induced ordinary Germans to kill unarmed, defenseless Jewish men, women, and children by the thousands, systematically and without pity.

For what developments would a comprehensive explanation of the Holocaust have to account? For the extermination of the Jews to occur, four principal things were necessary:

1. The Nazis—that is, the leadership, specifically Hitler—had to decide to undertake the extermination.
2. They had to gain control over the Jews, namely over the territory in which they resided.
3. They had to organize the extermination and devote to it sufficient resources.
4. They had to induce a large number of people to carry out the killings.

The vast literature on Nazism and the Holocaust treats in great depth the first three elements, as well as others, such as the origins and character of Hitler's genocidal beliefs, and the Nazis' ascendancy to power. Yet, as I have already indicated, it has treated the last element, the focus of this [selection], perfunctorily and mainly by assumption. It is therefore important to discuss here some analytical and interpretive issues that are central to studying the perpetrators.

Owing to the neglect of the perpetrators in the study of the Holocaust, it is no surprise that the existing interpretations of them have been generally produced in a near empirical vacuum. Until recently, virtually no research has been done on the perpetrators, save on the leaders of the Nazi regime. In the last few years, some publications have appeared that treat one group or another, yet the state of our knowledge about the perpetrators remains deficient. We know little about many of the institutions of killing, little about many aspects of the perpetration of the genocide, and still less about the perpetrators themselves. As a consequence, popular and scholarly myths and misconceptions about the perpetrators abound, including the following. It is commonly believed that the Germans slaughtered Jews by and large in the gas chambers, and that without gas chambers, modern means of transportation, and efficient bureaucracies, the Germans would have been unable to kill millions of Jews. The belief persists that somehow only technology made horror on this scale possible. "Assembly-line killing" is one of the stock phrases in discussions of the event. It is generally believed that gas chambers, because of their efficiency (which is itself greatly overstated), were a necessary instrument for the genocidal slaughter, and that the Germans chose to construct the gas chambers in the first place because they needed more efficient means of killing the Jews. It has been generally believed by scholars (at least until very recently) and non-scholars alike that the perpetrators were primarily, overwhelmingly SS men, the most devoted and brutal Nazis. It has been an unquestioned truism (again until recently) that had a German refused to kill Jews, then he himself would have been killed, sent to a concentration camp, or severely punished. All of these views, views that fundamentally shape people's understanding of the Holocaust, have been held unquestioningly as though they were self-evident truths. They have been virtual articles of faith (derived from sources other than historical inquiry), have substituted for knowledge, and have distorted the way in which this period is understood.

The absence of attention devoted to the perpetrators is surprising for a host of reasons, only one of which is the existence of a now over-ten-year-long debate about the genesis of the *initiation* of the Holocaust, which has come to be called by the misnomer the "intentionalist–functionalist" debate. For better or worse, this debate has become the organizing debate for much of the scholarship on the Holocaust. Although it has improved our understanding of the exact chronology of the Germans' persecution and mass murder of the Jews, it has also, because of the terms in which it has been cast, confused the analysis of the causes of the Germans' policies..., and it has done next to nothing to increase our knowledge of the perpetrators. Of those who defined this debate and made its central early contributions, only one saw fit to ask the question, Why, once the killing began (however it did), did those receiving the orders to kill do so? It appears that for one reason or another, all the participants in the debate assumed that executing such orders was unproblematic for the actors, and unproblematic for historians and social scientists. The limited character of our knowledge, and therefore our understanding, of this period is highlighted by the simple fact that (however the category of "perpetrator" is defined) the number of people who were perpetrators is unknown. No good estimate, virtually no estimate of any kind, exists of the number of people who knowingly contributed to the genocidal killing in some intimate way. Scholars who discuss them, inexplicably, neither attempt such an estimate nor point out that this, a topic of such great significance, is an important gap in our knowledge. If ten thousand Germans were perpetrators, then the perpetration of the Holocaust, perhaps the Holocaust itself, is a phenomenon of one kind, perhaps the deed of a select, unrepresentative group. If five hundred thousand or one million Germans were perpetrators, then it is a phenomenon of another kind, perhaps best conceived as a German national project. Depending on the number and identity of the Germans who contributed to the genocidal slaughter, different sorts of questions, inquiries, and bodies of theory might be appropriate or necessary in order to explain it.

This dearth of knowledge, not only about the perpetrators but also about the functioning of their host institutions has not stopped some interpreters from making assertions about them—although the most striking fact remains how few even bother to address the subject, let alone take it up at length. Still, from the literature a number of conjectured explanations can be distilled, even if they are not always clearly specified or elaborated upon in a sustained manner. (In fact, strands of different explanations are frequently intermingled without great coherence.) Some of them have been proposed to explain the actions of the German people generally and, by extension, they would apply to the perpetrators as well. Rather than laying out what each interpreter has posited about the perpetrators, an analytical account is provided here of the major arguments, with references to leading exemplars of each one. The most important of them can be classified into five categories:

One explanation argues for external compulsion: the perpetrators were coerced. They were left, by the threat of punishment, with no choice but to follow orders. After all, they were part of military or police-like institutions, institutions with a strict chain of command, demanding subordinate compliance to orders, which should have punished insubordination severely, perhaps with death. Put a gun to anyone's head, so goes the thinking, and he will shoot others to save himself.

A second explanation conceives of the perpetrators as having been blind followers of orders. A number of proposals have been made for the source or sources of this alleged propensity to obey: Hitler's charisma (the perpetrators were, so to speak, caught in his spell), a general human tendency to obey authority, a peculiarly German reverence for and propensity to obey authority, or a totalitarian society's blunting of the individual's moral sense and its conditioning of him or her to accept all tasks as necessary. So a common proposition exists, namely that people obey authority, with a variety of accounts of why this is so. Obviously, the notion that authority, particularly state authority, tends to elicit obedience merits consideration.

A third explanation holds the perpetrators to have been subject to tremendous social psychological pressure, placed upon each one by his comrades and/ or by the expectations that accompany the institutional roles that individuals occupy. It is, so goes the argument, extremely difficult for individuals to resist pressures to conform, pressures which can lead individuals to participate in acts which they on their own would not do, indeed would abhor. And a variety of psychological mechanisms are available for such people to rationalize their actions.

A fourth explanation sees the perpetrators as having been petty bureaucrats, or soulless technocrats, who pursued their self-interest or their technocratic goals and tasks with callous disregard for the victims. It can hold for administrators in Berlin as well as for concentration camp personnel. They all had careers to make, and because of the psychological propensity among those who are but cogs in a machine to attribute responsibility to others for overall policy, they could callously pursue their own careers or their own institutional or material interests. The deadening effects of institutions upon the sense of individual responsibility, on the one hand, and the frequent willingness of people to put their interests before those of others, on the other, need hardly be belabored.

A fifth explanation asserts that because tasks were so fragmented, the perpetrators could not understand what the real nature of their actions was; they could not comprehend that their small assignments were actually part of a global extermination program. To the extent that they could, this line of thinking continues, the fragmentation of tasks allowed them to deny the importance of their own contributions and to displace responsibility for them onto others. When engaged in unpleasant or morally dubious tasks, it is well known that people have a tendency to shift blame to others.

The explanations can be reconceptualized in terms of their accounts of the actors' capacity for volition: The first explanation (namely coercion) says that the killers could not say "no." The second explanation (obedience) and the third (situational pressure) maintain that Germans were psychologically incapable of saying "no." The fourth explanation (self-interest) contends that Germans had sufficient personal incentives to kill in order not to want to say "no." The fifth explanation (bureaucratic myopia) claims that it never even occurred to the perpetrators that they were engaged in an activity that might make them responsible for saying "no."

Each of these conventional explanations may sound plausible, and some of them obviously contain some truth, so what is wrong with them? While each suffers from particular defects, ... they share a number of dubious *common* assumptions and features worth mentioning here.

The conventional explanations *assume* a neutral or condemnatory attitude on the part of the perpetrators towards their actions. They therefore premise their interpretations on the assumption that it must be shown how people can be brought to commit acts to which they would not inwardly assent, acts which they would not agree are necessary or just. They either ignore, deny, or radically minimize the importance of Nazi and perhaps the perpetrators' ideology, moral values, and conception of the victims, for engendering the perpetrators' willingness to kill. Some of these conventional explanations also caricature the perpetrators, and Germans in general. The explanations treat them as if they had been people lacking a moral sense, lacking the ability to make decisions and take stances. They do not conceive of the actors as human agents, as people with wills, but as beings moved solely by external forces or by transhistorical and invariant psychological propensities, such as the slavish following of narrow "self-interest." The conventional explanations suffer from two other major conceptual failings. They do not sufficiently recognize the extraordinary nature of the deed: the mass killing of people. They *assume* and imply that inducing people to kill human beings is fundamentally no different from getting them to do any other unwanted or distasteful task. Also, none of the conventional explanations deems the *identity* of the victims to have mattered. The conventional explanations imply that the perpetrators would have treated any other group of intended victims in exactly the same way. That the victims were Jews —according to the logic of these explanations—is irrelevant.

I maintain that any explanation that fails to acknowledge the actors' capacity to know and to judge, namely to understand and to have views about the significance and the morality of their actions, that fails to hold the actors' beliefs and values as central, that fails to emphasize the autonomous motivating force of Nazi ideology, particularly its central component of antisemitism, cannot possibly succeed in telling us much about why the perpetrators acted as they did. Any explanation that ignores either the particular nature of the perpetrators' actions—the systematic, large-scale killing and brutalizing of people—or the identity of the victims is inadequate for a host of reasons. All explanations that adopt these positions, as do the conventional explanations, suffer a mirrored, double failure of recognition of the human aspect of the Holocaust: the humanity of the perpetrators, namely their capacity to judge and to choose to act inhumanely, and the humanity of the victims, that what the perpetrators did, they did to these people with their specific identities, and not to animals or things.

My explanation—which is new to the scholarly literature on the perpetrators—is that the perpetrators, "ordinary Germans," were animated by antisemitism, by a particular *type* of antisemitism that led them to conclude that the Jews *ought to die*. The perpetrators' beliefs, their particular brand of antisemitism, though obviously not the sole source, was, I maintain, a most significant and indispensable source of the perpetrators' actions and must be at the center of any explanation of them. Simply put, the perpetrators, having consulted their own convictions and morality and having judged the mass annihilation of Jews to be right, did not *want* to say "no." ...

The perpetrators were working within institutions that prescribed roles for them and assigned them specific tasks, yet they individually and collectively had latitude to make choices regarding their actions. Adopting a perspective which acknowledges this requires that their choices, especially the patterns of their choices, be discerned, analyzed, and incorporated into any overall explanation or interpretation. Ideal data would answer the following questions:

- What did the perpetrators actually do?
- What did they do in excess of what was "necessary"?
- What did they refuse to do?
- What could they have refused to do?
- What would they not have done?
- What was the manner in which they carried out their tasks?
- How smoothly did the overall operations proceed?

In examining the pattern of the perpetrators' actions in light of the institutional role requirements and incentive structure, two directions beyond the simple act of killing must be explored. First, in their treatment of Jews (and other victims), the Germans subjected them to a wide range of acts other than the lethal blow. It is important to understand the *gamut* of their actions towards Jews, if the genocidal slaughter is to be explicated. This is discussed in more detail presently. Second, the perpetrators' actions when they were *not* engaged in genocidal activities also shed light on the killing; the insights that an analysis of their non-killing activities offers into their general character and disposition to action, as well as the general social psychological milieu in which they lived might be crucial for understanding the patterns of their genocidal actions.

All of this points to a fundamental question: Which of the gamut of perpetrators' acts constitute the universe of the perpetrators' actions that need to be explained? Typically, the interpreters of the perpetrators have focused on one facet of the Germans' actions: the killing. This tunnel-vision perspective must be broadened. Imagine that the Germans had not undertaken to exterminate the Jews but had still mistreated them in all the other ways that they did, in concentration camps, in ghettos, as slaves. Imagine if, in our society today, people perpetrated against Jews or Christians, Whites or Blacks anything approaching one one-hundredth of the brutality and cruelty that Germans, independent of the killing, inflicted on Jews. Everyone would recognize the need for an explanation. Had the Germans not perpetrated a genocide, then the degree of privation and cruelty to which the Germans subjected Jews would in itself have come into focus and have been deemed an historic outrage, aberration, perversion that requires explanation. Yet these same actions have been lost in the genocide's shadow and neglected by previous attempts to explain the significant aspects of this event.

The fixation on the mass killing to the exclusion of the other related actions of the perpetrators has led to a radical misspecification of the explanatory task. The killing should be, for all the obvious reasons, at the center of scholarly attention. Yet it is not the only aspect of the Germans' treatment of the Jews that demands systematic scrutiny and explanation. Not only the killing but also *how* the Germans killed must be explained. The "how" frequently provides great insight into the "why." A killer can endeavor to render the deaths of others—whether he thinks the killing is just or unjust—more or less painful, both physically and emotionally. The ways in which Germans, collectively and individually, sought in their actions, or merely considered, to alleviate or intensify their victims' suffering must be accounted for in any explanation. An explanation that can seemingly make sense of Germans putting Jews to death, but not of the manner in which they did it, is a faulty explanation....

People must be motivated to kill others, or else they would not do so. What conditions of cognition and value made genocidal motivations plausible in this period of German history? What was the structure of beliefs and values that made a genocidal onslaught against Jews intelligible and sensible to the ordinary Germans who became perpetrators? Since any explanation must also account for the actions of tens of thousands of Germans of a wide variety of backgrounds working in different types of institutions, and must also account for a wide range of actions (and not merely the killing itself), a structure common to them must be found which is adequate to explaining the compass of their actions. This structure of cognition and value was located in and integral to German culture.

NO

Christopher R. Browning

Ordinary Germans or Ordinary Men?
A Reply to the Critics

In the spring of 1992, I published a book entitled *Ordinary Men,* the case study of a reserve police battalion from Hamburg that became the chief unit for killing Jews in the northern Lublin district of the General Government. In general, the book has been quite well-received, but it has not been without its critics in both the United States and Israel. While these critics have accepted the narrative presentation in the book that reveals the mode of operation and degree of choice within the battalion, they have objected to my use of sources, my portrayal of the perpetrators (particularly their motives and mindset) and, above all, the conclusions that I draw—the crux of which is summed up in the title *Ordinary Men.* As one friendly but critical letter-writer suggested, "Might not a preferable title... possibly have been Ordinary Germans?"

The argument of my critics for German singularity rests above all upon their assertion of a unique and particular German antisemitism. The letter-writer cited above argued that "cultural conditioning" shaped "specifically German behavioral modes." He continued, hypothesizing that "even many decidedly non-Nazi Germans... were so accustomed to the thought that Jews are less human than Germans, that they were capable of mass murder." Non-Germans in the same situation as the men of Reserve Police Battalion 101, he implies, would have behaved quite differently.

Daniel Goldhagen, the most severe critic of what he called my "essentially situational" explanation, put the matter more pointedly. The "Germans' singular and deeply rooted, racist anti-Semitism" was not "a common social psychological phenomenon" that can be analyzed in terms of "mere" negative racial stereotypes, as I had so "tepidly" done. "The men of Reserve Police Battalion 101 were not ordinary 'men,' but ordinary members of an extraordinary culture, the culture of Nazi Germany, which was possessed of a hallucinatory, lethal view of the Jews." Thus, ordinary Germans were "believers in the justice of the murder of the Jews." In their "inflamed imaginations," destruction of the Jews "was a redemptive act."

The issue raised here, namely the appropriate balance of situational, cultural, and ideological factors in explaining the behavior of Holocaust killers, is an important—indeed central—subject that merits further exploration. I would like to approach this issue along two lines of inquiry. First, what has the bulk of recent scholarship concluded about the nature, intensity, and alleged singularity of antisemitism within the German population at large? Second, what light can comparisons between German and non-German killers of Jews in the Holocaust shed on the issue of "specifically German behavioral modes"?

Let us turn to the first line of inquiry, namely the nature and intensity of antisemitism within Nazi Germany. Perhaps the most ardent advocate of an interpretation emphasizing the singularity and centrality of German antisemitism was Lucy S. Dawidowicz. In her book *The War against the Jews,* she argued that

> generations of anti-Semitism had prepared the Germans to accept Hitler as their redeemer.... Of the conglomerate social, economic, and political appeals that the NSDAP [National Socialist German Workers Party] directed at the German people, its racial doctrine was the most attractive.... Out of the whole corpus of racial teachings, the anti-Jewish doctrine had the greatest dynamic potency.... The insecurities of post–World War I Germany and the anxieties they produced provided an emotional milieu in which irrationality and hysteria became routine and illusions became transformed into delusions. The delusional disorder assumed mass proportions.... In modern Germany the mass psychosis of anti-Semitism deranged a whole people.

A large number of other scholars, however, have not shared this view. Three scholars in particular—Ian Kershaw, Otto Dov Kulka, and David Bankier—have devoted a significant portion of their scholarly lives to examining German popular attitudes toward National Socialism, antisemitism, and the Holocaust. While there are differences of emphasis, tone, and interpretation among them, the degree of consensus on the basic issues is impressive.

While Kulka and Bankier do not pick up the story until 1933, Kershaw argues that prior to the *Machtergreifung,* antisemitism was not a major factor in attracting support for Hitler and the Nazis. He cites Peter Merkl's study of the "old fighters," in which only about one-seventh of Merkl's sample considered antisemitism their most salient concern and even fewer were classified by Merkl as "strong ideological antisemites." Moreover, in the electoral breakthrough phase of 1929–1933, and indeed up to 1939, Hitler rarely spoke in public about the Jewish question. This reticence stood in stark contrast to the Hitler speeches of the early 1920s, in which his obsession with and hatred of the Jews was vented openly and repeatedly. Kershaw concludes that "antisemitism cannot... be allocated a decisive role in bringing Hitler to power, though... it did not do anything to hinder his rapidly growing popularity."

For the 1933–1939 period, all three historians characterize German popular response to antisemitism by two dichotomies. The first is a distinction between a minority of party activists, for whom antisemitism was an urgent priority, and the bulk of the German population, for whom it was not. Party activists clamored and pressed, often in violent and rowdy ways, for intensified persecution. The antisemitic measures of the regime, though often criticized as too mild by the radicals, served an integrating function within Hitler's movement: they helped to keep the momentum and enthusiasm of the party activists alive. Despite Hitler's pragmatic caution in public, most of these radicals correctly sensed that he was with them in spirit.

The second dichotomy characterizes the reaction of the general population to the antisemitic clamor of the movement and the antisemitic measures of the regime. The vast majority accepted the legal measures of the regime, which ended emancipation and drove Jews from public positions in 1933, socially ostracized the Jews in 1935, and completed the expropriation of their property in 1938–1939. Yet this same majority was critical of the hooliganistic violence of party radicals toward the same German Jews whose legal persecution they approved. The boycott of 1933, the vandalistic outbreaks of 1935, and above all the Kristallnacht pogrom of November 1938 produced a negative response among the German population. Bankier and Kulka emphasize the pragmatic concerns behind this negative response: destruction of property, foreign policy complications, damage to Germany's image, and general lawlessness offensive to societal notions of decorum. In Kershaw's opinion, the idea that the population discounted virtually any moral dimension is "a far too sweeping generalization." Nonetheless, these historians agree that a gulf had opened up between the Jewish minority and the general population. The latter, while they were not mobilized around strident and violent antisemitism, were increasingly "apathetic," "passive," and "indifferent" to the fate of the former. Antisemitic measures—if carried out in an orderly and legal manner—were widely accepted for two main reasons: such measures sustained the hope of curbing the violence most Germans found so distasteful, and most Germans ultimately agreed with the goal of limiting, and even ending, the role of Jews in German society.

The records of the war years upon which Kulka, Bankier, and Kershaw based their studies were sparser and more ambiguous. Accordingly, the difference in interpretation is greater. Kulka and Bankier deduce a more specific awareness of the Final Solution among the German people than does Kershaw. Kershaw and Bankier advocate a more critical and less literal reading of the SD [security service] reports than does Kulka. Kershaw sees a general "retreat into the private sphere" as the basis for widespread indifference and apathy toward Nazi Jewish policy. Kulka sees a greater internalization of Nazi antisemitism among the population at large, particularly concerning the acceptance of a solution to the Jewish Question through some unspecified kind of "elimination," and accordingly prefers the term "passive" or "objective complicity" over "indifference." Bankier emphasizes a greater sense of guilt and shame among Germans, widespread denial and repression, and a growing fear concerning the consequences of impending defeat and a commensurate rejection of the regime's antisemitic propaganda. But these differences are matters of nuance, degree, and diction. Fundamentally, the three scholars agree far more than they differ.

Above all, they agree that the fanatical antisemitism of the party "true believers" was not identical to the antisemitic attitudes of the general population and that the antisemitic priorities and genocidal commitment of the regime were not shared by ordinary Germans. Kershaw concludes that while

> the depersonalization of the Jew had been the real success story of Nazi propaganda and policy... the "Jewish question" was of no more than minimal interest to the vast majority of Germans during the war years.... Popular opinion, largely indifferent and infused with a latent anti-Jewish feeling... provided the climate within which spiralling Nazi aggression towards the Jews could take place unchallenged. But it did not provoke the radicalization in the first place.

Kershaw summarized his position in the memorable phrase that "the road to Auschwitz was built by hatred, but paved with indifference." ...

The general conclusions of Kershaw, Kulka, and Bankier—based on years of research and a wide array of empirical evidence—stand in stark contrast to the Dawidowicz/Goldhagen image of the entire German population "deranged" by a delusional mass psychosis and in the grips of a "hallucinatory, lethal view of the Jews." If "ordinary Germans" shared the same "latent," "traditional," or even "deep-seated" antisemitism that was widespread in European society but not the "fanatical" or "radical" antisemitism of Hitler, the Nazi leadership, and the party "true believers," then the behavior of the "ordinary Germans" of Reserve Police Battalion 101 cannot be explained by a singular German antisemitism that makes them different from other "ordinary men."

My characterization of the depersonalizing and dehumanizing antisemitism of the men of Reserve Police Battalion 101, which Goldhagen finds too "tepid," places them in the mainstream of German society as described by Kershaw, Kulka, and Bankier, distinct from an ideologically driven Nazi leadership. The implications of my study are that the existence of widespread negative racial stereotyping in a society—in no way unique to Nazi Germany—can provide fanatical regimes not only the freedom of action to pursue genocide (as both Kershaw and Kulka conclude) but also an ample supply of executioners.

In regard to the centrality of antisemitic motivation, it should be noted that German executioners were capable of killing millions of non-Jews targeted by the Nazi regime. Beginning in 1939, systematic and large-scale mass murder was initiated against the German handicapped and Polish intelligentsia. More than three million Soviet prisoners of war perished from hunger, exposure, disease, and outright execution—two-thirds of them in the first nine months after the launching of Barbarossa but before the death camps of Operation Reinhard had even opened. Tens of thousands fell victim to horrendous reprisal measures. Additionally, the Nazi regime included Gypsies in their genocidal assault. Clearly, something more than singular German antisemitism is needed to explain perpetrator behavior when the regime could find executioners to murder millions of non-Jewish victims.

Let us follow another approach to this issue as well by examining the behavior of non-German killing units in the Ukraine and Belorussia, which carried out killing actions quite similar to those performed by Reserve Police Battalion 101. I will not be looking at those elements that enthusiastically carried out the initial murderous pogroms in the summer of 1941—often at German instigation

—and were then frequently formed into full-time auxiliaries of the Einsatzgruppen for the subsequent large-scale systematic massacres. The zealous followers of Jonas Klimaitis in Lithuania or Viktors Arajs in Latvia, who eagerly rushed to help the invading Germans kill communists and Jews, are not appropriate counterparts of Reserve Police Battalion 101 for the purpose of cross-cultural comparison.

Instead, I will examine the rural police units in Belorussia and the Ukraine, which did not really take shape until 1942, when they participated in the "second wave" of killing on Soviet territory. Like the men of Reserve Police Battalion 101 in Poland, these policemen provided the essential manpower for the "mopping-up" killings of Jews in small towns and villages and for the "Jew hunts" that relentlessly tracked down escapees. . . .

In summary, the precinct-level Ukrainian police were first organized by the military administration in 1941. They were vastly expanded under the Order Police in 1942, whom they outnumbered in precinct service by at least a 10 to 1 ratio. The local police joined for numerous reasons, including pay, food for their families, release from POW camps, and especially a family exemption from deportation to forced labor in Germany. Although the Germans had difficulty recruiting as many Ukrainian police as they wanted, the Ukrainian police nonetheless numbered in the tens of thousands and constituted a major manpower source for the "second wave" of the Final Solution that swept through the Ukraine in 1942.

There is scant documentation from the precinct level on the day-to-day participation of the auxiliary police in the mass murder of Jews. From the Ukraine one series of police reports survives, from which we can see that the local Schutzmänner and their supervising German Gendarmerie performed precisely the same duties as Reserve Police Battalion 101 in Poland, with one exception—there were no deportations to death camps, only shooting actions. . . .

The Gendarmerie outpost in Mir, in Belorussia . . . reported the results of its killing activities to headquarters in Baranoviche. Its commander noted that "560 Jews were shot in the Jewish action carried out in Mir" on August 13, 1942. . . . Around Mir the Jew hunt continued. On September 29, 1942, a "patrol of the Mir Schutzmannschaft" found in the forest six Jews, who "had fled the previous Jewish action." They were shot on the spot. Six weeks later a forest keeper discovered a Jewish bunker. He led a patrol of three German gendarmes and sixty Schutzmänner to the site. Five Jews, including the former head of the Judenrat of Mir, were hauled from the bunker and shot. "The food"—including 100 kilos of potatoes—"as well as the tattered clothing were given to the Mir Schutzmannschaft."

In short, the role in the Final Solution of the precinct-level police recruited on Soviet territory seems scarcely distinguishable from that of German reserve police in Poland. The precinct-level Schutzmänner were not the eager pogromists and collaborators of mid-summer 1941, just as the German reserve police were not career SS and policemen but post–1939 conscripts. The role and behavior of the Ukrainian and Belorussian auxiliary police in carrying out the Final Solution do not lend support to the notion of "specifically German behavioral modes."

I would like to look into the particular case of the German Gendarmerie in Mir and their Belorussian auxiliaries in greater detail because this case pertains to a further criticism of my book, my alleged misuse of German sources and nonuse of Jewish sources. It has been suggested on the one hand that I was much too gullible and methodologically uncritical in my acceptance of German testimony, particularly that which I cited in support of my portrayal of a differentiated reaction by the perpetrators and a dramatic transformation in character of many of the policemen over time. I argued that most of the men were upset by the initial killing action, and that over time a considerable minority of the men became enthusiastic and zealous volunteers for the firing squads and Jew hunts; that the largest group within the battalion did not seek opportunities to kill but nonetheless routinely contributed to the murder operations in many ways with increasing numbness and callousness; and that a not insignificant minority remained nonshooters while still participating in cordons and roundups. On the other hand, both Goldhagen and a number of my Israeli colleagues have chided me for not using Jewish sources. If I had been more critical of my German sources and more inclusive in my use of Jewish sources, a more reliable image of a uniform and pervasive bestiality, sadism, and even "jocularity," "boyish joy," and "relish" on the part of the perpetrators would have resulted, they suggest.

After working with these German court testimony records for more than twenty years, I would readily concede that the vast bulk of it is pervasively mendacious and apologetic, especially concerning the motivation and attitude of the perpetrators. It was precisely on the basis of my previous experience with German court testimony, however, that I judged the court testimonies of Reserve Police Battalion 101 to be qualitatively different. The roster of the unit survived, more than 40 percent of the battalion members (most of them rank and file reservists rather than officers) were interrogated, and two able and persistent investigating attorneys spent five years carefully questioning the witnesses.

The resulting testimony provides a unique body of evidence that permits us to answer important questions for which previous court records did not provide adequate information. A historian would be wrong to lump this body of evidence together indiscriminately with other court records. Admittedly, these are subjective judgments on my part, and other honest and able historians could reach other conclusions. My critics' dismissal of my use of this particular German testimony as gullible and methodologically unsound, without giving due attention to the special character of these records, ought to be noted, however.

As for the nonuse of Jewish sources, I would make several observations. First, Jewish testimony was indispensable to my study in establishing the chronology for the fall of 1942. What became a blur of events for the perpetrators remained quite distinct days of horror for the victims. Also, while survivor testimony may be extremely valuable in many regards, it does not illuminate the internal dynamics of an itinerant killing unit. It would be difficult for the victim of such a unit to provide testimony concerning the various levels of participation of different perpetrators and any change in their character over time. Where long-term contact between victims and perpetrators did occur, survivors are able to and in fact do differentiate on such issues. Such long-term contact did not occur in the situations that I examined, however. The testimony of survivors and even Polish bystanders of a massacre or ghetto-clearing action by a unit such as Reserve Police Battalion 101 would inevitably focus on the brutality, sadism, and horror of the perpetrator unit, with little differentiation among its individual members. It would indeed support the conclusions of my critics concerning the uniform and enthusiastic behavior of the perpetrators, but that does not make those conclusions correct....

A remarkable testimony has recently been published by Nechama Tec in her book about Oswald Rufeisen. It is especially valuable because Rufeisen observed the internal workings of the Mir Gendarmerie post as a translator for the German sergeant in charge. Since some of Rufeisen's testimony so strikingly confirms the dynamics within the reserve police that I portrayed based on perpetrator testimony, I will quote it at length. Tec reports that, according to Rufeisen, there was:

> a visible difference in the Germans' participation in anti-Jewish and anti-partisan moves. A selected few Germans, three out of thirteen, consistently abstained from becoming a part of all anti-Jewish expeditions.... No one seemed to bother them. No one talked about their absences. It was as if they had a right to abstain.

Among these middle-aged gendarmes too old to be sent to the front, Rufeisen noted the presence of enthusiastic and sadistic killers, including the second-in-command, Karl Schultz, who was described as "a beast in the form of a man." "Not all the gendarmes, however, were as enthusiastic about murdering Jews as Schultz," Tec notes. Concerning the policemen's attitude toward killing Jews, she quotes Rufeisen directly:

> It was clear that there were differences in their outlooks. I think that the whole business of anti-Jewish moves, the business of Jewish extermination they considered unclean. The operations against the partisans were not in the same category. For them a confrontation with partisans was a battle, a military move. But a move against the Jews was something they might have experienced as "dirty." I have the impression that they felt that it would be better not to discuss the matter.

This is hardly the image of men uniformly possessed of a "lethal, hallucinatory view of the Jews" who viewed their killing of Jews as "a redemptive act."

Finally, I would like to look at a third example of crosscultural comparison that is very suggestive: the Luxembourgers. Reserve Police Battalion 101 was composed almost entirely of Germans from the Hamburg region, including some men from Bremen, Bremerhaven, and Wilhelmshaven, as well as a few Holsteiners from Rendsburg who felt like relative outsiders. In addition, the battalion included a contingent of young men from Luxembourg, which had been annexed to the Third Reich in 1940. The presence of the Luxembourgers in Reserve Police Battalion 101 offers the historian the unusual opportunity for a "controlled experiment" to measure the impact of the same situational factors upon men of differing cultural and ethnic background.

The problem is the scarcity of testimony. Only one German witness described the participation of the Luxembourgers in the battalion's activities in any detail. According to this witness, the Luxembourgers belonged to Lieutenant Buchmann's platoon in first company and were particularly active in the roundups before the first massacre at Józéfow. This was a period in late June and early July 1942 when the trains were not running to Belzec, and Jews in the southern Lublin district were being concentrated temporarily in transit ghettos such as Piaski and Izbica. On the night before the initial massacre at Józéfow, Lieutenant Buchmann was the sole officer who said he could not order his men to shoot unarmed women and children, and who asked for a different assignment. He was designated responsible for taking the work Jews to Lublin and, according to the witness, the Luxembourgers under his command provided the guard. Hence they did not participate in the massacre.

Thereafter Lieutenant Buchmann continued to refuse participation in any Jewish action. However, those in his platoon, including the Luxembourgers, were not exempted. Under the command of the first sergeant, who was a "110% Nazi" and real "go-getter," the Luxembourgers in particular became quite involved. According to the witness, the company captain took considerable care in the selection of personnel for assignments. "In general the older men remained behind," he noted. In contrast, "*the Luxembourgers were in fact present at every action* [emphasis mine]. With these people it was a matter of career police officials from the state of Luxembourg, who were all young men in their twenties." Despite their absence at Józéfow, it would appear that the Luxembourgers became the shock-troops of first company simply because of their younger age and greater police experience and training, the absence of "specifically German behavioral modes" and a singular German antisemitism notwithstanding....

I will conclude briefly. If the studies of Kershaw, Kulka, and Bankier are valid and most Germans did not share the fanatical antisemitism of Adolf Hitler and the hardcore Nazis, then an argument based on a singular German antisemitism to explain the murderous actions of low-level perpetrators does not hold up. If the Nazi regime could find executioners for millions of non-Jewish victims, the centrality of antisemitism as the crucial motive of the German perpetrators is also called into question. If tens of thousands of local policemen in Belorussia and the Ukraine—taken as needed by the Germans, who were desperate for help and offered a variety of inducements—basically performed the same duties and behaved in the same way as their German counterparts in Poland, then the argument of "specifically German behavioral modes" likewise fails. Finally, if Luxembourgers in Reserve Police Battalion 101 did not behave differently from their German comrades, then the immediate situational factors to which I gave considerable attention in the conclusion of my book must be given even greater weight. The preponderance of evidence suggests that in trying to understand the vast majority of the perpetrators, we are dealing not with "ordinary Germans" but rather with "ordinary men."

POSTSCRIPT

Was German "Eliminationist Antisemitism" Responsible for the Holocaust?

Both in the United States and Germany, the publicity engendered by Goldhagen's book has been overwhelming. Because of its seemingly anti-German message, the book has been surprisingly well received in Germany, and a book tour there was attended by largely enthusiastic audiences. However, when the book was translated into German, its title was translated as *Hitler's Willing Executors*, which gives quite a different slant to the book's thesis. Some have accused Goldhagen and his publisher of changing the German title in order to increase sales in Germany, adding their complaints to those who stated that Goldhagen's original title was intentionally inflammatory.

Many critical articles and reviews of *Hitler's Willing Executioners* have appeared—and Goldhagen has rebutted many of them in print. A most important one appeared in the *New Republic* (December 23, 1996) and is noteworthy because of the length, breadth, and depth of Goldhagen's response to his critics. It would provide a fitting and informative conclusion to this issue.

Needless to say, there have been so many books written about the Holocaust that to single out a few for mention can be a precarious operation. But a few general sources that should be consulted are Raul Hilberg, *The Destruction of the European Jews* (Holmes & Meier, 1985); Yehuda Bauer, *A History of the Holocaust* (Franklin Watts, 1982); and Martin Gilbert, *The Holocaust: A History of the Jews of Europe During the Second World War* (Holt, Rinehart & Winston, 1986). Michael Robert Marrus's, *The Holocaust in History* (University Press of New England, 1987) serves as one of the Holocaust's most thorough historiographical studies. Ron Rosenbaum's *Explaining Hitler: The Search for the Origins of His Evil* (Random House, 1998) provides an interesting and accessible look at Holocaust historiography, as the journalist/author interviews and writes about the world's leading Holocaust scholars and their works. For neophytes, this might be a good place to start. Also, the journal *Holocaust and Genocide Studies* always provides interesting and thought-provoking articles on the subject.

A book of essays critiquing Goldhagen's work is *Hyping the Holocaust: Scholars Answer Goldhagen* (Cummings and Hathaway, 1997). This book provides ample criticism of Goldhagen's scholarship. Finally, *Unwilling Germans? The Goldhagen Debate* (University of Minnesota Press, 1998), edited by Robert R. Shandley, offers a large sampling of German reaction to *Hitler's Willing Executioners*.

ISSUE 11

Should Emperor Hirohito Have Been Held Responsible for Japan's World War II Actions?

YES: Peter Wetzler, from *Hirohito and War: Imperial Tradition and Military Decision Making in Prewar Japan* (University of Hawai'i Press, 1998)

NO: Stephen S. Large, from *Emperor Hirohito and Shōwa Japan: A Political Biography* (Routledge, 1992)

ISSUE SUMMARY

YES: Professor Peter Wetzler states that Emperor Hirohito bears responsibility for World War II because he did not oppose the war effort. This was in order to guarantee the continued rule of his Japanese imperial family.

NO: Author Stephen S. Large argues that Emperor Hirohito's lack of real political power to effect change absolves him from any direct responsibility for World War II.

On August 15, 1945, Emperor Hirohito spoke to the Japanese people by way of a radio broadcast. It was the first time that many Japanese citizens had heard the voice of the man who was considered by many as descending from the gods. His message asked them to give up the fight that had begun almost four years earlier when the Japanese attacked Pearl Harbor, turning an Asian war into World War II. The word *surrender* was not used in Hirohito's speech, but it was clear to all that Japan had lost the war.

Few Japanese, including Hirohito, knew what lay in store for their country. The emperor felt that there was a possibility that he would be deposed and perhaps even tried as a war criminal. These prospects forced him to seriously consider abdication as an alternative.

Six weeks later Hirohito had a face-to-face meeting with United States general Douglas MacArthur, commander of Allied forces in Asia and soon-to-be Governor of Occupied Japan. Hirohito was informed that he would not be removed from office or tried as a war criminal. He would be allowed to remain as emperor, although he would have to renounce his right to divine origins. All of this was welcome news to a man whose fate was clearly in the hands of a general representing the United States government. To say that the emperor experienced a sense of relief would be an understatement.

Until his death in 1989 Hirohito was a model world citizen and the unofficial leader who presided over Japan's remarkable postwar recovery. A goodwill trip to the United States in 1975 was viewed by many as a symbolic end to World War II animosities held by both countries. Japan was a staunch, wealthy ally, and many Americans seemed willing to forgive and forget.

Hirohito's death also caused a historical reassessment of his career, which included a new look at his role in the planning and execution of Japan's war plans. Prior to this, it had been said that Hirohito was a constitutional monarch who possessed little political power, and even as emperor, he could have done little to control those who made the decisions for war. Some writers, however, looking at the question from a new perspective and with more sources of information available to them, began to draw a different picture of Hirohito. They concluded that he not only knew what Japan was doing during the prewar period, but actively participated in it and never spoke out against the war that was to come in 1941.

These writers seriously questioned the efficacy of MacArthur's (and the United States government's) decision to absolve Hirohito from all responsibility. They saw the decision as one of many American policies (our strong postwar support for West Germany was another) designed to create potential allies in the free world's struggle with world communism. They also believed that since the Japanese military and civilian leaders had been tried and found guilty of war crimes in 1946–1947—and many were even sentenced to death for their actions —absolving Hirohito from all responsibility was an unconscionable act.

Some have gone so far as to declare that a deliberate "cover-up" of Hirohito's participation in the war's planning and prosecution had occurred. To many this was corroborated by a 1989 British Broadcasting Corporation-produced film entitled *Hirohito: Behind the Myth,* which was televised in the United States by WGBH, the Public Broadcasting System's (PBS) Boston affiliate.

Although some were willing to give some credibility to the program's findings, a storm of protest arose from many influential American supporters of Japan and Hirohito, who saw the program as not only filled with errors, but as a deliberate attempt to sully the reputation of its subject. To those who welcomed the program's content, this response was part of another attempt to keep the truth hidden from the American people. This difference of opinion regarding Hirohito and his responsibility for the war frames the focus of this issue.

In the first selection, Peter Wetzler states that Hirohito refused to oppose the war plans of the Japanese military because he feared that if he did so, the military and political leaders in Japan would abolish the Japanese imperial throne, which Hirohito sought to protect at all costs. Steven S. Large argues that Japan's constitutional monarchy–based political system offered Hirohito few opportunities to actively oppose the Japanese plans for war.

Peter Wetzler  **YES**

Hirohito and War

Introduction

Emperor Hirohito (1901–1989) was the titular head of the Japanese government when the Imperial Army set up a puppet state in Manchuria in 1931–1932, when the war with China began in 1937, when the Japanese attacked Pearl Harbor and other targets in Southeast Asia without warning in late 1941 and early 1942, when Japan surrendered unconditionally in 1945, and when he visited Disneyland in the United States many years later. Of course, "titular head" meant different things to different people before and after the war. Accordingly, the debate about Emperor Hirohito's accountability for imperial government decisions and military operations up to the termination of World War II began before the end of the war and has continued even after his death in 1989. It is my contention that the debate is based on a false conception of the emperor's role in prewar decision making and how responsibility is to be assigned for those decisions. Supporters maintain that "the Emperor regarded his sanctioning of the war decision in 1941 as an act of political integrity required of a constitutional monarch." He therefore shared in the collective responsibility for the war, but only in a "formal legal sense." Critics assert that Hirohito personally approved the decision and is personally responsible for the war in the Pacific. Irokawa Daikichi, in a work recently translated into English, presents a more complicated picture: the emperor was not without authority, and on occasion he exercised it decisively. But due to his concern about constitutional monarchy, the emperor was "in a tragic position: the more he attempted to adhere to the principle of constitutional monarchy, the more he departed from the actual political situation and compromised his ability to lead." Each of these explanations contains an element of truth. But they all ignore a more important factor: contemporary concern about the survival of the imperial house and its position in the body politic.

Most conclusions about the Shōwa emperor's role in the prewar decision-making process are based on inferences drawn from postwar political policies and ideological preconceptions unrelated to those activities. Irokawa is to some extent an exception. My work agrees in part with his evaluations—but not

From Peter Wetzler, *Hirohito and War: Imperial Tradition and Military Decision Making in Prewar Japan* (University of Hawai'i Press, 1998). Copyright © 1998 by University of Hawai'i Press. Reprinted by permission. Notes omitted.

with his assessment of Hirohito's advisers or the way Irokawa assumes political and military decision making took place in the prewar years. I propose instead another decision-making process and alternative conclusions derived from primary source materials intimately related to the emperor's activities.

The Emperor and the Pacific War

Historian Carol Gluck wrote shortly after Hirohito's death: "Placing the Showa emperor in national history means dealing with the war." Nevertheless, few have dealt with the war and the emperor, including Gluck and the other scholars who contributed to the volume she and Stephen Graubard edited about this era. Indeed, the special issue of *Daedalus*, "Showa: The Japan of Hirohito," and the book of the same title are examples of what for the most part has been left undone—research into primary sources to ascertain what the emperor did and did not do in prewar Japan. Masataka Kosaka's comment is typical:

> Though the emperor himself was not responsible for the failure to change the [prewar] political order, it is undeniable that many of the acts that led to tragedy were carried out in his name, however painful they were to him.

That is, Hirohito was officially responsible for the tragedy, meaning the war, but not personally accountable for it. This is a compromise—neither fact nor fiction—that is profoundly unsatisfying because it exempts the emperor's role in prewar Japanese decision making from detailed analysis.

The debate about Hirohito's war responsibility revolves around the issues of war versus peace and constitutional monarchy versus direct imperial rule. Despite this trend, one cannot analyze Hirohito's actions only in terms of constitutionalism or militarism. Obviously these were significant issues for the emperor, but something else was even more important to him: the Japanese imperial house. The well-being and continued existence of Japan's imperial house were among the themes most often repeated by his teachers of ethics and history; were an overriding consideration of his two early advisers, Prince Saionji and Count Makino; and were of the utmost importance to the Shōwa emperor himself.

Hirohito affirmed the supreme importance of the imperial house by emphasizing his descent from the gods, even after Japan's defeat and occupation. Before his famous renunciation of divine status, the emperor told his vice-grand chamberlain, Kinoshita Michio (1887–1974):

> It is permissible to say that the idea that the Japanese are descendants of the gods is a false conception; but it is absolutely impermissible to call chimerical the idea that the emperor is a descendant of the gods.

Though Hirohito disavowed the divine origins of the Japanese people, he reaffirmed the special symbolic relation between the imperial house and Japan's gods. This folk belief was fundamental to Japan's war effort. It also coincided with the folkish ideals esteemed by the "war premier," General Tōjō Hideki (1884–1948). And it was these two very different men, Emperor Hirohito and Prime Minister Tōjō, who led Japan into a war it obviously could not win.

The Imperial Line, Imperial Legitimacy, and the Imperial Will

... The Meiji Constitution of 1889, a combination of Prussian constitutional theory and Japanese imperial line mythology based on Western principles, legitimized the modernization of the emperor's powers. Article 1 stated: "The Empire of Japan shall be reigned over and governed by a line of Emperors unbroken for ages eternal." The emperor was pronounced "sacred and inviolable" (Article 3). He "combined in his being the supreme rights of rule" (Article 4) and "exercised supreme command over the Army and Navy" (Article 11). As [David] Titus concludes: "The emperor thus became the source of executive, legislative, and judicial powers, and all government acts were issued in his name." At the same time, interpreters of this constitution strove to protect the emperor from personal responsibility for government acts. In particular, Article 55 of the constitution called for the various ministers of state to advise and assist the emperor within their respective areas of responsibility. This meant that they, not the emperor, were accountable for government acts. As Titus has observed about the refurbished titular head of state: "The traditional role of the emperor for 'ages eternal' as a medium between the Japanese people and the gods was therefore adopted as the basis of sovereignty in the Meiji Constitution." Titus continues: "The emperor was not to be the captive of inner court anachronisms but a modern symbol of old virtues." Japanese tradition— the emperor reigns but does not rule—was translated into modern terms: with respect to political policy, the emperor's personal will, which admittedly was fallible, was not identical with the imperial will. The imperial will was defined in theory as the will of the imperial ancestors extending into the past, and into the future, to infinity; in practice it was promulgated by government leaders. But this does not mean the emperor, in particular the Shōwa emperor, did not attempt to impress his personal will on the imperial will in prewar times.

The problem of Hirohito's war responsibility is related to questions about the imperial will, the legitimacy of the imperial house, and the nature and extent of his efforts to influence prewar political and military policy. Are these activities to be interpreted exclusively in the light of imperial line tradition as outlined here or in terms of constitutional monarchy—or was the emperor the state? In fact all three extremes, taken separately, are incorrect. They must be considered together. Even if the "emperor had not been sovereign for almost 1000 years" and the Meiji political system was an "aberration," between 1868 and 1945 the emperor "was the superintendent of the supreme right of rule— he was *perceived* as the locus of final political authority." Because of this widely shared view, the lacunae between the three positions—medium, sovereign, and constitutional monarch—gave rise to the possibility that the first and third ideals would be used to service the "sovereignty" of less exalted persons: civil and military leaders who assumed the right to declare to the Japanese people what the imperial will was in a given situation. Especially the militarists appealed to the former (emperor as medium), and civil authorities to the latter (emperor as constitutional monarch), in the 1930s and early 1940s.

Besides the military, certain politicians and high-ranking bureaucrats sought to appropriate for themselves the authority of the imperial will. This is well known. Less well known is the fact that Emperor Hirohito, who was personally fallible, was far more predisposed to acting behind the scenes to influence formation of the imperial will than he and his advisers acknowledged publicly. Therefore the question of his responsibility for political and military policies cannot be easily resolved. One must examine old and newly revealed sources to determine what in fact Hirohito did and did not do in prewar Japan. Moreover, the influences on these activities must be looked at anew.

Military Planning and Decision Making

With respect to the emperor's role in military planning, documents available at the Bōeichō Kenkyūjo (National Institute for Defense Studies, or NIDS) in Tokyo and studies by scholars there provide three new revelations. First, the emperor was regularly and extensively informed about military planning for at least six years before the attack on Pearl Harbor. Second, he was given a detailed explanation of the plan to attack Pearl Harbor by surprise one month before its execution. Third, he did not question military plans in imperial conferences because they were top secret and because he demanded the opportunity to suggest revisions in private before official approval. In short, handwritten records from the Imperial Army and Navy general staffs illustrate that the emperor was consulted about military planning, on occasion demanded and achieved revisions of specific plans, but was not able to dictate plans or basic strategy....

The emperor was not the ultimate or the only decision maker; he was part of the decision-marking process. Since he did not follow, in chambers, the advice of Saionji and Makino to avoid participating in these decisions, he was equally responsible with other leaders for them. Therefore, as titular head of the deciding body he might be expected to "take responsibility" for the decisions reached. The times when Hirohito did not act were as important as when he did. Both were expressions of his personal will. Absolute consistency with respect to a particular principle or set of ideals was, as in most political processes, impossible. But he did do his best to preserve the central position of the imperial house in this process....

Conclusion...

Beginning and Ending the War: Parallels

The same type of struggle can be seen in the adroitly orchestrated end to the war when the emperor was carefully presented with a constellation of balanced forces in the government. The issue was different, as were the people involved, but the decision-making mechanism was the same. A decision had to be made. But contrary to what is often asserted, the emperor did not make it alone. His advisers had prepared the way in advance and indicated what the decision should be—for the good of the nation and, more important, the imperial house. On 25 July 1945, for example, Kido [Kōichi] informed the undecided emperor that the army's plans for a decisive battle on the main islands were eyewash. Enemy airborne troops could isolate the emperor wherever he went. He could well be captured and the 2,600-year imperial dynasty terminated. This argument, as well as the atomic bombs of August, influenced "his" decision less than a month later. Four years earlier, when the war began, the imperial line was in no immediate danger and Hirohito was not called upon to enunciate a decision. But, in the manner of a traditional Japanese leader, he did participate in the policymaking process—exerting influence behind the scenes before decisions were made on, among other things, the military policies that led up to and included the decision to attack Pearl Harbor. At the same time he adhered to the principles of modern constitutional monarchy by sanctioning these decisions publicly when they were presented to him officially.

Hirohito and the Military

The emperor was presented with such a mountain of reports to sign that he could not review, critique, or remember them all. Nevertheless it seems safe to say he paid special attention to the annual operations plans presented to him by the army and navy. From well before the time Hirohito became emperor, the Imperial Army (1906) and Imperial Navy (1914) began drafting annual operations plans and presenting them to the emperor for approval. In certain periods, particularly during the Taishō emperor's reign, receiving imperial sanctions for these plans was purely a formal exercise. In the latter half of the 1930s, however, Hirohito used this process on a number of occasions to influence the plans—as documented in Imperial Army and Navy records from that time. These records also show the disagreements between the army and navy in minute detail. Not only were there disputes over the allocation of funds and raw materials, but leading generals and admirals were sharply divided on strategic issues as well. The emperor was well informed about these quarrels. He also knew that basic policy decisions were being delayed because there was no consensus. He did not take advantage of such stalemates and consistently intervene to prevent war. But he did consistently protect the interests of the imperial house and assert the emperor's right to be heard behind the scenes on these matters. Later, he was equally consistent in referring to his position as constitutional monarch to justify his public inaction and safeguard the position of his house. Finally, what he said and did in the late 1930s shows that Hirohito too was undecided about the proper course to take. This indecision is demonstrated by the contradictory policies he supported for over three years prior to the start of the Pacific War.

At the beginning of 1938, as we have seen, the annual operations plan could not be completed because of a dispute between the army and navy over the advisability of war with a third country before the war in China was won. Yet the emperor did not intervene. True, neither party had asked the emperor for a decision. But no one had asked him for his opinion on numerous other occasions when he freely voiced his mind and lobbied for specific measures. As emperor he did not have to wait to be asked. In 1939 he blocked temporarily the alliance with Nazi Germany; he required military planners to change plans that would have violated the neutrality of Thailand; he greatly influenced the selection of two prime ministers, Abe and Yonai. These moves improved the position of those opposed to an alliance with Germany and against war. But this was not the whole story. Hirohito usually acted very differently when dealing with military as opposed to political matters.

In the context of prewar consensus policymaking the emperor was not without influence, but he seems to have been concerned about something other than peace and constitutionalism. The gist of the oral reports presented to the throne by navy leaders in 1938 and 1939 show they would have welcomed some moderating influence from the emperor. This, however, was not readily forthcoming. The dispute between army and navy leaders over basic military strategy was the very type of impasse that the postwar Hirohito insisted had not existed before the war: a pat situation that would have allowed him to intervene on the side of peace. He allegedly blocked the alliance with Germany due to disunity in the government. Disunity in the high command, however, did not stimulate the emperor to act where it counted most—in military as opposed to political matters.

There seems to have been a significant discrepancy between Hirohito's perceptions of military and political policy-making at this time. The emperor vigorously opposed his foreign minister's plan (strongly supported by the army) for an alliance with Germany. But in 1938, when confronted with the possibility of war with England, America, and the Soviet Union, in addition to China, a dismaying prospect for any peace-loving man, he did nothing. Moreover, it is well to note that in 1938 the heart of the dispute between the army and navy—the navy's reluctance to fight a war with the United States versus the army's eagerness to do just that—was the same as the policy differences that precipitated the crisis between Prime Minister Konoe and Army Minister Tōjō in 1941. At that time the army for reasons of pride and prejudice insisted on pursuing a war against the United States. The navy, after looking at estimates of the economic and material aspects of prosecuting a modern war, was again less enthusiastic. On both occasions, in 1938 and 1941, the emperor acted not at all or indecisively. The reasons for this equivocation are difficult to ascertain, but the constitutional monarchy argument alone seems weak. After losing the war, of course, the emperor was against it. Before the fact he appears to have been undecided.

Following the debate and indecision in 1938–1939 the navy's operations became more ambitious with respect to fighting a war with the United States. Hirohito may have welcomed the increasing decisiveness. By 1941 he may have been mentally prepared to go to war after so many years of being readied for it by the general staffs. The oil embargo gave those favoring war a compelling argument. These developments, however, only brought out the ambivalent nature of the war issue. Hirohito appears to have been stimulated by the prospects of a greater, stronger empire—and, simultaneously, hesitant out of fear of losing a war. No doubt there also were thoughts about the possibility of a military putsch [a secretly plotted and suddenly executed attempt to overthrow a government] if the plans were not approved. A putsch would not only have endangered constitutional monarchy; it could also have had grave consequences for Hirohito and the imperial house. As he himself said, no doubt a regent or emperor more amenable to the desires of the army would have been selected. Then in the event of defeat, it would be even more difficult for the imperial house to avoid responsibility for the war, greatly jeopardizing its existence.

Tōjō and Hirohito

Another figure central to these events—the beginning of the Pacific War, its prosecution, and the survival of the emperor and his house—was Tōjō Hideki. Tōjō is not one of the more popular figures in Japanese history, modern or otherwise. He is known as an uncompromising Imperial Army general and the prime minister who led Japan for the greater part of the Pacific War. Many writers, particularly supporters of Hirohito, lament the demise of advisers like Saionji and all but ignore the relationship between Tōjō and the emperor. Tōjō deserves a better press.

Despite the conquering exploits of Jimmu, the first emperor of Japanese mythology, throughout history emperors have not enjoyed much loyalty from their military underlings. Tōjō was acutely aware of this situation and strove in his own way to be otherwise. This is not to say Tōjō had more conviction than his fellow officers. In the 1930s in Japan there was no lack of conviction, especially among young army officers. Tōjō, however, appears not only to have believed deeply in the Japanese national polity; he also had sufficient humility to honor Emperor Hirohito's representation of the *kokutai* [Japanese national polity] above his own interpretation of it. This does not mean he unquestioningly carried out orders from the emperor, however strange that may sound. He too was aware of the pluralistic nature of Japanese leadership—and, equally important, the "traditional position," beginning in the Meiji era, of the emperor in that body politic.

Emperors did not give orders; they guided the consensus-forming process. Therefore, although he had previously opposed it in the Konoe cabinet, Tōjō carried out the review mandated by the emperor when he was appointed prime minister: the review of the course set for war. When the group that conducted the review reached a conclusion he knew might be contrary to the emperor's feelings, he presented that conclusion in all sincerity to him. The outcome of this review made war in the Pacific, barring unexpected concessions from the United States, unavoidable from the Japanese point of view. No doubt Hirohito was moved to accept this conclusion not just by the threat to his position from army radicals, among whom Tōjō did not count himself, but also because of Tōjō's formal correctness and sincerity. Tōjō kept the emperor apprised of the proceedings. Not only did he send his cabinet ministers to him, but he reported to Hirohito himself as prime minister and army minister. The emperor was given ample opportunity to influence those making the review, therefore, and could not have been surprised by its outcome. This was constitutional monarchy, Japanese style, in action. The emperor was part of the process, not the victim of a plot, and was not presented with a fait accompli.

There are sufficient grounds for concluding that events at the end of October and beginning of November 1941 occurred in this way, for these reasons, and that the emperor was a party to the decision for war. The review itself has been described in detail by contemporary observers, corroborating the fact that

Tōjō sent his ministers repeatedly to report to the emperor. Chief of the General Affairs Section of the Prime Minister's Office Inada Shūichi, Tōjō's private secretary Akamatsu Sadao, and Lord Keeper of the Privy Seal Kido Kōichi, Hirohito's political adviser, all attest to this. Moreover, the content of the review was known to Hirohito then and is known to us now. For everyone involved, including the emperor, peace was not the primary topic of concern. The entire reexamination revolved around the question of whether the war could be won and under what conditions it would be prosecuted. Without thinking through the implications of his statement, Hirohito said in 1946 that the focal point of the discussions was oil. Unwittingly the emperor repeated the the arguments used by the military and right-wing leaders before and just after the beginning of the Pacific War. A lack of oil was the issue that led navy leaders to oppose war; acquiring oil and other strategic materials was the reason the army and others favored war; and the oil embargo was cited to shift the blame for starting the war away from Japan onto the United States. . . .

Pearl Harbor and the Decision for War

In addressing the question of the emperor's war responsibility, one must distinguish between legalistic assumptions in the postwar West and the emperor's responsibilities in prewar Japan. The question asked so frequently after the Pacific War—whether Emperor Hirohito was for or against it—often disregards the prewar context. Before the conflict, war was one aspect, albeit an important one, of policymaking and the struggle for power in Japan. Emperor Hirohito as head of the imperial family had a right to participate in these affairs. But this right, as he himself was fond of pointing out, was not that of a dictator. At the same time it was not the right of a Western monarch, constitutional or otherwise.

Arguments both for and against the emperor's constitutional powers can be made. But this line of discussion is confusing because many forget that Hirohito's stand for constitutional monarchy complemented—"modernized"—rather than contradicted his role as the head of the imperial house and emperor of Japan. Many tend to forget, as well, that the emperor's actual influence, and the restraints placed on his power, were defined in Japan, not in Western Europe. This was even more true of the obligations that accrued to the "office." As can be seen in Japanese history in general, the moral education of Hirohito in particular, and the advice of Makino and his other advisers, the emperor's primary responsibility was neither political nor military: it was the preservation and advancement of the imperial house itself.

Hirohito's postwar supporters and critics alike have assumed the perspective dictated by the atmosphere surrounding the war crimes trials. They focus on whether Hirohito was a militarist or a constitutionalist: was he personally accountable for the war? But peace and Western constitutionalism were not the main concerns of the emperor in Imperial Japan. They were important as ends in themselves, perhaps, but more important as a means to a greater end—the preservation of the imperial house. . . .

Taking into account the influence of the imperial house on decision making in prewar Japan means examining what the emperor stood for and what he did. During the crucial time immediately before the outbreak of war, he stood for the imperial line—and that meant asserting his right to participate in the decision-making process. Army and navy records clearly indicate this, as can be seen in the events leading up to the decision to go to war. In particular, consonant with his role as the emperor of Japan, Hirohito was told well in advance exactly how the attack on Pearl Harbor was to be carried out. This was done in a private audience on 3 November 1941. If Hirohito had any objections— as he had expressed unmistakably in similar private audiences previously—they were either not voiced or were made but not recorded later by the two military leaders present.

Prior to this audience the emperor ordered a review of the decision made in the 6 September imperial conference. Once again war was decided upon by Imperial Japan's pluralistic leadership. The disclaimers by Prime Minister Tōjō and the emperor about this decision not being the latter's will are well known. One Japanese authority has written: "The words of the emperor were not the words of the emperor." Stephen Large, expanding on these sentiments, says of the imperial conference of 1 December 1941 sanctioning war: "Tōjō and everyone else present that day knew perfectly well that the imperial will for war was not the Emperor's personal will and that the government, not the Emperor, had decided upon war." Both scholars adopt an idealized view of constitutional monarchy and overlook the emperor's long-standing participation, along with other leaders, in forming military and political policy behind the scenes before formal ratification. The emperor was not the government. But despite postwar protestations to the contrary, the emperor was a participating member of the government. If he was so adamantly opposed to the war, why did he not speak out one month earlier in audience with his military leaders, as he had done many times before? Hirohito was an integral part of the leadership that led Japan into war. Like any member of a collective group of leaders, he was not always able to prevail. But this does not mean he was not a party to the decisions, and responsible for them.

NO

Stephen S. Large

Emperor Hirohito and Shōwa Japan

Conclusion...

The Emperor's War Responsibility

Had the Emperor [Hirohito] been tried, it would have been logical for the IMTFE [International Military Tribunal, Far East] to convict and sentence him for formally sanctioning nearly every act of Japanese aggression and war in the 1931–1945 period, including, for example, the participation of Japanese army units from Korea in the Manchurian incident; the Japanese invasion of Jehol in 1933; the escalation of war with China in 1938; Japanese operations at Changkufeng in 1938; and the fateful decision for war which led to Japan's attack on Pearl Harbor in 1941. In addition, he sanctioned other Japanese initiatives which contributed in different ways to war: Japan's withdrawal from the League of Nations in 1933; Japan's entry into the Axis Alliance in 1940; and Japan's southern advance into French Indochina in 1940 and 1941.

For such critics of the Emperor as David Bergamini and Inoue Kiyoshi, his formal sanctions were emblematic of his deeper participation in a Japanese conspiracy to wage war. The strong implication is that he was as bloodthirsty as Kaiser Wilhelm II who, following the battle of Tannenberg in September 1914, 'proposed to kill 90,000 Russian prisoners of war by driving them onto the barren spit of land in the Baltic Sea known as the Kurische Nehrung, and letting them starve to death'.

The intense passions pervading this interpretation are readily understandable when we recall the carnage wrought by Japan in the Emperor's name. Yet, this interpretation is untenable. It ignores... that he personally opposed, and tried to use his influence privately at court to prevent, the acts of aggression that he ultimately sanctioned as representing the formal imperial will. He 'was absolutely consistent in using his personal influence to induce caution and to moderate, and even to obstruct, the accumulating, snowballing impetus towards war'. In retrospect, his only major success was the part he played at court in assisting the Hamaguchi cabinet on behalf of the London Naval Treaty in 1930.

Still, concerning the Emperor's war responsibility, Ishida Takeshi writes,

> since under the Meiji Constitution only the Emperor, as the supreme commander of the Imperial Army, was empowered to control the army, the emperor cannot be absolved of responsibility for Japan's invasion of China in the 1930s and other Asian countries in World War II, though it is true that these actions were planned by the militarists.

Similarly, Ōnuma Yasuaki concedes that the Emperor opposed war but agrees that he was accountable for war because the war crimes tribunal 'regarded as criminal not only positive acts but also "disregard" of the "legal duty" to prevent breaches of the laws of war...'. That the Emperor was accountable, not for acts of commission in conspiring to wage war, but for acts of omission in failing to prevent it, is therefore the central issue in considering his war responsibility. Could he have done more, should he have tried to do more, to oppose war?

For the historian, because of the methodological problems it poses, this question is as difficult to answer as it is necessary to ask. Not to ask it would imply a determinist view in which history is invariably governed by impersonal forces and structures over which individuals have little or no control; pushed to an extreme, the responsibility which individuals share for historical outcomes would be ignored.

On the other hand, to ask it implies a voluntarist view that individuals invariably matter more than impersonal forces and structures in the making of history. This assumption runs the twofold risk of over-simplifying the complexities of historical causation and making too much of individual responsibility for historical outcomes. Furthermore, it often leads to over-reliance on indirect and inconclusive evidence in making dubious counterfactual claims about what might have happened had individuals acted differently.

Clearly, an approach is needed which addresses the intricate interaction of impersonal forces, structures and individuals in shaping historical events and processes. Here, 'the problem that then confronts us has at its center the network of dependence within which scope for individual decisions opens to the individual, and which at the same time sets limits to his possible decisions'. [I] have considered this problem in probing how the Emperor perceived his political role, how he acted upon his perceptions, and with what consequences, while also exploring why his personal intentions for peace were so much at variance with the effects of his war-sanctioning.

More particularly,... this [selection emphasizes] the combination of 'external' and 'internal constraints'... that defined the political 'opportunities' available to the Emperor and his 'abilities' to respond to them when confronted by the issue of war in early Shōwa history. These constraints were both positive and negative: positive, in that some plainly obstructed action, and negative, in that some comprised 'an absence, such as lack of resources, strength, skill, or knowledge, that, equally, prevents a potential option from being realized'....

The formidable 'external constraints' on the Emperor make it unreasonable to hold that he could have done more to oppose war or that had he done more, war could have been averted. By way of a brief recapitulation, first, it was always clear that 'The emperor was to be neither a political partisan nor a policy maker. He was to ratify decisions produced by governmental leaders with the Imperial Seal'. He did not attend meetings of the cabinet or the liaison conferences, where decisions were made. Only when Japan's leaders competed in the process of 'working through the court' to declare the imperial will was he given opportunities to influence policy-making. Although he certainly was manipulated, especially by the military, he was no robot, for he exerted influence as he advised, encouraged, and warned. But his influence for peace was ignored, leaving him to confer automatically ritual sanction in the imperial conference on decisions reached elsewhere by others beforehand, as he was expected to do. Throughout prewar and wartime Shōwa, 'Far from being his personal decision-making powers, therefore, the Emperor's prerogatives were the source of authority for rule by others'.

Second, the military, which set the pace in developing a 'national defense state' and in determining Japanese foreign policy, not only ignored his opposition to war, it often presented him and the government with the *fait accompli* of war, only perfunctorily reported to him its strategic plans and operations, and frequently withheld information from him.

This last point bears directly on a question that is often asked: how much did the Emperor know about the military's policies and projects? What he could have done about what he knew is a more important issue, but that aside, we are left to speculate concerning the information at his disposal. . . . But did he know about such other infamous operations as the biological warfare experiments on prisoners of war that were carried out by the army's Unit 731 in Manchuria?

Probably not. It is true that Unit 731 was established, as an 'epidemic and water supply unit', under the authority of the imperial seal. However, the imperial seal was used to authorize a great many wartime activities of which the Emperor was unaware and it has not been established that he knew of the Unit's true purpose, which is unlikely, given the army's consistent deceitfulness in dealing with him. As Gavan McCormack writes, in an otherwise critical assessment of his career, 'The peculiar tragedy of Hirohito's life was to have been born and raised at the center of a web of deceit', which he continued to experience, and complain about, throughout the early Shōwa period.

Third, the Emperor's advisers constrained him in significant ways and on occasion, they, too, deliberately deceived him, as when, in 1931, Prince Saionji told the foreign minister, 'It is not necessary to lie but tell the Emperor things that will please him in order to ease his mind'. Moreover, on other occasions when he wanted to convene an imperial conference with the intention of speaking out against war, his advisers opposed the idea and thereby negated whatever imperial influence for peace he might have applied.

In 1939, Harada Kumao told the new prime minister, Hiranuma,

> It is regrettable to know that no knowledge of His Majesty's intelligence and virtues is being transmitted to the people. . . . For instance, in politics, it is the wish of the Emperor to respect and guard strictly the spirit of the Constitution, but this cannot be told to the people. . . . The Emperor's ideas are not at all evident either in politics or diplomacy. . . .

Harada continued,

> If one should explain that it is the Emperor's desire to conduct a completely constitutional government, it is said that Saionji, Makino, or other immediate officials do what they please behind the scenes by using the name of the Emperor. As a result, the spirit of the Constitution is ignored and matters are conducted in such a way that the Emperor's wishes cannot be conveyed to the people.

For all Harada's regret, he and other members of the court circle were mostly to blame for failing to communicate the Emperor's political wishes to the public and insofar as their fear of violence caused them to keep him out of controversial situations, the violent incidents of the early 1930s on the part of Shōwa Restoration extremists constituted a fourth, and very significant, 'external constraint' on the court, including the Emperor.

Fear of violent reprisals from the imperial way faction partly explains why he failed to follow through on his pledge to 'cleanse the army' following the suppression of the February 1936 rebellion. Similar fears of a possible coup also figured in his sanction of the decision for war in 1941. Throughout the prewar years of Shōwa, fear of 'riding a boat against the rapids', not only of army power but also of war-inspired popular nationalism, traumatized, and effectively neutralized, the Emperor and his advisers.

Finally, the most important 'external constraint' on the Emperor was the contradictory nature of the Meiji constitution. At best, 'Every constitutional monarchy has an element of ambiguity. In most cases the authority of the monarchy has been eroded in stages over time, so the limits of its power are not entirely clear.' This was true of Britain, too. For instance, Harold Nicolson writes of King George V that though he was determined to 'act strictly in accordance with his duties and responsibilities as a Constitutional Monarch', he 'was often driven by the winds and tides of events into these zones of uncertainty, and was obliged to determine, with little more than the stars to guide him, which was the true constitutional course to pursue'.

What made the Meiji constitution especially ambiguous was its provisions for both absolute and limited monarchy, to the point where, in 1932, the American political scientist, Kenneth Colegrove, justifiably preferred to call the Japanese system not a constitutional monarchy but a 'constitutional autocracy'. The Emperor's contradictory powers gave rise to an acute symbolic dissonance whereby the people saw him as an absolute monarch while Japan's political elites paid lipservice to the idea that he was a constitutional monarch. Until, that is, this latter perception was buried once and for all in prewar Shōwa by the 'Minobe incident' [attack on Minobe for having suggested that the emperor was an organ of the state] of 1935. Thereafter, imperial absolutism became national orthodoxy, not so that the Emperor would actually rule but so that the power of others who ruled in his name would be unassailable.

The confused and uncertain powers which the constitution ascribed to him forced the Shōwa Emperor to improvise in opposing the military and war. To be sure, article LV, which established the principle of ministerial responsibility, entitled him to expect that ministers of state would pay heed to his advice, warning, and encouragement in many areas of national policy. But whether they would do so was never guaranteed and in any case, where his relations with the military were concerned, article XI mattered more because it gave him the right of supreme command. It is this article which prompts the view that he should have been held accountable for failing to control the military, and in particular, the army and navy chief of staff offices.

Yet whether article XI ensured his control of the military was questionable. It, and article XII, which enabled the Emperor to determine the organization and peace standing of the armed forces, were originally meant 'to prevent cabinet intervention in affairs related to military strategy and operations; also to prohibit Diet [government] interference in determining the military strength needed for national defense. They were not framed to provide an institutional base for the Emperor's direction of military affairs'.

Regardless of its original purpose, article XI conceivably could still have been used by the Emperor to try and control the military. However, this would have been extremely difficult because 'there was absolutely no provision holding the supreme command responsible to the Tennō for its decisions or vice versa'. To recall Masuda Tomoko's similar point about article XI, 'there was no clear definition regarding either the scope of the right of supreme command or the person responsible for exercising it'. Thus, the Shōwa Emperor did not know how far he could go in using his supreme command prerogative to control the military. He evidently thought that the chiefs of staff should be responsible to him in the same way as ministers of state were responsible to him for their politics. But his concept of ministerial responsibility clashed with their political irresponsibility as the chiefs of staff repeatedly usurped his authority.

What does such usurpation signify when it comes to assessing the 'emperor system' in prewar Shōwa Japan? Many Japanese, and a minority of Western, historians have typically 'subsumed all aspects of the modern Japanese state and society under the category of "emperor system", or *tennōsei*, seeing it as the capstone' of power. But 'The construct of the emperor-system state ... is of little utility in terms of detailed historical inquiry, for it exaggerates the unity, strength, and rigidity of the Japanese state from 1890 to the nation's defeat'.

Given the prevalence of 'elite pluralism' and all of the political divisions, ... which made prewar Japan anything but totalitarian, if the 'emperor system' means anything, its distinguishing feature was is amorphousness. Takeyama Michio captures this reality when he writes, 'The history of the early Shōwa era demonstrates the absence of control. The government and the military were divided..., the emperor-system had become nominal and the insubordination of the military had usurped the Emperor's authority'....

In sum, the combination of 'external constraints' mentioned above make it doubtful that the Emperor could have done more to prevent war. But again, should he have tried to do more, and if so, why did he not do more, to prevent it? It is in pondering this problem that the 'internal constraints' discussed [earlier], which arose from his personality, temperament, political style and political beliefs, are important.

The rigid upbringing of the emperors in the Heian period was 'hardly designed to encourage the development of a vigorous personality, let alone any determination to challenge the political status quo'. Nor had much changed by the Tokugawa period when 'The training of imperial children bred in them habits of docility and rigidly patterned behavior'. Since rigid courtly precedents of protocol and ritual still obtained during his childhood, it is not surprising that his upbringing left the Shōwa Emperor a passive person who always was inclined to 'play by the rules', as when he performed Shintō rites whose underlying myths he personally rejected, or sanctioned war, despite his private hopes for peace.

This early conditioning to be passive was a long-term 'internal constraint' on his 'ability' to oppose war. Another was his scientific, rational world view as a marine biologist who was most at ease in his laboratory and when collecting specimens in Sagami Bay or elsewhere in Japan. Believing in the 'geometry' and orderly evolution of politics and government, which to him seemed comparable to the ordered and evolutionary patterns of the natural world, he was not the sort of man who could face, and deal effectively with, the reality of violence in domestic political life and foreign policy. His reliance on logical argument, and what Honjō Shigeru observed as his scholarly, almost pedantic, manner, made little impact on military men who subscribed to the different rationality of strategic ends and means and who were set on war.

It should be remembered, however, that although he was a naturalist who respected the sanctity of life, as when he once despaired that an officer had given him a pair of cranes which had been shot for his pleasure, he was not a pacifist. Despite his instinctive preference for international cooperation, the Shōwa Emperor was himself a nationalist whose abiding concern with national security ultimately made him susceptible to the argument in late 1941 that, encircled, Japan had to go to war to save itself and its overseas possessions.

[I have] also speculated that there were aspects of the Emperor's political style, including in particular his indirection and understatement, which rendered him more passive than assertive in expressing his opposition to war. It was suggested that these tendencies may have reflected certain general features of the political culture of the Japanese aristocracy. . . .

Another feature of aristocratic political culture in Japan which possibly impinged on the Emperor's 'ability' to oppose war is the ancient Chinese emphasis, translated into Japan, on the normative 'non-assertion' of monarchy. Herschel Webb quotes Han Fei Tzu as having written in the third century BC: 'The sceptre should not be shown. For its inner nature is non-assertion'. The sage-king merely 'remains empty' and relies on his ministers to govern: 'If the ruler has to exert any special skill of his own, it means that affairs are not going right'. Webb comments that in Japan, 'The *ideal* of non-assertion remained influential'.

To the extent that it influenced the Shōwa court, then this ideal helps to explain the Emperor's passive political style. And insofar as the Shōwa court was influenced by the ancient Japanese tradition in which emperors primarily used their religious authority to legitimize the secular power and policies of others, this tradition, too, informed his scrupulous sanctioning of policies, including those that led to aggression and war....

Perhaps the Emperor unconsciously used his constitutional scruples to disguise his inability to stand up to the military. Be that as it may, a major theme in this study has been the importance he consistently attached to upholding the example of Emperor Meiji as a constitutional monarch. The late Edwin Reischauer wrote in 1975, 'Since the present Emperor has always been a conscientious Constitutional monarch, it really is not proper to inquire what his own particular views may have been, even under the old system'. However, precisely because the Emperor so diligently operated as a constitutional monarch, it is absolutely essential 'to inquire what his own particular views may have been', if we wish to understand how, more than any other, this 'internal constraint' led him to tie his own hands politically even while others tied them.

... [T]he Shōwa Emperor was one of the 'very few' sovereigns who, for reasons of political conviction, made it a point to operate strictly as a limited monarch.... Sugiura Shigetake encouraged him to respect the principles of constitutional monarchy in emulation of Meiji. Later, after observing for himself the theory and practice of constitutional monarchy in Britain during his tour of Europe in 1921, the then Crown Prince 'conceived his own role as that of a constitutional monarch in the British mould, automatically sanctioning any bill approved by the cabinet', with King George V as his model.

This stance was in turn greatly reinforced by Saionji and his circle of constitutional monarchists who advised him during the Taishō regency and thereafter, well into the 1930s. Under their influence, he especially 'refrained from exercising the prerogative of supreme command... Deferring to parliamentary democracy based on constitutional government, he did not take the initiative'. Finally, through these advisers, and directly when Minobe Tatsukichi lectured at the palace, Minobe further strengthened the Emperor's resolve to function as a constitutional monarch with limited powers. The Emperor may not have followed Minobe's constitutional interpretation in every detail. But he firmly embraced Minobe's concept of the emperor as an 'organ' of the state.

He thus insisted on the rule of law, the principle of ministerial responsibility, and the need at all costs to avoid what he often referred to as 'the bane of despotism'. There is no question that 'In his own interpretation of the Constitution, the Emperor at all times acted constitutionally and it would have been out of character and contrary to his convictions about the rule of law to do otherwise'.

At times, in crisis situations, he acted and spoke as if he saw the possibility of using the absolute powers ascribed to him in the Meiji constitution to defend constitutional government, as when he reacted strongly to the exceptional political crisis of the February 1936 army insurrection. Furthermore, it will be recalled that during the Changkufeng crisis, he declared to the war minister and the army chief of staff, 'you may not move one soldier *without my command*'. And, when reflecting on the decision for war in 1941, he said in 1946, 'If at the time *I had suppressed* the advocacy of war' the public would have been incensed and a coup might have taken place. These statements suggest a more assertive model of imperial action.

Nevertheless, he deliberately rejected this model and instead virtually 'absolutized' the model of constitutional monarchy as he understood it. Thus, after dismissing Tanaka Giichi in 1929, and after helping to suppress the 1936 army rebellion, he worried that he had gone too far as a constitutional monarch. If anything, his determination to uphold his limited powers grew all the more as other elites sought to exploit his absolute powers in declaring the imperial will.... After Japan's defeat, Prince Konoe regretted that the Emperor had not boldly challenged the military:

> Out of reserve, the Emperor seldom expresses his own views. Prince Saionji and Count Makino taught His Majesty not to take the initiative, in adherence to the British-style constitutions, but the Japanese Constitution exists on the premise of the Emperor's personal administration.

The Emperor, Konoe complained, should have asserted his prerogative of supreme command to control the military. He concluded, 'If the Emperor merely gives encouragement or advice as in England, military affairs and political diplomacy cannot advance in unison'.

Konoe had exposed the contradictory nature of Japan's 'constitutional autocracy' but his criticism of the Emperor was self-serving. Konoe himself blocked the Emperor when he wanted to take the initiative: for example, when he told the Emperor not to speak at the crucial imperial conference of 11 January 1938, which ratified the decision to 'annihilate' the enemy in China. In fact, knowing of the Emperor's constitutional scruples, Konoe deliberately used the principle, that a constitutional monarch should not interfere with government policy, to prevent him from openly opposing all-out war in China. Kido, too, neutralized the Emperor politically in this way. When testifying on trial after the war, he said, 'I used to counsel the Emperor to approve [policy], trusting the government in accordance with constitutional government'....

The Shōwa Emperor... 'was actually downright stubborn in his observance of the Constitution'. Accordingly, he refused on 14 January 1938 to see the army chief of staff, Prince Kan'in, even though he knew that Kan'in shared his own opposition to the Konoe cabinet's pro-war stance on China. Of Kan'in's intentions, he said, 'I judged that this might surely be a plan to overturn what had already been determined [by the government] and I refused to see him'.

The same consideration convinced him that he had no choice as a constitutional monarch but to sanction the decision for war in 1941. There is thus a certain validity in Kamishima Jirō's remark. 'It is probably correct to say that he conducted himself generally in accordance with the "organ theory"' and that 'on that account, the war broke out' in December 1941. Ironically, however, his sanction served perfectly the interests of the militarists and it mattered little that he sanctioned war thinking that this was required of him as a constitutional monarch while to them he sanctioned it as an absolute monarch who, a god himself, spoke for the gods in commanding the destiny of imperial Japan.

After Japan attacked Pearl Harbor the Emperor, as 'manifest deity', was used by the government to sponsor Japan's 'holy war' and encourage the people in hard times. Yet his own constitutionalism still led him to support General Tōjō Hideki's leadership even after the war went badly for Japan and a 'peace party' had emerged, for he believed that it would be improper for a constitutional monarch to depose a prime minister, as he had once deposed Tanaka. And when he intervened to end the war in August 1945, he did so only at the request of the prime minister, after the government had reached a complete impasse in debating whether to carry on with a lost cause. His intervention was critical in ending the war but even at that point, 'the Emperor was only the instrument and not the prime mover, of Japan's momentous decision' to surrender.

Looking back on the prewar years of Shōwa,

> Should the Emperor have betrayed his own principles of Constitutional monarchy, which also served to preserve the Imperial institution by putting it, at least publicly, above politics? Should he have taken an inflexible stand, and suffered the consequences, including the probable assassination of his most trusted advisers, and his own captivity, or at least the loss of what freedom he had to influence politics?

The Emperor's consistent and principled adherence to constitutional monarchy was his strongest point and in modern times it would be strange indeed to criticize any sovereign for not acting in effect despotically. Also, if it takes a despotic intervention to avert the crisis of war, the crisis has probably already passed the point of no return in any case. All the same, however, in view of the terrible consequences of war fought in the Emperor's name, there is a strong case that, whatever the risks, he ought to have subordinated his constitutional principles to expediency, on the chance that a dramatic refusal to sanction war might have caused those who favored war to think twice.

The last chance to intervene with any hope of success was in the early stages of the Sino-Japanese War when there existed the potential, however slim, for mobilizing the caution of the army general staff to challenge the belligerent policy of Prime Minister Konoe and the generals who supported it. That the chance was missed made this arguably the darkest episode in the Emperor's career.

By late 1941, it was simply too late to intervene for peace with the United States and its allies, given that there was too much of a broad consensus on the part of military and civilian leaders that Western sanctions made war absolutely necessary. A failed imperial intervention for peace in 1941 might have ennobled him in the tradition of fallen heroes, which Ivan Morris has characterized as 'the nobility of failure' in Japanese history. But few men and women in history are cut out to be heroes and the Shōwa Emperor was not one of them.

The Emperor sanctioned war, but to conclude, this study confirms that 'Hirohito was neither the bloodthristy tyrant that David Bergamini has described, nor the reckless reactionary depicted by Inoue Kiyoshi'. Nor was he Edward Behr's devious sovereign who turned a blind eye to aggression while cleverly contriving to let others take responsibility for war. Rather, he exemplified what is more commonly found in history, major figures who, politically, were 'mediocre rather than great'. In the last analysis, the Shōwa Emperor was the unwilling symbol, not the maker, of chaos and catastrophe.

POSTSCRIPT

Should Emperor Hirohito Have Been Held Responsible for Japan's World War II Actions?

Many people today believe that the Japanese have never accepted its responsibility for World War II. First, the Japanese refused to acknowledge the commission of numerous atrocities in China, which included horrific medical experiments performed on prisoners of war, and the notorious "Rape of Nanking" in which thousands of innocent Chinese civilians were brutally killed by the Japanese armed forces. Later, the Japanese denied using Korean and other Asian women as sex slaves for their military personnel, until the evidence was too overwhelming to ignore. Negative accounts of Japanese troop behavior during the war seldom made their way into Japanese history books or movie houses. Some have stated that one reason the Japanese may have difficulty in accepting responsibility today is that they were never required to do so earlier. And today, with most Japanese citizens having no direct contact with the war, it is unlikely that they can be convinced that their country's armed forces committed atrocities and that the father of their present emperor may have been responsible for them. For more information about this subject, see Gavan McCormack, "Japan's Uncomfortable Past," *History Today* (May 1998).

One of the earliest works critical of Hirohito and Japan is David Bergamini, *Japan's Imperial Conspiracy*, 2 vols. (William Morrow, 1971), written by a man who suffered internment by the Japanese during the war. This was followed by Edward Behr, *Hirohito: Behind the Myth* (Villard, 1980), which provided the impetus for the BBC/PBS film mentioned in the introduction to this issue. Hirohito also had his defenders and among them are Charles D. Sheldon, "Japanese Aggression and the Emperor, 1931–1941, From Contemporary Diaries," *Modern Asian Studies* (vol. 10, no. 1, 1976); Jerrold M. Packard, *Sons of Heaven: A Portrait of the Japanese Monarchy* (Charles Scribner's Sons, 1987); and Edwin P. Hoyt, *Hirohito: The Emperor and the Man* (Bergin & Garvey, 1992).

Most of the recent books on Hirohito tend to be more condemning than exculpatory. This may be due to the loss of influence of those older historians who supported the American-directed post-war Japanese settlement and its concomitant exoneration of Hirohito. Some of the leading critical accounts are Herbert Bix, *Hirohito and the Making of Modern Japan* (HarperCollins, 2000); Daikichi Irokawa, *The Age of Hirohito: In Search of Modern Japan* (The Free Press, 1995); John W. Dower, *Embracing Defeat: Japan in the Wake of World War II* (W. W. Norton, 1999); and Richard B. Frank, *Downfall: The End of the Imperial Japanese Empire* (Random House, 1999).

More surprising than the sides taken by various historians regarding the question raised by this issue is the number of historians who have written books about twentieth-century Japan that cover the World War II era and are notoriously silent about the question of Hirohito's responsibility. In some of these works, his existence during the war is barely acknowledged.

ISSUE 12

Was Stalin Responsible for the Cold War?

YES: John Lewis Gaddis, from *We Now Know: Rethinking Cold War History* (Clarendon Press, 1997)

NO: Martin J. Sherwin, from "The Atomic Bomb and the Origins of the Cold War," in Melvyn P. Leffler and David S. Painter, eds., *Origins of the Cold War: An International History* (Routledge, 1994)

ISSUE SUMMARY

YES: Historian John Lewis Gaddis states that after more than a half a century of cold war scholarship, Joseph Stalin still deserves most of the responsibility for the onset of the cold war.

NO: Historian Martin J. Sherwin counters that the origins of the cold war can be found in the World War II diplomacy involving the use of the atomic bomb, and he places much of the blame for the cold war on the shoulders of Franklin D. Roosevelt, Harry S. Truman, and Winston Churchill.

It is hard to imagine that the cold war is over when it played such a pivotal role in world affairs for parts of five decades. But the disintegration of the Soviet Empire has ushered in a new era in strategic diplomacy. What shape this new international relations era will take has yet to be determined, but it is unlikely that it will influence our lives in the same manner as the cold war. It is now the job of historians to compose a reassessment of the cold war, which would cover questions of causes, effects, and responsibility.

The historiography of the cold war seemed to begin simultaneously with the onset of tensions between the democratic and communist worlds. With the question of responsibility looming large, the debate among historians seemed to center around two distinct groups of scholars. The first group, commonly referred to as the orthodox or traditional school, held the Soviet Union responsible for the cold war. Because some of the school's proponents were themselves participants (some were even policymakers) in the events of the era, it was easy for them to see Soviet culpability in the broken promises and duplicitous actions, which seemed to highlight the early cold war years. And as the Soviet Empire cast its menacing shadow over Eastern Europe, it became increasingly apparent to the traditionalists that Joseph Stalin could not be trusted. Also, the volatile nature of the postwar world—especially the vulnerability of the newly emerging nations of the postimperialist era—created tempting morsels for the "Russian Bear." A new policy, "containment," was created to control the voracious Soviet appetite. It would last for almost half a century and would lead to many crises, wars, and conflicts, which marked the cold war. Behind all of this loomed the towering figure of Stalin and, to a lesser degree, the men who succeeded him.

A new school of thought was created that opposed the cold war views of the traditionalists. Members of this school of thought became known as the revisionists, and they began to view the cold war from an entirely different perspective. From this would come a new set of assumptions, including (1) the postwar weakness of the Soviet Union, which prevented the Soviets from being the threat to world peace that many felt they were, (2) the obsession of free-world leaders in viewing any world problem as being Soviet-created, (3) the view that, after a careful examination of World War II diplomacy, many of the actions of the Western Allies, including the use of the atomic bomb, induced Soviet leaders to feel threatened and to react accordingly. Thus, much of the responsibility for the cold war, according to the revisionists, must be laid at the feet of the West and its leaders.

Subsequently, much of cold war historiography was dominated by this traditionalist/revisionist dichotomy. And, as the historical profession became more influenced by a conflict-oriented mode rather than a consensus-centered mode, the revisionists began to gain momentum in the crisis-laden 1960s and 1970s. The Vietnam War helped to trigger this response, as many began to see the mistakes of the cold war being played out again and again. There were no longer any "sacred cows" of the traditionalist variety.

The sudden decline of world communism seemed to usher in an aura of cold war justification. After all, in the eyes of many, the West had won; the enemy had been vanquished, and the end of the struggle seemed to have a ring of vindication to it. But the scars of the past were too deep to hide, and the critical examination of cold war politics continued.

New sources of information, especially those from the formerly secret Soviet archives, were opened up in order to assist historians in their search for answers. What was discovered was revelatory, but it changed few minds. Traditionalists and revisionists contined to hold the same opinions that they held a generation ago.

One historian, John Lewis Gaddis, author of the first selection, named this recent reexamination the "New Cold War." Having been involved in cold war historiography for most of its existence, he drew the conclusion that the Soviet Union and Stalin in particular still bear most of the responsibility for the cold war. Historians such as Gar Alperovitz, Gabriel Kolko, Martin J. Sherwin, and others continued to push the revisionist agenda, that the United States and its allies were responsible for the cold war, and Sherwin represents their viewpoint in his selection.

John Lewis Gaddis  **YES**

We Now Know:
Rethinking Cold War History

[Joseph] Stalin appears to have relished his role, along with [Franklin D.] Roosevelt and [Winston] Churchill, as one of the wartime Big Three. Such evidence as has surfaced from Soviet archives suggests that he received reassuring reports about Washington's intentions: "Roosevelt is more friendly to us than any other prominent American," Ambassador Litvinov commented in June 1943, "and it is quite obvious that he wishes to cooperate with us." Whoever was in the White House, Litvinov's successor Andrei Gromyko predicted a year later, the Soviet Union and the United States would "manage to find common issues for the solution of... problems emerging in the future and of interest to both countries." Even if Stalin's long-range thinking about security did clash with that of his Anglo-American allies, common military purposes provided the strongest possible inducements to smooth over such differences. It is worth asking why this *practice* of wartime cooperation did not become a *habit* that would extend into the postwar era.

The principal reason, it now appears, was Stalin's insistence on equating security with territory. Western diplomats had been surprised, upon arriving in Moscow soon after the German attack in the summer of 1941, to find the Soviet leader already demanding a postwar settlement that would retain what his pact with Hitler had yielded: the Baltic states, together with portions of Finland, Poland, and Romania. Stalin showed no sense of shame or even embarrassment about this, no awareness that the *methods* by which he had obtained these concessions could conceivably render them illegitimate in the eyes of anyone else. When it came to territorial aspirations, he made no distinction between adversaries and allies: what one had provided the other was expected to endorse....

On the surface, this strategy succeeded. After strong initial objections, Roosevelt and Churchill did eventually acknowledge the Soviet Union's right to the expanded borders it claimed; they also made it clear that they would not oppose the installation of "friendly" governments in adjoining states. This meant accepting a Soviet sphere of influence from the Baltic to the Adriatic, a concession not easily reconciled with the Atlantic Charter. But the authors of that document saw no feasible way to avoid that outcome: military necessity required continued Soviet cooperation against the Germans. Nor were they themselves prepared to relinquish spheres of influence in Western Europe and the Mediterranean, the Middle East, Latin America, and East Asia. Self-determination was a sufficiently malleable concept that each of the Big Three could have endorsed, without sleepless nights, what the Soviet government had said about the Atlantic Charter: "practical application of these principles will necessarily adapt itself to the circumstances, needs, and historic peculiarities of particular countries."

That, though, was precisely the problem. For unlike Stalin, Roosevelt and Churchill would have to defend their decisions before domestic constituencies. The *manner* in which Soviet influence expanded was therefore, for them, of no small significance. Stalin showed little understanding of this. Having no experience himself with democratic procedures, he dismissed requests that he respect democratic proprieties. "[S]ome propaganda work should be done," he advised Roosevelt at the Tehran conference after the president had hinted that the American public would welcome a plebiscite in the Baltic States. "It is all nonsense!" Stalin complained to [Soviet Foreign Minister V. M.] Molotov. "[Roosevelt] is their military leader and commander in chief. Who would dare object to him?" When at Yalta F.D.R. stressed the need for the first Polish election to be as pure as "Caesar's wife," Stalin responded with a joke: "They said that about her, but in fact she had her sins." Molotov warned his boss, on that occasion, that the Americans' insistence on free elections elsewhere in Eastern Europe was "going too far." "Don't worry," he recalls Stalin as replying, "work it out. We can deal with it in our own way later. The point is the correlation of forces."

The Soviet leader was, in one sense, right. Military strength would determine what happened in that part of the world, not the enunciation of lofty principles. But unilateral methods carried long-term costs Stalin did not foresee: the most significant of these was to ruin whatever prospects existed for a Soviet sphere of influence the East Europeans themselves might have accepted. This possibility was not as far-fetched as it would later seem. . . . [Stalin] would, after all, approve such a compromise as the basis for a permanent settlement with Finland. He would initially allow free elections in Hungary, Czechoslovakia, and the Soviet occupation zone in Germany. He may even have *anticipated an enthusiastic response* as he took over Eastern Europe. "He was, I think, surprised and hurt," [W. Averell] Harriman [one of Roosevelt's closest advisors] recalled, "when the Red Army was not welcomed in all the neighboring countries as an army of liberation." "We still had our hopes," [Nikita] Khrushchev remembered, that "after the catastrophe of World War II, Europe too might become Soviet. Everyone would take the path from capitalism to socialism." It could be that there was another form of romanticism at work here, quite apart from Stalin's affinity for fellow authoritarians: that he was unrealistic enough to expect ideological solidarity and gratitude for liberation to override old fears of Russian expansionism as well as remaining manifestations of nationalism among the Soviet Union's neighbors, perhaps as easily as he himself had overridden the latter—or so it then appeared—within the multinational empire that was the Soviet Union itself.

If the Red Army could have been welcomed in Poland and the rest of the countries it liberated with the same enthusiasm American, British, and Free French forces encountered when they landed in Italy and France in 1943 and 1944, then some kind of Czech–Finnish compromise might have been feasible. Whatever Stalin's expectations, though, this did not happen. That non-event, in turn, removed any possibility of a division of Europe all members of the Grand Alliance could have endorsed. It ensured that an American sphere of influence would arise there largely by consent, but that its Soviet counterpart could sustain itself only by coercion. The resulting asymmetry would account, more than anything else, for the origins, escalation, and ultimate outcome of the Cold War.

❦

. . . It has long been clear that, in addition to having had an authoritarian vision, Stalin also had an imperial one, which he proceeded to implement in at least as single-minded a way [as the American]. No comparably influential builder of empire came close to wielding power for so long, or with such striking results, on the Western side.

It was, of course, a matter of some awkwardness that Stalin came out of a revolutionary movement that had vowed to smash, not just tsarist imperialism, but all forms of imperialism throughout the world. The Soviet leader constructed his own logic, though, and throughout his career he devoted a surprising amount of attention to showing how a revolution and an empire might coexist. . . .

Stalin's fusion of Marxist internationalism with tsarist imperialism could only reinforce his tendency, in place well before World War II, to equate the advance of world revolution with the expanding influence of the Soviet state. He applied that linkage quite impartially: a major benefit of the 1939 pact with Hitler had been that it regained territories lost as a result of the Bolshevik Revolution and the World War I settlement. But Stalin's conflation of imperialism with ideology also explains the importance he attached, following the German attack in 1941, to having his new Anglo-American allies confirm these arrangements. He had similar goals in East Asia when he insisted on bringing the Soviet Union back to the position Russia had occupied in Manchuria prior to the Russo-Japanese War: this he finally achieved at the 1945 Yalta Conference in return for promising to enter the war against Japan. "My task as minister of foreign affairs was to expand the borders of our Fatherland," Molotov recalled proudly many years later. "And it seems that Stalin and I coped with this task quite well." . . .

❦

From the West's standpoint, the critical question was how far Moscow's influence would extend *beyond* whatever Soviet frontiers turned out to be at the end of the war. Stalin had suggested to Milovan Djilas that the Soviet Union would impose its own social system as far as its armies could reach, but he was also very cautious. Keenly aware of the military power the United States and its allies had accumulated, Stalin was determined to do nothing that might involve the USSR in another devastating war until it had recovered sufficiently to be certain of winning it. "I do not wish to begin the Third World War over the Trieste question," he explained to disappointed Yugoslavs, whom he ordered to evacuate that territory in June 1945. Five years later, he would justify his decision not to intervene in the Korean War on the grounds that "the Second World War ended not long ago, and we are not ready for the Third World War." Just how far the expansion of Soviet influence would proceed depended, therefore, upon a careful balancing of opportunities against risks....

Who or what was it, though, that set the limits? Did Stalin have a fixed list of countries he thought it necessary to dominate? Was he prepared to stop in the face of resistance within those countries to "squeezing out the capitalist order"? Or would expansion cease only when confronted with opposition from the remaining capitalist states, so that further advances risked war at a time when the Soviet Union was ill-prepared for it?

Stalin had been very precise about where he wanted Soviet boundaries changed; he was much less so on how far Moscow's sphere of influence was to extend. He insisted on having "friendly" countries around the periphery of the USSR, but he failed to specify how many would have to meet this standard. He called during the war for dismembering Germany, but by the end of it was denying that he had ever done so: that country would be temporarily divided, he told leading German communists in June 1945, and they themselves would eventually bring about its reunification. He never gave up on the idea of an eventual world revolution, but he expected this to result—as his comments to the Germans suggested—from an expansion of influence emanating from the Soviet Union itself. "[F]or the Kremlin," a well-placed spymaster recalled, "the mission of communism was primarily to consolidate the might of the Soviet state. Only military strength and domination of the countries on our borders could ensure us a superpower role."

But Stalin provided no indication—surely because he himself did not know —of how rapidly, or under what circumstances, this process would take place. He was certainly prepared to stop in the face of resistance from the West: at no point was he willing to challenge the Americans or even the British where they made their interests clear.... He quickly backed down when confronted with Anglo-American objections to his ambitions in Iran in the spring of 1946, as he did later that year after demanding Soviet bases in the Turkish Straits. This pattern of advance followed by retreat had shown up in the purges of the 1930s, which Stalin halted when the external threat from Germany became too great to ignore, and it would reappear with the Berlin Blockade and the Korean War, both situations in which the Soviet Union would show great caution after provoking an unexpectedly strong American response.

What all of this suggests, though, is not that Stalin had limited ambitions, only that he had no timetable for achieving them. Molotov retrospectively confirmed this: "Our ideology stands for offensive operations when possible, and if not, we wait." Given this combination of appetite with aversion to risk, one cannot help but wonder what would have happened had the West tried containment earlier. To the extent that it bears partial responsibility for the coming of the Cold War, the historian Vojtech Mastny has argued, that responsibility lies in its failure to do just that. . . .

Stalin's policy, then, was one of imperial expansion and consolidation differing from that of earlier empires only in the determination with which he pursued it, in the instruments of coercion with which he maintained it, and in the ostensibly anti-imperial justifications he put forward in support of it. It is a testimony to his skill, if not to his morality, that he was able to achieve so many of his imperial ambitions at a time when the tides of history were running against the idea of imperial domination—as colonial offices in London, Paris, Lisbon, and The Hague were finding out—and when his own country was recovering from one of the most brutal invasions in recorded history. The fact that Stalin was able to *expand* his empire when others were contracting and while the Soviet Union was as weak as it was requires explanation. Why did opposition to this process, within and outside Europe, take so long to develop?

One reason was that the colossal sacrifices the Soviet Union had made during the war against the Axis had, in effect, "purified" its reputation: the USSR and its leader had "earned" the right to throw their weight around, or so it seemed. Western governments found it difficult to switch quickly from viewing the Soviet Union as a glorious wartime ally to portraying it as a new and dangerous adversary. President Harry S. Truman and his future Secretary of State Dean Acheson—neither of them sympathetic in the slightest to communism—nonetheless tended to give the Soviet Union the benefit of the doubt well into the early postwar era. . . .

Resistance to Stalin's imperialism also developed slowly because Marxism-Leninism at the time had such widespread appeal. It is difficult now to recapture the admiration revolutionaries outside the Soviet Union felt for that country before they came to know it well. . . . Because the Bolsheviks themselves had overcome one empire and had made a career of condemning others, it would take decades for people who were struggling to overthrow British, French, Dutch, or Portuguese colonialism to see that there could also be such a thing as Soviet imperialism. European communists—notably the Yugoslavs—saw this much earlier, but even to most of them it had not been apparent at the end of the war.

Still another explanation for the initial lack of resistance to Soviet expansionism was the fact that its repressive character did not become immediately apparent to all who were subjected to it. . . .

One has the impression that Stalin and the Eastern Europeans got to know one another only gradually. The Kremlin leader was slow to recognize that Soviet authority would not be welcomed everywhere beyond Soviet borders; but as he did come to see this he became all the more determined to impose it everywhere. The Eastern Europeans were slow to recognize how confining incorporation within a Soviet sphere was going to be; but as they did come to see this they became all the more determined to resist it, even if only by withholding, in a passive but sullen manner, the consent any regime needs to establish itself by means other than coercion. Stalin's efforts to consolidate his empire therefore made it at once more repressive and less secure. Meanwhile, an alternative vision of postwar Europe was emerging from the other great empire that established itself in the wake of World War II, that of the United States, and this too gave Stalin grounds for concern. . . .

～◆◇◆～

What is there new to say about the old question of responsibility for the Cold War? Who actually started it? Could it have been averted? Here I think the "new" history is bringing us back to an old answer: that *as long as Stalin was running the Soviet Union a cold war was unavoidable.*

History is always the product of determined *and* contingent events: it is up to historians to find the proper balance between them. The Cold War could hardly have happened if there had not been a United States and a Soviet Union, if both had not emerged victorious from World War II, if they had not had conflicting visions of how to organize the postwar world. But these long-term trends did not in themselves *ensure* such a contest, because there is always room for the unexpected to undo what might appear to be inevitable. *Nothing* is ever completely predetermined, as real triceratops and other dinosaurs discovered 65 million years ago when the most recent large asteroid or comet or whatever it was hit the earth and wiped them out.

Individuals, not asteroids, more often personify contingency in history. Who can specify in advance—or unravel afterwards—the particular intersection of genetics, environment, and culture that makes each person unique? Who can foresee what weird conjunctions of design and circumstance may cause a very few individuals to rise so high as to shape great events, and so come to the attention of historians? Such people may set their sights on getting to the top, but an assassin, or a bacillus, or even a carelessly driven taxicab can always be lurking along the way. How entire countries fall into the hands of malevolent geniuses like Hitler and Stalin remains as unfathomable in the "new" Cold War history as in the "old."

Once leaders like these do gain power, however, certain things become highly probable. It is only to be expected that in an authoritarian state the chief authoritarian's personality will weigh much more heavily than those of democratic leaders, who have to share power. And whether because of social alienation, technological innovation, or economic desperation, the first half of the twentieth century was particularly susceptible to great authoritarians and all that resulted from their ascendancy. It is hardly possible to imagine Nazi Germany or the world war it caused without Hitler. I find it increasingly difficult, given what we know now, to imagine the Soviet Union or the Cold War without Stalin.

For the more we learn, the less sense it makes to distinguish Stalin's foreign policies from his domestic practices or even his personal behavior. Scientists have shown the natural world to be filled with examples of what they call "self-similarity across scale": patterns that persist whether one views them microscopically, macroscopically, or anywhere in between. Stalin was like that: he functioned in much the same manner whether operating within the international system, within his alliances, within his country, within his party, within his personal entourage, or even within his family. The Soviet leader waged cold wars on all of these fronts. The Cold War *we* came to know was only one of many from *his* point of view.

Nor did Stalin's influence diminish as quickly as that of most dictators after their deaths. He built a *system* sufficiently durable to survive not only his own demise but his successors' fitful and half-hearted efforts at "de-Stalinization." They were themselves its creatures, and they continued to work within it because they knew no other method of governing. Not until [Mikhail] Gorbachev was a Soviet leader fully prepared to dismantle Stalin's structural legacy. It tells us a lot that as it disappeared, so too did the Cold War and ultimately the Soviet Union itself.

This argument by no means absolves the United States and its allies of a considerable responsibility for how the Cold War was fought—hardly a surprising conclusion since they in fact won it. Nor is it to deny the feckless stupidity with which the Americans fell into peripheral conflicts like Vietnam, or their exorbitant expenditures on unusable weaponry: these certainly caused the Cold War to cost much more in money and lives than it otherwise might have. Nor is it to claim moral superiority for western statesmen. None was as bad as Stalin —or Mao—but the Cold War left no leader uncorrupted: the wielding of great power, even in the best of times, rarely does.

It is the case, though, that if one applies the always useful test of counterfactual history—drop a key variable and speculate as to what difference this might have made—Stalin's centrality to the origins of the Cold War becomes quite clear. For all of their importance, one could have removed Roosevelt, Churchill, Truman, Bevin, Marshall, or Acheson, and a cold war would still have probably followed the world war. If one could have eliminated Stalin, alternative paths become quite conceivable. For with the possible exception of Mao, no twentieth-century leader imprinted himself upon his country as thoroughly and with such lasting effect as Stalin did. And given his personal propensity for cold wars—a tendency firmly rooted long before he had even heard of Harry Truman—once Stalin wound up at the top in Moscow and once it was clear his state would survive the war, then it looks equally clear that there was going to be a Cold War whatever the west did. Who then was responsible? The answer, I think, is authoritarianism in general, and Stalin in particular.

NO

Martin J. Sherwin

The Atomic Bomb and the
Origins of the Cold War

During the Second World War the atomic bomb was seen and valued as
a potential rather than an actual instrument of policy. Responsible officials
believed that its impact on diplomacy had to await its development and, perhaps, even a demonstration of its power. As Henry L. Stimson, the Secretary of
War, observed in his memoirs: "The bomb as a merely probable weapon had
seemed a weak reed on which to rely, but the bomb as a colossal reality was
very different." That policymakers considered this difference before Hiroshima
has been well documented, but whether they based wartime diplomatic policies
upon an anticipated successful demonstration of the bomb's power remains a
source of controversy. Two questions delineate the issues in this debate. First,
did the development of the atomic bomb affect the way American policymakers
conducted diplomacy with the Soviet Union? Second, did diplomatic considerations related to the Soviet Union influence the decision to use the atomic bomb
against Japan?

These important questions relating the atomic bomb to American diplomacy, and ultimately to the origins of the Cold War, have been addressed almost
exclusively to the formulation of policy during the early months of the Truman administration. As a result, two anterior questions of equal importance,
questions with implications for those already posed, have been overlooked. Did
diplomatic considerations related to Soviet postwar behavior influence the formulation of [Franklin D.] Roosevelt's atomic energy policies? What effect did
the atomic legacy Truman inherited have on the diplomatic and atomic energy
policies of his administration?

Although Roosevelt left no definitive statement assigning a postwar role
to the atomic bomb, his expectations for its potential diplomatic value can be
recalled from the existing record. An analysis of the policies he chose from
among the alternatives he faced suggests that the potential diplomatic value of
the bomb began to shape his atomic energy policies as early as 1943. He may
have been cautious about counting on the bomb as a reality during the war,
but he nevertheless consistently chose policy alternatives that would promote
the postwar diplomatic potential of the bomb if the predictions of scientists

From Martin J. Sherwin, "The Atomic Bomb and the Origins of the Cold War," in Melvyn P. Lef-
fler and David S. Painter, eds., *Origins of the Cold War: An International History* (Routledge, 1994).
Copyright © 1994 by Martin J. Sherwin. Originally published in *American Historical Review*, no. 78
(October 1973). Reprinted and abridged by permission of the author. Notes omitted.

proved true. These policies were based on the assumption that the bomb could be used effectively to secure postwar diplomatic aims; and this assumption was carried over from the Roosevelt to the Truman administration.

Despite general agreement that the bomb would be an extraordinarily important diplomatic factor after the war, those closely associated with its development did not agree on how to use it most effectively as an instrument of diplomacy. Convinced that wartime atomic energy policies would have postwar diplomatic consequences, several scientists advised Roosevelt to adopt policies aimed at achieving a postwar international control system. [Winston] Churchill, on the other hand, urged the President to maintain the Anglo-American atomic monopoly as a diplomatic counter against the postwar ambitions of other nations—particularly against the Soviet Union. Roosevelt fashioned his atomic energy policies from the choices he made between these conflicting recommendations. In 1943 he rejected the counsel of his science advisers and began to consider the diplomatic component of atomic energy policy in consultation with Churchill alone. This decisionmaking procedure and Roosevelt's untimely death have left his motives ambiguous. Nevertheless it is clear that he pursued policies consistent with Churchill's monopolistic, anti-Soviet views.

The findings of this [selection] thus raise serious questions concerning generalizations historians have commonly made about Roosevelt's diplomacy: that it was consistent with his public reputation for cooperation and conciliation; that he was naive with respect to postwar Soviet behavior; that, like [Woodrow] Wilson, he believed in collective security as an effective guarantor of national safety; and that he made every possible effort to ensure that the Soviet Union and its allies would continue to function as postwar partners. Although this [selection] does not dispute the view that Roosevelt desired amicable postwar relations with the Soviet Union, or even that he worked hard to achieve them, it does suggest that historians have exaggerated his confidence in (and perhaps his commitment to) such an outcome. His most secret and among his most important long-range decisions—those responsible for prescribing a diplomatic role for the atomic bomb—reflected his lack of confidence. Finally, in light of this [selection's] conclusions, the widely held assumption that Truman's attitude toward the atomic bomb was substantially different from Roosevelt's must also be revised.

Like the grand alliance itself, the Anglo-American atomic energy partnership was forged by the war and its exigencies. The threat of a German atomic bomb precipitated a hasty marriage of convenience between British research and American resources. When scientists in Britain proposed a theory that explained how an atomic bomb might quickly be built, policymakers had to assume that German scientists were building one. "If such an explosive were made," Vannevar Bush, the director of the Office of Scientific Research and Development, told Roosevelt in July 1941, "it would be thousands of times more powerful than existing explosives, and its use might be determining." Roosevelt assumed nothing less. Even before the atomic energy project was fully organized he assigned it the highest priority.

The high stakes at issue during the war did not prevent officials in Great Britain or the United States from considering the postwar implications of their atomic energy decisions. As early as 1941, during the debate over whether to join the United States in an atomic energy partnership, members of the British government's atomic energy committee argued that the matter "was so important for the future that work should proceed in Britain." Weighing the obvious difficulties of proceeding alone against the possible advantages of working with the United States, Sir John Anderson, then Lord President of the Council and the minister responsible for atomic energy research, advocated the partnership. As he explained to Churchill, by working closely with the Americans British scientists would be able "to take up the work again [after the war], not where we left off, but where the combined effort had by then brought it."

As early as October 1942 Roosevelt's science advisers exhibited a similar concern with the potential postwar value of atomic energy. After conducting a full-scale review of the atomic energy project, James B. Conant, the president of Harvard University and Bush's deputy, recommended discontinuing the Anglo-American partnership "as far as development and manufacture is concerned." What prompted Conant's recommendations, however, was his suspicion—soon to be shared by other senior atomic energy administrators—that the British were rather more concerned with information for postwar industrial purposes than for wartime use. What right did the British have to the fruits of American labor? "We were doing nine-tenths of the work," Stimson told Roosevelt in October. Early in January 1943 the British were officially informed that the rules governing the Anglo-American atomic energy partnership had been altered on "orders from the top."

By approving the policy of "restricted interchange" Roosevelt undermined a major incentive for British cooperation. It is not surprising, therefore, that Churchill took up the matter directly with the President and with Harry Hopkins, "Roosevelt's own, personal Foreign Office."

Conant and Bush understood the implications of Churchill's intervention and sought to counter its effect. Information on manufacturing an atomic bomb, Conant noted, was a "military secret which is in a totally different class from anything the world has ever seen if the potentialities of this project are realised." Though British and American atomic energy policies might coincide during the war, Conant and Bush expected them to conflict afterward.

The controversy over the policy of "restricted interchange" of atomic energy information shifted attention to postwar diplomatic considerations. The central issue was clearly drawn. The atomic energy policy of the United States was related to the very fabric of Anglo-American postwar relations and, as Churchill would insist, to postwar relations between each of them and the Soviet Union. The specter of Soviet postwar military power played a major role in shaping the Prime Minister's attitude toward atomic energy policies in 1943.

Churchill could cite numerous reasons for this determination to acquire an independent atomic arsenal after the war, but Great Britain's postwar military-diplomatic position with respect to the Soviet Union invariably led the list. When Bush and Stimson visited London in July, Churchill told them quite frankly that he was "vitally interested in the possession of all [atomic energy] information because this will be necessary for Britain's independence in the future as well as for success during the war." Nor was Churchill evasive about his reasoning: "It would never do to have Germany or Russia win the race for something which might be used for international blackmail," he stated bluntly and then pointed out that "Russia might be in a position to accomplish this result unless we worked together." Convinced that the British attitude toward the bomb would undermine any possibility of postwar cooperation with the Soviet Union, Bush and Conant vigorously continued to oppose any revival of the Anglo-American atomic energy partnership.

On July 20, however, Roosevelt chose to accept a recommendation from Hopkins to restore full partnership, and he ordered Bush to "renew, in an inclusive manner, the full exchange of information with the British." At the Quebec Conference, the President and the Prime Minister agreed that the British would share the atomic bomb. The Quebec Agreement revived the principle of an Anglo-American atomic energy partnership, albeit the British were reinstated as junior rather than equal partners.

The debate that preceded the Quebec Agreement is noteworthy for another reason; it led to a new relationship between Roosevelt and his atomic energy advisers. After August 1943 the President did not consult with them about the diplomatic aspects of atomic energy policy. Though he responded politely when they offered their views, he acted decisively only in consultation with Churchill. Bush and Conant appear to have lost a large measure of their influence because they had used it to oppose Churchill's position. What they did not suspect was the extent to which the President had come to share the Prime Minister's view.

Roosevelt was perfectly comfortable with the concept Churchill advocated —that military power was a prerequisite to successful postwar diplomacy. As early as August 1941, during the Atlantic Conference, Roosevelt had rejected the idea that an "effective international organization" could be relied upon to keep the peace: an Anglo-American international police force would be far more effective, he told Churchill. By the spring of 1942 the concept had broadened: the two "policemen" became four, and the idea was added that every other nation would be totally disarmed. "The Four Policemen" would have "to build up a reservoir of force so powerful that no aggressor would dare to challenge it," Roosevelt told Author Sweetser, an ardent internationalist. Violators first would be quarantined, and, if they persisted in their disruptive activities, bombed at the rate of a city a day until they agreed to behave. A year later, at the Tehran Conference, Roosevelt again discussed his idea, this time with Stalin. As Robert A. Divine has noted: "Roosevelt's concept of big power domination remained the central idea in his approach to international organization throughout World War II."

Precisely how Roosevelt expected to integrate the atomic bomb into his plans for keeping the peace in the postwar world is not clear. However, against the background of his atomic energy policy decisions of 1943 and his peace-keeping concepts, his actions in 1944 suggest that he intended to take full advantage of the bomb's potential as a postwar instrument of Anglo-American diplomacy. If Roosevelt thought the bomb could be used to create a more peaceful world order, he seems to have considered the threat of its power more effective than any opportunities it offered for international cooperation. If Roosevelt was less worried than Churchill about Soviet postwar ambitions, he was no less determined than the Prime Minister to avoid any commitments to the Soviets for the international control of atomic energy. There could still be four policemen, but only two of them would have the bomb.

The atomic energy policies Roosevelt pursued during the remainder of his life reinforce this interpretation of his ideas for the postwar period. The following three questions offer a useful framework for analyzing his intentions. Did Roosevelt make any additional agreements with Churchill that would further support the view that he intended to maintain an Anglo-American monopoly after the war? Did Roosevelt demonstrate any interest in the international control of atomic energy? Was Roosevelt aware that an effort to maintain an Anglo-American monopoly of the atomic bomb might lead to a postwar atomic arms race with the Soviet Union?

The alternatives placed before Roosevelt posed a difficult dilemma. On the one hand, he could continue to exclude the Soviet government from any official information about the development of the bomb, a policy that would probably strengthen America's postwar military-diplomatic position. But such a policy would also encourage Soviet mistrust of Anglo-American intentions and was bound to make postwar cooperation more difficult. On the other hand, Roosevelt could use the atomic bomb project as an instrument of cooperation by informing Stalin of the American government's intention of cooperating in the development of a plan for the international control of atomic weapons, an objective that might never be achieved.

Either choice involved serious risks. Roosevelt had to balance the diplomatic advantages of being well ahead of the Soviet Union in atomic energy production after the war against the advantages of initiating wartime negotiations for postwar cooperation. The issue here, it must be emphasized, is not whether international control was likely to be successful, but rather whether Roosevelt demonstrated any serious interest in laying the groundwork for such a policy.

Roosevelt knew at this time, moreover, that the Soviets were finding out on their own about the development of the atomic bomb. Security personnel had reported an active Communist cell in the Radiation Laboratory at the University of California. Their reports indicated that at least one scientist at Berkeley was selling information to Russian agents. "They [Soviet agents] are already getting information about vital secrets and sending them to Russia," Stimson told the President on September 9, 1943. If Roosevelt was indeed worried to death about the effect the atomic bomb could have on Soviet-American postwar relations, he took no action to remove the potential danger, nor did he make any effort to explore the possibility of encouraging Soviet postwar cooperation on this problem.

Had Roosevelt avoided all postwar atomic energy commitments, his lack of support for international control could have been interpreted as an attempt to reserve his opinion on the best course to follow. But he had made commitments in 1943 supporting Churchill's monopolistic, anti-Soviet position, and he continued to make others in 1944. On June 13, for example, Roosevelt and Churchill signed an Agreement and Declaration of Trust, specifying that the United States and Great Britain would cooperate in seeking to control available supplies of uranium and thorium ore both during and after the war. This commitment, taken against the background of Roosevelt's peacekeeping ideas and his other commitments, suggests that the President's attitude toward the international control of atomic energy was similar to the Prime Minister's.

Churchill rejected the assumption that international control of atomic energy could be used as a cornerstone for constructing a peaceful world order. An atomic monopoly would be a significant diplomatic advantage in postwar diplomacy, and Churchill did not believe that anything useful could be gained by surrendering this advantage. The argument that a new weapon created a unique opportunity to refashion international affairs ignored every lesson Churchill read into history. "You can be quite sure," he would write in a memorandum less than a year later, "that any power that gets hold of the secret will try to make the article and this touches the existence of human society. This matter is out of all relation to anything else that exists in the world, and I could not think of participating in any disclosure to third or fourth parties at the present time."

When Roosevelt and Churchill met at Hyde Park in September 1944 following the second wartime conference at Quebec, they signed an *aide-mémoire* on atomic energy. The agreement bears the markings of Churchill's attitude toward the atomic bomb. It contained an explicit rejection of any wartime efforts toward international control: "The suggestion that the world should be informed regarding tube alloys [the atomic bomb], with a view to an international agreement regarding its control and use, is not accepted. The matter should continue to be regarded as of the utmost secrecy." The *aide-mémoire* then revealed the full extent of Roosevelt's agreement with Churchill's point of view. "Full collaboration between the United States and the British Government in developing tube alloys for military and commercial purposes," it noted, "should continue after the defeat of Japan unless and until terminated by joint agreement." Finally the *aide-mémoire* offers some insight into Roosevelt's intentions for the military use of the weapon in the war: "When a bomb is finally available, it might perhaps, after mature consideration, be used against the Japanese, who should be warned that this bombardment will be repeated until they surrender."

Within the context of the complex problem of the origins of the Cold War the Hyde Park meeting is far more important than historians of the war generally have recognized. Overshadowed by the Second Quebec Conference on one side and by the drama of Yalta on the other, its significance often has been overlooked. But the agreements reached in September 1944 reflect a set of attitudes, aims, and assumptions that guided the relationship between the atomic bomb and American diplomacy during the Roosevelt administration and, through the transfer of its atomic legacy, during the Truman administration as well. Two alternatives had been recognized long before Roosevelt and Churchill met in 1944 at Hyde Park: the bomb could have been used to initiate a diplomatic effort to work out a system for its international control, or it could remain isolated during the war from any cooperative initiatives and held in reserve should cooperation fail. Roosevelt consistently favored the latter alternative. An insight into his reasoning is found in a memorandum Bush wrote following a conversation with Roosevelt several days after the Hyde Park meeting: "The President evidently thought he could join with Churchill in bringing about a US-UK postwar agreement on this subject [the atomic bomb] by which it would be held closely and presumably to control the peace of the world." By 1944 Roosevelt's earlier musings about the Four Policemen had faded into the background. But the idea behind it, the concept of controlling the peace of the world by amassing overwhelming military power, appears to have remained a prominent feature of his postwar plans.

⋅⦿⋅

Harry S. Truman inherited a set of military and diplomatic atomic energy policies that included partially formulated intentions, several commitments to Churchill, and the assumption that the bomb would be a legitimate weapon to be used against Japan. But no policy was definitely settled. According to the Quebec Agreement the President had the option of deciding the future of the commercial aspects of the atomic energy partnership according to his own estimate of what was fair. Although the policy of "utmost secrecy" had been confirmed at Hyde Park the previous September, Roosevelt had not informed his atomic energy advisers about the *aide-mémoire* he and Churchill signed. Although the assumption that the bomb would be used in the war was shared by those privy to its development, assumptions formulated early in the war were not necessarily valid at its conclusion. Yet Truman was bound to the past by his own uncertain position and by the prestige of his predecessor. Since Roosevelt had refused to open negotiations with the Soviet government for the international control of atomic energy, and since he had never expressed any objection to the wartime use of the bomb, it would have required considerable political courage and confidence for Truman to alter those policies. Moreover it would have required the encouragement of his advisers, for under the circumstances the most serious constraint of the new President's choices was his dependence upon advice. So Truman's atomic legacy, while it included several options, did not necessarily entail complete freedom to choose from among all the possible alternatives.

"I think it is very important that I should have a talk with you as soon as possible on a highly secret matter," Stimson wrote to Truman on April 24. It has "such a bearing on our present foreign relations and has such an important effect upon all my thinking in this field that I think you ought to know about it without further delay." Stimson had been preparing to brief Truman on the atomic bomb for almost ten days, but in the preceding twenty-four hours he had been seized by a sense of urgency. Relations with the Soviet Union had declined precipitously. The State Department had been urging Truman to get tough with the Russians. He had. Twenty-four hours earlier the President met with the Soviet Foreign Minister, V. M. Molotov, and "with rather brutal frankness" accused his government of breaking the Yalta Agreement. Molotov was furious. "I have never been talked to like that in my life," he told the President before leaving.

With a memorandum on the "political aspects of the S-1 [atomic bomb's] performance" in hand, Stimson went to the White House on April 25. The document he carried was the distillation of numerous decisions already taken, each one the product of attitudes that developed along with the new weapon. The Secretary of War himself was not entirely aware of how various forces had shaped these decisions: the recommendations of Bush and Conant, the policies Roosevelt had followed, the uncertainties inherent in the wartime alliance, the oppressive concern for secrecy, and his own inclination to consider long-range implications. It was a curious document. Though its language revealed Stimson's sensitivity to the historic significance of the atomic bomb, he did not question the wisdom of using it against Japan. Nor did he suggest any concrete steps for developing a postwar policy. His objective was to inform Truman of the salient problems: the possibility of an atomic arms race, the danger of atomic war, and the necessity for international control if the United Nations Organization was to work. "If the problem of the proper use of this weapon can be solved," he wrote, "we would have the opportunity to bring the world into a pattern in which the peace of the world and our civilizations can be saved." To cope with this difficult challenge Stimson suggested the "establishment of a select committee" to consider the postwar problems inherent in the development of the bomb.

What emerges from a careful reading of Stimson's diary, his memorandum of April 25 to Truman, a summary by [Major General Leslie R.] Groves of the meeting, and Truman's recollections is an argument for overall caution in American diplomatic relations with the Soviet Union: it was an argument against any showdown. Since the atomic bomb was potentially the most dangerous issue facing the postwar world and since the most desirable resolution of the problem was some form of international control, Soviet cooperation had to be secured. It was imprudent, Stimson suggested, to pursue a policy that would preclude the possibility of international cooperation on atomic energy matters after the war ended. Truman's overall impression of Stimson's argument was that the Secretary of War was "at least as much concerned with the role of the atomic bomb in the shaping of history as in its capacity to shorten the war." These were indeed Stimson's dual concerns on April 25, and he could see no conflict between them.

Despite the profound consequences Stimson attributed to the development of the new weapon, he had not suggested that Truman reconsider its use against Japan. Nor had he thought to mention the possibility that chances of securing Soviet postwar cooperation might be diminished if Stalin did not receive a commitment to international control prior to an attack. Until the bomb's "actual certainty [was] fixed," Stimson considered any prior approach to Stalin as premature. As the uncertainties of impending peace became more apparent and worrisome, Stimson, Truman, and the Secretary of State-designate, James F. Byrnes, began to think of the bomb as something of a diplomatic panacea for their postwar problems. Byrnes had told Truman in April that the bomb "might well put us in a position to dictate our own terms at the end of the war." By

June, Truman and Stimson were discussing "further *quid pro quos* which should be established in consideration for our taking them [the Soviet Union] into [atomic energy] partnership." Assuming that the bomb's impact on diplomacy would be immediate and extraordinary, they agreed on no less than "the settlement of the Polish, Rumanian, Yugoslavian, and Manchurian problems." But they also concluded that no revelation would be made "to Russia or anyone else until the first bomb had been successfully laid on Japan."

Was an implicit warning to Moscow, then, the principal reason for deciding to use the atomic bomb against Japan? In light of the ambiguity of the available evidence the question defies an unequivocal answer. What can be said with certainty is that Truman, Stimson, Byrnes, and several others involved in the decision consciously considered two effects of a combat demonstration of the bomb's power: first, the impact of the atomic attack on Japan's leaders, who might be persuaded thereby to end the war; and second, the impact of that attack on the Soviet Union's leaders, who might then prove to be more cooperative. But if the assumption that the bomb might bring the war to a rapid conclusion was the principal motive for using the atomic bomb, the expectation that its use would also inhibit Soviet diplomatic ambitions clearly discouraged any inclination to question that assumption.

Thus by the end of the war the most influential and widely accepted attitude toward the bomb was a logical extension of how the weapon was seen and valued earlier—as a potential instrument of diplomacy. Caught between the remnants of war and the uncertainties of peace, policymakers were trapped by the logic of their own unquestioned assumptions. By the summer of 1945 not only the conclusion of the war but the organization of an acceptable peace seemed to depend upon the success of the atomic attacks against Japan. When news of the successful atomic test of July 16 reached the President at the Potsdam Conference, he was visibly elated. Stimson noted that Truman "was tremendously pepped up by it and spoke to me of it again and again when I saw him. He said it gave him an entirely new feeling of confidence." The day after receiving the complete report of the test Truman altered his negotiating style. According to Churchill the President "got to the meeting after having read this report [and] he was a changed man. He told the Russians just where they got on and off and generally bossed the whole meeting." After the plenary session on July 24 Truman "casually mentioned to Stalin" that the United States had "a new weapon of unusual destructive force." In less than three weeks the new weapon's destructive potential was demonstrated to the world. Upon learning of the raid against Hiroshima Truman exclaimed: "This is the greatest thing in history."

As Stimson had expected, as a colossal reality the bomb was very different. But had American diplomacy been altered by it? Those who conducted diplomacy became more confident, more certain that through the accomplishments of American science, technology, and industry the "new world" could be made into one better than the old. But just how the atomic bomb would be used to help accomplish this ideal remained unclear. Three months and one day after Hiroshima was bombed Bush wrote that the whole matter of international relations on atomic energy "is in a thoroughly chaotic condition." The wartime relationship between atomic energy policy and diplomacy had been based upon the simple assumption that the Soviet government would surrender important geographical, political, and ideological objectives in exchange for the neutralization of the new weapon. As a result of policies based on this assumption American diplomacy and prestige suffered grievously: an opportunity to gauge the Soviet Union's response during the war to the international control of atomic energy was missed, and an atomic energy policy for dealing with the Soviet government after the war was ignored. Instead of promoting American postwar aims, wartime atomic energy policies made them more difficult to achieve. As a group of scientists at the University of Chicago's atomic energy laboratory presciently warned the government in June 1945: "It may be difficult to persuade the world that a nation which was capable of secretly preparing and suddenly releasing a weapon as indiscriminate as the [German] rocket bomb and a million times more destructive, is to be trusted in its proclaimed desire of having such weapons abolished by international agreement." This reasoning, however, flowed from alternative assumptions formulated during the closing months of the war by scientists far removed from the wartime policymaking process. Hiroshima and Nagasaki, the culmination of that process, became the symbols of a new American barbarism, reinforcing charges, with dramatic circumstantial evidence, that the policies of the United States contributed to the origins of the Cold War.

POSTSCRIPT

Was Stalin Responsible for the Cold War?

Time, place, perspective—all play a role in historical assessment, and any analysis of responsibility for the cold war supports that statement. The cold war's first chroniclers were participants in postwar global politics, and their views were shaped by their personal experiences. Time provided distance, and the events of the coming decades nurtured a movement toward radical politics, which some have referred to as the "New Left." This paved the way for revisionist interpretations of the cold war's origins.

The use of the atomic bombs against Japan in 1945 created a cloud over cold war historiography. Some historians believe that this use was advocated not only to quickly end the war against Japan, but also to teach the Soviet Union a lesson in United States power politics. What course might the post–World War II era have followed if the West had sought different means to end the war? Many believe that the use of atomic weapons and the start of the cold war are inextricably connected.

Useful sources on cold war historiography should begin with the authors of the two selections. Gaddis's career as a cold war scholar can be traced from his *The United States and the Origins of the War, 1941–1947* (Columbia University Press, 1972) to *We Now Know: Rethinking Cold War History* (Routledge, 1997). Sherwin has extended the scholarship of his original *American Historical Review* article, "The Atomic Bomb and the Origins of the Cold War: U.S. Atomic Energy Policy and Diplomacy 1941–1945" (October 1973) in *A World Destroyed: The Atomic Bomb and the Grand Alliance* (Alfred A. Knopf, 1975).

Other significant works written in the traditionalist vein include Louis Halle, *The Cold War as History* (Harper & Row, 1967); Herbert Feis, *From Trust to Terror: The Onset of the Cold War, 1945–1950* (W. W. Norton, 1970); and Norman Graebner, *Cold War Diplomacy: American Foreign Policy 1945–1960* (Princeton University Press, 1962). Important revisionist works on the origins of the cold war include two books by Gar Alperovitz, *Atomic Diplomacy: Hiroshima and Potsdam* (Penguin Books, 1985) and *The Decision to Use the Bomb and the Architecture of an American Myth* (Alfred A. Knopf, 1995). Also included is Lloyd Gardner, *Architects of Illusion: Men and Ideas in American Foreign Policy, 1941–1949* (University of Chicago Press, 1970).

The many works of George F. Kennan, considered to be containment's prime mover, provide invaluable assistance to the study of this issue, as do the works of Russian diplomats Vyacheslav Molotov and Andrei Gromyko, both of whom were "present at the creation" of the cold war. Two recent cold war anthologies are David Reynolds, ed., *The Origins of the Cold War in Europe: International Perspectives* (Yale University Press, 1994) and Allan Hunter, ed., *Rethinking the Cold War* (Temple University Press, 1998).

Confucian Tradition(s)

Confucian Tradition(s) is a Web site that provides a primer on things Confucian; this site is good for both student and teacher, veteran and novice.

`http://www.clas.ufl.edu/users/gthursby/rel/kongfuzi.htm`

Islam, the Modern World, and the West

Islam, the Modern World, and the West is a Web site divided into four major sections: General Considerations; Islam in the United States; Islam, the Muslim World, and Contemporary Issues; and Islam Today in the Various Regions of the Muslim World.

`http://www.arches.uga.edu/~godlas/islamwest.html`

Naija Mall

Naija Mall is a comprehensive Web site developed by an international relations professor. This site contains much up-to-date information on Africa.

`http://www.naijamall.com/index.html`

The Center for Peace Studies in the Balkans

The Center for Peace Studies in the Balkans Web site provides a variety of sources of information on that part of Europe formerly called its "powder keg." This site consists of headlines that introduce relevant stories, studies, opinions and commentary, archives, a search engine, and links.

`http://balkanpeace.org/index.shtml`

The Euro—Europe's Single Common Currency

The Euro—Europe's Single Common Currency is a Web site that provides three full pages of links; many of them are business oriented, but some provide useful information for both student and teacher.

`http://www.ex.ac.uk/~RDavies/arian/euro.html`

Attack on America: Osama bin Laden, al-Qa'ida, and Terrorism

Attack on America: Osama bin Laden, al-Qa'ida, and Terrorism is a university-based Web site that provides a variety of links to the following subjects: Osama bin Laden and al-Qa'ida, the Taliban and Afganistan, terrorism research sources and government publications, and additional background on terrorism and the September 11, 2001, attacks.

`http://www.lib.ecu.edu/govdoc/terrorism.html`

PART 3

The Contemporary World

A s the world begins a new millennium, it is difficult to predict what the new century will bring. If some of the problems facing our world today continue to grow in seriousness, it is likely that the beginning of the millennium will not be a peaceful one, as the September 11, 2001, terrorist attacks on the United States seem to indicate.

- Are Chinese Confucianism and Western Capitalism Compatible?

- Does Islamic Revivalism Challenge a Stable World Order?

- Are Africa's Leaders Responsible for the Continent's Current Problems?

- Were Ethnic Leaders Responsible for the Death of Yugoslavia?

- Will the European Economic and Monetary Union Increase the Potential for Transatlantic Conflict?

- Do the Roots of Modern Terrorism Lie in Political Powerlessness, Economic Hopelessness, and Social Alienation?

ISSUE 13

Are Chinese Confucianism and Western Capitalism Compatible?

YES: A. T. Nuyen, from "Chinese Philosophy and Western Capitalism," *Asian Philosophy* (March 1999)

NO: Jack Scarborough, from "Comparing Chinese and Western Cultural Roots: Why 'East Is East and. . .'," *Business Horizons* (November 1998)

ISSUE SUMMARY

YES: Philosophy professor A. T. Nuyen maintains that the basic tenets of classical capitalism are perfectly compatible with the key elements of Chinese philosophy.

NO: Management professor Jack Scarborough contrasts the Western heritage of democracy, rationality, and individualism with Confucian values of harmony, filial loyalty, and legalism. Based on his comparison, Scarborough finds that Chinese Confucianism is incompatible with Western capitalism.

Why do Western nations play such a dominant role in the world economy? Are scientific materialism and aggressive individualism responsible for the West's economic prosperity? And, does the East need to abandon the conservative values of Confucianism and Taoism if it wishes to compete economically in the twenty-first century? There is widespread agreement that capitalism has been a successful economic ideology. What the authors of the following selections disagree about is whether classical capitalism, as articulated more than two hundred years ago, or a more modern form of capitalism should receive the credit. The resolution of this question will help us to understand whether or not Confucianism and capitalism are compatible.

When Scottish economist Adam Smith published *An Inquiry Into the Nature and Causes of the Wealth of Nations* in 1776, the same year as the Declaration of Independence, he inspired the Western economic system that came to be known as capitalism. Smith was profoundly influenced by the ideas of the French physiocrats. As the name suggests, these thinkers supported physiocracy

—"the rule of nature"—letting natural laws prevail in human society. Classical capitalism urges a hands-off approach, adopting the French term *laissez-faire* (to leave alone) as the best method of creating economic prosperity. Left unmolested, economic forces will be self-regulating, guided by what Smith called "the invisible hand" of the marketplace. Too much of a product drives prices down, discouraging further production; scarcity increases prices, stimulating production. Supply and demand naturally regulate the economy if government stays out of the process.

Smith encountered the ideas of François Quesnay on a trip to Europe around 1760. Quesnay was a brilliant French physician who originated the ideas of physiocracy after a long and thoughtful investigation into the functioning of the economic system. Smith, who had previously written on morals, turned his attention to what causes "the wealth of nations." Smith would have dedicated his masterpiece to Quesnay had Quesnay not died. Some scholars believe that Quesnay may have been inspired by the Chinese philosophy of wu-wei (literally translated as "no action"), which encourages individuals to allow the Tao to regulate everything with perfect efficiency, benefiting all.

Without pressing this point, A. T. Nuyen traces Quesnay's admiration of Confucius as a model human being and presents Quesnay's view that the Chinese system of government was an appropriate model for European nations to emulate. The emperor might have to enact "despotic laws" aimed at ensuring the smooth functioning of the natural laws regulating the economy. However, these laws would function simply to remove impediments and to allow natural forces to operate freely. Nuyen cites antitrust laws in the United States as a modern application of "legal despotism" in the service of natural laws. For Nuyen, classical capitalism arose from the same virtues that inspired the ancient Chinese philosophical systems of Confucianism and Taoism.

Jack Scarborough, by contrast, uses a couplet from a Rudyard Kipling poem about India and the West—"East is east and west is west and never the twain shall meet"—to explain the "enormous gulf" that he sees as separating Asia from Western capitalist economies. While the East, especially "once-great China," was reduced through imperial repression and Confucian discipline to "unrelenting poverty and hardship," the West went on to nearly conquer the world—first politically and later economically. Scarborough's selection is aimed at communicating the "cultural differences" that must be taken into account if one hopes to do business in China.

Scarborough has in mind present-day capitalism, which presumes an aggressive individualism that would have been equally foreign to both Confucius and Smith. He attributes China's economic weakness in the modern world to centuries of self-imposed isolation as well as to a cultural appreciation of harmony, communal loyalty, and an acknowledgement that nature acts with a superior wisdom.

Nuyen, having demonstrated the compatibility between Chinese philosophy and classical capitalism, counters that the economic gap between the West and Asia cannot be attributed to the "cultural factor." Instead, Nuyen suggests that colonialism and post-colonial ideologies are more likely factors.

A. T. Nuyen

Chinese Philosophy and Western Capitalism

As we stand now at the end of the 20th century, many nations in the East are well on their way along the path of economic growth and development. To be sure, the East, with the exception of Japan, still has a great deal of catching up to do before it can become the equal of the West in terms of economic prosperity. Also, progress has been uneven. On this score, economic commentators seem to agree that the nations that have done well are those that have adopted the capitalist model that has served the West well over the last hundred years. For instance, W. J. F. Jenner points out that, apart from Japan, "all the East Asian countries that have prospered in recent decades were colonies of either Britain or of Japan for generations before the Second World War", and as such inherited the capitalist structure of the West. Japan itself, Jenner contends, could not have prospered without "external conditions needed for rapid industrial growth", such as Western technology, capital and export markets.

Despite the fact that one can point to many obvious exceptions to Jenner's observations, there is fairly widespread support for his view. Thus, it is often enough said that what is holding back economic progress in the East is the "cultural" factor. Commentators frequently suggest that peoples of the East, particularly the ethnic Chinese, subscribe to values which are not conducive to economic progress, values that place the family and the community above individual interests, and spirituality above material well-being. By contrast, the West is said to subscribe to the kind of individualism and materialism that give its peoples a competitive edge. To do well in the economic arena, the suggestion goes, the East needs to embrace the Western capitalist model wholeheartedly by making fundamental changes in their cultural and philosophical outlook. If Asian, particularly Chinese, values had anything to do with economic success, they would have to be thoroughly cleansed through Western values and beliefs. Pace those commentators who credit the success in many Asian countries to Confucianism, Jenner insists that for Confucianism, or any other Chinese philosophical system, to work, "it needs dynamic, alien, Western institutions and forms of economic organization". Thus, in Jenner's view, only when "alien, Western factors came into play were certain elements within

From A. T. Nuyen, "Chinese Philosophy and Western Capitalism," *Asian Philosophy*, vol. 9, no. 1 (March 1999). Copyright © 1999 by *Asian Philosophy*. Reprinted by permission of Taylor & Francis Ltd., http://www.tandf.co.uk/journals, and the author. Notes omitted.

some inherited East Asian value systems able to bring about successful capitalist development". By themselves, such value systems are an obstacle to growth.

Behind views such as Jenner's is the supposition that capitalism is wholly a product of the West, that it is inherently an alien system from the point of view of the East, that it does not sit well with the traditions of the East and that the capitalist model cannot be successfully embraced without some violence being done to those traditions. The aim of this [selection] is to challenge such a notion. My thesis is that it is classical capitalism that first set the West on its course towards economic prosperity, and that the fundamental tenets of classical capitalism are perfectly compatible with the key elements of Chinese philosophy. Indeed, as we shall see, many historians of ideas have traced the origins of classical capitalism all the way back to Chinese thought. Setting aside whether anything can be made of the historical link, I shall attempt to show how classical capitalism could have developed from the fundamentals of Chinese philosophy. If I am right, the economic gap between the West and Asia has to be accounted for in terms other than the "cultural" factors, such as, perhaps, colonialism and post-colonialist ideologies.

By classical capitalism I mean an economic system based on unfettered competition, the unrestricted availability of productive technologies, the free movement of labour and other factors of production, and the smooth flow of information within both the producer and consumer groups. It is a system based on what economists call "perfect competition". Such a system would result in commodities being produced at the lowest possible costs and made available to consumers at the lowest possible prices. Under ideal conditions, the system would result in what economists call "Pareto efficiency", a state of affairs in which it is not possible to make someone better off, in the economic sense, without making someone else worse off. It is important to note that anti-competitive behaviour is an obstacle in the attainment of the economic benefits of the system. The most common form of anti-competitive behaviour is monopoly. This could result from the monopolisation of factors of production, or productive technologies, or the distribution of commodities. It is for this reason that anti-competitive behaviour has been outlawed in many capitalist nations. The USA, for instance, enforces its anti-trust law fairly vigorously, albeit with varying degrees of success. The other factor that tends to restrict competition is government intervention through burdensome rules and regulations, and the involvement of the state in the economy itself through state-owned companies. This is why capitalist nations such as the USA tend to make laws aimed at giving all economic agents a free reign and to minimize public ownership (in a process known as "privatisation"). The term "free enterprise", or the French equivalent, namely, laissez-faire, can be used as a name for the capitalist system I have described, provided that by "free" we mean free from anti-competitive forces, not free to engage in restrictive practices, and certainly not free to indulge in any kind of behaviour whatsoever in the pursuit of profit.

Classical capitalism as I have described it has evolved from the works of classical thinkers such as Francois Quesnay and the physiocrats, Bernard Mandeville and Adam Smith. It was Quesnay and his fellow physiocrats who persuaded the French government to overturn the interventionist policy of the mercantalists and to free up the market. It is true that Quesnay supported a governmental system known as "legal despotism", interpreted by some commentators as a model for absolute monarchy and thus might be taken as being against the spirit of free enterprise. However, Quesnay's intention in advocating legal despotism really was to set up the legal framework for free enterprise. The "despotic" laws were meant to ensure the smooth functioning of economic laws which were for the physiocrats, as we shall see later, identical with natural laws. The laws that Quesnay advocated have to be compared with the laws aimed at promoting free enterprise in modern capitalist nations, such as antitrust laws in the USA. It is for this reason that Quesnay is regarded by many commentators as undoubtedly the founder of modern capitalism. For instance, according to Weulerrse, Quesnay's doctrine expresses "the scientific principles of capitalism, pure and simple, of complete capitalism"; it represents "the triumph of the spirit of capitalism". At any rate, Quesnay's advocacy for free enterprise found a powerful support in Adam Smith in whose hands his economic/natural laws became the laws of the "invisible hand". I take for granted that Smith's doctrine of the wealth of nations is directly responsible for the wealth of modern capitalist nations. Given the theoretical connection between Smith and Quesnay, I shall restrict myself to Quesnay.

The brief excursion into economic history above may serve to confirm the impression that the intellectual roots of modern capitalism lie buried wholly in Western soil and that the Eat needs to make drastic internal changes if it is to adapt the alien capitalist model successfully. However, many historians have claimed that, at the philosophical level, Quesnay's ideas came directly from the East, from Chinese philosophy to be more precise. It is not altogether clear whether and to what extent Quesnay was influenced by Chinese thoughts, or whether he borrowed anything from the East. However, it is worth pursuing the historical link before turning to the more straightforward comparative reading of Quesnay and Chinese philosophers. What we do know is that Quesnay himself acknowledged his debt to Chinese philosophy, especially to Confucianism. His book, *Le Despotism de la Chine,* is not a critique of the Chinese system of government; rather, it is a description of a system on which he based his concept of legal despotism, mentioned [earlier]. According to J. J. Clarke, Quesnay

> regarded China as an ideal society that provided a model for Europe to follow, and in discussing Chinese despotism he wrote that 'I have concluded from the reports about China that the Chinese constitution is founded upon wise and irrevocable laws which the Emperor enforces and which he carefully observes himself'.

While the Chinese system of government was for Quesnay a model that Europe should follow, Confucius himself was for him a model of the perfect person. According to one historian, Quesnay modelled himself on Confucius, so much so that his disciples called him "The Confucius of Europe": "His manuscript for *Le Despotism de la Chine* contains a few pages on the life of Confucius which were deleted from the published version, but which provide a disarmingly close approximation to an autobiographical assessment and statement of personal purpose". In the manuscript, Quesnay expressed his admiration for Confucius's "grave, modest and serious air", his "most profound knowledge" and his "intent of spreading his doctrine and working for the reformation of men". Above all, Quesnay admired Confucius for the fact that by "his gravity, his modesty, his sweetness and his frugality, by his scorn of terrestrial pleasures, and by a continual vigilance on his own conduct, he was himself an example of the precepts he advanced in his writings and his discourses..."

Given what we know about Quesnay's respect and admiration for Confucius as a person, it is not surprising that historians go on to speculate that Quesnay freely made use of Confucius's philosophy and derived from it many useful ideas. What is evident is that he interpreted that philosophy as advocating the observance of the laws of nature and the adoption of nature's guiding principle, having in mind no doubt the notion of the tao. As Quesnay saw it, nature's guiding principle, in the philosophy of Confucius, is a force that commands "the respect, the fear [and] the recognition" in all of us, a force that "knows all, ... even the most secret recesses of the heart...". Furthermore, this force of nature, if allowed to operate unhindered, will result in the best for all, including human beings. From this it is but a small step to the conclusion that Quesnay either borrowed or was influenced by this view of Chinese philosophy, given his own doctrine that in economic affairs, it is best to follow the laws of nature, a doctrine for which Pierre-Samuel du Pont de Nemours aptly coined the term "physiocracy" in 1767, meaning literally "the rule of nature". It is certainly true that Quesnay thought that the laws of nature should not be interfered with, that nature should be left alone to operate, that in the economic sphere, we should let nature be, laissez-faire. Interestingly, one historian has speculated that the term "laissez-faire" is the French translation of the Chinese wu-wei: "Both lawmaker and law had to recognize the principle of... natural order, and in doing so conform to the Chinese ideal of wu-wei, which has ever inspired their theories of government".

It may be said that the historical evidence above is consistent with the thesis that Quesnay was influenced by Chinese philosophy as it is with a quite different thesis, namely, that Quesnay merely saw a parallel between his own doctrine and what he took to be the philosophy of Confucius. It is not my intention in this [selection] to settle this issue. My interest is confined to the question of whether capitalism is really so alien to the East that the East could not assimilate it without making some profound changes in its fundamental beliefs. However we interpret the historical evidence connecting physiocracy with Confucianism, or Quesnay with Confucius, the fact remains that the historical discussion above opens up the possibility for arguing that Chinese philosophy, and in particular Confucianism, provides a hospitable background for, rather than thwarting, the development of the kind of capitalism that has brought economic prosperity to the West. If the argument is successful then, as pointed out above, we have to look elsewhere for an explanation as to why such development failed to take place early enough in the East, thus resulting in the current economic gap between the East and the West. With this in mind, we can now take a closer look at Quesnay's doctrine of free enterprise, or the physiocrats' idea of laissez-faire, in order to see whether it could have grown out of Chinese philosophy.

From Quesnay's writings, it is clear that he saw the world as a self-regulating machine governed by a set of immutable laws ordained by God, its Creator. He also saw that the economy and its economic agents were part of that world and subject to the same laws. The economic part of the world in turn could be seen as a whole consisting of interdependent parts, such as production, consumption, exchange, etc. That part of the world, the economy, would function well if its component parts were to function in harmony with each other. As is well-known, Quesnay constructed the Tableau economique to model the interdependencies in the economy, thus allowing a greater understanding, better prediction and more effective regulation of economic activities. The key to it all is the harmony of the various component parts comprising the whole, a harmony that depends on the balancing of the oppositional forces exercised by the component parts. As Quesnay puts it in the essay "Hommes", in the case of the state, good government depends on "the balance of the bodies of the state, each restrained in turn by the other". What is true about the state is also true about the economy, indeed true generally. Thus, the general aim in human affairs is to achieve and maintain the "balance of bodies" comprising the whole. Since the whole is a self-regulating mechanism governed by natural laws, this is the same as saying that we should aim at restoring the natural order. Indeed, being a self-regulating mechanism, the economy possesses self-adjusting forces that tend to return it to the natural order and so in the usual course of events, the best policy turns out to be one of letting such forces operate unhindered, of letting nature be, of laissez-faire. Intervention is necessary only to restore the natural order.

Breaking down the component parts of the economy, we get to the ultimate economic unit, the individual person. The person too is a natural entity subject to natural laws. Quesnay knew this only too well, being a medical practitioner, a renown surgeon, for most of his life. Since the aim of the economy is, as Quesnay put it, the "perpetual reproduction of those goods necessary for the subsistence, conservation and convenience of men", it is important to understand the nature of "men". Influenced by the rationalist philosophy of Descartes, Quesnay saw the individual person as a rational creature who, naturally endowed with the capacity to reason, knew what he or she wanted and knew the best way to obtain it. It follows that the best economic policy is to allow the individual the freedom to pursue his or her own interests. However, it would be wrong to say that Quesnay advocated economic individualism. For Quesnay, the pursuit of self interest was never an end in itself; it was rather the means towards the goal of social harmony, and ultimately the harmony of the whole of nature. It is natural to let people engage in activities aimed at the satisfaction of natural needs and wants. To let people be, laissez-faire, is to follow the rule of nature, to be physiocratic. Self-interested economic activity should be permitted and assisted to take place unhindered, enterprise at the individual level should be free, only because it would lead to a good outcome at the social level, and a good society in turn would result in the well-being of the world. As is well-known, this doctrine is foreshadowed by Mandeville's Fable of the Bees and later received theoretical backing in Adam Smith, who turned it into the doctrine of the "invisible hand".

I have outlined the fundamental tenets of classical capitalism, or laissez-faire capitalism, as formulated by its founder, Francois Quesnay. By the time of Adam Smith, the economy of Western Europe, particularly that of Great Britain, had begun to reorganize itself along the lines of free enterprise, aided along in the process by Enlightenment ideas that emphasise personal freedom. In the case of France, the transition was facilitated by the presence of physiocrats in the government itself. Indeed, a well-known promoter of physiocracy, Anne Robert Turgot, became a finance minister of Louis XVI. The foundation stone was set for the economic prosperity of Western Europe. Why similar developments did not take place in Asia is a matter I happily leave to the historians. My purpose here is to show that it is not because the laissez-faire doctrine is philosophically alien to the East. Indeed, as pointed out [earlier], some historians even claim that Western thinkers responsible for the laissez-faire doctrine were influenced by Chinese philosophy—Turgot himself was described by Martin Bernal as a "promoter of Chinese economic ideas". Whatever can be made of this historical claim, we can certainly show that the fundamental tenets of classical capitalism could have grown out of Chinese philosophy, out of Confucianism in particular. I turn now to this task.

That the world is governed by a universal and natural force is a fundamental belief in Chinese philosophy. It is a part of most Chinese philosophical systems. This force is the tao. While Taoism and Confucianism draw different implications from the belief in the tao, both subscribe to the view that the tao is a creative force causally responsible for the existence of the world. The process of creation is described in the well-known chapter 42 of the Tao Te Ching. The tao is not only a creative force; it is also a regulative principle that maintains its own creation. Indeed, the tao permeates all aspects of the world and so can properly be equated with nature itself. Thus, the tao is God, nature and natural laws rolled into one. Where the laws of the tao operate unhindered, there is established the natural order and there is harmony. Where there are acts in defiance of the laws of the tao, the natural order is upset and there is chaos. Thus, for there to be harmony, all actions must comply with the laws of the tao, or with the rule of nature. To act in accordance with the tao is to let nature rule, to subscribe to physiocracy in the literal sense. Clearly then, the Chinese cosmology translates easily into the physiocratic belief in a natural order which regulates all aspects of life, including all human experiences.

As we saw [earlier], the French physiocrats considered the society and all the social units within it down to the individual persons as parts of the natural order subject to the same rule of nature. However, unlike other animals, humans have the capacity to reason and so can choose to act in ways that are contrary to the rule of nature. This gives rise to the physiocratic belief that the harmony of the world rests squarely on the individual person, that to establish the order of nature we have to start with the individual person. This idea could have grown out of Chinese philosophy. In both Taoism and Confucianism, the natural law, or the law of the tao, should be observed by all component parts of the natural whole, by all societies, groups of individuals, families and finally the individual people themselves. Given that the individual person has the power of choice, on his or her shoulders alone rests the responsibility to realise the law of the tao. Thus, as recorded in the Analects, Confucius said that "It is man that can make the Way [Tao] great, and not the Way that can make man great". This is echoed in the last few lines of chapter 25 of the Tao Te Ching: "Man models himself on earth, Earth on heaven, Heaven on the way, And the way on that which is naturally so". Clearly then, the focus of Chinese philosophy is on the individual, no less than is the case in physiocracy or in the Western tradition generally. If we understand "individualism" in this sense, there is no reason to think that Quesnay's "economic individualism" is alien to the Chinese tradition.

If it rests on the individual to "make the Way great" then, it follows, the individual should be left alone, if not encouraged, to do so. To interfere with the individual in his or her natural pursuits, particularly in the pursuits to secure the goods "necessary for their subsistence, conservation and convenience" (to borrow Quesnay's words), is to interfere with the way of nature itself. Thus, not only that the individual should let nature be if he or she is to follow the tao, or to "model himself on the earth", the government too should follow the tao by letting the individuals be. To let be is to take no action, or rather to do by not doing, wu-wei. This policy can be found advocated in many diverse philosophical systems. It is, as we would expect, most prominent in Taoism. Thus,

> The way never acts yet nothing is left undone. Should lords and princes be able to hold fast to it, The myriad creatures will be transformed of their own accord.

> — (Tao Te Ching, chapter 37)

Wu-wei is the way of the tao. For lords and princes to follow the way of the tao is for them to take no action, to let the people be. Lords and princes can "win the empire by not being meddlesome", and when they are "not meddlesome . . . the people prosper of themselves" (Tao Te Ching, chapter 57). This policy is endorsed by Confucius, who praised Shun for governing his empire well by taking "no [unnatural] action". Even the Legalists, who were well-known for their advocacy of a strong government, subscribed to the policy of wu-wei. As Wing-Tsit Chan puts it, the "Taoist ideal of taking no action (wu-wei) had a strong appeal to the Legalists because if laws worked effectively at all times, there would be no need for any actual government". Given the widespread philosophical support for the idea that "people prosper of themselves" if the government lets them be, it is surely perverse to suggest that any economic doctrine that advocates letting people be to pursue their economic interests, or laissez-faire, is alien to the East.

It may be said that the Chinese doctrine of wu-wei encourages passivity which is contrary to the qualities of drive and determination required for economic success. However, it should be noted that translating "wu-wei" as "taking no action" or "doing nothing" is highly misleading. Even within Taoism, wu-wei does not mean total passivity. Taking no action is not an end in itself but rather a means to achieving something positive. Thus, chapter 10 of the Tao Te

Ching speaks of not "resorting to action" in order to "govern the state", and chapter 51 speaks of taking no action to "give(s) [the myriad creatures] life", to "benefit(s) them". That positive things result from the non-action of the tao is due to its te, its "mysterious virtue", or "its "Dark Potency" as A. C. Graham has put it. It is true, though, that the Taoists, particularly Chuang Tzu, believe in the potency of the tao, and believe that nature will have its own way in the end and does not need much from humans to assert its own order. The Confucianists, by contrast, attribute to humans a greater capacity for departing from the order of nature. For them, wu-wei amounts to taking action to emulate the no-action way of nature itself. For this reason, some commentators describe the Confucian policy as wei-wu-wei, active inaction, rather than simply wu-wei. What this means is that the individual should be vigilant to correct his or her behaviour, and the government should take action to help the individual "make the way great". Clearly then, wu-wei does not translate into a lack of drive and determination. On the contrary, it entails the utmost determination to embrace the tao, and requires the constant drive to improve oneself by following the way of nature. The same thing applies to the state. Wu-wei does not mean inaction on the part of the government. Since humans have the capacity to act contrary to nature, to let nature be, wu-wei, is to intervene to keep recalcitrant humans in line. If restrictive behaviour in economic affairs is contrary to the way of nature then wu-wei calls for a positive action against it. Quesnay's advocacy for "despotic laws" to preserve and restore the natural order could have grown out of the Chinese doctrine of wu-wei. As we saw earlier, some historians are convinced that it did. Whether laissez-faire was in fact the physiocrats' translation of wu-wei, it could easily have been.

It may be said further that many different economic systems could have grown out of the Chinese metaphysics of the tao. What remains to be shown is how such metaphysics could have engendered classical capitalism described earlier. The key feature of classical capitalism is competition. However, this is not to be taken as a destructive relationship in which each economic agent is out to dominate others, to drive them out of business. Rather, it is a mutually dependent relationship in which each economic unit acts to check and to balance the actions of all other units. For instance, prices are kept at the lowest possible level because the action of raising the price by any one producer will be neutralised by the actions of other producers who will take the advantage of selling more of their own products by undercutting their rivals. Classical capitalism is a system of checks and balances, resulting in a state of equilibrium among the opposing forces. This is what Quesnay had in mind when he spoke of the "balance of the bodies". Such balance exists in nature. This is why, for Quesnay, there should be the same natural checks and balances in the economy. To let it be, laissez-faire, is to let the natural checks and balances operate to produce harmony, or equilibrium. Could this doctrine have grown out of Chinese philosophy? The answer is, once again, yes. It could have grown out of many Chinese philosophical systems, but more specifically, out of the Confucian doctrine of chung yung.

As Chung-ying Cheng has pointed out, the idea of harmony is embraced by all the major schools of Chinese philosophy. This idea is encapsulated in the

I Ching diagram of yin and yang forming a harmonious unity. The harmony in any unity rests on the balance of the forces exercised by the component parts, or the "bodies" of the whole. There is harmony if the force of one "body" is balanced by that of another. There is harmony in nature because

> ... Something and Nothing produce each other; The difficult and the easy complement each other; The long and the short off-set each other;
>
> — (Tao Te Ching, chapter 2)

The idea of harmony as the balance of oppositional forces is also endorsed in the book of Chung yung. For instance, taking a person's psychology as a unified whole, Chung yung declares that when the "passions awaken and each and all attain due measure and degree, that is harmony". There is harmony in nature because "the seasons succeed each other and the sun and the moon appear with the alternations of night and day". The human society is capable of attaining harmony insofar as its laws "form the same system" with the laws of nature. Harmony in society will be attained if laws are enacted to preserve the balance of opposing forces. This means in turn to keep to the middle path, the mean, between the extremes. Mapping all this onto the economy, we can draw the conclusion that economic harmony will be attained if the opposing forces in the economy are kept in a balance, if no one economic unit is allowed to dominate the others. Thus, only a competitive economic system is consistent with the Chinese idea of harmony. A system consisting of monopolies, state or private, lacks the checks and balances necessary for harmony. Such a system may be stable in the sense of producing a technical equilibrium with predictable and non-fluctuating outputs and prices, but it is not harmonious and is contrary to the order of nature, contrary to the tao. The Chinese notion of harmony entails that the state should make laws to ensure the balance of economic forces, laws that prevent anti-competitive behaviour, laws that strengthen the mutual dependencies of all economic units on each other. Such laws would be continuous with the laws of nature, the laws by which "the seasons succeed each other and the sun and the moon appear with the alternations of day and night".

I have argued that laissez-faire or free-enterprise capitalism is not alien to the Chinese way of thinking insofar as that way is informed by philosophical beliefs in the way of nature. What is certainly alien is an economic system that is driven by greed, ruthless individualism and the desire for absolute power. What is alien is a system of cut-throat competition without checks and balances, a system that allows extremes to develop rather than stays in the middle path, a system that encourages monstrous monopolies having the power to take over the laws of the market, to upset the order of nature. To be sure, the popular image of capitalism is closer to cut-throat competition than to free-enterprise in the classical sense. However, it is doubtful that the former has had anything to do with the economic prosperity of the West. If this is alien to the East then it is a reason to celebrate, not a cause of despair. Indeed, future historians could well attribute the economic crisis occurring in Asia at the end of the 20th century to Asia's attempt to embrace the greed-is-good mentality of cut-throat competition. I have argued that Asia need not sacrifice its philosophical soul at the altar of economic progress. On the contrary, if I am right in my reading of Chinese philosophy and if classical thinkers such as Quesnay and Smith are right about the causes of the wealth of nations, now that Asia has regained its power to determine its own destiny, economic prosperity depends on Asia's returning to its philosophical roots, maintaining the path of chung yung and embracing the way of the tao.

Jack Scarborough

 **NO**

Comparing Chinese and Western Cultural Roots: Why "East Is East and. . ."

"Oh, East is East, and West is West, and never the twain shall meet."

— Rudyard Kipling, The Ballad of East and West (1889)

Well, we meet now. As China accelerates into its inevitable place among the world's most important states and markets, the world is paying close attention. And as Westerners scrutinize China's pronouncements and actions, they become more aware of the great differences in how we think, what we believe, and how we behave. Although Kipling's familiar words applied to India, the thought expressed applies at least as well to China. Some might expect to see some convergence as trade, travel, and education bring us closer. But an enormous gulf remains because these differences have very deep and substantial roots that have produced highly divergent value systems.

The attitudes and behavior of a cohesive or otherwise unified group of people are shaped by the prevailing value system that defines for them what is good and bad, acceptable and unacceptable, desirable and undesirable, important and unimportant. We call this collectively shared value system that establishes behavioral norms a "culture": an artifact of a common experience and history, the dominant religion, political, social, and economic conditions, geographic, climatic, and topographic factors, and resource endowments. The ability to resist the tendency to judge another culture according to one's own values—the trap of ethnocentrism—can be strengthened by an understanding of how those differences came to be.

A brief review of the more salient differences between China and the West, as seen through Western eyes, is a good place to begin. Students of this topic, particularly those interested in Chinese ways of business and management practices, are familiar with such notions as "face," guanxi, and guo qing. "Face" generally is a matter of maintaining one's public dignity and standing. For the Chinese, there are two components of face: lien and mianzi. The former concerns one's reputation for integrity and morality; the latter is prestige attached to professional reputation, knowledge, wealth, and success.

A large component of lien is people's ability to live up to their obligations within the framework of Confucian hierarchy, social harmony, and strict behavioral ritual (li). The surest way to lose face is to act in a way that causes another to lose it. To avoid such uncivilized, disharmonious behavior, the Chinese practice a form of indirect speech that, to Westerners, seems overly modest and even self-effacing. The practice is sometimes so extreme as to appear disingenuous or even deliberately deceitful, as in overly optimistic promises and commitments. Another by-product of face-saving (or harmony-preserving) behavior is shaming, the ploy of getting one's way in negotiation by appealing to one's counterpart's obligation to conform to li. A common example is related to the Confucian ideal of the doting, overly solicitous parent and the resulting asymmetrical relationship of obligation whereby the parent expects much less from the child than the parent gives. A Chinese negotiator might attempt to portray a counterpart representing a large, accomplished company or developed country in the role of parent. Thus, an ostensibly weaker or technologically less advanced Chinese firm or governmental body assumes the role of the needy child to extract asymmetrical concessions.

Guanxi is the now well-known custom of relying on a network of fully committed personal relationships when conducting business or other affairs. A by-product is the need for go-betweens to establish a new business relationship. Another is that, unlike in Japan, personal loyalties and commitments take precedence over all others except family—including company ties. These asymmetrical relationships also favor the weaker party and must be cultivated assiduously. The obligations embodied in Confucian values and guanxi take the place of laws and contracts relied upon by Westerners to regulate business relationships.

Guo qing is a 2,000-year-old term meaning that China is special and the way things are done there are unique and, presumably, superior. This implies that outsiders (long considered barbarians) must learn these ways and adapt if they are to become functional in China. Such an attitude is to be expected from a people who constitute the world's oldest culture, the Middle Kingdom, and who lived for thousands of years largely in self-imposed isolation but who, nevertheless, accomplished much artistically, scientifically, and socially. Fan Xing sums up the observations and views of many with [a] comparison of common traits [in Table 1].

Hence, the Chinese lean toward a more holistic, systemic, nonlinear, fatalistic world view. Their attitude toward time is more relaxed; they tend to be humble and modest; and their culture is one of high-context communication and collectivism. . . .

Chinese and Western Cultural Roots Compared

. . . Confucian disdain for science and commerce has been an enormous constraint on economic development. Nevertheless, according to Paul Kennedy's 1987 *The Rise and Fall of the Great Powers,* in the Middle Ages the Chinese invented paper, printing by movable type, gunpowder, a mechanical clock, and the magnetic compass. And they were producing more iron than Great Britain

Table 1

Chinese	American
Intuitive	Rational
Aesthetic	Scientific
Introverted	Extroverted
Self-restrained	Aggressive
Dependent	Independent
Procrastinating	Active
Implicit	Explicit
Synthetic	Analytical
Patient	Impatient
Group-oriented	Individualistic
Desire for eternity (i.e., continuity)	Eager to change

did in the early years of the Industrial Revolution. With the exception of iron, used for arms, these technological advances were developed by Taoist alchemy, primarily for religious and ceremonial purposes.

Chinese ships were trading as far as the Indian Ocean a century before the Portuguese rounded the Cape of Good Hope. However, as the Ming dynasty sought to reestablish the ancient order after the Mongols were finally subdued at the end of the fourteenth century, the Mandarins put an end to foreign adventures and turned inward once again. In keeping with its relative isolation and highly ethnocentric self-concept as the Middle Kingdom, China has a strong tradition of xenophobia. Westerners have long been called yang gui zi, or "foreign devils" (gui lao in Cantonese). Even China's cultural progeny, the Japanese, are called "devils of the Eastern Sea." When Western adventurers, priests, and merchants finally arrived in some force in the nineteenth century, they were confined to a few coastal enclaves, and the Mandarins limited intercourse to the minimum necessary to sustain a tidy stream of tax revenue from trade.

This reaction to the West stands in stark contrast to Japan's. Once finally opened to the West after the Meiji Restoration in 1868, the Japanese aggressively sought Western expertise in industry, technology, and administration—a practice that still continues. One consequence was that relatively tiny Japan was able to invade and occupy much of China in the 1930s, the first nation to do so successfully since the Mongols.

As is typical of agrarian, subsistence economies, the large and extended family—essential to eke out an existence from the land—was and remains the primary social and economic unit. The ultimate source of security and refuge, the family was responsible for the debts and conduct of its members. Individual wrongdoing caused great loss of face (lien) for the entire family. The Confucian emphasis on social harmony was intended largely to maintain the family's central role and extend its organization to society as a whole. Many Chinese still feel very strong ties to their home villages, including those now living in urban, industrial environments. Typical Chinese enterprises remain relatively small, with simple functional structures built around the founding family.

Europeans had a very different experience that would be replicated in North America. A much more heterogeneous people, they are comprised of numerous indigenous tribes and many others that made their way into Europe primarily from Central Asia. Europe's topography and extensive river systems allowed great internal mobility, and its location and many ports made it a crossroads between Asia and Africa. Temperate climate and ample arable land supported surplus agriculture, which enabled the early development of towns and the attendant specialization of labor that impelled acceleration of trade and foreign exploration. These adventures made Europeans aware of new products and brought riches that stimulated still more exploration and, ultimately, mercantilism. Thus was made possible the accumulation of wealth that financed the artistic, technological, and political advances of the Renaissance. After the fall of the Roman Empire, there was no monolithic, centralized authority capable of enforcing an inward focus, as the imperial Mandarins did in China. The Roman's extensive financial, legal, and transportational infrastructure supported internal intercourse and opened the door to the external world.

Government

In the sixth century B.C., when the Greeks were contemplating protection of individual rights and the rule of law as the best means for rendering order and peace from chaos and oppression, Confucius was pondering the same problem. But although his intentions were equally benign, his solution was quite different. He concluded that social harmony would best be served not by a system of citizens' rights protected by law, but by a rigidly hierarchical system of reciprocal duties and highly regulated and ritualized behavior built around the principle of filial loyalty. This was the origin of guanxi, li, and face. Taught and perpetuated by the family, Confucianism established and enforced behavioral norms. Confucius believed leaders should earn their authority through a demonstration of learning, wisdom, and the virtues of humanity—benevolence, righteousness, propriety, and trustworthiness—in the way a good father commanded the respect of his children. In return, people would owe their leaders total loyalty and support. Analogous relationships could be established throughout society in a hierarchical cascade, thereby rendering it peaceful, harmonious, and productive.

Confucius believed leadership was too important to leave the accidents of heredity; the opportunity to lead should be open to all so that the most meritorious would rise to the top. He believed people were essentially good and that they required only education in the ways of a harmonious society. Education, then—including setting a proper example—was the most fundamental responsibility of leadership. Wisdom, along with character, was an important measure of merit. This is why knowledge and accomplishment are a major source of face (mianzi).

Leaders were expected to conduct themselves with placid reserve, modesty, and self-restraint, much like the Greek stoic ideal. The people had the right to question leaders who failed these tests, but not to question the fundamental order of society. However, no consideration was given to individual rights or due process. Rule was a matter of personality and preparation, not law.

Eventually, Confucius's views came to permeate China's culture and constitute the essence of its value system and that of all East Asia. One institution that did not adopt Confucian thinking, at least with respect to merit being the primary qualification for power, were the imperial dynasties that ruled China until Sun Yat-Sen's nationalist revolution in the early twentieth century. Nevertheless, the governmental structure that evolved was clearly Confucian, an elaborate bureaucracy replete with ministries, many hierarchical layers extending down to the local level, and a professional civil service with its own examination system and training academy (many centuries before Max Weber introduced merit-based bureaucracy to the West). It was much more elaborate than the Romans' administrative structure and more similar to that of the medieval Church. Portuguese traders labeled the top bureaucrats Mandarins, from the Latin mandare, "to command." Confucius's views were traditional and conservative, and the Confucian bureaucracy did what bureaucracies do best: preserve them.

Within the context of imperial rivalries and internal and external strife, the administrative decisions of the Mandarins have controlled day-to-day life in China for more than 2,000 years. Even under the most benign of rulers, Confucianism was applied as a kind of state orthodoxy. Under its rubric, China's highly centralized rule routinely confiscated and redistributed wealth, established state monopolies, price controls, and collective land ownership, and conscripted unwilling soldiers and forced labor (used in building the Great Wall).

Confucius saw commerce as a pursuit of low status, an attitude that would persist in China except for the small entrepreneurial class that emerged around the European enclaves in the late nineteenth century. These entrepreneurs became the "Overseas Chinese," the foundation of expatriate communities in Hong Kong, Singapore, Vietnam, and elsewhere after the communist victory in 1949. Of course, the long-standing, statist tradition had made China fertile ground for communism, which differed from the state orthodoxy more in name than in substance.

Many manmade hardships combined with frequent natural disasters made life miserable for the ordinary Chinese. According to LaTourette, average life expectancy remained below 30 years of age even as China entered the twentieth century. The depredations of Mao, including his purges and artificial famines (when, for example, during the "Great Leap Forward" every village was to manufacture steel regardless of the consequences of fields left untended) were but a recent example.

A stream of thought that emerged concurrently with Confucianism was legalism, offering a very different prescription for maintaining order. Unlike

Confucius, the legalists held that people were inherently bad and that a firm hand was needed to keep them in line. They believed that the primary responsibility of government (the king, and later the emperor) toward its subjects was to maximize their martial skills to help preserve and expand the state. Indeed, legalism was instrumental in first unifying the empire in the third century B.C. Although it soon dissipated as a philosophical discipline, the precedent it set cast China's emperors from that point forward with a much harder edge than Confucius would have envisioned or preferred.

The Romans applied Greek ideals to a large empire. Whereas Greek democracy, limited to the city-state and the upper class, took the form of a simple plebiscite or referendum, the Roman solution was representative democracy. The Romans elaborated and expanded the protection of law to more classes of citizens and developed the notion of checks and balances. All this may have come to naught after the Empire fell but for the towns that emerged during the Pax Romana, created by surplus agriculture and its handmaiden, specialized labor. The vitality of trade centered in these towns eventually produced sufficient wealth to finance the revival of classical art, science, and thinking known as the Renaissance and the great period of European exploration and empire-building. The ensuring Enlightenment refined classical political ideas, generated new ones (such as the social contract and the right of all people to own private property), and produced the philosophical rationale and impetus that led to the institutional arrangements governing Western democracies today.

It is an interesting coincidence that the sixth century B.C. witnessed the origins of the divergent value systems of East and West: Confucius's harmony and filial loyalty combined with legalism and Taoist fatalism on one hand, and Greek democracy, rationality, and individualism on the other. Thenceforth, imperial repression continued in once-great China, abetted by Confucian discipline, Taoist passivity, Buddhist introspection, and unrelenting poverty and hardship. But the West would go on to nearly conquer the world, at least for a time, first politically and then economically.

Cosmology

Taoism (pronounced "dowism") filled a spiritual void in the pragmatic Confucian world. It advocated simplicity, detachment from the concerns of everyday life, and harmony with nature as the means of establishing social unity and harmony. Like other agrarian societies perpetually struggling to eke out an existence and accustomed to frequent hardship, the Chinese felt dependent upon and subservient to nature and sought the protection of their ancestors. (In Chinese art, one never sees flower arrangements or a still life of fruit in a bowl representing an attempt to improve on nature.) Natural disasters were believed to be an expression of nature's wrath over human misdeeds.

According to the Tao (the "Way") taken from the ancient I. Ching, people must seek harmony with nature and accommodate its whims. This cosmology is embodied in the notion of yin and yang, the arrangement of nature into opposing but complementary and oscillating forces such as day and night, high and low tide, male and female. Time has no beginning or end; it does not lapse or expire; it is cyclical rather than linear. Time and phenomena simply happen; hence, they are to be sensed or experienced, not conserved or measured. Everything is related to everything else—what Trompenaars called a diffuse view of the world rather than a specific or compartmentalized view. A perception of interrelatedness promotes holistic thinking and a systemic view. Cyclical patterns of yin and yang, like a spinning gyroscope, create a sense of stability, whereas a more linear path trails off into the unknowable.

The application of accumulated wisdom and intuition rather than rationality is the normal way of thinking for the traditional Confucianist. The scientific method would be an alien and dangerous notion because, in the Taoist world view, it would tend to polarize rather than harmonize. Excessive knowledge was thought to make people ungovernable. The fatalism inherent in Taoist cosmology renders superfluous any search for cause-and-effect relationships—the essence of scientific inquiry. Moreover, science would be tantamount to tampering with nature and its natural rhythms. It would also present the risk of departure from the tradition and stability dear to Confucian bureaucrats. Many of China's technological advances were driven not by a search for understanding but by the efforts of Taoist priests to achieve immortality on earth—efforts the Confucianists considered frivolous and superstitious.

The contrast between Chinese and Western cosmology is stark. For the Westerner, there is no greater truth than what can be objectively measured and tested. The opposite of that shown to be true must be false. In other words, Western logic cannot accommodate the simultaneous validity of contradictory circumstances embodied in the Tao. Westerners tend to think in logical, linear patterns. For the Chinese, intuition, emotion, and the need to maintain harmonious relationships constitute truth; objective information is less important. Westerners assume they can employ and shape nature to their own ends. It is difficult to imagine the Chinese deciding, as did the medieval Dutch, that it was not only desirable but quite possible to push back the North Sea, reclaim much of its bottom, and convert it to cities and fertile farmland.

All of this, of course, traces back to a very different cosmological view with roots in ancient Greece. Aristotle thought that by observation and experimentation, man could begin to understand how nature worked. Once that understanding began to accumulate, it was quite natural for the Greeks and their heirs to find ways to employ this knowledge. Early success gave Westerners confidence that they could harness nature and its resources rather than submit to it.

Religion and Ethical Standards

By Western standards, China is a secular society; most Chinese do not "belong" to a faith in the sense of being a Christian, a Jew, or a Muslim. Little thought is given to supreme beings, other than venerated ancestors, or to such matters as holiness or life after death. There is a dearth of universal ethical principles or moral absolutes other than maintaining the security and well-being of the family and living up to one's Confucian obligations. These remain the primary normative prescriptions for correct behavior. Because maintaining social harmony and order is the highest ideal, minimization of conflict is essential and absolutes are seen as sources of conflict.

Like the ancient Greeks, Confucius advocated a "golden mean," a moderation and balance in all things. But unlike the Greeks, Confucius and his followers believed this meant being reasonable rather than relying on reason. They held no relentless quest for the "truth," which many Westerners search for in the spiritual realm as diligently as they do in the scientific. Such a search would be futile, for when and where the yang prevails, its opposite yin will follow, and so on.

Behavior that maintained one's system of relationships was expected, rather than adherence to abstract principles. The "right" decision was the one that best served the present circumstances, not some code of temporal or religious law. Ethics were largely relative or situational, particularistic rather than universal. In any given circumstances, one might invoke Confucius, Buddha, the Tao, a venerated ancestor, or an animistic spirit, depending on whatever seemed to provide the most appropriate guidance. Europeans found this lack of "principle" barbarian. On the other hand, the Chinese considered barbarian the Europeans' aggressive, disharmonious behavior and ignorance of li.

Confucianism makes no pretense as a religion. Rather, it is a system of values that govern interpersonal behavior with an eye toward building a civil society. It does not speak to humanity's relationship with any supreme being. Taoism and Buddhism are more concerned with obtaining release from worldly cares and woe than with holiness or heavenly aspirations. The asceticism and mendicancy of Buddhist monks is not consistent with Confucian humanism and its ideals of hard work, order, and propriety. Celibacy attacks the bedrock of the Chinese society, the family.

Nevertheless, even as Buddhism declined in its home on the Indian subcontinent, it spread rapidly throughout East Asia. Buddha's first principle, that life is pain, certainly rang true with the vast majority of Chinese, who lived largely miserable lives. His prescription for escape into a state of enlightenment had great appeal. Accordingly, the more inclusive Mahayana form of Buddhism was more welcome in China because it held that a good Buddhist in any walk of life could reach an enlightened state, nirvana, and freedom from the needs and desires that made life so painful. In contrast, the more rigorous Theravada form held the pursuit of enlightenment to be a full-time pursuit and thus possible only for cloistered monks. In practice, the Chinese tended to set aside the search for enlightenment and settled for abiding by the behavioral standards embodied in Buddha's prescriptive "Eightfold Path"—standards that were consistent with those of Confucius. Buddhism's most significant impact on the Chinese value system lay in teaching that life is in a state of constant flux and a sorrow-free life of serenity and peace means accepting rather than resisting change. Any sense of individuality, self, ego, or soul was made transient and meaningless by this flux. Thus, Buddhism served to amplify the importance of Confucian behavioral norms and collectivism and Taoist receptivity to change.

Chinese religion has evolved in ways that support and advance the maintenance of social harmony. In contrast, Judaism and Christianity (and Islam as well) prescribe behavioral and ethical standards intended to allow the faithful an opportunity to please and prove their worthiness to their Creator and Supreme Being. While banning behavior detrimental to maintaining a civil society (though perhaps one not quite as well-mannered as China's), these religions also prescribe how the Supreme Being should be worshipped and require followers to hold certain beliefs, make certain expressions of faith, and participate in various rituals.

Secular authorities in the West, particularly the Romans building on the precedent set by the ancient Greeks, extended ecclesiastical law into a natural law that dealt with practices, abstract principles, and beliefs beyond the spiritual domain. From natural law, greatly elaborated during the Enlightenment, were derived such notions as liberty, justice, equity, fairness, the binding contact, and, ultimately, the social contract between people and their governments. These important social and political virtues, binding governments as well as citizens, acquired the force of principle as important to many—and perhaps more so to some—as the tenets of sacred scripture. Though Westerners might disagree on what is "fair" in any set of circumstances, few would argue against the worth of "fairness."

The Chinese, like most human beings, will recognize the evil of a wanton crime, but they will have trouble responding to the invocation of abstractions such as "fair trade." What is fair to the Chinese is whatever works, whatever action or manner of speech is necessary to execute a transaction satisfactorily for both parties. Westerners are taught to place the principle of honesty above the nicety of harmony; for them, constructive criticism is the "right" thing to do, even if painful. For the Chinese, this threat to harmony is antisocial. Likewise, most Westerners would be appalled that a manager could be so unprincipled as to show favoritism in hiring a relative. A Chinese would be equally appalled by any reluctance to do so.

Managerial Implications

The Chinese are not necessarily better or worse than Westerners, only different. As we have seen, this is the result of a very different set of traditions, not of inherent flaws in the Asian or national character or even of communism. An appreciation of these actual attitudinal and behavioral differences is obviously of great interest to those who would negotiate with the Chinese, teach or learn from them, do business in China, or find themselves working with them in any capacity. Table 2 encapsulates some of these differences and the ways in which they may affect working relationships....

The Chinese mind is accustomed to coping comfortably with dichotomies and accepting both poles as valid. Such bipolar conundrums as effectiveness and efficiency, high quality and low cost, short-term and long-term, profit and growth, stability and progress, may come easier to the Chinese. They intuit a holistic and mutually complementary, dependent, or symbiotic relationship among all things. Accordingly, they may be better strategic thinkers than Westerners because they can come to terms with the attendant multiplicity of variables and mental trade-offs, recognize and adapt to what "nature" gives

Table 2

A Summary of Western and Chinese Cultural Differences and the Implications for Management

Comparing pertinent features of the history of the West with that of China, we can make the following distinctions:

The West	China
Individual rights	Individual duty and collective obligations
Rule by law	Rule by personality and imperial authority
The collective right to grant, question, and reject political authority	Unquestioning submission to hereditary authority backed by force
Political and ethnic pluralism	Monolithic power and homogeneity
Cultural interaction	Cultural isolation
Sufficient resources to support early urbanization, specialization of labor, and large-scale trade	An agrarian, subsistence economy and endless hardship, both natural and imposed
An external orientation	An internal orientation
Physical and social mobility	Permanence in situ
Reliance on reason and the scientific method	Reliance on precedent, intuition, and wisdom
An aggressive, active approach to nature, technology, and progress	Passive, fatalistic submission

---

them (recall the strategic lessons of the Vietnam War), be comfortable with flux, and stay less encumbered by the urge to find the "truth" before acting.

Another manifestation of holistic thinking is the Chinese sense that the relationship among the parties to a business transaction is part of that transaction, not preliminary to it. When you want to get beyond the social niceties and relationship-building and get down to business, you must step back and recognize that the social interaction is an essential part of the process. All Chinese seek to cement such relationships into their guanxi networks, building a system of reciprocal, mutual obligation and dependency (renqing).

The Chinese will respect and appreciate a Westerner's knowledge of their culture. However, it is probably better to act with good manners and a sincere respect for Chinese culture than as an expert if, as a result, one comes across as self-assured to the point of arrogance. Remember that, like the Japanese, the Chinese tend to think of themselves as so unique that foreigners cannot comprehend them and their ways completely. It is probably wise to accept that proposition and, accordingly, be open-minded and meticulously well-mannered, listen more and speak less, learn at least as much as you try to teach, and avoid any form of aggressiveness, arrogance, individual competitiveness, self-promotion, or ostentation.

It is worth repeating here that interpersonal relationships, rather than the content and practice of business, are affected most by these cultural differences. Your domestic success can be replicated in China if you learn and adapt to Chinese ways of building and maintaining relationships. You can introduce Western practices successfully, but you must first build trust. This is best done by demonstrating your sincerity in working for some common good that accrues to your Chinese counterparts, to their enterprise, and to the Chinese people.

POSTSCRIPT

Are Chinese Confucianism and Western Capitalism Compatible?

Both Confucianism and capitalism can be confusing concepts. For further insight into the former, see Issue 12 of *Taking Sides: Clashing Views on Controversial Issues in World History, Volume I.* This issue discusses the role of Confucianism in shaping the warrior code of the Japanese samurai. Along with Shinto and Zen Buddhism, Confucian values contributed to the formation of the Japanese worldview. Any good translation of *The Analects* will introduce the teachings of Confucius, a Chinese master from the sixth century B.C.E., and allow him to speak for himself. A very complete resource for Chinese thought in general is *Sources of Chinese Tradition*, 2 vols., compiled by William Theodore de Bary and Irene Bloom (Columbia University Press, 1999). The first volume extends from earliest times to 1600 C.E.

Capitalism can be equally daunting. Issue 1 in this volume provides a context for the modern world with its look at the role of capitalism in launching the Industrial Revolution. Smith's classic *The Wealth of Nations* is available from the University of Chicago Press (1976) and also in a Modern Library edition (Random House, 1994). A good, straightforward introduction to the field of economics is *Economics Explained* by Robert Heilbruner and Lester Thurow (Simon & Schuster, 1998). This book describes the influence of Quesnay on Smith as well as the key components of classical capitalism in simple, engaging prose. A good backup source for terms is John Black, *Oxford Dictionary of Economics* (Oxford University Press, 1997).

For greater depth, see "The Physiocrats: Six Lectures on the French Economistes of the 18th Century," originally delivered at the London School of Economics in 1897 and reprinted by Augustus M. Kelley publishers in 1989. Elizabeth Fox-Genovese's *The Origins of Physiocracy* (Cornell University Press, 1976) provides a modern historical account of the works of Quesnay and his unacknowledged collaborator Victor Riqueti, marquis de Mirabeau. Gianni Vaggi's *The Economics of François Quesnay* (Duke University Press, 1987) offers a reconsideration of Quesnay's theories in the light of contemporary economic theory. *François Quesnay (1694–1774)*, Mark Blaug, ed. (Edward Elgar Publishing Limited, 1991), is Volume II of the Pioneers in Economics series, which presents "critical appraisals of influential economists." And, finally, Quesnay's *Tableau Economique,* Marguerite Kuczynski and Ronald L. Meek, eds. (Augustus M. Kelley Publishers, 1972), explores the history of the several editions of Quesnay's conceptual construct—the tableau economique—which lays out the ideas on which classical capitalism is constructed.

ISSUE 14

Does Islamic Revivalism Challenge a Stable World Order?

YES: John L. Esposito, from *The Islamic Threat: Myth or Reality?* 2d ed. (Oxford University Press, 1995)

NO: Sharif Shuja, from "Islam and the West: From Discord to Understanding," *Contemporary Review* (May 2001)

ISSUE SUMMARY

YES: Professor of Middle East studies John L. Esposito sees the Iranian Revolution against Western-inspired modernization and Egypt's "holy war" against Israel as examples of the Islamic quest for a more authentic society and culture, which challenges a stable world order.

NO: Professor of international relations Sharif Shuja identifies the rise of Islamic movements as resistance to Western domination rather than as a threat to the West as such and traces Western fears of a monolithic Islamic entity to the errors of an "Orientalist" mindset.

For many Westerners the adjective *Islamic* seems to be linked inexorably with either *fundamentalist* or *terrorist*. Particularly since the Islamic revolution of 1978–1979 in Iran, images of Western hostages and calls for a *jihad*, or holy war, have created a climate of fear and mistrust between the West and Islam. Are the two on a collision course, rooted in history and driven by an absolute incompatibility of beliefs and lifestyles? Or can Islam play a role in a stable world order that affirms Islam's own tradition while accommodating secularism and pluralism? The two selections that follow acknowledge the flash points and conclude by placing the emphasis at different places.

Because Islam sees itself as the fulfillment of both Judaism and Christianity—as the final word of God for human beings—it has from the beginning sought to spread its truth throughout the world. In the tradition of jihad, those who died in the attempt to bring Islam to nonbelievers were ensured a place in Paradise. Early successes came during Europe's so-called Dark Ages. Muslim learning and culture were more advanced, and it was only natural for conquering armies to assume that their religion enjoyed a comparable superiority. Unlike Christianity, Islam gained secular power within the founder Muhammad's lifetime (c. 570–632), and the rulers that followed him, known as caliphs, combined secular and religious power. There could be no conflict between church and state because the church and the state were one.

For many Muslims in the modern world, the political and military domination of the West has brought a secularism that is repugnant to all they hold sacred. It seems to them that Westerners—with their lack of respect for traditional authority, their emancipated and exploited women, and their shallow and materialistic values—have won. Becoming modern is generally equated with embracing the consumer culture and values of the West. The question seems to be whether or not Islamic countries can modernize without giving up their core values and embracing those of the West.

Both of the following selections point out that people in the West must begin by understanding the history and idea systems of modern Islam, whose believers constitute one-fifth of the world's population. In the first selection, John L. Esposito notes that the clout provided by oil has brought the Islamic Middle East into the world economy and given it the power to be a significant player in either supporting or destabilizing a peaceful world order. Believing that Islam has superseded both Judaism and Christianity calls Muslims to impose the law of God on all the world. In the search for an authentic Islamic culture, Esposito concludes, Muslims present a strong challenge to the political and cultural values of the West.

In the second selection, Sharif Shuja acknowledges the points of potential conflict between Islam and the West. However, he insists that the rise of Islamic movements signals resistance to Western domination and control over Muslim territories and resources and does not necessarily pose a threat to the West as such. He describes the Westernization that colonized more than two-thirds of the Muslim world during the first half of the twentieth century as one major globalizing force. There is now under way another globalizing force, which he calls the demographic Islamization of the Western world, represented by dramatic increases in the Muslim populations of Europe and the United States. Shuja counters Samuel P. Huntington's contention that the Islamic threat has been going on for 1300 years. What is wrong with Huntington's thesis, according to Shuja, is the depiction of Islamic countries as "part of a wider pan-Islamic movement, united in their hostility to the West and the United States." This kind of phobia can arise out of an "Orientalist" mindset that glosses over the diversity within Islam. Shuja sees Islamic revivalism as a successor to failed nationalist programs that in their own way tried to chart a third alternative between the undesirable poles of capitalism and communism. The best way to reduce extremism, Shuja contends, is through gradual democratisation. He points to hopeful signs, such as the voices of moderate Muslims who joined a worldwide outcry against the Islamicist regime in Afghanistan that decided to blow up centuries-old statues of the Buddha during the early months of 2001.

John L. Esposito  **YES**

The Islamic Threat:
Myth or Reality?

Are Islam and the West on an inevitable collision course? Are Islamic fundamentalists medieval fanatics? Are Islam and democracy incompatible? Is Islamic fundamentalism a threat to stability in the Muslim world and to American interests in the region? These are critical questions for our times that come from a history of mutual distrust and condemnation.

From the Ayatollah Khomeini to Saddam Hussein, for more than a decade the vision of Islamic fundamentalism or militant Islam as a threat to the West has gripped the imaginations of Western governments and the media. Khomeini's denunciation of America as the "Great Satan," chants of "Death to America," the condemnation of Salman Rushdie and his *Satanic Verses,* and Saddam Hussein's call for a jihad against foreign infidels have reinforced images of Islam as a militant, expansionist religion, rabidly anti-American and intent upon war with the West.

Despite many common theological roots and beliefs, throughout history Muslim-Christian relations have often been overshadowed by conflict as the armies and missionaries of Islam and Christendom have struggled for power and for souls. This confrontation has involved such events as the defeat of the early Byzantine (eastern Roman) empire by Islam in the seventh century; the fierce battles and polemics of the Crusades during the eleventh and twelfth centuries; the expulsion of the Moors from Spain and the Inquisition; the Ottoman threat to Europe; European (Christian) colonial expansion and domination in the eighteenth and nineteenth centuries; the political and cultural challenge of the superpowers (America and the Soviet Union) in the latter half of the twentieth century; the creation of the state of Israel; the competition of Christian and Muslim missionaries for converts in Africa today; and the contemporary reassertion of Islam in politics.

"Islamic fundamentalism" has often been regarded as a major threat to the regional stability of the Middle East and to Western interests in the broader Muslim world. The Iranian Revolution, attacks on Western embassies, hijackings and hostage taking, and violent acts by groups with names like the Army of God (Jund Allah), Holy War (al-Jihad), the Party of God (Hizbullah), and Salvation from Hell have all signaled a militant Islam on a collision course with the West. Uprisings in the Muslim republics of the Soviet Union, in Kosovo in Yugoslavia, in Indian Kashmir, in Sinkiang in China, and on the West Bank and in Gaza, and more recently, Saddam Hussein's attempted annexation of Kuwait, have reinforced images of an expansive and potentially explosive Islam in global politics.

With the triumph of the democratization movement in Eastern Europe and the breakup of the Soviet empire, Islam constitutes the most pervasive and powerful transnational force in the world, with one billion adherents spread out across the globe. Muslims are a majority in some forty-five countries ranging from Africa to Southeast Asia, and they exist in growing and significant numbers in the United States, the Soviet Union, and Europe. For a Western world long accustomed to a global vision and foreign policy predicated upon superpower rivalry for global influence if not dominance—a U.S.–Soviet conflict often portrayed as a struggle between good and evil, capitalism and communism—it is all too tempting to identify another global ideological menace to fill the "threat vacuum" created by the demise of communism.

However diverse in reality, the existence of Islam as a worldwide religion and ideological force embracing one fifth of the world's population, and its continued vitality and power in a Muslim world stretching from Africa to Southeast Asia, will continue to raise the specter of an Islamic threat....

As Western leaders attempt to forge the New World Order, transnational Islam may increasingly come to be regarded as the new global monolithic enemy of the West: "To some Americans, searching for a new enemy against whom to test our mettle and power, after the death of communism, Islam is the preferred antagonist. But, to declare Islam an enemy of the United States is to declare a second Cold War that is unlikely to end in the same resounding victory as the first." Fear of the Green Menace (green being the color of Islam) may well replace that of the Red Menace of world communism.

Islam and Islamic movements constitute a religious and ideological alternative or challenge and in some instances a potential danger to Christianity and the West. However, distinguishing between a religious or ideological alternative or challenge and a direct political threat requires walking the fine line between myth and reality, between the unity of Islam and the diversity of its multiple and complex manifestations in the world today, between the violent actions of the few and the legitimate aspirations and policies of the many. Unfortunately, American policymakers, like the media, have too often proved surprisingly myopic, viewing the Muslim world and Islamic movements as a monolith and seeing them solely in terms of extremism and terrorism. While this is understandable in light of events in Iran and Lebanon and the Gulf crisis of 1990–91, it fails to do justice to the complex realities of the Muslim world and can undermine relations between the West and Islam....

The Islamic Resurgence

Islam reemerged as a potent global force in Muslim politics during the 1970s and 1980s. The scope of the Islamic resurgence has been worldwide, embracing much of the Muslim world from the Sudan to Indonesia. Heads of Muslim governments as well as opposition groups increasingly appealed to religion for legitimacy and to mobilize popular support. Islamic activists have held cabinet-level positions in Jordan, the Sudan, Iran, Malaysia, and Pakistan. Islamic organizations constitute the leading opposition parties and organizations in Egypt, Tunisia, Algeria, Morocco, the West Bank and Gaza, and Indonesia. Where permitted, they have participated in elections and served in parliament and in city government. Islam has been a significant ingredient in nationalist struggles and resistance movements in Afghanistan, the Muslim republics of the former Soviet Central Asia, and Kashmir, and in the communal politics of Lebanon, India, Thailand, China, and the Philippines.

Islamically oriented governments have been counted among America's staunchest allies (Saudi Arabia and Pakistan) and most vitriolic enemies (Libya and Iran). Islamic activist organizations have run the spectrum from those who work within the system—such as the Muslim Brotherhoods in Egypt, Jordan, and the Sudan—to radical revolutionaries like Egypt's Society of Muslims (known more popularly as Takfir wal-Hijra, Excommunication and Flight) and al-Jihad (Holy War), or Lebanon's Hizbullah (Party of God) and Islamic Jihad, which have resorted to violence in their attempts to overthrow prevailing political systems.

Yet to speak of a contemporary Islamic revival can be deceptive, if this implies that Islam had somehow disappeared or been absent from the Muslim world. It is more correct to view Islamic revivalism as having led to a higher profile of Islam in Muslim politics and society. Thus what had previously seemed to be an increasingly marginalized force in Muslim public life reemerged in the seventies—often dramatically—as a vibrant sociopolitical reality. Islam's resurgence in Muslim politics reflected a growing religious revivalism in both personal and public life that would sweep across much of the Muslim world and have a substantial impact on the West in world politics.

The indices of an Islamic reawakening in personal life are many: increased attention to religious observances (mosque attendance, prayer, fasting), proliferation of religious programming and publications, more emphasis upon Islamic dress and values, the revitalization of Sufism (mysticism). This broader-based renewal has also been accompanied by Islam's reassertion in public life: an increase in Islamically oriented governments, organizations, laws, banks, social welfare services, and educational institutions. Both governments and opposition movements have turned to Islam to enhance their authority and muster popular support. Governmental use of Islam has been illustrated by a great spectrum of leaders in the Middle East and Asia: Libya's Muammar Qaddafi, Sudan's Gaafar Muhammad Nimeiri, Egypt's Anwar Sadat, Iran's Ayatollah Khomeini, Pakistan's Zia ul-Haq, Bangladesh's Muhammad Ershad, Malaysia's Muhammad Mahathir. Most rulers and governments, including more secular states such as Turkey and Tunisia, becoming aware of the potential strength of Islam, have shown increased sensitivity to and anxiety about Islamic issues. The Iranian Revolution of 1978–79 focused attention on "Islamic fundamentalism" and with it the spread and vitality of political Islam in other parts of the Muslim world. However, the contemporary revival has its origins and roots in the late sixties and early seventies, when events in such disparate areas as Egypt and Libya as well as Pakistan and Malaysia contributed to experiences of crisis and failure, as well as power and success, which served as catalysts for a more visible reassertion of Islam in both public and private life.

The Experience of Failure and the Quest for Identity

Several conflicts (e.g., the 1967 Arab–Israeli war, Chinese–Malay riots in Malaysia in 1969, the Pakistan–Bangladesh civil war of 1971, and the Lebanese civil war of the midseventies) illustrate the breadth and diversity of these turning points or catalysts for change. For many in the Arab and broader Muslim world, 1967 proved to be a year of catastrophe as well as a historic turning point. Israel's quick and decisive defeat of Arab forces in what was remembered as the Six-Day War, the Israeli capture and occupation of the Golan Heights, Sinai, Gaza, the West Bank, and East Jerusalem, constituted a devastating blow to Arab/Muslim pride, identity, and self-esteem. Most important, the loss of Jerusalem, the third holiest city of Islam, assured that Palestine and the liberation of Jerusalem would not be regarded as a regional (Arab) issue but rather as an Islamic cause throughout the Muslim world. The defense of Israel is dear to many Jews throughout the world. Likewise, for Muslims who retain a sense of membership in a transnational community of believers (the *ummah*), Palestine and the liberation of Jerusalem are strongly seen as issues of Islamic solidarity. As anyone who works in the Muslim world can attest, Israeli control of the West Bank, Gaza, and Jerusalem as well as U.S.–Israeli relations are topics of concern and bitter debate among Muslims from Nigeria and the Sudan to Pakistan and Malaysia, as well as among the Muslims of Europe and the United States.

The aftermath of the 1967 war, remembered in Arab literature as the "disaster," witnessed a sense of disillusionment and soul-searching that gripped both Western-oriented secular elites as well as the more Islamically committed, striking at their sense of pride, identity, and history. Where had they gone wrong? Both the secular and the Islamically oriented sectors of society now questioned the effectiveness of nationalist ideologies, Western models of development, and Western allies who had persisted in supporting Israel. Despite several decades of independence and modernization, Arab forces (consisting of the combined military might of Egypt, Jordan, and Syria) had proved impotent. A common critique of the military, political, and sociocultural failures of Western-oriented development and a quest for a more authentic society and culture emerged—an Arab identity less dependent upon the West and rooted more indigenously in an Arab/Islamic heritage and values. Examples from Malaysia, Pakistan, and Lebanon reflect the turmoil and soul-searching that occurred in many parts of the Muslim world....

From Failure to Success

During the seventies Islamic politics seemed to explode on the scene, as events in the Middle East (the Egyptian–Israeli war and the Arab oil embargo of 1973, as well as the Iranian Revolution of 1978–79) shocked many into recognition of a powerful new force that threatened Western interests. Heads of state and opposition movements appealed to Islam to enhance their legitimacy and popular support; Islamic organizations and institutions proliferated.

In 1973 Egypt's Anwar Sadat initiated a "holy war" against Israel. In contrast to the 1967 Arab–Israeli war which was fought by Gamal Abdel Nasser in the name of Arab nationalism/socialism, this war was fought under the banner of Islam. Sadat generously employed Islamic symbols and history to rally his forces. Despite their loss of the war, the relative success of Egyptian forces led many Muslims to regard it as a moral victory, since most had believed that a U.S.-backed Israel could not be beaten.

Military vindication in the Middle East was accompanied by economic muscle, the power of the Arab oil boycott. For the first time since the dawn of colonialism, the West had to contend with and acknowledge, however begrudgingly, its dependence on the Middle East. For many in the Muslim world the new wealth, success, and power of the oil-rich countries seemed to indicate a return of the power of Islam to a community whose centuries-long political and cultural ascendence had been shattered by European colonialism and, despite independence, by second-class status in a superpower-dominated world. A number of factors enhanced the Islamic character of oil power. Most of the oil wealth was located in the Arab heartland, where Muhammad had received the revelation of the Quran and established the first Islamic community-state. The largest deposits were found in Saudi Arabia, a self-styled Islamic state which had asserted its role as keeper of the holy cities of Mecca and Medina, protector of the annual pilgrimage *(hajj),* and leader and benefactor of the Islamic world. The House of Saud used its oil wealth to establish numerous international Islamic organizations, promote the preaching and spread of Islam, support Islamic causes, and subsidize Islamic activities undertaken by Muslim governments.

No event demonstrated more dramatically the power of a resurgent Islam than the Iranian Revolution of 1978–79. For many in the West and the Muslim world, the unthinkable became a reality. The powerful, modernizing, and Western-oriented regime of the Shah came crashing down. This was an oil-rich Iran whose wealth had been used to build the best-equipped military in the Middle East (next to Israel's) and to support an ambitious modernization program, the Shah's White Revolution. Assisted by Western-trained elites and advisers, the Shah had governed a state which the United States regarded as its most stable ally in the Muslim world. The fact that a revolution against him and against the West was effectively mounted in the name of Islam, organizing disparate groups and relying upon the mullah–mosque network for support, generated euphoria among many in the Muslim world and convinced Islamic activists that these were lessons for success to be emulated. Strength and victory would belong to those who pursued change in the name of Islam, whatever the odds and however formidable the regime.

For many in the broader Muslim world, the successes of the seventies resonated with an idealized perception of early Islam, the Islamic paradigm to be found in the time of the Prophet Muhammad, the Golden Age of Islam. Muhammad's successful union of disparate tribal forces under the banner of Islam, his creation of an Islamic state and society in which social justice prevailed, and the extraordinary early expansion of Islam were primal events to be remembered and, as the example of the Iranian Revolution seemingly verified, to be successfully emulated by those who adhered to Islam. Herein lies the initial attraction of the Iranian Revolution for many Muslims, Sunni and Shii alike. Iran provided the first example of a modern Islamic revolution, a revolt against impiety, oppression, and injustice. The call of the Ayatollah Khomeini for an Islamic revolution struck a chord among many who identified with his message of anti-imperialism, his condemnation of failed, unjust, and oppressive regimes, and his vision of a morally just society.

By contrast, the West stood incredulous before this challenge to the Shah's "enlightened" development of his seemingly backward nation, and the resurrection of an anachronistic, irrational medieval force that threatened to hurtle modern Iran back to the Middle Ages. Nothing symbolized this belief more than the black-robed, bearded mullahs and the dour countenance of their leader, the Ayatollah Khomeini, who dominated the media, reinforcing in Western minds the irrational nature of the entire movement.

The Ideological Worldview of Islamic Revivalism

At the heart of the revivalist worldview is the belief that the Muslim world is in a state of decline. Its cause is departure from the straight path of Islam; its cure, a return to Islam in personal and public life which will ensure the restoration of Islamic identity, values, and power. For Islamic political activists Islam is a total or comprehensive way of life as stipulated in the Quran, God's revelation, mirrored in the example of Muhammad and the nature of the first Muslim community-state, and embodied in the comprehensive nature of the Sharia, God's revealed law. Thus the revitalization of Muslim governments and societies requires the reimplementation of Islamic law, the blueprint for an Islamically guided and socially just state and society.

While Westernization and secularization of society are condemned, modernization as such is not. Science and technology are accepted, but the pace, direction, and extent of change are to be subordinated to Islamic belief and values in order to guard against the penetration of Western values and excessive dependence on them.

Radical movements go beyond these principles and often operate according to two basic assumptions. They assume that Islam and the West are locked in an ongoing battle, dating back to the early days of Islam, which is heavily influenced by the legacy of the Crusades and European colonialism, and which today is the product of a Judaeo-Christian conspiracy. This conspiracy is the result of superpower neocolonialism and the power of Zionism. The West

(Britain, France, and especially the United States) is blamed for its support of un-Islamic or unjust regimes (Egypt, Iran, Lebanon) and also for its biased support for Israel in the face of Palestinian displacement. Violence against such governments and their representatives as well as Western multinationals is legitimate self-defense.

Second, these radical movements assume that Islam is not simply an ideological alternative for Muslim societies but a theological and political imperative. Since Islam is God's command, implementation must be immediate, not gradual, and the obligation to do so is incumbent on all true Muslims. Therefore individuals and governments who hesitate, remain apolitical, or resist are no longer to be regarded as Muslim. They are atheists or unbelievers, enemies of God against whom all true Muslims must wage jihad (holy war). . . .

As some dream of the creation of a New World Order, and many millions in North Africa, the Middle East, Central Asia, and southern and Southeast Asia aspire to greater political liberalization and democratization, the continued vitality of Islam and Islamic movements need not be a threat but a challenge. For many Muslims, Islamic revivalism is a social rather than a political movement whose goal is a more Islamically minded and oriented society, but not necessarily the creation of an Islamic state. For others, the establishment of an Islamic order requires the creation of an Islamic state. In either case, Islam and most Islamic movements are not necessarily anti-Western, anti-American, or anti-democratic. While they are a challenge to the outdated assumptions of the established order and to autocratic regimes, they do not necessarily threaten American interests. Our challenge is to better understand the history and realities of the Muslim world. Recognizing the diversity and many faces of Islam counters our image of a unified Islamic threat. It lessens the risk of creating self-fulfilling prophecies about the battle of the West against a radical Islam. Guided by our stated ideals and goals of freedom and self-determination, the West has an ideal vantage point for appreciating the aspirations of many in the Muslim world as they seek to define new paths for their future.

Sharif Shuja

Islam and the West:
From Discord to Understanding

The spread of Islam has had an impact on the globalisation of culture. Islam has spread not only as a religion but has also helped to give birth to languages which are spoken by many more non-Muslims than Muslims. Kiswahili in Africa is today the most important indigenous language to have emerged out of Africa—but its origins lie in the interaction between Islam and African culture. Islam and the Arabic language have bequeathed the Arabic alphabet for languages like Farsi, Urdu, Old Hausa and others. The Arabs have given the world the so-called Arabic numerals through which the twentieth century has computerised the human experience. Today the Quran (Koran) is the most widely read book in its original language in human history. Muslims are expected to read the Quran in the original Arabic and not a translation that may change the intended meaning. The Bible is the most widely read book in translation.

As the twenty-first century begins, almost one out of every five human beings is a Muslim. In the course of the 21st century a quarter of the human race will probably be Muslim. The new demographic presence of Islam within the Western world is indicative that Islamisation is now a major globalising force.

Perspectives on Islamisation/Westernisation

In the second half of the twentieth century both Muslim migration to the West and conversions to Islam within the West consolidated a new Islamic presence. In Europe as a whole, there are now 20 million Muslims, eight million of whom are in Western Europe. These figures exclude the Muslims of the Republic of Turkey, who number some 50 million. There are new mosques from Munich to Marseilles.

Also as a manifestation of the demographic Islamisation of the Western world, there are now over a thousand mosques and Islamic centres in the United States alone. And the country has professional associations for Muslim engineers, Muslim social scientists and Muslim educators. There are some six million American muslims—and the number is rising impressively. Indeed,

From Sharif Shuja, "Islam and the West: From Discord to Understanding," *Contemporary Review*, vol. 278, no. 1624 (May 2001). Copyright © 2001 by *Contemporary Review*. Reprinted by permission of The Contemporary Review Company Limited.

the American society in general is now coping with this issue, which creates cultural tensions between Islam and the West, as some observers have noted.

Currently Islam is the fastest growing religion in Central Asia. After the collapse of the U.S.S.R., all five states of Central Asia—Kazakhastan, Kyrghystan, Uzbekistan, Turkemenistan and Tajikistan—made an official place for Islam as the dominant religion. In France, Islam is becoming the second most important religion numerically after Catholicism. In Britain, Muslims have been demanding state subsidies for Muslim denominational schools. In Germany it has been belatedly realised that the importation of Turkish workers in the 1970s was also an invitation to the muezzin and the minaret to establish themselves in German cities. Australia has discovered that it is a neighbour to the largest Muslim country in the world in terms of population (Indonesia). There are new mosques, Islamic schools and Quranic centres from Brisbane to Perth.

Westernisation, on the other hand, is also a major globalising force. In the first half of the twentieth century, the West had colonised more than two-thirds of the Muslim world, from Africa to Asia. The first half of the twentieth century also witnessed the collapse of the Ottoman Empire and the complete de-Islamisation of the European state-system. The aftermath included the abolition of the caliphate as the symbolic centre of Islamic authority. The ummah (Islamic community) became more fragmented than ever and became even more receptive to Western cultural penetration. Other forces which facilitated the cultural Westernisation of the Muslim world included the replacement of Islamic and Quranic schools with Western style schools; the increasing use of European languages in major Muslim countries; and the impact of the Western media upon the distribution of news, information and entertainment. In other words, the West has in turn spread not only its technology and market ideology but also its languages (especially English, French and Spanish), its educational systems, consumer culture, including the dress code for men world-wide, and its mass media. The net result has indeed been a form of globalisation of aspects of Western culture. But at what cost?

In almost every liberal country in the West, crime is escalating, violence sometimes quadrupling, street mugging is on the rise, and the culture of the fortress city is developing. Suicide is now the second leading cause of death among American adolescents, the causes including the decline of family values and a more general national malaise. By comparison, suicide is a rare form of violence in the Muslim world.

There are scholars who feel that there is another way of looking at globalisation—and that is to focus on the three techno-systemic revolutions of all human history. There was first the agricultural revolution which started before Islamic and Western civilisations and transformed the relationship between man and plants. Millennia later there was the industrial revolution for which Islamic science helped to prepare the ground but which was essentially led by the West. This transformed the relationship between man and all material resources.

And now there is the emerging information revolution which leaves the West both triumphant and vulnerable—but is also leaving Islam marginalised.

This is the revolution which is transforming the relationship between man and knowledge itself. But the question arises: can the Muslim world enter the positive sphere of globalisation without risking the negative aspects of Westernisation?

One of the remarkable things about the twentieth century is that it combined the cultural Westernisation of the Muslim world, on the one hand, and the more recent demographic Islamisation in the Western world, on the other. The foundations for the cultural Westernisation of the Muslim world were laid mainly in the first half of the twentieth century. The foundations for the demographic Islamisation in the Western world were laid in the second half of the twentieth century. The cultural Westernisation of Muslims contributed to the brain drain of Muslim professionals and experts from their homes in Muslim countries to jobs and educational institutions in North America and Europe. It is in this sense that the cultural Westernisation of the Muslim world in the first half of the twentieth century was part of the preparation for the demographic Islamisation in the West in the last fifty years.

Islamic Revivalism in Context

There are scholars and policy makers in the West who are concerned with recent Islamic revivalism and face tensions about how Islam is to be treated in Western textbooks and the media, especially as Islam becomes a more integral part of Western society. As one observer (Ali Mazrui) put it:

> Judaism, Christianity and Islam are the three Abrahamic creeds of world history. In the twentieth century the Western world has often been described as a 'Judeo-Christian civilisation', thus linking the West to two of those Abrahamic faiths. But if in countries like the US Muslims will soon outnumber Jews, is Islam becoming the second most important Abrahamic religion after Christianity? Numerically Islam may overshadow Judaism in much of the West, regardless of future immigration policies.

The question has therefore arisen about how Islam is to be treated in Western classrooms. In the Muslim world, 'education has become substantially Westernised. Is it now the turn of education in the West to become partly Islamised?' Can the Western world enter the positive sphere of globalisation and draw on the traditional wisdom of cultures such as Islam which point towards a more integrated society with drastically decreased levels of crime and violence?

The rise of Islamic movements in different parts of the world, aimed at resisting Western domination and control over Muslim territories and resources, Muslim cultures and communities, has provoked a new wave of aggressive emotions against the religion and its practitioners. That it is resistance to Western domination and control—and not some threat to the West as such—which is taking place within the Muslim world is a reality that is concealed from the general public. What Islamic movements are opposed to is the annexation and occupation of their lands as in the case of Palestine and Lebanon, the usurpation of their rights over their own natural resources as in the case of the Gulf

Sheikhdoms, and the denigration of their religion as often happens in the Western media, sometimes abetted by local elites and writers.

Salman Rushdie's *The Satanic Verses* is a case in point. The results were terrifying. A holy man called for the author's death. Thousands were engaged in riots, dozens were killed, and normally brave defenders of free expression hunkered down or bent with the wind. Undoubtedly, the book is offensive to many Muslims. But books are published, plays are written and movies produced throughout the year that are deemed offensive by some group or other. And civilised people have learned not to murder the librarian or bomb the theatre to express their distaste. In this case, the intolerant reach of the Ayatollah has touched us all. Islamic groups and some individuals have expressed strong resentment and anger over Rushdie, the publisher of the book and Western media, and demanded the immediate ban of this book. Broadly speaking, they see their struggle as part of the still unfulfilled quest for self-determination and for genuine sovereignty. Such Muslim resistance is portrayed as an 'Islamic threat' by some Western academics, including Samuel P. Huntington. Conflict between Western and Islamic civilisations, Huntington in his article 'The Clash of Civilizations' points out, 'has been going on for 1300 years. The Gulf War is only the most recent important example'. His argument has been the centre of controversy for the last decade.

At the turn of the Western millennium, it is crucial to consider whether Islam is a monolithic force; whether the clash between Islam and the West is inevitable; and whether the so-called Islamic civilisation poses a credible threat to the West.

Huntington depicts the Islamic countries as part of a wider pan-Islamic movement, united in their hostility to the West and the United States. So convinced is Huntington of the 'kin-country' syndrome that even the Gulf War of 1990 becomes clear evidence of the brewing clash between Islam and the West.

The depiction of Islam and the Islamic countries as a monolithic entity may reflect the errors of the Orientalist mind-set, which refuses to understand the diversity within Islam for the convenience of a simple explanation. The assumed identity, through segregation and confinement of the Islamic civilisation, is a product of the Western imagination and sustains a deep phobia because the simple explanation, ironically, renders Islam both 'unknown' and mysterious.

It is orientalist scholarship that has invested Islam both with internal unity and an external political ambition. Orientalists have reconstructed Islam as a political religion despite the fact that there is little in original Islamic sources on how to form states or run governments. It also produced a particular reading of the 'orient' that was at odds with reality. Edward Said, in his article 'Orientalism Reconsidered' argued that 'designations like Islam and the Arabs ... represented interests, claims, projects, ambitions, and rhetorics that were not only in violent disagreement, but were in situation of open warfare'. These diversions, however, were quickly glossed over and the myth that the Islamic countries possessed a fundamental unity of purpose that transcended national boundaries became the accepted consensus. The myth has, so far, refused to adapt itself to reason.

If the notion of a political and monolithic Islam should be taken with some scepticism, it is still true that a fundamentalist movement has emerged with the specific political task of reforming Muslim societies. This, however, is essentially a reaction to Westernisation, though not modernisation, and constitutes an attempt to check a perceived social drift and weakening of morals. In the West, modernisation is synonymous with Westernisation, but Muslim 'fundamentalists' clearly dissociate the two. This discordant understanding of modernisation has given Western analysts the impression that a rejection of Westernisation is the equivalent of a battle-cry against the West.

It should also be mentioned that the fundamentalist movement, most active in the Shi'ite countries of Iran, Iraq and Lebanon, is diverse and a minority movement in most Islamic countries. Even assuming Islamic fundamentalism would spread significantly, it is not inevitable that it will inexorably lead to a clash with the West. After all, the West, and particularly the United States, has maintained a very special relationship with Saudi Arabia, one of the most fundamentalist Arab States.

Therefore, even if we grant that Islam forms a united movement in comparison to Western culture, it is not certain whether the Islamic civilisations will constitute a true adversary to the West. However, it would be helpful if commentators in the West recognised that the pursuit of modernisation need not be accompanied by Westernisation, and that a rejection of Westernisation is not an inevitable call to do battle with the West.

It is helpful here to recognise that Islamic revivalism is in many ways the successor to failed nationalist programmes and offers an Islamic alternative or solution, a third way distinct from capitalism and communism. Islamists argue that Islam is not just a collection of beliefs and ritual actions, but rather a comprehensive ideology embracing public as well as personal life. It is important to understand that Islamic activism in some countries is a cause of concern but not for alarm. It is not a challenge to any civilisation. Like radicals throughout history, Islamic radicals become moderate once accommodated and incorporated into the socio-political mainstream. If they do not, they perish or become sociologically irrelevant cults. Therefore, extremism can best be reduced through gradual democratisation, a process and a system of governance which the West is not actively encouraging in the Muslim world, and particularly not in the Middle East.

So far the reality is that Islamic revivalism is neither a product of the Iranian revolution nor a result of Libyan extremist policies. The depth of frustration and anger is a reaction against European colonial rule, support for unpopular regimes and the internal weaknesses of the Muslim governments. Although some scholars argue that the present awakening in the Muslim world is a response to the decline of power and the loss of divine favour, in fact, the current revolt is a product of the weak economies of the Muslim countries, illiteracy and high unemployment, especially among the younger generation. The lack of political institutions, absence of democracies and good governments in the Muslim world is also an immediate cause of extremism. In this context, the Muslim demands for change are no different from the demands in Eastern Europe.

In many Muslim countries the secular nationalists and Islamists are united in the common cause of popular democracy. They are demanding the right to gain legitimate power with ballots rather than bullets. These forces are also cooperating with each other to topple monarchies, military dictators and authoritarian governments. They blamed their governments for their countries' backwardness and failure to achieve economic self-sufficiency and development. In addition to these internal reasons, there are also some external factors which push the Islamists to struggle for the rights and protection of Muslims which are under the siege of oppressive rule. Muslims are worried about the people of Palestine and they cannot ignore the inhuman massacres of Muslims in Bosnia, Chechnya and Kashmir. Such experiences tend to make Muslims think that the West is against them.

This author believes that the conflicts in Bosnia, Chechnya and Kashmir are political in nature. Others could say that the current conflict is either directly based on religious differences or at least involves an element of religion which contributes to the conflict. Military means, however, is not a solution. Devising appropriate mechanisms for their resolution continues to require the application of scientific method, rational inquiry and balanced argument. Because you dislike war does not mean you should not study it. And because we don't like the behaviour of politicians does not mean we can ignore them.

The Road Ahead

We should start from the premise that there is a need for all members of our global village to work towards harmony, cohesion and a peaceful world. We need to emphasise that the expressed goal of all religions is to achieve peace in the world. Conflict often arises in the way in which representatives of religions interpret these principles and the way they should be applied.

In this context one needs to be clear about the teachings of Islam. Some analysts in the West take the view that the rapidly growing Muslim population in Europe and the United States, and Islamic revivalism generally, are potential threats to Western culture. The study of Islam demonstrates that this is not a violent doctrine. Islam, like other world religions, is a faith of peace and social justice. In fact, Islam is as universalist as Christianity, and offers generous consolation when it comes to finding purpose and guiding the soul in a confusing world. It does not turn to fundamentalist militancy, because it has always been a tolerant religion and dislikes extremism and killing. Islam does not encourage terrorism and threatening behaviour. These violent concepts do not originate in Islam as a faith. Those groups who practise terror under the flag of Islam are a small minority, rejected by the great majority of Muslims. In relation to aggressive attitudes, the key message to Western scholars is to oppose the extremist Muslims but not blame all Islam.

Today's tensions would lead to tomorrow's aspirations. What we need now is the culture of peace that would help broaden cross-cultural understanding between Islam and the West. With proper knowledge of the culture of the Arab and Muslim worlds, this understanding would help foster tolerance and resolve conflict. We need to 'sustain a diversity of cultures, not a diversity of imagined clashes and conflicts.'

Now that the Muslim world, through Pakistan, has an 'Islamic nuclear bomb', Muslim leadership matters more than ever. There is every likelihood of other Muslim nations joining Pakistan in the near future. The West should not ignore the danger. The world will become an even more dangerous and unstable place.

President [Bill] Clinton predicted that the events of 1998 (when Pakistan/ India exploded nuclear devices) were a foretaste of things to come, that this is the way that the wars of the future will be fought. He may be right. But the response of the Muslim world will depend on whether the militancy model prevails, or that of moderation. Therefore, the need for the West to understand Islam and to actively encourage moderation and democratisation in the Muslim world has again arisen.

Indeed, extremism can best be reduced through gradual democratisation. Efforts should be directed to expedite the transition to democracy in the Muslim world. They should be made to feel that the West is on their side, particularly if the movements that precisely champion the values of democracy arise there.

The New Millennium brings fresh challenges and opportunities in relations between Islam and the West. Religious leaders now must re-establish the will to implement the true essence of their religion and to find those factors which provide common ground with other religions. It is then required for them to initiate dialogue with other religious leaders with the purpose of finding commonalities and joining forces in setting standards for dealing with the wider issues of cultural diversity. It is pointed out that governments must have a strong interest in supporting such moves. Moderate Muslims showed a good example of this recently when they joined in worldwide protests against the action of the Islamicist regime in Afganistan's decision to blow up statues of the Buddha.

This process has to be on-going because as conditions in our world change, so does the need to find new responses. Now we are thinking in terms of 'cultural diversity'. The message is that people are not all the same, but that their differences are of mutual interest; their societies and cultures are often historically interdependent in surprising ways; and that seeking to understand one another is an intrinsically enlightening process whose fruits are material, political and cultural.

POSTSCRIPT

Does Islamic Revivalism Challenge a Stable World Order?

Understanding how Islam sees itself and its place in the world might make us fearful or hopeful. If Islam cannot accommodate to Western, secular values, as Esposito points out, does it challenge a stable world order? Shuja is more hopeful, believing that through a process of political maturation Islamic states may become more fully integrated into an increasingly globalized world civilization. One key is a fuller understanding among Western nations of the goals of Islamic revivalism. Furthermore, the West must understand its own image in the Muslim world and not expect a commitment to secularism that would appear to Muslims as blasphemy. Whether deeper dialogue will bring Islam and the West closer together or push them further apart is not yet clear.

A fascinating survey of how people have perceived God from the time of Abraham to the present can be found in Karen Armstrong, *A History of God* (Ballantine Books, 1993). Since Judaism exists in its own right and is the foundation for both Christianity and Islam, this "4000-year quest" provides insight into key similarities and points of difference. Any good text on world religions will provide an introduction to Islam; particularly accessible is Huston Smith, *Illustrated World's Religions: A Guide to Our Wisdom Traditions* (HarperSanFrancisco, 1994), which is also available on videocassette. Students who have not read the Qur'an might like to explore these scriptures, which are available in English translation in paperback.

The dilemma of becoming modern without becoming Western is addressed by Bernard Lewis in "The West and the Middle East," *Foreign Affairs* (January/February 1997). Other books by Lewis include *Islam and the West* (Oxford University Press, 1993) and *The Middle East: A Brief History of the Last 2,000 Years* (Scribner, 1995).

Director of Columbia University's Middle East Institute Richard Bulliet has written an account of Islam's success among people who live far from the political center, such as those in Iran. In *Islam: The View From the Edge* (Columbia University Press, 1994), Bulliet argues that the origins of today's Islamic resurgence are to be found in the eleventh century. Other books of note are *Orientalism* by Edward Said (Pantheon, 1978) and *Islam and the Cultural Accommodation to Social Change* by Bassam Tibi (Westview Press, 1991). In Francis Fukuyama's influential book *The End of History and the Last Man* (Free Press, 1992), the chapter entitled "The Worldwide Liberal Revolution" considers Islam as an alternative to liberalism and communism.

ISSUE 15

Are Africa's Leaders Responsible for the Continent's Current Problems?

YES: George B. N. Ayittey, from *Africa Betrayed* (St. Martin's Press, 1992)

NO: A. Adu Boahen, from *African Perspectives on Colonialism* (Johns Hopkins University Press, 1987)

ISSUE SUMMARY

YES: Economics professor George B. N. Ayittey states that, since achieving independence, many African countries' interests have been betrayed by their own incompetent, corrupt, power-hungry leaders.

NO: African history professor A. Adu Boahen argues that major problems left to Africa by the departing colonial powers are at the root of many of the continent's current problems.

To say that Africa has been exploited by outsiders throughout its history is an understatement. Beginning with the East and West African slave trades and continuing through the age of imperialism, it is difficult to fathom the price that Africa has had to pay for its geographic location and richness of resources.

When European imperialists invaded Africa in the late nineteenth century, the exploitation was blatant and all-encompassing. Every conceivable reason—economic, political, social, cultural, religious—was used by Europeans to justify their actions. By the time the imperialists were finished carving up the continent, only two states, Ethiopia and Liberia, could be called free and independent nations.

The post–World War II era marked the end of worldwide imperialism. Gradually, most of the continent's nations achieved independence, some peacefully, some through armed resistance or the threat of it. As these former colonies entered nationhood, hopes were high that Africa's future would be a bright and glorious one.

One only needs to look at the continent today, almost a half-century since the demise of colonialism, to see that Africa's problems far outweigh the continent's promise. In a recent civil war in central Africa, where members of the

Hutu tribe murdered so many of the rival Tutsi tribe members, charges of genocide were brought against some Hutus by the International Criminal Tribunal for Rwanda.

When Mobutu Sese Seko, long-time ruler of Zaire (now referred to as the Congo Republic), was finally deposed in 1997, military strongman Laurent Kabila replaced him and did not work hard to bring needed change to one of Africa's wealthiest—and most exploited—nations. Kabila's assassination by a deranged bodyguard in 2001 brought his 29-year-old son Joseph to power. Joseph was placed there by military forces who for days denied Kabila's death until Joseph could be safely ensconced in power. Sadly, little immediate help is likely to come to a nation's people who are so desperate for it.

Also, illnesses caused by *E. coli* bacteria and HIV (human immunodeficiency virus) continue to ravage the continent, causing deaths in epic proportions. Every day 6,000 Africans succumb to AIDS (acquired immunodeficiency syndrome); another 11,000 become HIV infected. And future projections are far worse, for few resources are available to stem this tide of annihilation.

In regard to this myriad of problems throughout the continent, questions need to be answered, one of the most important being: Who or what is responsible for all of this?

It would be hard to find anyone who would state that colonialism was a positive force in the development of Africa or that its negative impact was minimal. Therefore, the standard argument is that many of the continent's problems are part and parcel of the colonial legacy. Recently, however, the focus of attention has turned to many African leaders, who some argue have betrayed their people's trust and exploited their country's wealth in the name of power and self-aggrandizement. Today the continent seems to be filled with military dictators and political tyrants who refuse to serve anyone but themselves and their cronies and who neglect to share power with anyone, including their own people.

The authors of the following selections, George B. N. Ayittey and A. Adu Boahen—both Ghanaians—agree that the colonial legacy was damaging to Africa's people and their interests. Their differences lie in determining who or what is responsible for the continent's current problems. For Ayittey, the answer is simple: African leaders who have come to power since independence have betrayed their own people through usurpation of power, political corruptness, and a failure to enact democratic principles. He finds that the continent today is generally worse off than it was under colonial rule. The policies of the outside world toward Africa have not helped the situation, maintains Ayittey, but the problems that the continent faces today are more internal than external.

Boahen argues that although colonialism made some beneficial achievements possible, on the whole it created a series of political, economic, social, and psychological problems that plague African nations today. African leaders may be responsible for some of the continent's current problems, but some of these woes can be traced back to the legacy that colonialism bequeathed.

Aluta Continua!
(*The Struggle Continues!*)

This [is an attempt] to present the true story about Africa's postcolonial experience. It is a grisly picture of one betrayal after another: economic disintegration, political chaos, inane civil wars, and infrastructural and institutional decay. These were not what Africans hoped for when they asked for their independence from colonial rule in the 1960s. It is difficult to convey their outrage and sense of indignation at the leaders who have failed them.

By the beginning of the 1990s economic and political conditions in Africa had become intolerable. African socialism has been a dismal failure, one-party rule has been a disaster, and international blindness to the nearly universal corruption of the continent's leaders has made matters immeasurably worse.

Various actors, foreign as well as domestic, participated, wittingly or not, in the devastation of Africa. It is easy for African leaders to put the blame somewhere else; for example, on Western aid donors or on an allegedly hostile international economic environment. But as the World Bank observed in its 1984 report, *Toward Sustained Development in Sub-Saharan Africa,* "genuine donor mistakes and misfortunes alone cannot explain the excessive number of 'white elephants'" (p. 24). Certainly, donor blunders and other external factors have contributed to the crisis in Africa, but in my view the internal factors have played a far greater role than the external ones.

Of the internal factors, the main culprit has been the failure of leadership. In many cases African leaders themselves created "black elephants" and state enterprises that were dictated more by considerations of prestige than by concerns for economic efficiency. Mobutu Sese Seko of Zaire once declared, "I know my people. They like grandeur. They want us to have respect abroad in the eyes of other countries" (*The Wall Street Journal,* Oct 15, 1986). Accordingly, half of Zaire's foreign debt of $6 billion went to build two big dams and the Inga-Shaba powerline, as well as a $1 billion double-decked suspension bridge over the Congo River. The upper level is for a railroad that does not exist. In many other cases elite *bazongas* (raiders of the public treasury) blatantly squandered part of the foreign aid money. Does Africa need more foreign aid?

In truth, Africa needs less—not more—foreign aid. David Karanja of Kenya wrote: "Foreign aid has done more harm to Africa than we care to admit. It has led to a situation where Africa has failed to set its own pace and direction of development free of external interference. Today, Africa's development plans are drawn thousands of miles away in the corridors of the IMF and World Bank" (*New African,* Jun 1992; p. 20).

Moreover, there are a number of ways that aid resources Africa desperately needs can be found in Africa itself. Maritu Wagaw wrote: "Let Africa look inside Africa for the solution of its economic problems. Solutions to our predicament should come from within not from outside" (*New African,* Mar 1992; p. 19). Indeed.

First, in 1989 Africa was spending $12 billion annually to import arms and to maintain the military. Second, the elites illegally transferred from Africa at least $15 billion annually during the latter part of the 1980s. Third, at least $5 billion annually could be saved if Africa could feed itself. Foreign exchange saved is foreign exchange earned. Fourth, another $5 billion could be saved from waste and inefficiencies in Africa's 3,200-odd state enterprises. This might entail selling off some of them or placing them under new management. Fifth, the civil wars raging in Africa exact a heavy toll in lost output, economic development, and destroyed property. If Angola's civil war alone cost the country $1 billion annually, $10 billion would not be an unreasonable estimate of the average annual cost of civil wars throughout the continent. Adding up these savings and the foreign exchange generated from internal sources would yield at least $47 billion annually, compared with the $12.4 billion in aid Africa received from all sources in 1990.

A bucket full of holes can only hold a certain amount of water for a certain amount of time. Pouring in more water makes little sense as it will all drain away. To the extent that there are internal leaks in Africa—corruption, senseless civil wars, wasteful military expenditures, capital flight, and government wastes—pouring in more foreign aid is futile. As a first order of priority, the leaks should be plugged to ensure that the little aid that comes in, stays. But African dictators, impervious to reason, continue to wage destructive wars.

In 1990 the OAU [Organization of African Unity] finally began to show signs of awakening from its slumber. Delegates to the OAU summit in July of that year, which Nelson Mandela addressed, observed that the summit demonstrated realism and a laudable determination to make progress in the resolution of Africa's intractable problems. Delegates realized that if Africa is to resist Western pressure for reforms and find its own solutions, it must first put its house in order. There was a genuine desire to end civil wars and disputes between neighbors, to increase regional cooperation, and to advance development.

The delegates signed a declaration, pledging to establish more democracy on the continent. According to the *Washington Times,* the incoming OAU chairman, President Yoweri Museveni of Uganda, averred, "Africa must find African solutions to its problems." Emphasizing that democracy could take many forms, he said that all states must have regular, free elections, a free press, and respect for human rights. In addition, the *Washington Times* reported that Nigerian President Ibrahim Babangida told the assembly that Africa's leaders had failed their people. "Ever since the majority of our countries became independent in the 1960s we have conducted our lives as if the world owes us a living," he said. According to one African political analyst, the delegates realized that "unless they change they won't be coming to any other summits because they will no longer be in power" *(Washington Times,* Jul 13, 1990; p. A11). But rhetoric is one thing and action another.

While the delegates were speaking, the Babangida administration was continuing its crackdown on journalists and anyone suspected to be involved in the abortive April 22, 1990, coup attempt. In Uganda it may be recalled that journalists who put tough questions to visiting President Kaunda were arrested in spite of the free press that President Museveni called for.

If Africa is in a mess, the fault does not lie in any innate inferiority of the African people but rather in the alien, defective political systems instituted across much of the continent. It is not the charisma or the rhetoric of African leaders which makes a political system democratic and accountable. The *institutional approach* . . . is far superior.

Kwame Nkrumah, Julius Nyerere, Kenneth Kaunda and other nationalists were all great heroes with charisma. But they all established regimes which lacked the institutions of a free press, an independent judiciary, freedom of political association, and the most basic standards of accountability. Political systems which lack these institutions have the tendency to produce despots. . . . [V]irtually all African regimes have been characterized by an enormous concentration of both economic and political power in the hands of the state and, therefore, one individual.

Africa has more than its share of civilian autocrats, military dictators, and rapacious elites. . . . Africa's indigenous system of government produced few tyrants. The modern leadership is a far cry from the traditional. In fact, by Africa's indigenous standards the modern leadership in much of Africa has been a disgraceful failure. They refuse to learn and keep repeating not only their own mistakes but those of others as well.

In an address to the Rotary International in Accra, retired Lt. Gen. Emmanuel Erskine, former commander of the United Nations Forces in Lebanon, remarked: "The fact that some African leaders get themselves emotionally identified with their country which they consider their personal property and that they and their minority ethnic clientele should lead the country and that they should rule until death is the single major phenomenon creating serious political crisis on the continent. Not even bulldozers can dislodge some of these leaders from office" (West Africa, May 6–12, 1991; p. 722).

Why African Dictators Cling to Power

[B]etween 1957 and 1990, there were more than 150 African heads of state and only six relinquished power voluntarily. There are three main reasons why African heads of state refuse to step down when their people get fed up with them. First, they somehow get this absurd notion that the country belongs to them and them alone. Witness their pictures on the currency and in every nook and cranny in the country. Every monument or building of some significance is named after them: Houphouet-Boigny this, Houphouet-Boigny that, Moi National Park, and on and on. In Malawi, "President Hastings Kamuzu Banda's face is everywhere, from the buttons on Youth League uniforms to the dresses of dancers. Highways, stadiums and schools are named for him. A national holiday honors him. It is forbidden to call him by his last name; only 'Ngwazi,' meaning lion or protector, or 'the life president' are allowed" *(Washington Post,* May 5, 1992; p. A22).

Second, insecure African heads of state surround themselves with loyal supporters, often drawn from their own tribes: the late Doe from the Krahn tribe, Mobutu of Zaire from the Gbande, Biya of Cameroon from the Bamileke, Moi of Kenya from the Kalenjin and Babangida of Nigeria from the Muslims. In Togoland, about 70 percent of General Eyadema's army were drawn from his own Kabye tribe *(Africa Report,* Jan–Feb 1992; p. 5).

Other supporters are simply bought: soldiers with fat paychecks and perks; urban workers with cheap rice and sardines ("essential commodities"); students with free tuition and hefty allowances; and intellectuals, opposition leaders and lawyers with big government posts and Mercedes-Benzes.

Even when the head of state is contemplating stepping down, these supporters and lackeys fiercely resist any cutbacks in government largesse or any attempt to open up the political system. This was precisely the case in The Gambia when Sir Dawda Jawara—in power since the country's independence in 1965—announced in March 1992 his intention to step down. Freeloaders and patronage junkies urged him to stay on! In Sierra Leone, Mr. Musa Gendemeh, the deputy agriculture minister, was quite explicit. On the BBC "Focus on Africa" program (Apr 24, 1990), he declared that,

> "He won't give up his present privileged position for the sake of a multiparty system nor would one expect a policeman or soldier to give up his one bag of rice at the end of every month for the same. . . .
>
> He warned that anyone talking about another party would be committing treason . . . that ministers and MPs suspected of having something to do with the multiparty movement are now under surveillance . . . and that whenever there has been trouble in the country, his people, the Mende, have suffered the most and he warned them to be careful" *(West Africa,* Jun 4–10, 1990; p. 934).

To protect their perks and benefits, these sycophants lie, deceive, and misinform the head of state. They continually praise him to the sky, even when his own tail is on fire! Kenneth Kaunda was informed that he would have "no problem" winning the October 1991 elections as he had 80 percent of the popular vote and "everything else had been taken care of." But when the actual voting took place, he was resoundingly humiliated, garnering a pitiful 25 percent of the vote. Ghanaians would recall that "party stooges" and "sycophants" also misled Nkrumah. African leaders should remember that "it is better to have wise people reprimand you than have stupid people sing you praises" (Ecclesiastes 7:5).

The third reason why African heads of state are reluctant to relinquish power is *fear.* Many of them have their hands so steeped in blood and their pockets so full of booty that they are afraid all their past gory misdeeds will be exposed. So they cling to power, regardless of the cost and consequences. But eventually they are dislodged, and only few subsequently are able to live peacefully in their own countries, much less to enjoy the loot.

Three Ways of Removing African Tyrants

In the ouster of Africa's dictators, three scenarios have emerged since 1990. By the "Doe scenario," those leaders who foolishly refused to accede to popular demands for democracy only did so at their own peril and at the destruction of their countries: Doe of Liberia, Traore of Mali, Barre of Somalia and Mengistu of Ethiopia. (Doe was killed in September 1990; Barre fled Mogadishu in a tank in January 1991; and Mengistu to Zimbabwe in February 1991.) African countries where this scenario is most likely to be repeated are Algeria, Cameroon, Djibouti, Equatorial Guinea, Libya, Malawi, Sudan, Tunisia, and Uganda.

In the "Kerekou scenario," those African leaders who wisely yielded to popular pressure managed to save not only their own lives but their countries as well: Kerekou of Benin, Kaunda of Zambia, Sassou-Nguesso of Central African Republic, and Pereira of Cape Verde Islands. Unfortunately, they are the exceptions.

The "Eyadema scenario," the third, is by far the most common. In this scenario, they yield initially after considerable domestic and international pressure but then attempt to manipulate the rules and the transition process to their advantage, believing that they could fool their people. In the end, they only fool themselves and are thrown out of office in disgrace. African countries likely to follow this route are: Angola, Burkina Faso, Burundi, Ghana, Ivory Coast, Kenya, Mozambique, Nigeria, Rwanda, Sierra Leone, Tanzania, Zaire, Zambia, and Zimbabwe. Recent events in Togo and Zaire also show that the outcome of the Eyadema scenario is highly unpredictable and its impact on economic development deleterious. Political uncertainty discourages business investment and trade....

Education of Opposition Leaders

It is sad and painful to admit that the level of political sophistication and intellectual maturity of some of our opposition leaders is disgustingly low. All opposition groups and leaders must recognize that the political arena is a free marketplace and they are like merchants, peddling political ideas and solutions. If they demand the right to propagate their political philosophy, they cannot deny anyone else the right to do so. If their philosophy has any merit, the people will buy it. If not, they will reject it. It is not up to the opposition leaders to make this determination, but the people.

Furthermore, most opposition leaders define "democracy" only in terms of their right to form political parties, to hold rallies, and to criticize foolish government policies.... [I]nstitutions such as the rule of law, freedom of expression, and an independent judiciary are far more important.

Focus

The primary focus of all opposition groups in Africa should be on removing the tyrant in power and establishing a level political playing field. If the tyrant is crafting a dubious transition process, the focus should be on halting or changing that process. All other issues (such as who should be president, what type of ideology the country should follow, a political platform, whether the country should have a new currency or flag) are secondary.

The Covenant

Quite clearly, the opposition in Africa needs to "get its act together." One effective way of doing this is to draw up a covenant, a set of rules by which all opposition groups agree to abide. At a meeting of all opposition leaders, a covenant should be signed containing the following stipulations:

1. Politics is a competitive game, and therefore the rules of competition must be established and respected by all. The term of the president will be limited to two terms (of four years each) in office.
2. All must agree on the safeguards and the necessary structures to be adopted to ensure free and fair elections. Political maturity requires accepting electoral defeat graciously and congratulating the winner. Political violence and voter intimidation must be eschewed. Severe sanctions, such as disqualification or heavy fines, must be imposed against any political party that is guilty of murder of political opponents.
3. Ultimately, it is the African people themselves who must determine what is best for them; not what one person imposes upon them. To do this, the African people need the means and the forum as well as the freedom to participate in the decisionmaking process.
4. Each opposition leader must agree to respect and honor the OAU's Charter of People's and Human Rights. This Charter is explicit on freedom of expression, freedom from arbitrary arrests, press freedoms, and so forth.
5. No one person or party shall monopolize the means or the forum by which the people can participate. All leaders will undertake to respect the right of every African to air his opinion freely, without harassment or intimidation, even if his view diverges from that of the head of state. Tolerance of diversity of opinion is a sign of intellectual maturity.
6. The media shall be taken out of the hands of the government. Religion and foreign ideology must be kept out of government. All leaders must pledge to build on or improve Africa's indigenous institutions and culture.
7. All must agree on sanctions to be applied against any leader or political party acting in violation of this covenant. Such sanctions must be determined by the leaders themselves.

After all is said and done, it becomes apparent that it is the educated elites —the leaders and the intellectuals—who have failed Africa. The Vai of Liberia have a proverb most appropriate for this situation. If after spending their meager savings to educate a child, he returns to the village an ignoramus, Vais elders may look upon him and ruefully remark: "The moon shines brightly but it is still dark in some places." Doesn't this describe postcolonial Africa and its elites?

Common sense has probably been the scarcest commodity among the elite in postcolonial Africa. Most of the "educated" leaders lacked it, intellectuals flouted it, and the opposition, in many cases, was woefully deficient in it. The peasants may be "illiterate and backward," but at least they can use their common sense. Obviously, a *common sense revolution* is what is urgently needed in African government....

While battling current despots, Africans should be vigilant, think ahead, and formulate strategies against the next buffoon. Since the winds of democratic change began sweeping across Africa in 1990, all sorts of intellectual crackpots, corrupt former politicians, charlatans, and unsavory elements have suddenly jumped on to the "democracy bandwagon" to hijack the democratic revolution. In 1992, Kaunda, and Nyerere, for example, were all preaching multiparty democracy. Where were they back in 1985 when true democrats were laying their lives on the line to demand political pluralism?... The African story is one of betrayal—by one buffoon after another.

NO

A. Adu Boahen

The Colonial Impact

Nothing has become more controversial now than the question of the nature of the impact of colonialism on Africa. Many European and Eurocentric historians—such as L. H. Gann, P. Duignan, Margery Perham, P. C. Lloyd, and more recently D. K. Fieldhouse—have contended that the impact was both positive and negative, with positive aspects far outweighing the negative ones. Gann and Duignan, who appear to have devoted themselves to the defense of colonialism in Africa, concluded in 1967 that "the imperial system stands out as one of the most powerful engines for cultural diffusion in the history of Africa; its credit balance far outweighs its debit account."

Other historians—mainly African, black, and Marxist scholars and especially the development and the underdevelopment theorists—have maintained that colonialism made no positive impact on Africa. The great exponents of this rather extreme position are Walter Rodney, the black Guianese historian and activist, and the Ugandan historian T. B. Kabwegyere. According to the former, "the argument suggests that, on the one hand, there was exploitation and oppression but on the other hand colonial governments did much for the benefit of Africans and they developed Africa. It is our contention that this is completely false. Colonialism had only one hand—it was a one-armed bandit." Before deciding one way or the other, let us examine the colonial balance sheet in the political, social, and economic fields.

The first obvious positive political legacy was undoubtedly the establishment of continuous peace and stability in Africa, especially after the First World War. Let me hasten to add, first, that Africa was certainly not in a Hobbesian state of nature at the dawn of the colonial era and, secondly, that the first three decades of the colonial era... introduced into Africa far more violence, instability, anarchy, and loss of African lives than probably any other period in its history. The population of the Belgian Congo fell by 50 percent, and that of the Herero by 80 percent, as a result of the oppressive and inhuman treatment of the Africans by the colonizers during the period. There is no doubt, however, that after the wars of occupation and the repression of African opposition and resistance, an era of continuous peace, order, and stability set in. This certainly facilitated and accelerated the economic and social changes that occurred on the continent during the colonial period.

The second positive political impact has been the very appearance of the independent African states of today. The partition of Africa by the imperial colonial powers led ultimately to the establishment of some forty-eight new states, most of them with clearly defined boundaries, in place of the existing innumerable lineage and clan groups, city-states, kingdoms, and empires without any fixed boundaries. It is significant that the boundaries of these states have been maintained ever since independence.

However, the creation of the states has proved to be more of a liability than an asset to the present independent African nations. Had the boundaries of these states been laid down in accordance with any well-defined, rational criteria and in full cognizance of the ethnocultural, geographical, and ecological realities of Africa, the outcome would have been wholesome. Unfortunately, many of these boundaries were arbitrarily drawn on African maps in the chancelleries of the imperial powers in Europe. The result has been that most of these states are artificial creations, and this very artificiality has created very serious problems, many of which have still not been solved. One of these problems is that of nation-state building. Because of the artificiality of these boundaries, each independent African state is made up of a whole host of different ethnocultural groups and nations having different historical traditions and cultures and speaking different languages. One can imagine, then, how stupendous the problem of developing the independent states of Africa into true nation-states is.

A second problem has been that of interstate boundary disputes. Not only did these artificial boundaries create multi-ethnic states, but worse still, they often run across preexisting nations, ethnicities, states, kingdoms, and empires....

A third problem has been the uneven sizes and unequal natural resources and economic potentialities of these states. Some of the states that emerged from the partition were really giants, like the Sudan, with an area of approximately 967,000 square miles, Zaire with 906,000, Algeria with 920,000, and Nigeria with 357,000; others were midgets, like the Gambia, with a total area of 4,000 square miles, and Lesotho and Burundi with 11,000 each. Moreover, some states have miles and miles of coastline, while others are landlocked, with no access to the sea.... Some have very fertile lands and several mineral resources, but others... are mere desert. Finally, while some states, like the Gambia and Somalia, have only a border or two to police, others have four or more, and Zaire has seven. Here, again, how can such handicapped states solve their problems of development? How can a state without access to the sea or without fertile land really develop? Can one imagine the problems of security and of smuggling confronting these states with so many borders to patrol?

The third positive political impact of colonialism was its introduction into Africa of two new institutions—a new bureaucracy of civil servants and a new judicial system. On the first score, the contribution of the Europeans was uneven: the British bequeathed a far better trained and numerically stronger civil service to its former colonies than the French, while the record of the Belgians and the Portuguese is the worst in this field. However, the judicial systems, bequeathed by the colonial administrations, have not undergone any fundamental changes in any of the independent African states.

Another positive colonial impact was the generation of a sense of nationalism as well as the intensification of the spirit of Pan-Africanism. The colonial system generated a sense of identity and consciousness among the different ethnic groups of each colonial state, while the anticolonial literary activities of some of the educated Africans and more especially the Fascist attack on Ethiopia and the connivance of the other European imperial powers diffused and strengthened the spirit of Pan-Africanism throughout the black world.

But it should be immediately pointed out that African nationalism was one of the accidental by-products of colonialism. No colonial power ever deliberately set out to generate or promote that consciousness. Moreover, the nationalism that was generated by colonialism was not a positive but a negative one, arising out of the sense of anger, frustration, and humiliation produced by the oppressive, discriminatory, and exploitative measures and activities of the colonial administrators. It is rather unfortunate that with the overthrow of colonialism, this negative sentiment of nationalism or, rather, anticolonialism has almost lost its cohesive force. Independent African states are therefore now saddled with the crucial problem of how to forge a new and more positive force of nationalism in place of the negative one generated by colonialism, or, as Ali Mazrui and M. Tidy have recently put it, how to move "from modern nationalism to modern nationhood."

Another political legacy bequeathed to independent African states was the professional army. In traditional Africa, there were hardly any full-time, standing armies. In the whole of West Africa, it was probably only the kings of Dahomey and Samori Ture who developed real full-time, well-trained armies. However, all the imperial powers developed professional armies, which they used first to occupy and police their colonies, then in the First and Second World Wars, and finally in the campaigns against African independence; and these armies were among the most conspicuous legacies apart from physical structures bequeathed to independent African states. And what a legacy these armies have turned out to be! In retrospect, they have become nothing but a chronic source of instability, confusion, and anarchy as a result of their often unnecessary and unjustifiable interventions in the political processes of African countries. Indeed, African armies are the greatest millstones around the necks of African leaders, and the future of the continent is going to be determined very much on how these armies are dealt with.

The final political impact—and a very negative and regrettable one—is the delay that colonialism caused in the political development and maturity of African states. If colonialism meant anything at all politically, it was the loss of sovereignty and independence by the colonized peoples. This loss of sovereignty, in turn, implied the loss of the right of a state to control its own destiny; to plan its own development; to decide which outside nations to borrow from or associate with or emulate; to conduct its own diplomacy and international relations; and above all, to manage or even mismanage its own affairs, derive pride and pleasure from its successes, and derive lessons, frustrations, and experience from its failures. As Rodney has pointed out, the seventy-year colonial era was one of the most dynamic and scientific periods in world history. It was the period, for instance, that witnessed Europe's entry into the age of the motor vehicle, of the airplane, and finally of nuclear power. Had African states been in control of their own destinies . . . there is no reason why, judging from the very healthy and promising trends . . . , they could not also have followed the Japanese mode, as indeed some of their educated sons, like Mensah Sarbah and the Malagasi scholar Ravelojaona, were advocating. But colonialism completely isolated and insulated Africa from all these changes. It is in this loss of sovereignty and the consequent isolation from the outside world that one finds one of the most pernicious impacts of colonialism on Africa and one of the fundamental causes of its present underdevelopment and technological backwardness.

The impact of colonialism in the economic field, as in the political field, was clearly a mixed one. The most important economic benefit was the provision of an infrastructure of roads, railways, harbors, the telegraph, and the telephone. The basic infrastructure of every modern African state was completed during the colonial period, and in most countries, not even a mile of railroad has been constructed since independence. A second important economic impact was the development of the primary sector of Africa's economy. It was during this period that the mineral potential of many African countries was discovered and modern scientific mining introduced. Above all, it was during this period that the production of such cash crops as cotton, peanuts, palm oil, coffee, tobacco, rubber, and cocoa, became the main feature of the political economy of many an African state.

These fundamental economic changes, in turn, had some far-reaching consequences. In the first place, land acquired great commercial value and assumed far greater importance than it had ever had before. Secondly, the spread of cash-crop agriculture enabled Africans of whatever social status, and especially rural Africans in many regions, to acquire wealth and raise their standard of living. Another significant impact was the spread and consolidation of the money economy in Africa and with it not only a change in the traditional standards of wealth and status but also a phenomenal increase (as will be seen [in subsequent sections]) in the class of wage earners and salaried persons. In the wake of the money economy came the banking activities which have become such a feature in the economies of independent African states. The sum total of all these colonial economic reforms was what has been described by economists as the completion of the integration of the African economy into the world economy in general and into the capitalist economy of the former colonial powers in particular.

But the economic changes introduced by colonialism had a negative side also. First, the transportation and communications infrastructure that was provided was not only inadequate but was also very unevenly distributed in nearly all the colonies. The roads and railways were by and large constructed to link areas with the potential for cash crops and with mineral deposits with the sea or the world commodity market. In other words, the infrastructures were meant to facilitate the exploitation of the natural resources but not to promote the accessibility and development of all regions of the colony. The outcome of this has been uneven regional economic development in most African countries, still a major stumbling block in the way of nation-building in Africa today.

Secondly, the colonial system led to the delay of industrial and technological developments in Africa. As has been pointed out already, one of the typical features of the colonial political economy was the total neglect of industrialization and of the processing of locally produced raw materials and agricultural products in the colonies. It should not be forgotten that before the colonial period, Africans were producing their own building materials, their pottery and crockery, their soap, beads, iron tools, and especially cloth; above all, they were producing the gold that was exported to Europe and the Mediterranean world. Had the traditional production techniques in all these areas been modernized and had industrialization been promoted, African industrial and technological development would have commenced much earlier than it did. But they were not. Instead, preexisting industries were almost all eradicated by the importation of cheap and even better substitutes from Europe and India, while Africans were driven out of the mining industry as it became an exclusive preserve of Europeans. This neglect of industrialization, destruction of the existing industries and handicrafts in Africa, and elimination of Africans from the mining field further explain Africa's present technological backwardness.

Thirdly, colonialism saddled most colonies with monocrop economies. During the colonial period, as may be recalled, each colony was made to produce a single cash crop or two, and no attempts were made to diversify the agricultural economy. The habit of producing these single cash crops appears to have become so ingrained that it has not been changed to any appreciable degree since independence. The other consequence of this concentration on the production of cash crops for export was the neglect of the internal sector of the economy and, in particular, of the production of food for internal consumption, so that rice, maize, fish, and other foods had to be imported. Thus, during the colonial period, Africans were encouraged to produce what they did not consume and to consume what they did not produce, a clear proof of the exploitative nature of the colonial political economy. It is lamentable that this legacy has not changed materially in most African countries. To this day, they have to rely on the importation of rice, maize, edible oil, flour, and other foodstuffs to survive.

Nor did the commercialization of land turn out to be an unqualified asset. In its trail followed a whole series of litigations over the ownership of land, which caused widespread poverty, especially among the ruling houses and landowning families. Again, litigation over land has continued to this day.

Colonialism also put an end to inter-African trade. I pointed out [elsewhere] that on the eve of the imperial scramble and occupation, the commercial unification of the African continent had been completed. There is no doubt that Africans would have continued to trade among themselves as they had been doing from time immemorial. One of the consequences of this interregional and intraregional trade would have been the continuing spread of, say, the Swahili language and culture in eastern and central Africa, the Hausa language and culture in western Africa, and the Arabic language and culture in northern Africa. What a beneficial development this would have been for the whole continent!

But colonialism put an end to all this. The new artificial boundaries not only divided peoples but also blocked the centuries-old transregional and regional caravan routes. Trading between even members of the same ethnic group on either side of new borders suddenly became no longer trading but smuggling, which was heavily punished. On the contrary, the flow of trade in each colony was now oriented to the relevant metropolitan country. The sad thing is that even after twenty years of independence, this orientation has not ended, thanks to the neocolonialist activities of the former metropolitan countries and their African allies.

Finally, the monetary policies pursued by all the colonial powers must be held partly responsible for the present underdeveloped state of the continent. Under these policies, all the colonial currencies were tied to those of the metropolitan countries, and all their foreign exchange earnings were kept in the metropolitan countries and not used for internal development. The expatriate commercial banks and companies were also allowed to repatriate their deposits, savings, and profits instead of reinvesting them in the colonies for further development. The consequence of all this was that at the time of independence, no African state apart from the Union of South Africa had the strong economic or industrial base needed for a real economic takeoff. And if this base could not be provided during the eighty-year period of colonial rule, should we expect it to have been done in twenty years of independence, especially in the light of the changing international economic order? . . .

But the last and the most serious negative impact of colonialism has been psychological. This is seen, first, in the creation of a colonial mentality among educated Africans in particular and also among the populace in general. This mentality manifests itself in the condemnation of anything traditional, in the preference for imported goods to locally manufactured goods (since independence), and in the style of dress—such as the wearing of three-piece suits in a climate where temperatures routinely exceed eighty degrees Fahrenheit. Above all, it manifests itself in the belief so prevalent among Africans, both literate and illiterate, that government and all public property and finance belong, not to the people, but to the colonial government, and could and should therefore be taken advantage of at the least opportunity, a belief which leads to the often reckless dissipation and misuse of public funds and property.

Another psychological impact is apparent in ostentatious and flamboyant life-styles, especially on the part of the elite and businessmen. All this arose from the fact that while the colonialists taught their colonial subjects the Protestant work ethic, the drive for worldly success, and the acquisitive instinct, they did not, for obvious reasons, inculcate in them the puritanical spirit which emphasized frugality and very little consumption. In other words, colonialism taught its subjects only part of the puritanical lesson of "make money," not the full one of "make money but do not spend it," which, according to Ali Mazrui, "seemed to be the ultimate commercial imperative operating within the Protestant ethic." Thus, while in Europe this full ethic led to the rise of capitalism, as both [Max] Weber and [Richard H.] Tawney have clearly shown, and with it the scientific and technological breakthrough, in the African colonies it only generated the ostentatious consumption habits which are still very much with us.

The final and worst psychological impact has been the generation of a deep feeling of inferiority as well as the loss of a sense of human dignity among Africans. Both complexes were surely the outcome not only of the wholesale condemnation of everything African already referred to but, above all, of the practice of racial discrimination and the constant humiliation and oppression to which Africans were subjected throughout the colonial period. The sense of human dignity seems to have been regained, but the feeling of inferiority has not entirely disappeared even after two decades of independence.

It should be obvious from the above, then, that all those historians who see colonialism as a "one-armed bandit" are totally wrong. Equally guilty of exaggeration are those colonial apologists who see colonialism as an unqualified blessing for Africa as well as those who see its record as a balanced one. Colonialism definitely did have its credit and debit sides, but quite clearly the debit side far outweighs the credit side. Indeed, my charge against colonialism is not that it did not do anything for Africa, but that it did so little and that little so accidentally and indirectly; not that the economy of Africa under colonialism did not grow but that it grew more to the advantage of the colonial powers and the expatriate owners and shareholders of the companies operating in Africa than to the Africans; not that improvements did not take place in the lives of the African peoples but that such improvements were so limited and largely confined to the urban areas; not that education was not provided but that what was provided was so inadequate and so irrelevant to the needs and demands of the African themselves; not that there was no upward social mobility but that such a relatively small number of Africans did get to the top. In short, given the opportunities, the resources, and the power and influence of the colonial rulers, they could and should have done far more than they did for Africa. And it is for this failure that the colonial era will go down in history as a period of wasted opportunities, of ruthless exploitation of the resources of Africa, and on balance of the underdevelopment and humiliation of the peoples of Africa. . . .

In the light of all the above, we may safely conclude that though colonialism was a mere episode lasting no more than a hundred years anywhere in Africa, it was nonetheless an extremely important one. It marks a clear watershed in the history of the continent, and Africa's subsequent development is bound to be very much determined by some of its legacies. Ali Mazrui has recently speculated that "African culture may reclaim its own and help Africa retreat back to its ancestral authenticity, or Africa may struggle to find a third way." I do not agree with the first alternative, since any such retreat is exceedingly unlikely if not utterly impracticable. I find the second alternative more realistic, but even here, I am convinced that any third way that would be found would still bear some of the impregnations and scars of colonialism. It would be most expedient, then, for African leaders to take the colonial impact very much into account in the formulation of their future development programs and strategies.

POSTSCRIPT

Are Africa's Leaders Responsible for the Continent's Current Problems?

$\mathbf{A}$good way to approach this subject is to identify the problems facing Africa today and to use contemporary sources to determine responsibility for them.

Problem 1: As evidenced by the massacre in Rwanda of Tutsi tribe members by Hutus, long-standing tribal differences still plague Africa today. Who or what is responsible for this situation: the leaders who permitted it to happen or the circumstances that placed rival tribes in the same country? For information see Francis M. Deng, "Ethnicity: An African Predicament," *Brookings Review* (Summer 1997) and Leo J. DeSouza, "Assigning Blame in Rwanda: How to Break the Cycle of Revenge in Ethnic Conflict," *Washington Monthly* (September 1997).

Problem 2: Most African nations achieved independence in the 1955–1975 period. Since then they have been ignored by the West (including the United States) for a variety of reasons. Consult William Minter, "America and Africa: Beyond the Double Standard," *Current History* (May 2000); John Stremlau, "Ending Africa's Wars," *Foreign Affairs* (July–August 2000); Balih Booker, "Thinking Regionally About Africa," *Current History* (May 1998); and Silih Booker, "Bush's Global Agenda: Bad News for Africa," *Current History* (May 2001).

Problem 3: Western aid, given to African nations since independence, has mainly gone to strong military dictators because of their staunch opposition to communism. To use the Congo Republic as a case study, see Herbert Weiss, "Civil War in the Congo," *Society* (March 2001) and Norimitsu Onishi, "Death in Congo," *New York Times Upfront* (March 5, 2000).

Problem 4: The AIDS epidemic threatens to overwhelm Africa's limited financial resources and requires a large infusion of foreign assistance to keep up with it. Refer to Sandra L. Thurman, "Joining Forces to Fight HIV and AIDS," *The Washington Quarterly* (Winter 2001) and Stephen Morrison, "The African Pandemic Hits Washington," *The Washington Quarterly* (Winter 2001).

Problem 5: Globalization and resultant economic policies have proven to be of little benefit to Africa. See Olufemi Vaughan, "The Politics of Global Marginalization," *Journal of Asian and African Studies* (November 2000).

Problem 6: African leaders are the continent's most significant current problem. Consult Marina Ottaway, "Africa's 'New Leaders': African Solution or African Problem?" *Current History* (May 1998); Dan Connell and Frank Smyth, "Africa's New Bloc," *Foreign Affairs* (March–April 1998); Joel D. Barkin and David F. Gordon, "Democracy in Africa: No Time to Forsake It," *Foreign Affairs* (July/August 1998); and Anver Versi, "On Knocking African Leaders," *African Business* (February 1998).

Problem 7: Africa's future is a bleak and pessimistic one. Refer to Steven Friedman, "Agreeing to Differ: African Democracy, Its Obstacles and Prospects,"

Social Research (Fall 1999); John W. De Gruchy, "Christian Witness at a Time of African Renaissance," *The Ecumenical Review* (October 1997); and Abiodun Onadipe, "Africa: Building on Hopes?" *Contemporary Review* (February 2000).

Exploring these problems will not only help to cover the questions posed by this issue, it will also expand knowledge of contemporary Africa in areas separate from, but certainly related to, these problems.

ISSUE 16

Were Ethnic Leaders Responsible for the Death of Yugoslavia?

YES: Warren Zimmermann, from *Origins of a Catastrophe* (Times Books, 1996)

NO: Steven Majstorovic, from "Ancient Hatreds or Elite Manipulation? Memory and Politics in the Former Yugoslavia," *World Affairs* (Spring 1997)

ISSUE SUMMARY

YES: Career diplomat Warren Zimmermann, the United States' last ambassador to Yugoslavia, argues that the republic's ethnic leaders, especially Slobodan Milosevic, bear primary responsibility for the nation's demise.

NO: Political science professor Steven Majstorovic contends that while manipulation by elite ethnic leaders played a role in the death of Yugoslavia, the fragile ethnic divisions, formed by memory and myth, also played an important role in the country's demise.

It is not often that the world can witness the death of a country, but that is precisely what many say we witnessed in the 1990s with the passing of Yugoslavia. In a graduated series of events, various areas broke from the Yugoslav republic until only Serbia and Montenegro remained. This was only the latest move in the complex and confusing game of Balkan politics.

Because of its volatile history, the Balkans were once referred to as Europe's "powder keg." The area's history began when the Balkans were settled by the southern branch of the Slavic family tree a millennium ago. During Europe's medieval period, Serbs, Croats, and Bosnians established ethnic kingdoms, which were soon overrun and conquered by the forces of the Ottoman Empire, which maintained control over part of the area for almost 500 years. When Ottoman power began to erode in the eighteenth and nineteenth centuries, one result was a gradual loss of Turkish control over their Balkan lands. The Ottomans were replaced by the Austrian Hapsburg Empire, one of their traditional rivals. While many of the Slavic citizens preferred a Christian-based rule to a Muslim one, some would only be satisfied with independence accomplished along ethnic lines.

Balkan opposition to Hapsburg hegemony manifested itself in June 1914, when the heir to the Hapsburg Empire was assassinated by a Serbian nationalist group. This event proved to be the immediate cause of World War I, as Europe's nations blundered into a costly conflict. (For background information on World War I and its causes, see Issue 8 in this volume.)

At the war's conclusion, the victorious Allies decided that the solution to the Balkan quagmire was a federal republic comprising the disparate ethnic and religious groups, many of whom had been there for a thousand years. Thus, Serbs, Croats, Slovenes, Bosnians, Herzegovenians, Montenegrins, Ottomans, Macedonians, and Albanians were asked to live together in the new nation of Yugoslavia.

The nation's initial period of establishment was brief, as World War II brought Nazi occupation to Yugoslavia. Complicating things further was the fact that while most "Yugoslavs" fought against the German occupation, others (Croats and Bosnian-Herzegovinians) actually collaborated with the Nazis, resulting in numerous atrocities. The main victims would be the Jews and the Serbs, many of whom were massacred by the Croat Ustashas and their Nazi cohorts. The Serbs would not forget this.

After the war, Yugoslavia once again became a federal republic, with separate states established in Slovenia, Croatia, Bosnia-Herzegovina, Serbia, Montenegro, and Macedonia. Its leader was Josip Broz (Tito), a World War II hero to many, whose leadership held the republic together until his death in 1980. The gradual decline of Yugoslavia began in the 1980s; by 1995 it had virtually disintegrated.

The problems that brought about Yugoslavia's disintegration are many. The ancient ethnic rivalries and conflicts were extremely difficult to overcome. Complicating matters were the religious differences, with Eastern Christian Orthodoxy, Roman Catholicism, and Islam claiming the allegiance of the area's peoples. And of course there is the history—who did what to whom and when they did it—which has influenced the myths and realities of the Balkan landscape.

Contemporary leaders of Yugoslavia during the post–Tito era represented neither ideology nor country, but ethnic constituencies. They acted on the latter's behalf in their own quest for power. To what extent are these leaders personally responsible for Yugoslavia's demise? Or, was the country eventually doomed to failure by ethno-religious-historical forces beyond anyone's control?

Two responses regarding who and what was responsible for the demise of Yugoslavia are expressed by Warren Zimmermann and Steven Majstorovic in the following selections. Zimmermann holds the former Yugoslavia's ethnic leaders primarily responsible for the country's demise. Majstorovic accepts that "elite manipulation" played a role in Yugoslavia's demise, but he states that the "ancient hatreds" that have become embedded in the Balkan psyches are difficult to ignore as factors.

Warren Zimmermann

Origins of a Catastrophe

Preface

This is a story with villains—villains guilty of destroying the multiethnic state of Yugoslavia, of provoking three wars, and of throwing some twenty million people into a distress unknown since the Second World War. How could this tragedy have happened to a country that by most standards was more prosperous and more open than any other in Eastern Europe? My thesis is that the Yugoslav catastrophe was not mainly the result of ancient ethnic or religious hostilities, nor of the collapse of communism at the end of the cold war, nor even of the failures of the Western countries. Those factors undeniably made things worse. But Yugoslavia's death and the violence that followed resulted from the conscious actions of nationalist leaders who coopted, intimidated, circumvented, or eliminated all opposition to their demagogic designs. Yugoslavia was destroyed from the top down.

This [selection] is primarily about those destroyers. As American ambassador between 1989 and 1992, I saw them frequently and came to know them well. Speaking with me before their faces had become familiar to Western television viewers, they hadn't yet learned the full panoply of defenses against questions from foreigners. They described their plans, sometimes honestly, sometimes deceitfully, but always passionately and with a cynical disregard for playing by any set of rules. This record of their words and actions provides evidence for a coroner's report on the death of Yugoslavia....

The prime agent of Yugoslavia's destruction was Slobodan Milošević, president of Serbia. Milošević claimed to defend Yugoslavia even as he spun plans to turn it into a Serb-dominated dictatorship. His initial objective was to establish Serbian rule over the whole country. When Slovenia and Croatia blocked this aim by deciding to secede, the Serbian leader fell back on an alternative strategy. He would bring all of Yugoslavia's Serbs, who lived in five of its six republics, under the authority of Serbia, that is, of himself.

Milošević initiated this strategy in Croatia, using the Yugoslav army to seal off Serbian areas from the reach of Croatian authority. His plan in Bosnia was even bolder—to establish by force a Serbian state on two-thirds of the territory of a republic in which Serbs weren't even a plurality, much less a majority.

In league with Radovan Karadžić, the Bosnian Serb leader with whom he later broke, Milošević was responsible for the deaths of tens of thousands of Bosnians and for the creation of the largest refugee population in Europe since the Second World War.

Franjo Tudjman, elected president of Croatia in 1990, also played a leading role in the destruction of Yugoslavia. A fanatic Croatian nationalist, Tudjman hated Yugoslavia and its multiethnic values. He wanted a Croatian state for Croatians, and he was unwilling to guarantee equal rights to the 12 percent of Croatia's citizens who were Serbs. Tudjman's arrogance in declaring independence without adequate provisions for minority rights gave Milošević and the Yugoslav army a pretext for their war of aggression in Croatia in 1991. And Tudjman's greed in seeking to annex Croatian areas of Bosnia prolonged the war and increased the casualties in that ill-starred republic.

Slovenian nationalism was different from the Serbian or Croatian sort. With a nearly homogeneous population and a location in the westernmost part of Yugoslavia, Slovenia was more democratically inclined and more economically developed than any other republic in Yugoslavia. The Slovenes wanted to be free of the poverty and intrigue of the rest of Yugoslavia. They particularly detested Milošević, charging him with making Yugoslavia uninhabitable for non-Serbs. Under the presidency of Milan Kučan—a conflicted figure buffeted toward secession by the winds of Slovenian politics—Slovenia unilaterally declared its independence on June 25, 1991. The predictable result, irresponsibly disregarded by Kučan and the other Slovene leaders, was to bring war closer to Croatia and Bosnia. . . .

Decline . . .

A law graduate of Belgrade University, Milošević began his career as a communist apparatchik with an authoritarian personality already noticed by schoolmates. He was too young and too junior to have been close to [Josip Broz] Tito, but he was old enough (thirty-eight when Tito died) to have prospered in the Titoist system. I never saw in him the personal animus against Tito that many other Serbs felt. In fact, on my first visit to his office I noticed a large painting of Tito behind his desk; significantly, he took it down in 1991, the year Yugoslavia fell apart.

As he cultivated a nationalist persona, Milošević dropped the external aspects of his communist formation. He purged himself of the wooden language that makes communists the world over such hapless communicators. He dropped all references to communism. And he renamed the League of Communists of Serbia the Serbian Socialist Party.

In two ways, however, Milošević failed to break the ties. The first was his continued reliance on communist techniques of control over his party, the Serbian police, the media, and the economic sector. The second was his highly visible wife, Mirjana Marković, a Belgrade University professor and frequent author of turgid Leninist essays in glossy Serbian magazines. Marković flaunted her communism; in fact, she cofounded a communist party in 1990. She was thought to have the influence of a Lady Macbeth over her husband, particularly with regard to his frequent abrupt dismissals of hitherto trusted subordinates. Liberal Serbs described her variously as flaky, crafty, amoral, or vicious.

Whatever his real views of Tito, Milošević was nevertheless the vessel for the Serbian claim that Tito had denied Serbs the role to which destiny had entitled them. The charge may have been partly true, but it was certainly exaggerated. Serbs were a major element of Tito's partisan army during World War II, including its first two elite units, and played a prominent role in the Yugoslav army and police afterward. At his death, however, Tito left Yugoslavia so decentralized that no ethnic group—and certainly not the Serbs—could possibly dominate it. Given Serbian messianism, it became inevitable that a Serbian nationalist would rise up to redress the imagined wrongs dealt his nation. It was a tragedy for Serbia, its neighbors, and Europe as a whole that this nationalist turned out to be Slobodan Milošević. . . .

Milošević deploys his arguments with force and apparent conviction. They're always internally consistent, even when based on fallacies or delusions. "You see, Mr. Zimmermann," he would say, "only we Serbs really believe in Yugoslavia. We're not trying to secede like the Croats and Slovenes, we're not tied to a foreign country like the Albanians in Kosovo, and we're not trying to create an Islamic state like the Muslims in Bosnia. They all fought against you in World War II. We were your allies." . . .

In my view, Milošević is an opportunist rather than an ideologue, a man driven by power rather than nationalism. In the late 1980s he was a communist official in search of a legitimation less disreputable than communism, an alternative philosophy to help him consolidate his hold on Serbia, and a myth that would excite and energize Serbs behind him. He calculated that the way to achieve and maintain power in Serbia was to seize the nationalist pot that Serbian intellectuals were brewing and bring it to a boil.

I don't see Milošević as the same kind of ethnic exclusivist as Croatia's President Franjo Tudjman, who dislikes Serbs, or Bosnian Serb politician Radovan Karadžić, who hates everybody who isn't a Serb. Milošević felt no discomfort in bragging to me, no matter how fraudulently, about Serbia as a multiethnic paradise. Nor, I'm sure, did it disturb his conscience to move ruthlessly against Serbian nationalists like Karadžić when they got in his way. He has made a compact with nationalism as a way to bring him power. He can't break the compact without causing political damage to himself, but it has a utilitarian rather than an emotional value for him.

I can't recall ever seeing a cooler politician under pressure than Slobodan Milošević. In March 1991 he lunched with me and six other Western ambassadors. The meeting came during one of the most explosive crises of his political career. The week before, he had weathered the largest street demonstration ever mounted against his rule, had lost a bid to overthrow the leaderships of Slovenia and Croatia, and was in the process of trying to destroy the presidency of Yugoslavia.

He had come to our lunch from a four-hour meeting with hostile Belgrade University students. Yet he looked and acted as if nothing gave him greater pleasure than to sit down for a long conversation with us. He addressed all our questions with equanimity, asserting with good humor that the Kosovo Albanians were the most pampered minority in Europe, that street demonstrations (which had brought him to power) were wrong, and that Serbia had the freest media and the freest election system in Yugoslavia.

As I pondered the surreal quality of Milošević's remarks, I couldn't help admiring his imperturbability. I went back to the embassy and wrote a facetious cable saying that I had finally penetrated the mystery of the man. There were really two Milošević's. Milošević One was hard-line, authoritarian, belligerent, bent on chaos, and wedded to the use of force to create a Greater Serbia. Personally, he was apoplectic, he hated Westerners, and he spoke in Serbian. Milošević Two was polite, affable, cooperative, and always looking for reasonable solutions to Yugoslavia's problems. He was calm, he liked to reminisce about his banking days in New York, and he spoke good English.

I did note that Milošević One and Milošević Two had several traits in common: they disliked Albanians, they were strong in the defense of Serbian interests, and they seemed to believe that the world was ganging up against Serbia. Milošević Two, I wrote, would often be summoned to repair the horrendous damage caused to Serbia's reputation by Milošević One, who would be sent back to the locker room. There his handlers would salve his wounds and get him ready for the next round. The one sure thing, I concluded, was that Milošević One would always be back.

The strategy of this schizoid figure was based on the fact that Serbs were spread among five of Yugoslavia's six republics. Slovenia was the only exception. At the foundation of Yugoslavia after World War I, Serbia's chief interest was that all these Serbs live in a single state. Before Tito, Serbia had dominated that state. Now, after Tito, Milošević wanted to restore that dominance. His chief obstacle in the late 1980s was Slovenia, ironically the only republic without large numbers of Serbs. The Slovenes were the first to challenge the unity of Yugoslavia.

Milošević, no supporter of Yugoslav unity except as a vehicle for Serbian influence, wrapped himself in the mantle of unity as he sharpened his duel with the Slovenes. His concept of unity was Serbian nationalism buttressed by communist methods of control. It tolerated neither democracy nor power-sharing with other national groups. Because it was unacceptable to all Yugoslavs who wanted real unity or real democracy, or both, it was bound to be divisive. In fact, Milošević's pursuit of a narrow Serbian agenda made him the major wrecker of Yugoslavia....

Departures

On May 12, 1992, the State Department announced that I was being recalled to Washington in protest against the Serbian aggression in Bosnia....

The days before our departure and the weeks after gave us time for introspection about a country where we had lived six years and that had affected us deeply. How was it possible that such attractive people, on whom the gods of nature and fortune had smiled, could have plowed their way straight to hell? Shortly before we left Belgrade, I tried to answer that question in a cable entitled

"Who Killed Yugoslavia?" It was intended as an analysis of the fatal elements in Yugoslavia's distant and recent past, laced with some nostalgia for what had been lost. I used as a framework the old English folk song "Who Killed Cock Robin?" a tale of murder complete with witnesses, grave-diggers, and mourners, but nobody to save the victim or bring him back to life. . . .

With the perspective of years, of the Bosnian war, and of many gross mis-representations of Yugoslavia's collapse, it's important to eliminate some of the reasons often cited. First, Yugoslavia was not destroyed by ancient Balkan ha-treds. This doesn't mean that the Balkans don't seethe with violence. The First World War was touched off by the assassination in Sarajevo of an Austrian arch-duke by a Bosnian Serb; the Second was for Yugoslavia not only a liberation war but a civil war with over half a million Yugoslav deaths.

But is Yugoslavia so unique? Europe, taken as a whole, has endured two civil wars in this century, involving sixty million deaths, including the genoci-dal annihilation of six million European Jews. Placid England suffered in the fifteenth century the Wars of the Roses, which moved Charles Dickens to re-mark: "When men continually fight against their own countrymen, they are always observed to be more unnaturally cruel and filled with rage than they are against any other enemy." The English lived through an even bloodier pe-riod in the seventeenth century: a king was executed and many of the people of Ireland massacred by Cromwell's forces. France had its wars of religion in the sixteenth century and its blood-drenched revolution in the eighteenth. Nor has the United States been immune from domestic conflict. More Americans died in our civil war than in any foreign war we have ever fought.

Balkan genes aren't abnormally savage. Bosnia enjoyed long periods of tranquility as a multiethnic community. Serbs and Croats, the most antago-nistic of adversaries today, had never fought each other before the twentieth century. The millennium they spent as neighbors was marked more by mutual indifference than by mutual hostility. Serbs, though demonized by many as incorrigibly xenophobic, don't fit that stereotype. Milovan Djilas's son Aleksa, author of a brilliant history of nationalism in Yugoslavia, points out that, with all the manipulative tools at Milošević's disposal, it still took him four years to arouse the Serbian population and that, even then, thousands of Serbs fled the country to avoid fighting in Croatia.

The Yugoslav wars can't be explained by theories of inevitable ethnic ha-treds, even when such explanations conveniently excuse outsiders from the responsibilities of intervening. There was plenty of racial and historical tin-der available in Yugoslavia. But the conflagrations didn't break out through spontaneous combustion. Pyromaniacs were required.

Second, religion wasn't at the heart of Yugoslavia's demise. The Yugoslav wars were primarily ethnic, not religious, wars. The major proponents of de-structive nationalism weren't driven by religious faith. Franjo Tudjman had been a communist most of his life; he converted to Catholicism when he turned to nationalist activities. Milošević, a lifelong communist, never, as far as I know, entered a Serbian Orthodox church except for blatant political purposes. I re-call a visit he made for electoral reasons to a Serbian monastery on Mt. Athos in northern Greece. Not even the official photographs could disguise the disconcerted and uncomfortable look on his face. Even Bosnia was largely a secular society; a 1985 survey found that only 17 percent of its people considered themselves believers.

None of this absolves the Serbian and Croatian churches. There were many religious people in Yugoslavia, particularly among rural folk. The Serbian Orthodox Church and the Catholic Church in Croatia were willing accomplices of the political leaders in coopting their parishioners for racist designs. These two churches were national churches, in effect arms of their respective states when it came to ethnic matters. They played a disgraceful role by exacerbating racial tensions when they could have urged their faithful toward Christian healing.

With regard to Bosnia, both the Serbian and Croatian regimes felt the need to impute fanatic religiosity to the Muslims in order to satanize them. But the portrayal was false. The Bosnia I knew was probably the most secular Muslim society in the world. The growing number of Muslim adherents today is a consequence of the war, not one of its root causes.

Third, Yugoslavia was not a victim of communism or even of its demise. Yugoslavs didn't live under the Soviet yoke, unlike their neighbors in the Warsaw Pact, for whom communism was an alien and evil implant. Gorbachev's withdrawal from Eastern Europe liberated whole countries but had little direct effect on Yugoslavia, whose communism, whatever its defects, was homegrown. In Eastern Europe the fault line was between communism and Western-style democracy; in Yugoslavia it was between ethnic groups. Tito's relative liberalism within the European communist world coopted many people for the Yugoslav party who would have been Western-oriented dissidents in Czechoslovakia or Poland.

In Yugoslavia the dissidents were for the most part nationalists, not liberals, and they marched to domestic drummers beating out racist, not Western, themes. Communists in Yugoslavia wore black hats or white hats, depending on whether they were nationalists or not. The most rabid nationalists, like Milošević or Tudjman, were or had been communists. So had many antinationalist, democratic figures, like Drnovšek, Gligorov, Tupurkovski, and many courageous journalists and human rights activists. In most of Eastern Europe, the word "communist" explained a good deal about a person; in Yugoslavia it explained next to nothing.

Fourth, Yugoslavia wasn't destroyed by foreign intervention or the lack of it. General Kadijević, in his paranoid account of the end of Yugoslavia, blames the United States, Germany, and the European Community, acting in collusion with traitors in Slovenia, Croatia, and Kosovo. Foreign countries did make serious mistakes in Yugoslavia, but they didn't destroy it. The failure to do more to support Prime Minister Marković, the lack of a forceful Western reaction to the shelling of Dubrovnik, and the European Community's premature decision to recognize the independence of Yugoslavia's republics were all mistakes, but not fatal ones. Whatever inducements or penalties the West might have devised, they wouldn't have been enough to suppress the nationalistic rage that was overwhelming the country. The war in Bosnia was another matter; there the West could have saved the situation and didn't. But the murder of Yugoslavia was a crime of domestic violence.

The victim itself had congenital defects. Yugoslavia was a state, but not a nation. Few felt much loyalty to Yugoslavia itself. Tito sought to encourage fealty by guaranteeing ethnic autonomy rather than by trying to create an ethnic melting pot. Political energy was directed more toward gaining a better position in Yugoslavia for one's ethnic group than toward preserving the viability of the state. Nobody wanted to be a member of a minority; nobody expected minorities automatically to be protected. Vladimir Gligorov, son of the wise president of Macedonia and a perceptive scholar, captured this feeling when he asked ironically, "Why should I be a minority in your state when you can be a minority in mine?"

These character traits damaged, but didn't doom, Yugoslavia. The country didn't commit suicide. As the court of history pursues its investigation of the death of Yugoslavia, I can imagine the following indictments: Slovenia for selfishness toward its fellow Yugoslavs; Tudjman's Croatia for insensitivity toward its Serbian population and greed toward its Bosnian neighbors; the Yugoslav army for ideological rigidity and arrogance, culminating in war crimes; Radovan Karadžić for attacking the principle of tolerance in Yugoslavia's most ethnically mixed republic; and—most of all—Slobodan Milošević for devising and pursuing a strategy that led directly to the breakup of the country and to the deaths of over a hundred thousand of its citizens. Nationalism was the arrow that killed Yugoslavia. Milošević was the principal bowman.

The Serbian leader made Yugoslavia intolerable for anybody who wasn't a Serb. He is hated among Albanians, Slovenes, Croats, Muslims, Macedonians, and Hungarians. And he has brought his own people into poverty and despair. The potentially prosperous and influential Serbia on which he expatiated in our last meeting in April 1992 is now an economic and civil shambles. Much of its youth and middle class—the foundation of democratic construction— has fled to the west. Milošević's dream of "all Serbs in one state" is a nightmare today; Serbs are now scattered among four states—"Yugoslavia" (Serbia and Montenegro), Bosnia, Croatia, and Macedonia. In seeking to dominate Yugoslavia, Milošević destroyed it. In seeking to tear out the pieces where Serbs lived, he wrecked, for a generation or more, the future of all Serbs.

NO

Steven Majstorovic

Ancient Hatreds or Elite Manipulation? Memory and Politics in the Former Yugoslavia

Any optimism generated by the Dayton peace accords in late 1995 was substantially eroded by events during the spring and summer of 1996. These events marked a protracted and tragic endgame in the former Yugoslavia. The flight from Sarajevo by Bosnian Serbs in February and March 1996 was the first indication of things to come. During the summer, refugees who tried to return to their former homes were harassed and attacked by paramilitary gangs. The early focus was on the behavior of the Bosnian Serbs, but now it is apparent that a policy of ethnic apartheid is being pursued by all sides in Bosnia....

The complexity of the Yugoslav conflict illustrates that the genesis of the war and the issues of ethnonational identity that fed the flames of conflict are far from being understood in any way that reflects some set of shared perspectives among scholars and pundits. For example, the exodus from Sarajevo by the Serbs in February and March 1996 seems to defy logic and rationality. One analytic perspective contends that the war is a product of "ancient hatreds" rooted in primordial identity and consequently any national group that falls under the political control of another is in mortal danger. The experience of some Serbs who left Sarajevo certainly reinforces this contention, as they ran a gauntlet of hostile Bosnian Muslims, supposedly bent on revenge. An opposing perspective views the war as the product of elite manipulation and fear-mongering by ethnic entrepreneurs who fanned the flames of hatred for their own purposes and who manipulated ethnonational identity issues that are themselves just a product of an "invented tradition." Analysts who adhere to the second perspective suggested that Serbs should take hold of their senses, accept the guarantees of the Bosnian-Croat Federation, ignore their leader's warnings, and stay in Sarajevo. Despite assurances, however, the Serbs who stayed in Sarajevo have been continually threatened. Bosnian Prime Minister Hasan Muratovic promised that the violence against Serbs in Sarajevo would be stopped. But unfortunately, most of the Serbs in Sarajevo now want to leave, including many who were loyal to the Bosnian government during the war.

From Steven Majstorovic, "Ancient Hatreds or Elite Manipulation? Memory and Politics in the Former Yugoslavia," *World Affairs*, vol. 159, no. 4 (Spring 1997). Copyright © 1997 by The American Peace Society. Reprinted by permission of *World Affairs*. Notes omitted.

Clearly, the Yugoslav conflict is an almost ideal laboratory for addressing some of the central questions that scholars of nationalism and ethnicity pose. Those who espouse a primordialist conception of national identity have ample evidence to support their position, while the constructionists also have abundant data that support their contention that national identity is essentially an artificial and modern phenomenon that is often at the mercy of ambitious leaders who manipulate and instrumentalize ethnonational identity.

This [selection] argues that prevailing analyses of ethnic conflict in the former Yugoslavia that focus either on a notion of ancient, primordial hatreds rooted in centuries-old identities, or on the premise that ethnic identity in the Balkans is a modern social construction that has been instrumentalized by political elites, miss the essential nature of the ongoing struggle. Historical memory constrains the options that leaders exercise in conflict creation and in peacemaking. Ethnic identity in the former Yugoslavia, however, has also been and will continue [to] be somewhat flexible and politically adaptive but only within a framework that does not threaten the constraints imposed by myth and memory. The constraints on masses and elites imposed by historical experience are particularly applicable for the Serbs, somewhat less so for the Croats, and even less so for the Bosnian Muslims. The Balkan conflict has both premodern, primordial characteristics and modern, constructed/instrumentalized elements in which ancient antagonisms (sometimes hatreds) and modern politics have both contributed appreciably to the tragedy, and an overemphasis on either perspective misrepresents the nature of ethnic conflict and politics in the former Yugoslavia....

Memory and Myth in Serbian, Croatian, and Bosnian Muslim Ethnonational Identity

When the term "Balkan politics" is conjured up, a mental picture that many people might have is one of incessant conflict, ethnic tinderboxes, and terrorist plots. This stereotypical view of Balkan politics is not wholly inaccurate. The Balkans have historically been a crossroads for conquest and occupation. The area that is now Yugoslavia was settled by the migration of Slavic tribes during the sixth century. Those tribes were independent until the beginning of the twelfth century, when the Croatians yielded to Hungarian political dominance, and until the beginning of the fifteenth century when the Serbians were defeated by the Ottoman Turks. External rule from Austria, Hungary, Italy, or Turkey lasted until the beginning of the twentieth century, although in a series of revolts the Serbs had formed an independent state by the middle of the nineteenth century.

In addition to being distinguished from each other by self-defined differences in tribal custom and culture, the South Slavs were further differentiated by the split in the Christian church. As a consequence, the Croats and Slovenes identified with Roman Catholicism, while the Serbs were under the jurisdiction of Byzantium and had formed by the thirteenth century an independent Serbian Orthodox Church. This division between East and West was reinforced when the Eastern Orthodox Serbs fell under Turkish rule, while the Croats and Slovenes answered to Rome and Hungary, and eventually to the Austro-Hungarian Empire. Thus, when the South Slavs were brought into a common state in 1918, the stage for ethnonational conflict had been set by a thousand years of history.

Serbian identity can best be understood as a combination of three historical experiences: the memory of the Battle of Kosovo in 1389 and the subsequent five hundred years of servitude and resistance against the Ottoman Turks; the successful revolts against the Turks early in the nineteenth century that culminated in an independent Serbian state by the middle of the century; and the role of the Serbs as allies of the West in two World Wars.

By the fourteenth century, the Serbs under Tsar Dusan had grown into a medieval empire that spanned the Balkans from the Adriatic to Western Bulgaria and to most of Albania and some areas in northern Greece. After his death in 1355, centralized power started to ebb, and various Serb nobles started to unravel the system set up by Dusan. In 1371, however, Prince Lazar came to power and a temporary recentralization of control was established. This short period ended at Kosovo Polje (The Field of Blackbirds) on 28 June 1389.

The battle between the Serb forces of Prince Lazar and the Ottoman Turks was at the time perceived as either a pyrrhic victory for the Turks or indecisive. The Serbian state survived for another seventy years before finally succumbing to Ottoman rule. However, the cataclysmic nature of a battle in which Prince Lazar and his son were beheaded, the Turkish Sultan Murad disemboweled by the Serbian knight Milos Obilic, and in which there were horrific losses on both sides (over 100,000 deaths in an eight-to-ten-hour battle) created a myth-making apparatus that has shaped Serbian consciousness to this day.

The battle decimated the Serb nobility and cost the Ottomans dearly. Almost immediately, Serbian poets, priests, and peasants started to propagate the notion of Christian martyrdom by the Serbian people, Prince Lazar, and Milos Oblic. The primordialization of the event had all the elements of a passion play played out in real life. Interestingly enough, the perspective of the Ottoman Turks only reinforces the Serbian myths:

> Yet this Ottoman view in some ways mirrors traditional Serbian views. Both the Ottoman and Serbian accounts emphasize the battle's cataclysmic nature. Both traditions have martyrdom as a theme.

Added to this vision shared between the Serbs and the Turks, the battle itself is routinely listed in historical surveys as one of the most important events in history. The result of all this valorization is an identity marker that is so rooted in real historical events that it is almost impossible for Serbs to escape its ubiquitous presence in Serbian identity.

Also a part of the Kosovo myth is the tale of migration by Serbs from Kosovo, the failed attempts to migrate back over a period of centuries, and the final triumphant return to Kosovo in 1912. Taken together, these events, which were kept alive by the Serbian Orthodox church in the liturgy and by traveling troubadours who annually embellished the story in an ever-growing epic poem ("The Kosovo Cycle"), suggest that even the horrible events in Bosnia may have been less destructive than the potential for catastrophe in the Serbian province of Kosovo that is today 90 percent Albanian.

The memory of an independent state that was relinquished to form the Kingdom of South Slavs is also a critical part of Serb identity. The theme of successful revolt and emancipation dominates the mythicizing of the Balkan Wars. Finally, the Serbian role in World War I and World War II completes the picture. Serbs suffered enormous losses in both wars and continually stress their part in the Allied victories, comparing their role to Croat, Bosnian Muslim, and Albanian collaboration. In particular, the role of General Draza Mihailovich and the Chetnik resistance in World War II is highlighted, as archival evidence has suggested a reassessment of [Josip Broz] Tito and the role of the partisans.

Surprisingly, Serbs do not consider the genocidal policies of the Croatian Ustasha state and their Bosnian Muslim allies during World War II as an important element of Serbian identity. Instead, the events are often used as a way to stereotype all Croatians and Muslims by both Serb masses and elites. In particular, the Ustasha- and Muslim-led genocide of Serbs in Croatia and Bosnia in World War II has been the key to understanding Bosnian Serb and Croatian Serb propaganda and military mobilization strategies against Croats and Muslims in the contemporary period. Both Rodovan Karadzic and Ratko Mladic, the Bosnian Serb military leader, have used the events of World War II to successfully demonize Croats and Muslims in the eyes of the Serbs.

Croatian identity also has a memory of a medieval kingdom, but one that peacefully gave up its sovereignty to the Hungarian crown in 1102. The project of identity primordialization by the Croats has been to present events since 1102 as evidence for the continuity of a Croatian state in waiting. The keys to this continuity are peasant uprisings, a succession of Croatian kings, advances in Croatian culture and learning that depict Croatia as a part of a Western European culture that is distinct from the Serbs, and the unbroken reality of Croatian national consciousness that goes back to the seventh century. What is often ignored by Serbs is that it was the efforts of Croat intellectuals and church leaders in the nineteenth century that first broached the idea of a single South Slav state.

Croatian identity is also tied to the Catholic church and its role in resisting Serbian dominance in the interwar period. The issue of Serbian dominance is hotly debated between Serbs and Croats. While Croats refer to Serbian dominance, Serbs refer to Croat obstructionism. The debate has no resolution, but by 1938 Croatia did win considerable autonomy from Belgrade and was, effectively, a state within a state.

Another part of the Croatian primordialization project is to address the events of World War II by minimizing the Ustasha aspect and emphasizing the role of the Croats in the partisan resistance led by Tito. This interpretation, however, is also open for debate between Croats and Serbs, since most sources that address Tito's partisan movement make it clear that an overwhelming majority of the partisans were Serbs, and that many Croatians did not join until Tito, a Croat, offered a pardon at the end of 1943 to anyone who joined the partisans, although Tito's action did alienate many Serb partisans. It should also be noted that many Serb renegade units participated in revenge massacres against

Croatian and Muslim civilians toward the end of World War II. These killings numbered in the thousands and are remembered by Croats and Muslims who insist that the slaughter was mutual and that the world has tended to ignore Croatian and Muslim victims of World War II.

Croatian identity is also reinforced by the failure of the Croatian Republic to separate from Yugoslavia during what is called the Croatian Crises or Croatian Spring of 1968–72. The crises started out as an attempt to liberalize the economic and political system. But the movement was eventually taken over by nationalist elements who pushed for Croatian independence. An alarmed Tito brutally ended the movement and purged the Croatian party of liberals. He then did the same thing to the Serbian party to effect some semblance of ethnic symmetry. Unfortunately, many of the liberals who were purged in both the Serbian and Croatian Communist parties were the type of leaders who might have been effective in heading off the level of conflict in the Yugoslav conflict of 1991–95. But it is from the experience of 1968–72 that many Croatians today stereotype Serbs as conservative Communists while Croats see themselves as liberal democrats in the Western tradition. It was also during the period of the Croatian Crises that Franjo Tudjman became a staunch nationalist who started to write revisionist tracts about what he labeled the myth of the number of Serbian deaths in World War II.

The next element in the continual primordialization of Croatian identity will become the successful secession from Yugoslavia in 1991, Croatian suffering at the hands of the Serbs, and the German-led recognition by the world community. Pronouncements from Zagreb seem to support this view, although it is still too early for any complete evaluation.

Until the Bosnian war and the siege of Sarajevo began in 1992, Bosnian Muslim identity was essentially a tug of war between Serbian, Croatian, and Bosnian Muslim interpretations of history. The Serb perspective is that the Muslims are Islamicized Slavs who were mostly Serbs. The Croat view is that these same Slavs were Catholic Croats. Some Bosnian Muslims, however, claim that they are descended from the Bogomils, who were a heretic Manechean sect. Moreover, many Muslim intellectuals during the nineteenth century started to claim that the Bogomils were really Turks from Anatolia and that the "only thing Slavic about the Bosnian Muslims is their language, which they absorbed from the indigenous population." There are also perspectives that contend that the Bogomils were much more than a sect and that contemporary Bosnian Serbs are not really Serbs but an offshoot of the Vlachs, a sheep-herding people related to the Rumanians.

Muslim ethnic identity got a boost in 1971 when they were officially declared a nationality by the Tito regime. He thought that this declaration might end the warring claims for Muslim identity by the Serbs and Croats. Tito's rationale was that the creation of Bosnia-Hercegovina as a republic at the end of World War II had outlived its usefulness as a buffer between the Croats and the Serbs and that some other policy was necessary.

There are many recent works that present the history of Bosnia as generally one of interethnic harmony and cooperation. But it is [Robert J.] Donia and [John V. A.] Fine's thorough research that, despite their contentions, highlights very ancient roots of the conflict in Bosnia. They present a rich chronology of Bosnian life from antiquity to the present tragedy. Their most important contribution is the thorough and impressive debunking of the incessant claims of Croatian and Serbian chauvinists. Serb nationalists produce evidence that most Bosnian Muslims are Orthodox Serbs who were forcibly converted to Islam by the Ottoman Turks, while Croat nationalists argue that Bosnian Muslims are by blood the "truest" and "purest" of Catholic Croats who were led astray by the Turks.

The conversion to Islam in Bosnia was characterized by a very complex process. Bosnian Muslims were once Slavic Christians who were neither Serbs nor Croats but had a distinct Bosnian identity and belonged to a Bosnian church that ostensibly bowed toward Rome, a fact that Croats seize upon to make their claims. But the rites of this church closely followed the Eastern Orthodox model, which Serbs contend establishes Serbian identity. But what is most evident is that the Bosnian church was never well established, there were few priests, and the Bosnian Slavic peasants maintained only a tenuous tie to Christianity. Thus, with the Ottoman penetration into Bosnia in the fifteenth century, these peasants began a gradual conversion to Islam in a pragmatic decisionmaking process that took between one and two centuries. Moreover, the contention by some modern Bosnian Muslim scholars that Muslim identity was never Christian but instead sprang from the Bogomils, a sect that rejected Christianity and its rituals, is also refuted by evidence that the Bogomils in Bosnia were very few in number and were never influential in the development of Bosnian history.

Eventually, Muslims adapted to the erosion of Ottoman hegemony, the nineteenth century influence of the Austro-Hungarian empire, the Balkan Wars and World War I, the first Yugoslavia in which Serbs predominated, World War II, the Tito period in which the Muslims finally gained official status as a nation in Bosnia, and the final degeneration into civil war. During this period, the Muslims often exhibited a predilection for compromise and pragmatism, especially after the fall of the Ottoman empire, as the Muslims formed political parties and interest groups whose purpose was to tread the narrow balance point between blatant Croat and Serb attempts to capture their loyalty. Throughout the period, the tolerant, cooperative, and multicultural nature of Bosnian society is stressed by Bosnian Muslim nationalists. But a closer examination reveals that Bosnian society was somewhat less tolerant and harmonious than some would contend.

The constructionist and instrumentalist perspectives suggest that Croat and Serb ethnic consciousness did not exist in Bosnia prior to the nineteenth century and that the often mentioned notion that the current war is based on "ancient hatreds" is false. But history presents a more complex picture. It is clear that the development of medieval Bosnia did not occur in isolation and was closely connected to events in Serbia and Croatia. Also, the Ottoman millet system identified ethnic groups by religion instead of ethnicity. Consequently, it is often mistakenly assumed that since the Turks used a non-ethnic marker to identify Croats and Serbs, a pre-nineteenth-century Croat and Bosnian ethnicity did not exist. But Serbian settlers started moving into Bosnia by the early fifteenth century to escape Ottoman expansion into Kosovo, the Serbian heartland. After some initial migration of Croats out of Bosnia, the Franciscan order successfully helped to maintain a Croat presence in the area of western Bosnia known as Hercegovina. Furthermore, the Austrians offered Serbs land to act as a military buffer against the Turks, and by the seventeenth century Serbs occupied the Krajina in Croatia and adjacent areas in Bosnia. Croat and Serb consciousness was well established and was not simply a construction of nineteenth-century nationalism.

In the social system built by the Ottomans, the Muslim converts were landowners and freeholders, and the overwhelming majority of peasants, who were taxed heavily and lived as second-class citizens, were Serbs, along with a number of Croats. The peasants, especially the Serbs, who lived in this Jim Crow system chafed at the inequities and started to revolt by the nineteenth century. Of particular interest to a contemporary understanding of ethnic frictions is that, as the Ottoman empire eroded and was forced to make concessions to subject populations, it was in Bosnia where the local Muslim landlords were the most reactionary and hostile to any changes that threatened their paramountcy.

If the above-recounted issues are not evidence of "ancient hatreds," then at least there was fertile ground in Bosnia for ancient antagonisms. When it came to manipulating public opinion, Milosevic in Serbia and Tudjman in Croatia are often cited as architects of the war in Bosnia. However, Bosnian President Alija Izetbegovic should not be left off the hook. His role in the war, his rather radical political views, and his reneging on the Lisbon Agreement of 1992 that would have maintained a multiethnic Bosnia need to be examined closely. Still, it is clear from the evidence that despite the protestations of extremist Serbs and Croats, the reality of a Muslim national identity is undeniable. The notion of a Bosnia in multiethnic harmony before the current struggle is an insupportable myth that could be maintained only by a centralized Communist system. When Tito died and the system collapsed, history started to catch up rather quickly.

It should be apparent that at this point Muslim identity is still in the process of primordialization. The sieges of Sarajevo and Mostar and the killing fields of Srebrenica will be the building blocks as Kosovo was for the Serbs. Instead of historical records and oral history, the Bosnian Muslims will have access to videotapes, and Benedict Anderson's notion of the printing press as a vehicle for the imaging of identity has evolved to NPR and PBS. The Bosnian Muslims are quickly moving from being Yugoslavs to Bosnian Muslims, and women wearing veils have started to appear in villages and even on the streets of Sarajevo. Moreover, the flirtation with Islamic forces from the Middle East, particularly Iran, has been recently documented.

In contrast to Muslim identity, Serbian identity is rooted in a centuries-old primordialization project. Despite Milosevic's manipulation of the Serbian media and elections, the force of elite manipulation in an instrumentalist fashion is not as significant as one would think for Serbian identity today because Milosevic, or any democratic alternative to him, would be constrained by history from stepping too far outside the successful Kosovo-inspired primordialization of identity. There are even arguments that in the case of the Serbs it is the elites who have been shaped by the memories and the myths of the masses.

The Serbs, more than the Croats or Muslims, are shackled by their view of history and may not be able to escape what they see as an apocalyptic destiny, a destiny that unfortunately combines national paranoia with a sense of a messianic mission to defend Christianity from the mounting forces of Islam.

The Croatian model represents an ethnic identity that is still in the process of primordialization, which is committed to reinforce the notion of a thousand-year history. This project is augmented by a heavy dose of instrumentalism as President Tudjman and his supporters on the Right try to hold onto the power and privileges that they enjoyed during the Communist era. An example of this effort is the release of the new Croatian currency during May 1994. The new currency is called the "Kuna" and refers to a forest marten. The only memory of this currency dates back to the Ustasha regime, and Jews and Serbs in Croatia have protested in vain. Croatian historians, some quite reluctantly, have scrambled to discover or perhaps imagine instances where marten skins have been used in trade within Croatia during the past thousand years. Some isolated instances have been discovered and so the process of primordialization continues.

Moreover, the Croats, as they did during the 1960s, have recently declared that Croat is a separate language from Serbian and have introduced numerous words that go back to Slavic anachronisms from the past. Differences in dialect between Serbian, Croatian, and Bosnian are probably less pronounced, according to most linguists, than between American and British English. But the process of identity differentiation through language policy is in high gear. In reaction, the Serbs and the Bosnian Muslims have also jumped on the bandwagon, and perhaps in five hundred years there will be three different languages created from the current Serbo-Croation.

The Muslims are in some sense the most free to pursue their own vision of an ethnic identity. Without a Kosovo or a thousand-year state to guide them, they are in a Big Bang period of imagining their place in the world. The process of primordialization occurs under the watchful eye of the world, and the instrumental policies of the government in Sarajevo are profoundly tied to this process. Primordialist, constructivist, and instrumentalist categories have collapsed upon each other in Sarajevo, and the Bosnian Muslims have the luxury of picking and choosing, although there is growing evidence that their role as absolute victim is starting to come under question as more recent evidence has started to point toward a more symmetrical structure of suffering in the current conflict. Choices for the Croats are more limited but still possible.

The Serbs are fanatically committed to a mythic identity that may not allow choices, even if they desire them. Moreover, the Serbs have already started to mythicize the expulsion of 250,000 civilians from the Krajina region of Croatia, an expulsion that the United States refrained from labeling "ethnic cleansing." The Serbs have also started to focus on the slaughter of Serbs in the Srebrenica area before the Bosnian Serb army atrocities of July 1995 as new fodder for their continued vision of martyrdom. If the Serbs cannot break out of a primordialization process that has exhausted itself, then the outlook for the Balkans is very bleak indeed, and the post-Dayton events of 1996 may be the harbinger of tragedy when the NATO forces leave Bosnia.

   The complexity of the ethnic conflict in the former Yugoslavia has illustrated the difficulty of mono-causal analyses. Despite the penchant in postmodern analysis for stressing the decentered person who can change identities like clothing, ethnonational identity often predisposes people to dispense with rational decisionmaking and instead embrace a policy of radical ethnic altruism in which lives are sacrificed. And although the examination of elite behavior is part and parcel of the methodology of social scientists, this methodology falls short when historically rooted conflicts are examined. In the dark street of available data, it is elite behavior that is lit by the lamp at the end of the street. But it is the rest of the street in which the richness and cultural thickness of memory, myth, and shared experience lurks in shadows. The data in these shadows are often difficult to measure empirically. We must, however, seriously consider their validity lest we ignore them at great cost to future peacemaking and conflict resolution.

POSTSCRIPT

Were Ethnic Leaders Responsible for the Death of Yugoslavia?

The biggest loss caused by the disintegration of Yugoslavia is to the country's people. They are the ones who have been driven from their homes, placed in "detention centers," beaten, humiliated, raped, and brutally murdered in frighteningly high numbers. The actual number of the displaced, humiliated, tortured, and dead is hard to come by, given the fluid and anarchic nature of the Yugoslavian battleground. Most chilling has been the use of the term *ethnic cleansing* to describe the "Balkan killing fields," conjuring up memories of the Nazi Holocaust. In support of such indictments, charges of genocide and "crimes against humanity" have been leveled against many former Yugoslavs, both participants in the crimes and the leaders who may have ordered or permitted them. Several Yugoslav political and military leaders, including former president Slobodan Milosevic, have been presently brought to trial for war crimes committed in Bosnia-Herzegovina and Kosovo.

After years of neglect by the outside world, it is ironic that it took the demise of Yugoslavia to bring the country the attention it deserved. Many books on the subject have been written recently, and some writers have attempted to look at this crisis through the eyes of its victims, such as Roger Cohen in *Hearts Grow Brutal: Sagas of Sarajevo* (Random House, 1998). Laura Silber and Allan Little's *Yugoslavia: Death of a Nation* (Penguin Books, 1997) gives a blow-by-blow account of Yugoslavia's death and is a concise, chronological account of the last 10 years of its life. Some works have examined the genocide factor; a useful anthology on this subject is Thomas Cushman and Stjepan Mestrovic, eds., *This Time We Knew: Western Responses to Genocide in Bosnia* (New York University Press, 1998). For those who need some historical background on Yugoslavia's past, see John R. Lampe, *Yugoslavia as History: Twice There Was a Country* (Cambridge University Press, 1996).

For information on Kosovo, the Balkans' latest casualty, see Tim Judah, *Kosovo: War and Revenge* (Yale University Press, 2000) and William J. Buckley, ed., *Kosovo: Contending Voices on Balkan Interventions* (William B. Eerdmans Publishing, 2000). For an account of the war from a military/diplomatic perspective, consult Ivo H. Daalder and Michael E. O'Hanlon, *Winning Ugly: NATO's War to Save Kosovo* (Brookings Institute, 2000).

Whether the trial of Slobodan Milosevic and others on charges of war crimes and crimes against humanity will bring relief to the Balkans remains to be seen. The troubled 1000-year history of the area indicates that any settlement will be neither quick nor acceptable to all concerned parties.

ISSUE 17

Will the European Economic and Monetary Union Increase the Potential for Transatlantic Conflict?

YES: Steven Everts, from "America and Euroland," *World Policy Journal* (Winter 1999/2000)

NO: Werner Weidenfeld, from "The Euro and the New Face of the European Union," *The Washington Quarterly* (Winter 1999)

ISSUE SUMMARY

YES: Steven Everts, research fellow at the Centre for European Reform in London, argues that the emergence of the *euro* as a world currency and Euroland as a united voice may lead to increasing rivalry between Europe and the United States, as both seek economic and political influence in the rest of the world.

NO: Werner Weidenfeld, director of the Munich Center for Applied Policy Research, sees the European Union as a vehicle for restructuring the transatlantic relationship between Europe and the United States. If they develop a partnership between equals, they will be positioned for international crisis management and other global challenges.

Starting in January 1999, 11 European states (Austria, Belgium, Finland, France, Germany, Ireland, Italy, Luxembourg, the Netherlands, Portugal, and Spain) began using a common European currency called the *euro* in electronic transactions. In 2002 the euro replaced coin and paper currencies in these nations. What impact will this European Economic and Monetary Union (EMU) have on world politics? A united Europe, with a population of 300 million and an economy equal in size to that of the United States, will become another superpower, capable of safeguarding Europe's interests politically and militarily in a worldwide balance of power. The most intriguing question is whether an economically and politically united Europe will find its own interests diverging from or converging with those of the United States.

The European Union had a modest beginning as the European Coal and Steel Community in 1952. The so-called Common Market countries of Belgium, France, Italy, Luxembourg, the Netherlands, and West Germany signed the Treaty of Rome in 1958, forming the European Economic Community, and new members have gradually been added (Austria, Britain, Denmark, Finland, Greece, Ireland, Portugal, Spain, and Sweden), bringing the present total to 15 member nations. In 1992 a Treaty of European Union was signed at Maastricht in the Netherlands, with the goal of creating a more comprehensive economic and political union through (1) a common European citizenship, (2) a single European currency (the euro), and (3) a central European bank.

Displaced persons from the prison and concentration camps of World War II, "guestworkers" who helped rebuild postwar Europe, and the subjects of former colonies arriving in Europe as citizens have all contributed to population mixing over the past 50 years. Since 1968 workers have been free to seek the best opportunities available within the Common Market, and a 12-year-old scholarship program (Socrates-Erasmus) has permitted European university students to study in other countries within the Union for up to a year tuition-free. Faces of European political leaders are widely seen on the news and even in television ad campaigns throughout Europe. Over the past 20 years, a number of European business schools have started offering American-style MBA programs. What will this economic and cultural amalgamation mean as Europe begins to see itself as a single political entity?

Is it possible to imagine a Europe in which moving from one country to another or living in one country and working in another would be as routine as living in New Jersey and working in New York? Will a common currency and increasingly common economic and political interests forge a European supernation that does not need the military power of the United States to resolve its internal conflicts and does not want either American culture or American pressure to marginalize rogue nations such as Libya, Iran, and Iraq? Will the world order following the breakup of the Soviet Union be one of increased transatlantic tension or enhanced transatlantic cooperation?

Steven Everts predicts that the emergence of an economically powerful Euroland will bring an end to the asymmetrical advantages that the dollar has enjoyed as the world's only truly global currency. The United States may find it more difficult to engage in "dollar diplomacy" (pressuring other countries into dampening or reflating their own economies), Everts observes. With Europe as a more cohesive and more assertive international actor, Everts concludes, the transatlantic partnership will need to be recast into a more diversified and equal partnership that will require some adjustments.

Werner Weidenfeld is more optimistic. With Europe and the United States as the only reliable guarantors of stability in the world today, the need for a restructured transatlantic partnership between equals is greater than ever. Faced with similar challenges regarding reform of social security and education as well as common issues of environmental management, crime, and migration, Europe and the United States must find a way to share solutions and assume joint responsibility on the world stage.

Steven Everts  **YES**

America and Euroland

The start of Economic and Monetary Union (EMU) has produced a sea change in European affairs. After all, for 11 countries to voluntarily share their monetary policy is an unprecedented endeavor. And while some aspects of EMU are, by necessity, shrouded in uncertainty, the signs are that this gamble has paid off.

Let's be clear about this: EMU has been a success. The doomsayers got it wrong. It has boosted investment and innovation in the euro zone, strengthened cooperation among its participants on budgetary policies, facilitated progress toward the creation of an integrated European capital market, and advanced the broader process of economic reform.

Given the substantive importance of the issues involved, it is logical that EMU has, for some years now, been a hotly debated topic. Unfortunately, this active debate has largely ignored EMU's effects on the outside world. And yet, analyzing these external repercussions is vital. It is obvious that EMU is having a significant impact on monetary and financial policy, trade relations, and in the broader geostrategic sphere.

It is therefore imperative for both Europeans and Americans to think through the implications, both economic and political, of this bold project. This exercise should be based on the recognition that the start of EMU, on time, with as many as 11 countries, was never a foregone conclusion. Indeed, until early 1998 many seasoned observers—especially those in the English-speaking world—thought it would never happen, or would at least be postponed. But strategic commitment and political determination saw the project through.

The corollary of this emphasis on willpower is that EMU is the monetary equivalent of the romantics' blood pact. To the wider world, EMU often represents an act of European self-assertion even if its origins can clearly be located in intra-European considerations. Some, especially on the political right in the United States, seem disturbed or even opposed to EMU and warn of its possible detrimental effects for U.S.-European relations.[1] However, if managed adroitly, EMU will promote, not obstruct, effective transatlantic cooperation. But before we can assess EMU's external implications, we must first establish what exactly has changed with the launch of the euro.

The New Dollar-Euro Order

U.S.-European economic relations have experienced a significant transformation. Some figures will illustrate how they have moved in the direction of rough equality. The current Euroland population is somewhat larger than that of the United States, making the euro the currency of the world's largest group of affluent customers. Total merchandise trade with the rest of the world is about 25 percent larger than that of the United States (and more than double that of Japan), although GDP per capita in Euroland remains lower than in the United States.[2] However, in the coming years, as more countries enter EMU and its poorer countries catch up economically, Euroland's overall GDP will exceed that of the United States. "Euroland," the economist C. Fred Bergsten argues, "will equal or exceed the United States on every key measure of economic strength and will speak increasingly with a single voice on a wide array of economic issues. . . . Economic relations between the United States and the European Union will rest increasingly on a foundation of virtual equality."[3]

In the world of high finance, EMU will essentially challenge and transform the existing dollar-centered global financial system, gradually forcing its transformation into a bipolar, dollar-euro order, with Japan as a distant third. In this context, people often wonder what kind of currency the euro will become. Many have made predictions on the euro's future exchange rate: will it go up or down, and when and by how much? Others ask to what extent international investors, exporters and central bankers will use the euro. Though linked, these are actually very different questions and we should not confuse the two. The first asks whether the euro will be strong or weak against other currencies, principally the U.S. dollar, while the second asks whether the euro will be a "big" or a "small" currency.

The "Size" Question

For public policy purposes, it is probably more important and fruitful to gauge whether the euro will be a big or a small currency rather than to second-guess the markets and speculate on its future exchange rate. After all, the scope and importance of EMU's medium-term, external effects—on monetary, trade, and foreign policy—will depend in part on whether the euro becomes a global currency or remains a regional one. The "larger" the euro is as a currency, the more serious a challenge it will pose to the dollar, dollar-denominated assets, and the American government's freedom of maneuver.

On this "size" question, the euro is doing well. In international bond markets in particular, it has already been something of a runaway success. In the first half of 1999, euro-denominated bonds accounted for slightly more than 44 percent of total bond issues worldwide, compared to 43 percent for the dollar. Thus, in capital markets, the euro is much "bigger" than the sum of its parts.

Furthermore, given the size and significance of their trade links with the euro zone, many countries in Eastern Europe, North Africa, but also in Asia and Latin America will want to diversify the composition of their currency reserves by reducing their dollar holdings. All in all, the euro stands to become a currency with a significant international role, challenging but not ending the dominance of the dollar.

If so, this will imply an end to the asymmetrical advantages the United States has enjoyed and which accrued from the dollar's status as the world's only global currency. Over time, the United States may find it harder to attract foreign capital to finance its large and growing external deficits. Until now, the United States could run large fiscal and trade imbalances because it had preferential access to "cheap" money abroad. Because of the preeminent status of the dollar, foreigners have been willing to buy U.S. debt in greater quantities and at lower interest rates than that of any other government. But with the advent of a credible alternative in the form of euro-assets, the price of money for the United States—reflected in higher interest rates—may well go up.

U.S. policymakers will also find it more difficult to engage in "dollar diplomacy," that is, attempts to pressure other countries into dampening or reflating their economies in accordance to U.S. preferences by threatening precipitous exchange-rate movements of the dollar. And international investors could become less forgiving of Washington's policy mistakes, such as the excessive fiscal loosening—i.e., unfunded tax cuts—of the early 1980s, because now the euro will offer them an alternative to dollar-denominated and U.S.-linked assets. The bottom line is that the United States and the dollar will no longer be in a class of their own. No longer shielded to the same extent from the competitive forces of the global economy, they will have to compete more directly than before.

By the same token, the Europeans can expect some benefits from the probable global role of the euro. Apart from the small but interesting benefit called "seigniorage" (the fact that anyone who holds a banknote is making an interest-free loan to the issuing bank), the real advantage will lie in the greater degree of control Europeans will have over their own economies.

EMU of course also means that Europeans will no longer have to struggle with the havoc that large swings in the dollar have historically brought to European foreign exchange markets. In the past, the gyrations of the dollar would send the deutschmark and the Italian lira in opposite directions, putting great strains on the European Exchange Rate Mechanism (ERM) and, by extension, on Europe's single market.

Treasury Thinking

Since the stakes are so high, it is right to ask whether EMU is, on balance, a help or a hindrance to effective transatlantic cooperation. To answer this, let us look at the dominant American view of EMU at a strategic level.

First, it is important to note that few American policymakers are thinking about EMU at all. When asked, European diplomats in Washington vent their frustrations regarding the lack of interest on the part of their American colleagues. The latter for their part concede that it does not come up on their proverbial radar screens. Moreover, the city's strategists have maintained a studied silence on the matter. Consequently, the debate, such as it is, has been dominated and its terms set by the U.S. Treasury.

Treasury thinking actually takes place along two separate lines. On the one hand, there is considerable skepticism whether EMU can function with existing levels of labor mobility and fiscal transfers to assist regions within the euro area that experience an economic downturn. It is the familiar mantra of the neo-liberal school. The catch phrase one hears at the Treasury is that "the jury is still out on whether EMU will be successful." There is also a lot of talk that EMU, a project of dubious economic merit, will distract policymakers' attention from what really matters: structural reform. What this view ignores is that EMU makes these reforms much more likely.

On the other hand, there is the strand of thought, usually emphasized in public, which says that what is good for Europe is also good for the United States. While true at a metaphysical level, this is also somewhat banal. After all, EMU raises important policy challenges.

Actually, broad American attitudes toward EMU have followed a pattern that is eerily familiar to those that have followed U.S. perceptions of European affairs in general. As the European commentators William Wallace and Jan Zielonka wrote in *Foreign Affairs:* "First inattention, then assertions that it cannot succeed, then warnings of danger once success appears imminent."[4] For decades, the U.S. position on European integration has suffered from a degree of schizophrenia. To acknowledge this is not to indulge in anti-American rhetoric. Many Americans themselves recognize that while American governments have long supported the idea of European unification, they have simultaneously also reverted to classic "divide-and rule" practices when expedient.

Likewise, U.S. leaders have often voiced their frustrations at the slow pace of the integration process and the unwieldy Brussels arrangements it relied upon. Why can't Europeans simply be like us? is the underlying—and deeply ahistorical—exhortation. However, whenever Europe has spoken with a single voice and said something of which Washington disapproved, America's reaction has invariably been a blend of surprise and indignant disapproval. U.S. attitudes toward European economic integration have, for some time now, veered between proclamations of Europe's decline and complaints of European threats to American interests.

EMU will not, cannot, change this underlying ambivalence and ambiguity. So we will continue to hear from the Americans that EMU cannot work, that it is a distraction, that it is a threat to U.S. interests and "leadership," and at the same time that it is a positive if belated step toward unification that will strengthen the Western alliance. Euroland should downplay the first three responses and seize upon the fourth.

Peter W. Rodman, director of national security studies at the Nixon Center, argues that "it is a commonplace that the EMU ... reflects a new stage in the desire to build the EU into an economic and financial equal to the U.S." Its success will mean "freeing Europe from disadvantageous subordination to the dollar and subjecting the United States, finally, to some of the same financial discipline which it hitherto escaped."[5] The British journalist Martin Walker essentially agrees: "If the adjustment process is pursued with care and forethought, it will involve a sobering though not humiliating decline in the dollar's prestige, a small price to pay for the economic and strategic benefits involved."[6] On that point, Europeans and Americans can agree.

Dispelling the Anti-American Myth

Yet Rodman also makes another, more contentious point, which harks back to conservative attitudes toward European integration that have a long pedigree. He claims that European policies in general and EMU in particular have been conceived, in part, as anti-American moves. In line with many analysts of the realist persuasion, Rodman points to the possible emergence of a new hegemon, with EMU merely being the latest tool Europeans are employing to distance themselves from the United States. He goes out of his way to deplore the self-indulgent "infantile disorder" of anti-Americanism and warns of the dangers it presents to Atlantic unity.[7]

William Pfaff, another self-styled realist, has echoed this alarm. In an article for the winter 1998/99 issue of this journal, "The Coming Clash of Europe with America," he wrote: "It is interest, not volition, that will produce a deepening rivalry between Europe and the United States during the decades to come, with competitive searches for economic and political influence in the rest of the world."[8] Reginald Dale, a columnist for the *International Herald Tribune,* has talked of the "small cottage industry of American experts scouring European pronouncements on the euro and other moves toward a stronger Europe, almost in the hope of finding anti-American sentiments that could give the US cause for offense."[9]

In truth, the situation need not be so dramatic. But since this view of EMU being actually or potentially anti-American is so prevalent, it needs to be tackled head on. To do this, a brief historical detour is necessary. It will show that EMU was never conceived as an anti-American move, nor even aimed at minimizing the asymmetrical advantages the United States enjoyed. These are merely the unintended—yet for Europeans beneficial—by-products of a project that clearly found its origins in intra-European developments.

First among these is the aim not just to "finish the single market," as Europeans often stress, but also to solve the dilemma of combining the exchange rate mechanism (a system of fixed, but adjustable, pegs) with the free flow of capital. Back in 1987, Tommaso Padoa-Schioppa, a European Commission official, had already predicted that this combination would lead to damaging speculative attacks on the weaker currencies in the system. The only way for the ERM to survive the liberalization of capital flows, he argued in a seminal report that convinced Commission president Jacques Delors, was to move to full monetary union. Subsequent attacks on the Italian lira, the British pound, and the French franc in 1992 and 1993 proved Padoa-Schioppa right."[10]

Of course, the Europeans had talked about the merits of a monetary union since the late 1960s. But despite a steady stream of reports and blueprints, the project lacked political commitment and so remained in the realm of academic aspirations. It was something people referred to at seminars, but it was quite distinct from practical politics.

All that changed in November 1989. Then, the prospect of a hegemonic united Germany rediscovering the dubious virtues of *Sonderweg*—of its "special path"—moving away from its commitment to the West and the EC in particular had gripped Parisian imaginations. But true to the maxim of French foreign policy that whatever the problem, the answer is always "Europe," President Francois Mitterrand offered German chancellor Helmut Kohl a quid pro quo. He essentially traded his assent to German unification for a West German accord to fix a date for an agreement on a possible starting date of EMU. That was when Chancellor Kohl crossed the Rubicon, as he realized that EMU was a price well worth paying to allay fears among Germany's neighbors—however misplaced these might have been. Mitterrand got half the deutschmark, Kohl the whole of Germany.

America's Dependable Ally

The United States, or rather the alleged need to balance American preponderance, played no salient role in the calculations of Europe's leaders in that crucial phase. Therefore, this charge of EMU being anti-American in its origins and objectives is misplaced. American conservatives who nonetheless insist on this flawed argument should remember that it could, if repeated often enough, become a self-fulfilling prophecy.

Instead, the United States should drop its paranoia and ambivalence and welcome Europe as a truly equal partner. Real allies are rare in today's world, and on the grand strategic issues, the Europeans are closer to the United States and have more diplomatic and economic clout to offer than any other country, or group of countries. As Wallace and Zeilonka remind us, "The European allies—with all their evident flaws and weaknesses—are the United States' only dependable partners, sharing America's values and burdens."[11]

If and when Europe is recognized as America's natural ally, it will also become evident that more respect for European views in Washington is desirable and possible. This means a bit less boasting about alleged or real U.S. successes and less lecturing about Europe's actual or imagined defects. Consider for instance publisher Mortimer Zuckerman's claim that the United States dominates the knowledge industries of the future: "Some 90 percent of web sites are American. U.S. companies are the major suppliers of the information age's silicon brains and sinews.... [U.S. companies]...spend more than twice as much per capita on 'infotech' as Western European firms...." France, Zuckerman concludes, "had the seventeenth century, Britain the nineteenth, and America the twentieth. It will also have the twenty-first."[12]

This self-satisfaction may be excessive in light of the less than impressive U.S. record on crime, healthcare and social cohesion. But it is particularly hard to combine with the incessant American emphasis that it can no longer bear the economic burden of global responsibilities and that "Europe should pay more."

Appointing Mr. Euroland

EMU is making Europe more coherent. If handled well, it could empower Europe's leaders, regaining for them collectively a margin of maneuver they had each lost individually. It will force the Americans to take European preferences and positions more seriously.

Against this background, it is tempting from a European perspective to believe that coming to terms with EMU's external effects is mainly a task for non-Europeans. But this view is misguided. EMU's participants will also have to enact serious reforms in policies, attitudes, and institutions to manage successfully the euro's external repercussions. More specifically, the Europeans need to rethink their external representation and create the position of "Mr. (or Ms.) Euroland," that is, an individual who can speak authoritatively for the euro zone.

The case for Mr. Euroland starts from the assessment that the euro is enabling Euroland to raise its stature in global financial diplomacy. After all, EMU's participants now share a single external balance of trade as well as a single monetary policy. Over time, the euro will become a currency with a significant international role. And the rest of the world will increasingly expect the euro zone to speak with a single voice in the management of financial crises such as those that wracked Asia in 1997–98.

The handling of those crises led to some harsh words between the United States and European governments. The Americans remember then U.S. deputy treasury secretary Lawrence Summers shuttling around the region, and the U.S. Treasury providing the intellectual input for the International Monetary Fund (IMF) rescue packages. Many Americans felt that the Europeans were conspicuously absent from the region, hopelessly divided, and focused on their own internal priorities.

The Europeans, in contrast, remember that they were asked to pay a great deal for U.S.-inspired measures, without having had much say over their conception. And yet the European banks were owed far more money than American banks. More Europeans also reckoned that the IMF rescue packages for the Asian countries were too fiscally restrictive.

To reduce the scope for such disputes and misunderstandings, Euroland needs to develop a strategic view of its wider responsibilities in co-managing the global economy. To their credit, many American policymakers want the Europeans to overcome their internal divisions and nominate a political representative that could speak for the euro zone. No doubt U.S. support for such an authoritative spokesman would depend on what he or she said. But the creation of such a post would—on balance—facilitate the striking of bargains and increase the chances of making them stick.

Euroland thus needs a political figure who could operate alongside European Central Bank (ECB) president Wim Duisenberg. The point of such a post should not be merely to deal with the old American grumbles about European divisions and provincialism. Now that the Asian financial crises are history, and the euro has emerged as a solid currency, the time has come for Europe to make its presence felt at the high tables of global finance.

Until now, Europe's ministers and officials have merely tried to forge "common understandings" on international financial questions. Such efforts are necessary but not sufficient: cooperation of this kind remains slow, reactive, and often vacuous. Furthermore, the current procedures for external representation show that Euroland is unable to make painful choices. In G-7 negotiations, for example, the euro zone is represented not only by three central bank governors (from France, Germany, and Italy) and the ECB president, but also by the finance minister of the country that holds the rotating EU presidency and the EU commissioner in charge of monetary affairs, "to lend assistance." This unwieldy arrangement has—predictably—drawn a negative U.S. reaction. The Americans point out, with some justification, that despite the lofty talk of European integration, there are now more Europeans around the table at every international meeting.

The Politics of Action

So who exactly should be the political voice of Euroland? The commissioner in charge of EMU, Pedro Solbes, say many euro-enthusiasts. But in reality any commissioner, however brilliant, will lack political clout because the large member-states in particular will not accept that he speaks for Euroland. Nor does public opinion seem ready for such a step. It might seem sensible for the Council of Ministers, which groups the EU finance ministers, to take prime responsibility for external representation, because of the sensitivity of the issues, and because the member-states still control the money needed for international rescue operations. However, the rotating presidency of the council also seems ill-suited to perform this task. It lacks continuity and credibility, and is seen by many non-Europeans, especially Americans, as a complicating irrelevancy. They have a point.

The U.S. secretary of the treasury is simply not going to treat the finance minister of Luxembourg as a serious interlocutor. There is also the problem that when the rotating president arrives at international meetings, he comes with a carefully prepared position from which he cannot budge without further consultations with his peers, the other finance ministers of the euro zone. This rigidity is not exactly conducive to flexible diplomacy, and certainly not in dealing with international financial crises.

So we need a Mr. Euroland unanimously appointed by the finance ministers of the euro zone and answerable to them. The job would be comparable to the new post of EU high representative for foreign policy. The U.S. treasury secretary or the IMF's managing director could call Mr. Euroland if, say, Russia were on the verge of defaulting on its international debt payments, or simply to review the global financial scene. The Euro-11 Council, the informal body of the finance ministers of the EMU countries, should give Mr. Euroland a mandate to negotiate agreements with other political authorities. And it should then speedily ratify (or reject) any international agreement thus negotiated.

This proposal would require a matching reform of EU rules so that the Euro-11 Council would have the power to make formal decisions affecting the workings of EMU. If there were a single euro-zone representative to put forward a common position in international forums such as G-7 meetings, Euroland would gain the credibility and strength it evidently lacked during the Asian crises. Over time, it would also make sense for Mr. Euroland to become the euro zone's political representative at the IMF.

Evidently, the EU governments are some way away from creating the post of Mr. Euroland. Distinctive national outlooks, shaped by history and habit, not to mention matters of prestige, preclude a rapid agreement. Nonetheless, the Europeans should work toward giving themselves a single voice, for the benefit of the rest of the world as much as for themselves. If they can do it in trade, then why not on international financial questions?

Recasting the Transatlantic Bargain

EMU will be a test for the transatlantic relationship. Overall, it will probably make Europe a more cohesive and assertive international actor. This will be truer if Britain ends its prevarication and decides to join. But even without the British, Euroland is fast becoming a formidable financial power.

This development, in turn, will mean that the existing transatlantic "bargain" will have to be recast. What is needed is a streamlining and transformation of the transatlantic relationship into a more diversified and equal partnership: one where consultation is genuine and not a one-way street. The United States, in short, should stop hedging its bets, shake off its ambivalence, and positively welcome the advent of the euro.

But the Europeans as well will have some tough choices to make. Much will depend on whether Euroland will choose to perform its anticipated greater role in global finance and on whether it can get away with not doing so. Future financial crises, especially those on its geographic doorstep, will play a significant role in this equation. Such crises (for example, another Russian default) will probably act as catalysts for further integration and force Euroland to act, just as other external or disruptive events (German unification, the war in Kosovo) have done in the not-so-distant past. As Malvolio says in Shakespeare's *Twelfth Night:* "Some are born great, some achieve greatness, and some have greatness thrust upon 'em." Euroland is likely to fall into that third category. When that moment comes, Euroland politicians should realize that in order to manage "greatness," important—sometimes painful—reforms will be necessary. The Europeans should also recognize, more than they do at present, that power is linked to responsibility, greater power to greater responsibility. Provincialism and abdication will not suffice, if indeed they ever did. Finally, a more balanced relationship requires an understanding by both Americans and Europeans that they are, in a very real sense, condemned to live together.

Notes

1. For the most flamboyant of this kind of analysis, see Martin Feldstein, "EMU and International Conflict," *Foreign Affairs,* vol. 76 (November–December 1997).

2. For additional figures, see "The Euro Area in the Global Economy," a speech delivered by Christian Noyer, vice president of the European Central Bank, at the London Business School, July 19, 1999.

3. C. Fred Bergsten, "America and Europe: Clash of the Titans?" *Foreign Affairs,* vol. 78 (March–April 1999), p. 20.

4. William Wallace and Jan Zielonka, "Misunderstanding Europe," *Foreign Affairs,* vol. 77 (November–December 1998), p. 67.

5. Peter W. Rodman, *Drifting Apart? Trends in US-European Relations* (Washington, DC.: Nixon Center, June 1999).

6. Martin Walker, "The Euro: Why It's Bad for the Dollar But Good for America," *World Policy Journal,* vol. 15 (Fall 1998), p. 1.

7. See Rodman, *Drifting Apart?*

8. William Pfaff, "The Coming Clash of Europe with America," *World Policy Journal,* vol. 15 (Winter 1998/99), p. 8.

9. Reginald Dale, "Ambivalence Reigns in U.S.-EU Ties," *International Herald Tribune,* September 17, 1999.

10. Tommaso Padoa-Schioppa, *Efficiency, Stability and Equity: A Strategy for the Evolution of the Economic System of the European Community* (Oxford: Oxford University Press, 1987).

11. Wallace and Zielonka, "Misunderstanding Europe," p. 77.

12. Mortimer Zuckerman, "A Second American Century," *Foreign Affairs,* vol. 77 (May/June 1998), pp. 20–21, 31.

Werner Weidenfeld

The Euro and the New Face of the European Union

Future generations of historians will consider the introduction of the euro an historic turning point. The boldest integration project of the European Union (EU) to date, it will change the map of Europe as fundamentally as the end of World War II and the demise of the communist bloc. But not until some time has passed will the curious fabric of the debate over the introduction of the single European currency become truly transparent. Pronouncements both for and against the euro, doubts and fears, speculation and insinuations obscure rather than illuminate a complicated issue. The filibustering over the stability criteria was always strangely superficial and has hardly created confidence. Anyone noticing this quickly realizes that the euro enterprise has not been based on truthfulness.

Among euro supporters, for example, even those with doubts about the timetable of the Maastricht Treaty, had to publicly profess their commitment to it if they were not to risk panicking the financial markets. Even those who did not believe that the stability criteria could be strictly observed had to laud them if budgetary discipline was not to erode. Even those who invested a great deal of effort into considering how to restructure budgets and reinterpret expenditure items had to strongly condemn any form of "creative accounting" to meet the stability criteria. Even those who knew that the stability criteria were relatively arbitrary and say very little about the future stability of the currency had to revere them as European icons, because the central players would otherwise have suffered a loss in credibility.

Euro opponents engaged in the same tactics. Even those who were aware of the German mark's integration into international structures and its dependency on global economic and monetary trends had to hail it as a paragon of stability in favorable contrast to the euro. Even those who doubted the mark's long-term stability had to hide their doubts to make their attack on the idea of the euro more effective.

The debate on the euro was therefore marked by rationality rather than truthfulness. Every comment on the euro was not simply a statement of fact, but a form of speculation about the new reality. Merely hinting that the euro would eventually be introduced "in accordance with provisions in the Maastricht Treaty," for example, was regarded as a step away from the stability criteria, because the treaty left considerable leeway for their interpretation. Indeed, the sage intention of the signatories of the Maastricht Treaty was to develop a culture of monetary stability rather than to follow preestablished criteria to the letter by use of creative budget statistics. Any financial expert worth his or her salt would have known these elementary facts but had to be careful of the chain reaction that might be set off by reference to "the introduction of the euro as provided for in the treaty." Thus the perceived move away from the stability criteria gave rise to doubts about the euro's credibility before it had even got off the ground.

Every remark about the euro therefore had an effect on several levels—it was not merely a comment on the issue itself but also provided a focus for speculative conjectures and helped create a new reality. Rarely has the phenomenon that sociologists call the "reciprocity of perspectives"—what does the other think I am thinking that the other thinks I think—been as tangible as in this case. Any remark had to take into account the possible chain of escalating reactions. That is why the euro debate has seemed so sterile and ritualized: Every new term, every new nuance on the part of decisionmakers could have uncontrollable consequences. The creators of the euro therefore found themselves maneuvering on very difficult territory between multiple reflections of facts and ambiguous descriptions of reality.

The Euro as the Key to a New European Solidarity

But even the ritualized debate cannot explain the seriousness, breadth, and depth of Europeans' concern about the introduction of the euro. Suddenly, a new kind of interest in Europe has developed. After the age of visionary ideas and pancontinental dreams, after the era of those of little faith, after the celebrations marking the end of continental division, greater personal involvement in the European reality can now be observed. The times in which Europe sparked off solemn rhetoric are long gone—as are the years when European developments served primarily as a reason for bureaucracy bashing and egoism over national contributions. More essential matters are now at stake. What is the secret of the euro that is so much on the minds of Europeans?

Evidently Europeans sense that the introduction of the euro concerns much more than the financial details—the question of identity is of greater urgency now than it has ever been. At all times Europeans have had various sources of identity, both positive and negative: the great cultural conflicts, empires, and dynasties; religious and philosophical hegemonies; and finally, major power struggles, such as the East-West conflict, that divided the continent. With the end of this conflict the last important tool for interpreting the political and cultural map of Europe has disappeared. Hitherto Europe was held together by the need for the political classes to forge links between their societies and by external threats; these ties are growing weaker now that the threat is gone. There are noticeable symptoms of renationalization, and national interests allow for only minimal steps forward on the European project, as the 1997 Amsterdam Treaty makes abundantly clear.

Since then we have found ourselves in a kind of a limbo without a clearly defined mission. How should we organize our lives together? What does a left or right standpoint mean? Why should we integrate nation-states into a European framework if there is no longer a serious threat? Without future-oriented options the old modes of perception will return. Old thinking about the balance of power is experiencing a renaissance; the major European powers are again deciding matters among themselves. Old dividing lines such as those between Habsburgs and Ottomans, between Catholicism and Orthodoxy, have reemerged. Nationalist and ethnic tensions are erupting into violent conflicts involving minorities. All of this is gnawing at and wearing out a Europe that finally has an opportunity to grow together in freedom.

This does not, however, mean that a return to earlier disasters is unavoidable, if we succeed in giving Europe a plausible form and a tangible identity. Identities develop from various sources: from experiences of being a stranger, from threats to one's very existence, and from positive experiences of solidarity. At a time when serious threats no longer provide a basic rationale for a united Europe, we are left with a peaceful link: the new currency. This currency is both a symbolic tie and a day-to-day, concrete link that in the future can make the interdependence of Europeans tangible. The vacuum that emerged with the end of the menacing East-West conflict will be filled by the magnetic field of the euro. The struggles surrounding the euro will become the core of Europe's common cause; the currency will be the key to our identity. Many people will define Europe as the area in which the single currency is in circulation, and conditions in this area will become an integral part of citizens' assessment of their own situation. Crises in distant EU regions will be felt more directly and urgently; events in all parts of the common currency area will influence the stability of the area and its currency as a whole. Buffers provided by information filters at the national level will disappear—Europe will move closer together, to both the approval and disapproval of its citizens.

From the outset European integration has always been about more than merely maximizing the benefits for its member states. The EU combines economic prosperity and political stability with structures aimed at reconciling interests in a productive manner. Linking these elements also adds a further dimension to integration: integration means sharing a common destiny. From joint control of coal and steel—industries formerly essential to the war effort —to the Common Market, the development of cooperation in foreign policy, and the creation of a single currency, Europeans are increasingly uniting their economic and political needs, interests, objectives, and thus their future.

The concept of European solidarity, which today is embedded in many facets of the EU's policies and institutions, forms part of the basic idea of a shared destiny. It is to be found in the EU's political sphere—above all in the structural funds, the cohesion fund, the agricultural sector, and a host of backup policies governing everything from vocational training to the promotion of small languages. It is to be found in the financing of the community on the basis of the economic performance of its members. And it is to be found in the institutional balance between the community and state and the balance between large, medium-size, and small member states in the EU's institutions.

This concept of solidarity-based Europe will be faced with difficult tasks in the years ahead. Increased competition in the global economy has restricted the scope for distribution in Europe, too. The social security network of the classic welfare state is stretched to the breaking point, and the old solidarity models are already being called into question at the national level. Countries are keener than ever before to ensure that they are the net beneficiaries of European integration. Nevertheless, the expansion of the prosperous Western European community cannot be postponed: the accession of the reforming states of Central and Eastern Europe is an historic mandate that the EU cannot reject. In all areas, from a common agricultural policy to the distribution of power in the EU institutions, this mandate will sorely test European solidarity. What can the single currency contribute to the future viability and enhancement of European solidarity?

New Currency—and a New Urgency to Modernize

. . . Monetary union will generate an accompanying need for legitimization on the part of the other time-honored union institutions: the European Parliament, the European Commission, and, above all, the European Council. Their democratic legitimization rests, at best, on shaky ground—this is true even of the Parliament, which is directly elected but invariably with a low voter turnout. They therefore must justify their powerful intervention in the affairs of citizens by their efficiency and the tangible benefits they produce for the common good. Questions about the efficiency of European institutions in economic, employment, or social policy will become louder as the public grows accustomed to regarding economic issues and the single monetary policy from a European perspective. The fact that the European treaties and the consensus of the member states have granted only limited powers in these areas has little influence on public expectations—a fact vividly illustrated by the community's impotence in the Yugoslav conflict.

If the EU wants to avoid losing its legitimacy in the eyes of its citizens, then, it will need more effective powers in the field of economic policy, powers beyond its current authority to monitor the budgets of member states. Leaving sovereignty over economic issues in the hands of the nation-states may be reassuring for citizens as long as the quantum leap toward the single currency has not yet been visibly completed. Once it has taken place, however, and the inefficiencies of competing national economic policies are evident, the public will quickly become frustrated with the again seeming inactivity of the EU—all the more so if the EU wants to tackle the task of leading the European community to success after the enlargement eastward.

The euro should be viewed as a great historic project—by both supporters and opponents. Those who regard this project as a mundane enterprise, who merely juggle figures or even distort them, have failed to recognize the true consequences of the decision. Opponents of the euro must understand that the failure of the single currency will not bring back the supposed idyll of the nation-state. Supporters must make it clear that the introduction of the single currency will bring about a radical transformation in Europe: The euro will create a genuinely European community without external threats, and it will force large-scale financial transfers Europe-wide, thus triggering off newly intense conflicts. They should be fully aware of this now rather than discovering it later with alarm when the euro has come in through the back door. Opponents must openly admit what the consequences of the failure of this historic project could be—namely, that Europeans could turn their backs on further integration and revert to fighting among themselves without a binding consensus or any clear rules. Europe has no comparable alternative should this project fail.

This is the key point. The old and new Europes are vying for ascendancy —but this has not been openly discussed. Europe must begin to discuss these opposing concepts out in the open.

Europe's Response to Globalization

The euro will alter Europe's image not only insofar as it is the motor of internal modernization. The EU must also redefine its role in world politics once it has completed the transformation to monetary union. It will have new opportunities as well as new responsibilities when the euro assumes its position beside the dollar in the global financial system.

The economic performance of the enlarged EU will exceed that of the United States. Already today the EU produces 31 percent of worldwide output and handles more than 20 percent of world trade. Europe's global role will be enhanced by the euro as a world-power factor. Alongside the dollar the European currency will become a major world reserve currency, a trading currency, and an international investment currency—the European response to globalization. The current small-scale national currency areas seem like impotent dwarfs in the face of the immense flows of capital that circulate daily in the world. The vast euro area will force Europe to think globally: the continent will become a key region in the world currency market. A new bipolar world currency system dominated by Europe and the United States will replace the old hegemony of the dollar.

One result will be that the euro will exert enormous pressure on Europe to live up to its new role as a world power. Whether Europeans can summon the required will and solidarity remains to be seen. Global thinking will have to be redefined in the wake of the eastward enlargement of the EU. Three factors mitigate against the EU's development of a global orientation:

- The conflicts on distribution inherent in the enlargement policy will direct attention to internal issues, European policy will be dominated by EU internal policy.
- Differences in interests and efficiency will increase. The new members will only partly share old members' experiences of taking action and dealing with conflicts (for example, in Bosnia); the new members have shown little willingness to relinquish sovereignty. After integration they could endeavor to compensate for their loss of power

over economic and domestic policies by insisting on preserving their sovereignty in foreign policy.

- The ambition to act on the global stage will be shared by only a minority of states.

Several competing factors foster global orientation: The expanded power base of a larger EU; its vicinity to the former superpower Russia in the East; its growing economic interests in the Asian arena; the global economic and political impact of the euro; and, last but not least, the readiness of some new members such as Poland to take action and make a considerable commitment to peacekeeping operations over the last few years. A European global role would have three immediate objectives: to widen the area of political stability around the union, to maintain the EU's key role in maintaining order in the region, and to safeguard Europe's interests at a global level. In addition, a European world policy should develop strategic partnerships with other major international players. In the surrounding area such a policy would involve major states such as Russia, Ukraine, and Turkey; in the Middle East it would mean safeguarding the security and integrity of Israel and supporting Palestinian independence; and in Asia it would give strategic priority to Japan and China.

If the euro transforms Europe into a world power, then the transatlantic relationship will also have to be restructured. The challenge lies not only in overcoming the deficiencies in Europe's global policies but also in redefining the transatlantic partnership as a whole. The security link between Europe and the United States will continue to exist, but without the presence and mentality of a defense organization always on standby to repulse a large-scale attack. The political community across the Atlantic will continue to exist but it will lack the challenge of competition with an antagonistic value system and a special sensitivity to the development of transatlantic relations. Europe and the United States still share values and a Western identity but lack a definition of what they have in common and of their specific contribution to the new issues in international politics. On the other hand, no political ideology challenges the supremacy of pluralist democracy worldwide, and the existing fundamentalist movements in the Islamic world, the ethno-ideologies and movements with charismatic leaders, are not of an antagonistic nature, nor do they possess the power to threaten the West militarily. The West's stabilizing policy now has an opportunity to actively shape conditions instead of merely reacting by repelling threats.

Western states are more involved in international cooperation and supranational integration than other players in world politics. However, within European societies this policy is not consolidating and being accepted at the same rate. Politicians are reacting to the globalization of challenges with regional integration, the phases of which have to be justified on a national level. Problems, decisions, and legitimization must be made to coincide.

A new order of international politics, new norms aimed at ensuring peace and at reconciling interests, and a new conflict-prevention strategy cannot emerge from ad hoc coalitions. Such coalitions can be thwarted at any time by calculated aggression if they are not supported and credibly protected by visibly cohesive communities of nations. Europe and the United States are the only reliable guarantors of stability in the world today; their readiness and ability to impose order will be needed in the future, especially in regions and spheres that lie beyond the current structures of transatlantic cooperation. Many necessary solutions are feasible only if the burden is shared, a high degree of political coordination is developed, and an adequately dense communications network is built.

The advent of the euro will considerably increase the need for consultation and coordination in the transatlantic relationship. With the introduction of the single currency Europe will, at least in economic terms, move into the newly structured league of world powers. At the same time, the transatlantic partners will become more interdependent. Awareness of internal economic developments will increase on both sides. This will have at least two consequences for the transatlantic relationship.

- First, monetary policy. The United States will observe Europe closely to see whether the euro is being deliberately manipulated for the benefit of European interests and to the detriment of its own. If Europe and the United States use the external value of their currencies to increase their own competitiveness, the transatlantic community will face new conflicts. This is a potential source of mistrust that, if not tackled, could slowly poison relations.
- Second, there is the question of global responsibility. The United States will ask itself to what extent a monetary power such as Europe must also assume responsibility for global security, and the issue of burdensharing will become more pressing with the introduction of the euro. A gap will open between the demands on Europe and the staying power of European foreign policy. Further tensions can then be expected if Europe's effectiveness and power increase internationally but its preferences and actions are not in harmony with Washington's interests.

The start of monetary union will mean more joint responsibility for the transatlantic partners, including responsibility for developing a reliable set of rules for the world economy. While a tried and tested system of rules and arbitration for world trade exists in the form of the World Trade Organization, there is no comparable framework for the global financial markets. The fact that capital circulates globally within a matter of minutes presents not only opportunities but also risks, as has been vividly illustrated by the Asian crisis. The United States realized even more readily than the EU that the impact of such financial slumps can no longer be limited regionally. They have a detrimental effect on the global economy and quickly reach dimensions no longer controlled with the traditional international instruments for fighting balance of payments crises, in particular those available to the International Monetary Fund. The United States and Europe, the two largest global players in the world's financial markets, are therefore faced with an important task: they must join forces and work to create a global framework for recognizing and combating crises such as the one in Asia even before they develop. Furthermore, the growing funding difficulties of the International Monetary Fund show that new methods that can be financed over the long term are needed to control the debt crises that have already emerged.

Restructuring Transatlantic Relations

In the light of this array of tasks, it would seem that the increasing institutionalization of transatlantic communications is unavoidable as the need for consultations and coordination between Europe and America grows. Several proposals for this have already been put forward.

A transatlantic process of mutual learning. Now that the common threat presented by the Soviet Union has evaporated, societal relations between Europe and America offer a special chance to place Atlantic integration on a long-term, stable basis. The internal challenges facing European and American societies have determined their common agenda during the last few years. It is obvious that there is a need for common action in cross-border problems affecting both regions in equal measure—for example, crime and migration. However, Europe and the United States are also faced with common challenges in the reform of social security systems and education. Frequently, the approach of each side to these problems is very different, which means that conditions for establishing a transatlantic process of mutual learning are ideal. Only through a systematic exchange of experiences can the potential for innovation on both sides of the Atlantic be put to maximum use. A transatlantic process of mutual learning could do this by providing a structural framework for the currently rather random contacts at the social level.

European-American political cooperation. At the level of political cooperation our task is to create a framework for relations that can act as a catalyst rather than an obstacle to greater integration. Such new political structures can no longer be based on the rationale of defense against a common enemy. International crisis management and global challenges are the issues in which the partners have a prime interest in cooperating. The approach to rogue states such as Iraq, Iran, or Libya, international environmental policy, and, after the introduction of the euro, monetary policy all clearly illustrate the need for close coordination. The establishment of a process of European-American political cooperation along the lines of European political cooperation could give our joint endeavors a future-oriented structure. Even a minimal institutional framework—for example, a secretariat—could guarantee continuity and effectiveness. It could provide a modern forum for mastering the issues that the international community now takes to the transatlantic partners and for which an appropriate organizational form is lacking.

A new transatlantic market. Nowhere is the degree of transatlantic interdependence and the potential for future cooperation more apparent than in economic relations. Economically Europe and the United States are the most closely integrated regions in the world. New regulatory mechanisms are required if the full potential of transatlantic economic relations is to be realized in the context of growth and crises in East and Southeast Asia and trade and monetary competition. The development of a new transatlantic market is overdue. Although most bilateral trade is no longer subject to restrictions, there are important exceptions and nontariff trade barriers. A joint liberalization initiative on the part of Americans and Europeans could help in the development of the World Trade Organization, in the creation of a common strategy for dealing with the consequences of opening up markets, in the preparation of international standards, and in the coordination of the economic policies of Europe and the United States. Such an initiative would be a stepping stone to a transatlantic internal market in which goods, capital, services, and persons circulate freely. It could also defuse conflicts in trade and monetary policy.

Until we have a new transatlantic market, a process of European-American political cooperation, and a transatlantic process of mutual learning, European-American relations will not acquire the substance and vitality they urgently need to master the challenges of the twenty-first century. In the light of the risks involved, the completion of European integration could be delayed or even hindered if the transatlantic partnership is not intensified. The United States needs Europe as a world power that, despite its cultural, historical, and political diversity, is in a position to safeguard its interests and pool its resources. However, Europe's importance to the United States cannot lie in seconding U.S. global policies. The distribution of burdens and responsibility, a partnership between equals, is the prerequisite of a future alliance.

The dynamic process of economic and monetary union offers us an opportunity to revitalize transatlantic structures of cooperation. If we boldly seize this chance, the introduction of the euro could stimulate a new era in relations between Europe and the United States. Entry into the third stage of EMU marks the last important milestone of European integration in this century. Which road the EU chooses to take from here will determine its destiny, both internally and externally, for decades to come. If the EU wants to continue its success story, the states of Europe must keep to the path of cooperation—both with one another and with their partners across the Atlantic.

POSTSCRIPT

Will the European Economic and Monetary Union Increase the Potential for Transatlantic Conflict?

A good place to begin unraveling the complicated process that has led to the European Monetary Union is Michael Maclay, *The European Union* (Sutton Publishing, 1998). This 100-page book begins with a timeline of important dates and a map of member states, includes dates of their joining the Union, and ends with a glossary of terms and abbreviations and an annotated bibliography. In between are six clearly written chapters that follow the development of the European Union from 1945 to the present.

Weidenfeld, author of the No-side selection, is coeditor with Wolfgang Wessels of *Europe From A to Z* (European Commission, 1997), a mini-encyclopedia of events translated from the German. For a useful guide to the treaties that have created the present Union, see Alexander Noble, *From Rome to Maastricht: Essential Guide to the European Union* (Warner Books, 1996).

Britain's decision to opt out of the common currency is explained in Michael Charlton, *The Price of Victory* (Parkwest Publications, 1985). Robert Mundell and Armand Clesse, eds., *The Euro as a Stabilizer in the International Economic System* (Kluwer, 2000) compile papers presented at an international conference held at the Luxembourg Institute for European and International Studies, which speak directly to questions raised in this issue.

Effects of the EMU on gender conventions are explored in Barbara Hobson, ed., *Gender and Citizenship in Transition* (Routledge, 2000) and Graham Dawson et al., *Market, State and Feminism: The Economics of Feminist Policy* (Edward Elgar, 2000). In the Social Charter annexed to the Maastricht Treaty, fundamental social rights are extended to people not in the paid workforce on the grounds of their European citizenship—a pathbreaking opportunity for women.

Analysis of the current situation is best studied through journals. University of Chicago professor Stephen M. Walt explains why Europe and America are drifting apart in "The Ties That Fray," *The National Interest* (Winter 1998/1999). C. Fred Bergsten, director of the Institute for International Economics, sees a looming clash between the euro and the dollar in "America and Europe: Clash of the Titans," *Foreign Affairs* (March/April 1999). For a look at conflicting views on the status of the euro as of late 2000, see Justin Fox Fortune, "The Euro Is a Raging Success—Really It Is," *International Economy* (October 30, 2000) and Janet Bush, "Euro Blues?" *International Economy* (November 2000).

ISSUE 18

Do the Roots of Modern Terrorism Lie in Political Powerlessness, Economic Hopelessness, and Social Alienation?

YES: Anatol Lieven, from "Strategy for Terror," *Prospect* (October 2001)

NO: Mark Juergensmeyer, from "Terror in the Name of God," *Current History* (November 2001)

ISSUE SUMMARY

YES: World policy analyst Anatol Lieven states that dated United States cold war policies and despair-inducing political, economic, and social conditions have contributed to the rise of radical Islamists, some of whom were responsible for the September 11, 2001, attacks.

NO: International relations specialist Mark Juergensmeyer contends that the roots of the September 11, 2001, attacks lie in the radical views of the terrorists, especially the symbolism of cosmic war and the battle between good and evil.

W hat is the relationship between modern terrorist acts (such as the sarin gas attack initiated by Aum Shinrikyo in Tokyo, Timothy McVeigh's assault on the Murragh Federal Building in Oklahoma City, the actions of Afghanistan's Taliban and the wider al Qaeda network) and the religions (Buddhism, militant Christianity, and revivalist Islam) invoked to justify terrorist acts? Do the roots of all of these acts lie in feelings of despair, alienation, and powerlessness? Is the ancient pull of religion as a force in an increasingly secular world simply reasserting itself? This issue traces the roots of twenty-first-century terrorism by exploring the intellectual and cultural environments that produce it.

When Osama bin Laden spoke about the "humiliation and disgrace" suffered by Islam for "more than 80 years," he was evoking a bitter past that culminated in the occupation of Constantinople in 1918 and the subsequent carving up of the Ottoman Empire by European powers into what we call the modern Middle East. The countries created, the frontiers drawn, and even the system of independent secular states, based on national citizenship, were

European creations and quite foreign to the Islamic worldview that had prevailed since the time of the prophet Muhammad in the seventh century. At that time Islam unified a people who lived in many geographical areas. It is hardly surprising, then, that residents of the modern Middle East would find the imposition of secular states, based not on religion or on tribal identity, to be confusing at best.

As the inheritor of Western world dominance, the United States is seen by many in the Muslim world as playing a similar game—propping up corrupt leaders who serve its own purposes, while allowing disparities in wealth and power between the haves and the have-nots to increase. With the collapse of the Soviet Union in 1989, the Muslim Middle East, bereft of outside allies, was forced to create indigenous bases from which to oppose what it views as the latest foreign hegemon, the United States.

To many in the Middle East, modernization has meant the importation of corrupt Western values and a decadent Western lifestyle. Communism and democracy seem to have been eclipsed by a global market, larger and more powerful than any nation-state and responsible to neither law nor moral ideal. For some the only hope seems to lie in a return to an idealized version of the early, pure form of Islam, which existed at the time of the prophet Muhammad. Wahhabism, a strict, eighteenth-century movement that sought to purify and renew Islam, was embraced first by the rulers of Saudi Arabia and has also inspired such extremist reformers as the Taliban in Afghanistan and the Muslim Brotherhood in Egypt.

Moderate, mainstream Islam has rules governing warfare that are quite similar to the so-called "just war" theory articulated by the Christian theologian Augustine in the fifth century. War may be undertaken only under specific circumstances (in defense of the faith or to right a great wrong), noncombatants should be protected, and prisoners must be fairly treated. There is nothing in the Qur'an to justify steering airplanes into skyscrapers. Nonetheless, the impulse behind these acts has received intense and emotional support from a surprising variety of sources.

In a world that seems godless to many, the globalization of Western popular culture and the unresponsiveness of national governments have led some to take matters into their own hands. Afghanistan, the battleground for control of the vast oil and gas reserves of Central Asia, is merely the latest focus in an ongoing struggle between tribal and global impulses. Can aggressive, violent forms of religion thrive when people are basically content with their lot? As we discuss in Issue 14 of this volume, Islamic revivalism does not necessarily represent a threat to a stable world order. What motivates people to participate in terrorist acts is the major question posed by this issue.

In the following selections, Anatol Lieven faults despair-inducing economic, social, and political conditions in the Middle East for facilitating the rise of radical Islamists, some of whom carried out the September 11th attacks. Mark Juergensmeyer counters that the roots of the attacks lie in the radical religious views of the terrorists, especially their use of the powerful symbolism of cosmic war—the battle between good and evil.

Anatol Lieven

Strategy for Terror

The US has been the target of a very serious act of war, conducted by a formidably cruel, brave, fanatical and well-organised enemy with a terrifying capacity for both savagery and self-sacrifice. At the time of writing, a few hours after the attacks, the casualty figures are not known, but it is clear that this has been by far the worst terrorist attack in history and the worst attack of any kind ever directed against the American mainland.

On the assumption that the perpetrators are identified and traced to some physical space a ferocious military response will be necessary. Not to do this would be to betray the victims and display weakness. However, successful war requires both a capacity for ruthlessness and an intelligent political strategy, including the attraction and conciliation of essential allies. So what we also desperately need is a fundamental reassessment of many of the attitudes which have guided American policies since the end of the cold war. In some areas at least, we may get this. For while war produces strongly emotional responses, it can also provoke stark clarity of thought and a radical re-ordering of previous priorities.

Such new thinking is essential, not only on the part of the US, but also of Britain and other American allies. This is not just because the US will expect our full support in hunting down and destroying the perpetrators of this atrocity. It is also because our own cities are under the same threat, and the extent of this threat may be determined by what actions and policies America now pursues. We therefore have to work with the US to shape common strategies.

The attack has underlined the irrelevance of America's dominant security priorities, which are still rooted in cold war attitudes and structures. This is true of three areas: first, the attempt to cast Russia and China as major threats to vital US interests. Second, the strategy of National Missile Defence (NMD) and the militarisation of space. And third, policy towards Israel and its occupation of the West Bank and Gaza—since this attack originated in the Muslim world and was clearly motivated by hatred of Israel and of US support for Israel.

Very much against its will, America is now effectively at war alongside Israel. That gives it the right, and, perhaps, the possibility of finally controlling some of its ally's more outrageous actions. But while some Americans in private are already placing the blame for what has happened on blind US support for

Israel, the short-term tendency will be to back Israel to the hilt in whatever action it now takes. This temptation will of course be increased by the ugly popular celebrations of "victory" in parts of the Arab world.

A hardline response from the US is appropriate in the short-term. Moreover it would be wrong to execute any significant policy shifts that could be construed as a victory for the terrorists. But if the US response results in too much pressure on the governments of Pakistan and other fragile states (in the case of Pakistan, by forcing the Taleban to hand over Osama bin Laden) these states may collapse—with radical Islamists left to pick up the pieces. This is where American allies need to play a part. Above all, a new US policy needs to be shaped by three linked realisations. First, that since the end of the cold war, there has come into being the basis of a unified world system in which the world's other leading states are partners, not enemies, and in which all these states are under threat from similar forces. In other words, there really is the makings of an "international community"—or would be, if the US could stop acting as if it alone constituted this community. The community is based on shared adherence to western-led modernity. The only categorical opponents of this modernisation project are indeed religious maniacs—who are not to be found in Moscow or Beijing. Second, that with the exception of certain middle eastern states, the real threat to the world order comes not from states, but from below: from alienated populations. And third, since the US cannot occupy and police the Muslim world in the struggle against Muslim terrorism, it is essential to have the co-operation of leading Muslim states. This is something which was already emphasised by the aftermath of the attacks on Khobar Towers and the USS Cole.

The reordering of policy towards Israel is a slender hope, at least in the short term. But when it comes to NMD and policy towards Russia and China, a shift is more likely.

The failure, until now, to move away from the cold war has its roots not only in various forms of inherited bigotry, but also in very strong interests within the US security establishment. This establishment was a product of the cold war, and it needs a cold war-type enemy: huge, identifiable, and, most importantly, armed with either high-tech conventional arms or with old-style nuclear missiles. Hence the endless insistence on the danger of a restoration of the Soviet Union.

Russia is no longer strong enough to fulfil that role, so China has been widely promoted as a replacement. But a pathological loathing of Russia remains in important parts of the US establishment and, until last week at least, some bizarre arguments were still made concerning Russia.

Thus the leaders of the only institute in Washington explicitly devoted to the study of the Caucasus and central Asia has been arguing for an American reconciliation with the Taleban as part of a new strategy of driving Russian influence out of the region. In other words, these people wanted to revive American policies of the 1980s—with which some of them were closely associated —of support for the Afghan Mujahedin; despite the fact that the Soviet global threat has disappeared, Russia is not in occupation of Afghanistan, and this past American policy has helped to produce Osama bin Laden and the safe haven given to him by the Taleban. Such people have sought to deny the presence of international Muslim radicals in Chechnya—though the latter have a website which publicises its victories and casualties, and despite the fact that Osama bin Laden's aides have spoken publicly of sending volunteers and supplies to Chechnya. Hopefully, we will now be hearing less of such stupidity.

Concerning NMD, no more argument should be necessary. For years now, both critics and allies of the US, plus other states, have been arguing that the real threat to the American mainland comes not from ballistic missiles, but from terrorism; that a ballistic missile defence system would therefore be a form of Maginot Line which our enemies would simply outflank. After all, if a missile had been fired at the US last week, the country responsible would have been obliterated by an American counter-strike hours later. Given the nature of the actual attack, we may never be exactly sure which group or combination of groups was responsible and, therefore, of how and where to retaliate. More than five years after the bomb attack on the US barracks at Khobar Towers in Saudi Arabia in 1996, which killed 19 US servicemen, American intelligence analysts are still at odds over whether the perpetrators were agents of Osama bin Laden, of Saddam Hussein, or Iran—and if so which Iranian-backed group—or even of some combination between them. One reason for this failure has been the attitude of the Saudi authorities and intelligence services, who for their own security reasons have refused to seriously investigate an Iranian role. An even less helpful stance was taken by the Yemeni authorities after the attack on the USS Cole.

One way of combating the kind of attacks we saw is of course better security in the US; but this will not necessarily prevent a terrorist attack, as long as that terrorist is prepared to die. In the end, the key to fighting this war successfully has to be good intelligence—and given the difficulty that American agents have of penetrating the world of the Islamist extremists, for such intelligence the west desperately needs Arab and Muslim allies. The Saudis in particular will have to be persuaded to drop the decades-old strategy begun by Saudi Arabia's founder, Kind Ibn Saud, according to which the House of Saud has turned a blind eye to Saudi-based radicalism beyond the borders of the kingdom, as long as the radicals do not cause trouble within Saudi Arabia itself.

The help of leading Muslim states will also be essential if there is to be an invasion and occupation of some part of the Muslim world. For, in their different ways, the US bombardment of targets in Sudan and Afghanistan, and the aftermath of the Nato bombardment of Yugoslavia, have shown the inadequacy of long-range bombardment when it comes to destroying enemies on the ground, who are dispersed and hidden in a friendly civilian population.

Unfortunately, over the past ten years, US Muslim allies have been severely undermined by Israeli policies and American refusal to act against those policies while continuing massively to help Israel with financial and military aid. This primarily refers to the failure quickly and honestly to honour the Oslo agreement, the continuation of Jewish settlement in the occupied territories and the failure of the west in general to offer generous financial aid to Palestinian refugees. This has been in defiance of UN resolutions, of the wishes of almost all other US allies, including all allies in the middle east—and of America's professed principles and the rules it insists on elsewhere. The result of this has been the collapse of the peace process and renewed mass protest and terror —including, for the first time, by Israeli Arab citizens.

Israel and its US backers have stuck with policies which were necessary at a time of threats to Israel's existence; the threats came not only from its Arab neighbours, but indirectly from their superpower backer, the Soviet Union. Over the past generation, this has changed—but basic American policies do not appear to have changed in any way. With American military backing, Israel crushingly defeated its Arab neighbours and forced two of them to make peace. By far the largest, Egypt, became an American client state. The Soviet Union collapsed, not only crippling the remaining radical Arab states militarily, but releasing an immense flood of Soviet Jewish emigrants to Israel. This established Jewish demographic superiority (within Israel's pre-1967 borders) beyond challenge. Due to this link, but more importantly because of a common threat from Islamist extremism, Russia has actually become in many ways a de facto ally of Israel (at least when it comes to intelligence sharing).

Saddam Hussein's invasion of Kuwait in 1990 united most of the Arab world behind the west's response. A key part of the price the US had to pay for putting this broad anti-Saddam coalition together was to promise its Arab allies to push Israel towards a just peace with the Palestinians. Largely as a result of the American failure to do this, US Arab allies have been reduced to what a Jordanian ex-minister described to me as "shell regimes." This pro-western figure—he was a senior fellow at an American think tank at the time— said that the repeated humiliations of the Arab world by Israel had destroyed the domestic prestige of his own and other Arab elites seen as pro-American, and hollowed out the entire state system. "The only reason we are still standing is because no one is strong enough yet to push us over."

It is not only unyielding American policy towards Israel which has undermined its diplomacy in much of the Muslim world—there has also been a failure to exploit opportunities. Sections of the Iranian regime remain bitterly hostile to the US—but they are far more hostile to Iraq and the Taleban, who just happen to be America's own greatest enemies in the region. In 1998, after Taleban massacres of Iranian diplomats and Afghan Shias, Iran nearly went to war with Afghanistan. Up to now, this has not been made the basis for any new American strategy with regard to Iran—partly because so few US analysts have even noticed it. A chance to gain a new ally in the fight against Sunni terrorism has been lost. Instead, the US is risking new action in the Persian Gulf in the face of Iraqi, Afghan and Iranian hostility, with Iran armed by Russia—despite the fact that all these states loathe and fear each other. American policy in the region is officially described as "dual containment" (of Iraq and Iran). Up until last week at least, it was more like quadruple containment (of Iraq, Iran, Russia and Afghanistan), in obedience to policies laid down by a profoundly ignorant US Congress, under the sway of domestic lobbies.

To blame Muslim-based terrorism on Israel would be unfair and inadequate, for a whole set of reasons. The humiliation of the Arab and Muslim worlds by Israel is so infuriating to them, in part because it is only the last in a long history of defeats starting in the 17th century and extending far into the

20th—overwhelmingly at the hands of the Christian or western worlds. It is of course true that the west has often played a disgraceful role—at least in the 20th century, when it repeatedly betrayed its own professed ideals in its behaviour towards Muslim peoples. However, the key reason for these defeats has been the prolonged decline of the Muslim world relative to the west—defeats which were already producing radical Muslim responses (whether in Sufi or Wahabi guise) in the last decades of the 18th century. The key reason for this decline has been the multiple failures of development and progress within the Muslim world.

It is the pathologies produced by these failures, as well as the appearance of Israel and the US as objects of hatred, which have produced the phenomenon of modern Muslim extremist. Though they have found their most widespread and powerful expressions in the Muslim world, these pathologies are not restricted to that world. They are to be found wherever proud people, with strong but in part irrational traditions, feel defeated or radically unsettled by aspects of western-dominated modernity....

The danger to world order comes not from the ruling elites, who are increasingly integrated into the global market order (even in China, Russia and India), but from the excluded: those numerous social and ethnic groups who, for whatever reasons of culture, history or geography, are unable to take part in the world banquet—or who have declined in status, even if they have benefited economically. After all, the great European political pathologies of the 20th century did not have their roots in underdevelopment as such; rather they stemmed from the effects of uneven development and cultural change on deeply conservative societies.

Many of these excluded groups and individuals are simply pitiable, far too weak and miserable to threaten anyone. Others, however, have proud cultural traditions which make it very difficult for them to accept second-class status. Their strong fighting traditions give them a distinct edge in certain kinds of warfare, in organised crime and in the areas where the two intersect. Such groups give hostile states the chance to hit at the west without exposing their hands directly and thereby suffering retaliation.

Of course, such alienated groups form a relatively small minority of the world's population. The greater part of humanity has benefited to a greater or lesser extent from economic growth and "globalisation" in recent decades. But those who have not—or think they have not—are still too numerous. They can certainly not be mastered by the high-tech fighter aircraft, heavy battle tanks and enormous aircraft carriers on which the post-cold war US military remains determined to spend so much money.

This then is the dark side of the global village—the ability of that village's alienated minorities to hit out at their perceived oppressors over huge distances. Because the Muslim world was the oldest and grandest rival of the west and its greatest "victim," because "fundamentalist" Islam provides a singularly tough and yet flexible ideological framework for modern extremism, and because of the role of Israel and the US as a focus on hatred, it is in the Muslim world that these pathologies have assumed their greatest and more dangerous forms.

It would be wrong to copy Samuel Huntington and posit one single Muslim cultural-political world united in difference from and hostility to the west.

The Muslim world is immensely varied, both in its own cultures and in its attitudes to the west. In the largest Muslim state by far—Indonesia—radical Islam as yet plays a rather limited role. But, sadly, one thing which does unite most Muslim countries is relative political and socio-economic failure.

With the exception of some of the oil-endowed Gulf states and—to a limited degree—Turkey and Malaysia, every single Muslim country has failed to enter the developed world, whether in its western or east Asian variant. Almost all are menaced by rapid, and in some cases, virtually uncontrolled population growth, flooding inadequate labour markets with unemployable and embittered young men. Almost all are failing to educate or use their female populations, in some cases disgracefully so. Afghanistan has collapsed altogether, becoming a murderous theocracy and international menace. Others are threatened with this fate. The behaviour of elites and state services across most of the region presents a deeply depressing picture. Most importantly, this has been true of regimes across the political spectrum, from authoritarian traditional monarchies and western-backed semi-democracies through anti-western radical nationalist and military regimes to ex-communist ones in the former Soviet Union.

It is not surprising in these circumstances that many people in the region have fallen back on revolutionary Islam as a last resort when everything else has failed, and on belief in a supposedly "Koranic" or Shariah system. As a result of this, the Muslim world finds itself in a profoundly peripheral position vis-à-vis the western-dominated world. At the same time (unlike Africa or Latin America) it retains a deeply-felt—and assiduously cultivated—collective memory of the Islamic sphere as a great cultural, economic and political metropolis in its own right.

So in attacking America, Muslim terrorists would certainly not only be attacking Israel's key backer, but also the central symbol of their own failure. And anti-American Arab nationalism is—in the classical fashion of all nationalisms—an ideology which is capable of sucking up and drawing strength from a whole set of other, unconnected resentments, including bitter resentment of the corruption and oppression of the Arabs' own regimes. Israeli and American behaviour has provided a dangerous focus for this.

The Chinese have some of the same historically-based feelings and, in the past, this contributed to the appalling pathologies of Maoism; but China has the largest population on earth, with one of the world's fastest growing economies. Economic success has been the hallmark of the other Chinese states, Taiwan, Singapore and Hong Kong. Indeed the Chinese diaspora has been one of the most economically successful groups in world history. China is a genuinely powerful, relatively orderly state under a nationalist and authoritarian, but rational and pragmatic leadership. It has become a successful participant in the western-defined modernisation project. The position of the Muslim world is very different.

I gained certain insights into the roots of Muslim extremism during my work as a stringer for *The Times* in Pakistan and Afghanistan in the late 1980s —not only through meeting some precursors of the Taleban among the Afghan Mujahedin, but among radical groups in Pakistan. I especially remember a long conversation with some young members of a "fundamentalist" group in

Lahore. None were from the bottom of society. They came from that classical breeding group of fascistic and religious extremism, the struggling lower middle class and upper peasantry.

They were under threat not only of sinking into the immiserated, semi-employed proletariat—with the Hira Mandi, or prostitutes' quarter, as the possible destiny of their womenfolk—but of being able to escape and rise only through entry into the junior ranks of organised crime, especially heroin smuggling. Given the state of the Pakistani economy, legitimate economic opportunities were few. Their traditional communities and cultures were being undermined by urbanisation and "atomisation." The semi-western, semi-modern new culture being thrust on them was of the most repulsive kind, especially concerning the treatment of women—a mixture of western licentiousness with local brutality, crudity and chauvinism.

In these depressing circumstances, adherence to a radical Islamist network provides a sense of cultural security, a new community and some degree of social support—modest, but still better than anything the state can provide. Poverty is recast as religious simplicity and austerity. Perhaps, even more importantly, belief provides a measure of pride: a reason to keep a stiff back amidst continual humiliations and temptations. In the blaring, stinking, violent world of the modern "third world" Muslim city, the architecture and aesthetic mood of the mosque is (like the Catholic churches in central America described by Graham Greene in *The Lawless Roads*) the only oasis, not only of beauty but of an ordered and coherent culture and guide to living. Of course this is true ten times over for a young male inhabitant of an Afghan, Chechen or Palestinian refugee camp.

NO

Mark Juergensmeyer

Terror in the Name of God

P erhaps the first question that came to mind on September 11 when the horrific images of the aerial assaults on the World Trade Center and the Pentagon were conveyed around the world was: Why would anyone want to do such a thing? As the twin towers crumbled in clouds of dust and the identities and motives of the perpetrators began to emerge, a second question arose: Why would anyone want to do such a thing in the name of God?

These are the questions that have arisen frequently in the post–cold war world. Religion seems to be connected with violence everywhere—from the World Trade Center bombings to suicide attacks in Israel and the Palestinian Authority; assassinations in India, Israel, Egypt, and Algeria; nerve gas in the Tokyo subways; unending battles in Northern Ireland; abortion-clinic killings in Florida; and the bombing of Oklahoma City's federal building.

What does religion have to with this virtually global rise of religious violence? In one sense, very little. If the activists involved in the World Trade Center bombing are associated with Osama bin Laden's al Qaeda, they are a small network at the extreme end of a subculture of dissatisfied Muslims who are in turn a small minority within the world of Islam. Osama bin Laden is no more representative of Islam than Timothy McVeigh is of Christianity, or Japan's Skoko Asahara is of Buddhism.

Still, one cannot deny that the ideals and ideas of these vicious activists are permeated with religion. The authority of religion has given bin Laden's cadres what they believe is the moral standing to employ violence in their assault on the very symbol of global economic power. It has also provided the metaphor of cosmic war, an image of spiritual struggle that every religion has within its repository of symbols: the fight between good and bad, truth and evil. In this sense, the attack on the World Trade Center was very religious. It was meant to be catastrophic, an act of biblical proportions.

What is striking about the World Trade Center assault and many other recent acts of religious terrorism is that they have no obvious military goal. These are acts meant for television. They are a kind of perverse performance of power meant to ennoble the perpetrators' views of the world and to draw us into their notions of cosmic war.

From Mark Juergensmeyer, "Terror in the Name of God," *Current History*, vol. 100, no. 649 (November 2001). Copyright © 2001 by Current History, Inc. Reprinted by permission.

The recent attacks in New York City and Washington, D. C.—although unusual in the scale of the assault—are remarkably similar to many other acts of religious terrorism around the world. In my recent comparative study of religious terrorism, *Terror in the Mind of God,* I have found a strikingly familiar pattern. In each case, concepts of cosmic war are accompanied by strong claims of moral justification and an enduring absolutism that transforms worldly struggles into sacred battles. It is not so much that religion has become politicized but that politics has become religionized. Worldly struggles have been lifted onto the high proscenium of sacred battle.

This is what makes religious terrorism so difficult to combat. Its enemies have become satanized: one cannot negotiate with them or easily compromise. The rewards for those who fight for the cause are transtemporal, and the time lines of their struggles are vast. Most social and political struggles look for conclusions within the lifetimes of their participants, but religious struggles can take generations to succeed. When I pointed out to political leaders of the Hamas movement in the Palestinian Authority that Israel's military force was such that a Palestinian military effort could never succeed, I was told that "Palestine was occupied before, for two hundred years." The Hamas official assured me that he and his Palestinian comrades "can wait again—at least that long," for the struggles of God can endure for eons. Ultimately, however, Hamas members "knew" they would succeed.

In such battles, waged in divine time and with heaven's rewards, there is no need to compromise one's goals. No need, also, to contend with society's laws and limitations when one is obeying a higher authority. In spirtualizing violence, religion gives terrorism a remarkable power.

Ironically, the reverse is also true: terrorism can give religion power as well. Although sporadic acts of terrorism do not lead to the establishment of new religious states, they make the political potency of religious ideology impossible to ignore. Terrorism not only gives individuals the illusion of empowerment, it also gives religious organizations and ideas a public attention and importance that they have not enjoyed for many years. In modern America and Europe it has given religion a prominence in public life that it has not held since before the Enlightenment over two centuries ago.

Empowering Religion

The radical religious movements that have emerged from cultures of violence around the world have three elements in common. First, they reject the compromises with liberal values and secular institutions that most mainstream religion has made, be it Christian, Muslim, Jewish, Hindu, Sikh, or Buddhist. Second, radical religious movements refuse to observe the boundaries that secular society has set around religion—keeping it private rather than allowing it to intrude into public spaces. And third, these radical movements try to create a new form of religiosity that rejects what they regard as weak, modern substitutes for the more vibrant and demanding forms of religion that they imagine to be essential to their religions' origins.

One of the men accused of bombing the World Trade Center in 1993 told me in a prison interview that the critical moment in his religious life came when he realized that he could not compromise his Islamic integrity with the easy vices offered by modern society. The convicted terrorist, Mahmud Abouhalima, claimed that the early part of his life was spent running away from himself. Although involved in radical Egyptian Islamic movements since his college years in Alexandria, he felt there was no place where he could settle down. He told me that the low point came when he was in Germany, trying to live the way that he imagined Europeans and Americans did: a life where the superficial comforts of sex and inebriates masked an internal emptiness and despair. Abouhalima said his return to Islam as the center of his life carried with it a renewed sense of obligation to make Islamic society truly Islamic—to "struggle against oppression and injustice" wherever it existed. What was now constant, Abouhalima said, was his family and his faith. Islam was both a "rock and a pillar of mercy." But it was not the Islam of liberal, modern Muslims—they, he felt, had compromised the tough and disciplined life the faith demanded.

In Abouhalima's case, he wanted his religion to be hard, not soft like the humiliating, mindnumbing comforts of secular modernity. Activists such as Abouhalima—and Osama bin Laden—imagine themselves defenders of ancient faiths. But in fact they have created new forms of religiosity: like many present-day religious leaders they have used the language of traditional religion to build bulwarks around aspects of modernity that have threatened them, and to suggest ways out of the mindless humiliation of modern life. Vital to their image of religion, however, was that it be perceived as ancient.

The need for religion—a "hard" religion as Abouhalima called it—was a response to the soft treachery they had observed in the new societies around them. The modern secular world that Abouhalima and the others inhabited was a chaotic and violent sea for which religion offered an anchor in a harbor of calm. At some deep and almost transcendent level of their consciousnesses, they sensed their lives slipping out of control, and they felt both responsible for the disarray and a victim of it. To be abandoned by religion in such a world would mean a loss of their own individual locations and identities. In fashioning a "traditional religion" of their own making, they exposed their concerns not so much with their religious, ethnic, or national communities, but with their own personal, perilous selves.

Assaults on Secularism

These intimate concerns have been prompted by the perceived failures of public institutions. As the French sociologist Pierre Bourdieu has observed, social structures never have a disembodied reality; they are always negotiated by individuals in their own strategies for maintaining self-identity and success in life. Such institutions are legitimized by the "symbolic capital" they accrue through the collective trust of many individuals. When that symbolic capital is devalued, when political and religious institutions undergo what German philosopher Jurgen Habermas has called a "crisis of legitimacy," the devaluation of authority is experienced not only as a political problem but as an intensely personal one, as a loss of agency.

This sense of a personal loss of power in the face of chaotic political and religious authorities is common, and I believe critical to Osama bin Laden's al Qaeda group and most other movements for Christian, Muslim, Jewish, Sikh, Buddhist, and Hindu nationalism around the world. The syndrome begins with the perception that the public world has gone awry, and the suspicion that behind this social confusion lies a great spiritual and moral conflict, a cosmic battle between the forces of order and chaos, good and evil. Such a conflict is understandably violent, a violence that is often felt by the victimized activist as powerlessness, either individually or in association with others of his gender, race, or ethnicity. The government—already delegitimized—is perceived to be in league with the forces of chaos and evil.

One of the reasons why secular government is easily labeled as the enemy of religion is that to some degree it is. By its nature, the secular state is opposed to the idea that religion should have a role in public life. From the time that modern secular nationalism emerged in the eighteenth century as a product of the European Engilghtenment's political values, it did so with a distinctly antireligious, or at least anticlerical, posture. The ideas of John Locke about the origins of a civil community and the "social contract" theories of Jean Jacques Rousseau required very little commitment to religious belief. Although they allowed for a divine order that made the rights of humans possible, their ideas had the effect of taking religion—at least church religion—out of public life. At the time, religious "Enemies of the Enlightenment"—as the historian Darrin McMahon describes them in a new book with this title—protested religion's public demise. But their views were submerged in a wave of approval for a new view of social order in which secular nationalism was thought to be virtually a natural law, universally applicable and morally right.

Post-Enlightenment modernity proclaimed the death of religion. Modernity signaled not only the demise of the church's institutional authority and clerical control, but also the loosening of religion's ideological and intellectual grip on society. Scientific reasoning and the moral claims of the secular social contract replaced theology and the church as the bases for truth and social identity. The result of religion's devaluation has been a "general crisis of religious belief," as Bourdieu has put it.

In countering this disintegration, resurgent religious activists have proclaimed the death of secularism. They have dismissed the efforts of secular culture and its forms of nationalism to replace religion. They have challenged the idea that secular society and the modern nation-state are able to provide the moral fiber that unites national communities or give the ideological strength to sustain states buffeted by ethical, economic, and military failures. Their message has been easy to believe and has been widely received because the failures of the secular state have been so real.

Antiglobalism

The moral leadership of the secular state was increasingly challenged in the last decade of the twentieth century following the end of the cold war and the rise of a global economy. The cold war provided contesting models of moral politics—communism and democracy—that were replaced with a global market that weakened national sovereignty and was conspicuously devoid of political ideals. The global economy became controlled by transnational businesses accountable to no single governmental authority and with no clear ideological or moral standards of behavior. But while both Christian and Enlightenment values were left behind, transnational commerce transported aspects of Westernized popular culture to the rest of the world. American and European music, videos, and films were beamed across national boundaries, where they threatened to obliterate local and traditional forms of artistic expression.

Added to this social confusion were convulsive shifts in political power that followed the breakup of the Soviet Union and the collapse of Asian economies at the end of the twentieth century. The public sense of insecurity that came in the wake of these cataclysmic global changes was felt not only in the societies of those nations that were economically devastated by them—especially countries in the former Soviet Union—but also in economically stronger industrialized societies. The United States, for example, saw a remarkable degree of disaffection with its political leaders and witnessed the rise of right-wing religious movements that fed on the public's perception of the inherent immorality of government.

Is the rise of religious terrorism related to these global changes? We know that some groups associated with violence in industrialized societies have had an antimodernist political agenda. At the extreme end of this religious rejection in the United States were members of the American anti-abortion group Defensive Action; the Christian militia and Christian Identity movement; and isolated groups such as the Branch Davidian sect in Waco, Texas. Similar attitudes toward secular government emerged in Israel—the religious nationalist ideology of the Kach party was an extreme example—and in Japan with the Aum Shinrikyo movement. Like the United States, contentious groups within these countries were disillusioned about the ability of secular leaders to guide their countries' destinies. They identified government as the enemy.

The global shifts that have given rise to antimodernist movements have also affected less-developed nations. India's Jawaharlal Nehru, Egypt's Gamal Abdel Nasser, and Iran's Riza Shah Pahlavi once were committed to creating versions of America—or a kind of cross between America and the Soviet Union—in their own countries. But new generations of leaders no longer believed in the Westernized visions of Nehru, Nasser, or the Shah. Rather, they were eager to complete the process of decolonization and build new, indigenous nationalisms.

When activists in Algeria who demonstrated against the crackdown against the Islamic Salvation Front in 1991 proclaimed that they were continuing the war of liberation against French colonialism, they had the ideological rather than political reach of European influence in mind. Religious activists such as the Algerian leaders; the Ayatollah Khomeini in Iran; Sheikh Ahmen Yassin in the Palestinian Authority; Maulana Abu al-Ala Mawdudi in Pakistan; Sayyid Qutb and his disciple, Sheik Omar Abdul Rahman, in Egypt; L. K. Advani in India; and Sant Jarnail Singh Bhindranwale in India's Punjab have asserted the legitimacy of a postcolonial national identity based on traditional culture.

The result of this disaffection with the values of the modern West has been what I described in my earlier book, *The New Cold War?*, as a "loss of faith" in the ideological form of that culture, secular nationalism. Although a few years ago it would have been a startling notion, the idea has now become virtually commonplace that secular nationalism—the idea that the nation is rooted in a secular compact rather than religious or ethnic identity—is in crisis. In many parts of the world it is seen as an alien cultural construction, one closely linked with what has been called the "project of modernity." In such cases, religious alternatives to secular ideologies have had extraordinary appeal.

This uncertainty about what constitutes a valid basis for national identity is a political form of post-modernism. In Iran it has resulted in the rejection of a modern Western political regime and the creation of a successful religious state. Increasingly, even secular scholars in the West have recognized that religious ideologies might offer an alternative to modernity in the political sphere. Yet, what lies beyond modernity is not necessarily a new form of political order, religious or not. In nations formerly under Soviet control, for example, the specter of the future beyond the socialist form of modernity has been one of cultural anarchism.

The al Qaeda network associated with Osama bin Laden takes religious violence to yet another level. The implicit attack on global economic and political systems that are leveled by religious nationalists from Algeria to Indonesia are made explicit: America is the enemy. Moreover, it is a war waged not on a national plane but a transnational one. Their agenda is not for any specific form of religious nation-state but an inchoate vision of a global rule of religious law. Rather than religious nationalists, transnational activists like bin Laden are guerrilla antiglobalists.

Postmodern Terror

Bin Laden and his vicious acts have a credibility in some quarters of the world because of the uncertainties of this moment of global history. Both violence and religion historically have appeared when authority is in question, since they are both ways of challenging and replacing authority. One gains its power from force, and the other from its claims to ultimate order. The combination of the two in acts of religious terrorism has been a potent assertion indeed.

Regardless of whether the perpetrators consciously intended them to be political acts, all public acts of violence have political consequences. Insofar as they are attempts to reshape the public order, they are examples of what the sociologist Jose Casanova has called the increasing "deprivatization" of religion. In various parts of the world where defenders of religion have attempted to reclaim the center of public attention and authority, religious terrorism is often the violent face of these attempts.

The postmodern religious rebels such as those who rally to the side of Osama bin Laden have therefore been neither anomalies nor anachronisms. From Algeria to Idaho, their small but potent groups of violent activists have represented masses of supporters, and they have exemplified currents of thinking and cultures of commitment that have risen to counter the prevailing modernism—the ideology of individualism and skepticism—that in the past three centuries emerged from the European Enlightenment and spread throughout the world. They have come to hate secular governments with an almost transcendent passion. They have dreamed of revolutionary changes that would establish a godly social order in the rubble of what the citizens of most secular societies have regarded as modern, egalitarian democracies. Their enemies have seemed to most people to be both benign and banal: symbols of prosperity and authority such as the World Trade Center. The logic of this kind of militant religiosity has therefore been difficult for many people to comprehend. Yet its challenge has been profound, for it has contained a fundamental critique of the world's post-Enlightenment secular culture and politics.

Acts of religious terrorism have thus been attempts to purchase public recognition of the legitimacy of religious world views with the currency of violence. Since religious authority can provide a ready-made replacement for secular leadership, it is no surprise that when secular authority has been deemed to be morally insufficient, the challenges to its legitimacy and the attempts to gain support for its rivals have been based in religion. When the proponents of religion have asserted their claims to be the moral force undergirding public order, they sometimes have done so with the kind of power that a confused society can graphically recognize: the force of terror.

POSTSCRIPT

Do the Roots of Modern Terrorism Lie in Political Powerlessness, Economic Hopelessness, and Social Alienation?

The two arguments represented in this issue seem intertwined. The religious goals and motivations of those who are responsible for the September 11th attacks in the United States have been clearly stated; at the same time, the recruitment of terrorists from the young, disillusioned male population in the Islamic world cannot be denied. The answer to the question of what lies at the roots of modern terrorism depends on which of the two forces plays a more important role in creating modern terrorism.

Answers to the questions raised in this issue extend beyond the boundaries of academic debate; the future of the Middle East as we know it may be at stake. If the religious radicalism of the terrorists was primarily responsible for the September 11th attacks, the present attempt to eradicate them will not permanently solve the current crisis. However, if the environmentally-induced terrorist argument is correct, amelioration of the conditions that create a fertile ground for terrorism could remove the need for its desperate tactics.

Needless to say, the literature on terrorism is vast and diverse. The following recommendations include sources from the past that have proven to be all too prophetic as well as contemporary sources that deepen our understanding of both sides of this issue.

Originally published in 1989 David Fromkin's *A Peace to End All Peace: The Fall of the Ottoman Empire and the Creation of the Modern Middle East* (Henry Holt & Company, 2001) provides a readable, scholarly account of the creation of the modern Middle East in the years following World War I. Two articles by Middle East scholar Bernard Lewis provide supplementary material that brings the situation up-to-date. See "The Roots of Muslim Rage," *The Atlantic Monthly* (September 1990) and "The Revolt of Islam," *The New Yorker* (November 19, 2001).

Works that provide a useful introduction to the religious nature of Middle Eastern society include Judith Miller, *God Has Ninety-Nine Names: Reporting From a Militant Middle East* (Simon & Schuster, 1997). This book investigates militant Islamic movements in ten countries with an emphasis on Islamic diversity. Also see Karen Armstrong's *The Battle for God* (Ballantine Books, 2000), which considers historical and modern fundamentalist movements in Judaism, Christianity, and Islam. Juergensmeyer's *Terror in the Mind of God: The Global Rise of Religious Violence* (University of California Press, 2001) explores the relationship between religious fundamentalism and violence. An article by Walter

Laqueur, "The New Face of Terrorism," *The Washington Quarterly* (Autumn 1998) examines how religious fundamentalism has changed the nature of modern terrorism.

For the environmentally induced terrorism argument, consult Benjamin R. Barber, *Jihad vs. McWorld: How Globalism and Tribalism Are Shaping the World* (Ballantine Books, 1996), which considers the dialectical nature of these two forces, as each creates the other. Barber also wrote an article entitled "Jihad vs. McWorld," *The Atlantic Monthly* (March 1992) that encapsulizes the arguments in his book. Finally, Ahmed Rashid's *Taliban: Militant Islam, Oil and Fundamentalism in Central Asia* (Yale University Press, 2001), written by a Pakistani journalist well experienced in current Middle Eastern affairs, explores the role of the Taliban in the current crisis.

Contributors to This Volume

EDITORS

JOSEPH R. MITCHELL is a history instructor at Howard Community College in Columbia, Maryland, and a popular regional speaker. He received an M.A. in history from Loyola College in Maryland and an M.A. in African American History from Morgan State University, also in Maryland. He is the principal coeditor of *The Holocaust: Readings and Interpretations* (McGraw-Hill/Dushkin, 2001).

HELEN BUSS MITCHELL is a professor of philosophy and director of the women's studies program at Howard Community College in Columbia, Maryland. She is the author of *Roots of Wisdom* and *Readings From the Roots of Wisdom*. Both books were published by Wadsworth Publishing Company and are now in their third editions. She has also created, written, and hosted a philosophy telecourse, *For the Love of Wisdom*, which is distributed throughout the country by PBS. She has earned numerous degrees, including a Ph.D. in women's history from the University of Maryland.

STAFF

Theodore Knight List Manager
David Brackley Senior Developmental Editor
Juliana Gribbins Developmental Editor
Rose Gleich Administrative Assistant
Brenda S. Filley Director of Production/Design
Juliana Arbo Typesetting Supervisor
Diane Barker Proofreader
Richard Tietjen Publishing Systems Manager
Larry Killian Copier Coordinator

AUTHORS

GEORGE B. N. AYITTEY is a distinguished economist at the American University and president of the Free Africa Foundation, both in Washington, D.C. He is the author of *African Institutions* (Transnational, 1991) and *Africa in Chaos* (St. Martin's Press, 1998).

W. G. BEASLEY is emeritus professor of the history of the Far East at the University of London. He is the author of many works on Japan, including *The Rise of Modern Japan* (St. Martin's Press, 1995).

V. R. BERGHAHN is professor of history at Brown University. He is the author of fifteen books, including the forthcoming *German Big Business and Europe, 1918-1992.*

A. ADU BOAHEN is a native of Ghana who won the 1997 Noma Prize, Africa's premier book prize. He edited Volume 7 of UNESCO'S General History of Africa series, entitled *Africa Under Colonial Domination* (University of California Press, 1990).

CHRISTOPHER R. BROWNING is professor of history at the University of North Carolina, Chapel Hill. A leading Holocaust historian, his most recent book is *Nazi Policy, Jewish Workers, German Killers* (Cambridge University Press, 2000).

PAUL A. COHEN is professor of Asian studies and history at Wellesley College in Massachusetts. He is the author of *Discovering History in China: American Historical Writing on the Recent Chinese Past* (Columbia University Press, 1984).

LANCE E. DAVIS is a professor at the California Institute of Technology. He is the coauthor of *In Pursuit of Leviathan: Institutions, Productivity, and Profits in American Whaling, 1818-1906* (University of Chicago Press, 1997).

HASIA R. DINER is professor of history at New York University. Her research interests include American Jewish history, immigration-ethnic history, and women's history.

JOHN L. ESPOSITO is a professor of religion and international affairs at Georgetown University in Washington, D.C., and director of the Center for Muslim Understanding at Georgetown's Edmund A. Walsh School of Foreign Service. His publications include *Islam and Democracy* (Oxford University Press, 1996).

STEVEN EVERTS is a senior research fellow at the Centre for European Reform in London and an economist with a strong interest in the European Economic and Monetary Union.

JOHN LEWIS GADDIS is Robert Lovett Professor of History at Yale University. He has contributed extensively to cold war historiography with at least six major works on the subject.

DANIEL JONAH GOLDHAGEN is a professor of government and social studies at Harvard University. He has written articles and reviews on subjects related to the Holocaust.

HENRIETTA HARRISON is a lecturer in Chinese at the University of Leeds in England. She is the author of *The Making of Republican China: Political Ceremonies and Symbols in China, 1861–1911* (Oxford University Press, 2000).

THOMAS M. HUBER is a historian for the United States Army. He is the author of *Strategic Economy in Japan* (Westview Press, 1994).

ROBERT A. HUTTENBACK was a professor of history at the University of California at Santa Barbara, where he was chancellor from 1977 to 1986.

DENIS JUDD is professor of history at the University of North London and is a fellow of the Royal Historical Society. He is the author of *Evolution of the Modern Commonwealth* (Macmillan, 1982).

MARK JUERGENSMEYER is professor of sociology and director of global and international studies at the University of California at Santa Barbara. He is the author of *Terror in the Mind of God: The Global Rise of Religious Violence* (University of California Press, 2000).

CHRISTINE KINEALY is a fellow of the University of Liverpool, where she lectures on Irish and British history. She is the author of *A Death-Dealing Famine: The Great Hunger in Ireland* (Pluto Press, 1997).

PETER KROPOTKIN (1842–1921) was a Russian revolutionary who wrote his autobiography entitled *Memoirs of a Revolutionist* in 1899.

STEPHEN S. LARGE is lecturer in modern Japanese studies and reader in modern Japanese history at the University of Cambridge in England. He is the author of *Emperors of the Rising Sun: Three Biographies* (Kodansha International, 1997).

ANATOL LIEVEN is a senior associate at the Carnegie Endowment for International Peace. His latest book is *Chechnya: Tombstone of Russian Power* (Yale University Press, 1998).

JOHN M. MacKENZIE is a professor of imperial history at Lancaster University in England. He is the editor of *Imperialism and Popular Culture* (Manchester University Press, 1986).

STEVEN MAJSTOROVIC is an assistant professor of political science at the University of Wisconsin, Eau Claire. He has written and lectured extensively on modern European politics.

FRANÇOISE NAVAILH is a Russian film historian at the University of Paris. She teaches Russian language and is a specialist in Russian cinema.

A. T. NUYEN is a member of the Department of Philosophy at the University of Queensland in Brisbane, Australia.

JACK SCARBOROUGH is a management educator at Barry University in Florida and a retired U.S. Coast Guard commander.

SIMON SCHAMA is a professor of art and art history at Columbia University. He is the author of *The Embarrassment of Riches: An Interpretation of Dutch Culture During the Golden Age* (Alfred A. Knopf, 1987).

JOAN W. SCOTT is a professor of social science at Princeton University's Institute for Advanced Study. She is the author of *Gender and the Politics of History* (Columbia University Press, 1988).

MARTIN J. SHERWIN is professor of history at Tufts University. He is the author of *A World Destroyed: The Atomic Bomb and the Grand Alliance* (Random House, 1977).

EDWARD SHORTER directs the history of medicine program at the University of Toronto. He is the author of *From the Mind Into the Body* (Free Press, 1996).

SHARIF SHUJA is adjunct assistant professor of international relations at Bond University in Australia. He has contributed numerous articles to professional journals that specialize in Asian affairs.

RICHARD STITES is a professor of history at Georgetown University. He is the author of *Revolutionary Dreams* (Oxford University Press, 1989) and *Russian Popular Culture* (Cambridge University Press, 1992).

LOUISE A. TILLY is an assistant professor of history and director of the women's studies program at the University of Washington. She is the author of numerous articles on social history.

WERNER WEIDENFELD is director of the Center for Applied Policy Research at Ludwig Maximilians University in Munich, Germany.

PETER WETZLER is professor of Japanese business, politics, and language at the East Asia Institute of the Ludwigshafen School of Business Administration in Germany. He has published works on Japanese history both in English and German.

LUISE WHITE wrote her doctoral dissertation for Cambridge University on "The History of Prostitution in Nairobi, Kenya." She currently teaches African history at Rice University in Texas.

SAMUEL R. WILLIAMSON, JR. is professor of history at the University of the South. He is the author of *Austria-Hungary and the Origins of the First World War* (St. Martin's Press, 1991).

WARREN ZIMMERMANN served as the last U.S. ambassador to Yugoslavia, and, after retirement from the Foreign Service, is now a professor of international diplomacy at Columbia University.

Index